Lee Meriwether

Afloat and Ashore on the Mediterranean

Lee Meriwether

Afloat and Ashore on the Mediterranean

ISBN/EAN: 9783337111298

Printed in Europe, USA, Canada, Australia, Japan

Cover: Foto ©ninafisch / pixelio.de

More available books at **www.hansebooks.com**

AFLOAT AND ASHORE ON THE MEDITERRANEAN

BY

LEE MERIWETHER

AUTHOR OF "A TRAMP TRIP; OR, EUROPE ON FIFTY CENTS A DAY,"
"A TRAMP AT HOME," ETC.

"The grand object of all travelling is to see the shores of the Mediterranean. On those shores were the four great empires of the world: the Assyrian, the Persian, the Grecian, and the Roman. All our religion, almost all our law, almost all our arts, almost all that sets us above savages, has come to us from the shores of the Mediterranean." — *Samuel Johnson.*

NEW YORK
CHARLES SCRIBNER'S SONS
1892

TO
MY MOTHER
MY TRUEST FRIEND AND WISEST COUNSELLOR
THIS BOOK IS DEDICATED
BY
HER GRATEFUL AND AFFECTIONATE SON
THE AUTHOR

PREFACE

In his "History of Civilization" Buckle speaks rather disparagingly of the mere narrator of events, remarking that for every original thinker there are a dozen trained observers. Having small claim to being even a trained observer, it would be no easy matter to defend this book before Buckle; to the general reader, however, I shall feel that no apology is due should the perusal of the adventures herein related afford a tithe of the pleasure experienced in the adventures themselves. The manner in which the trip was taken is not without novelty, nor are all the places described visited by summer tourists to Europe. No railroads reach the extreme southwest coast of Italy; some of the islands of the Ægean are also difficult of access, except in private yachts. These facts embolden me to hope that the chapters of this book, if twice-told tales to the few, may not be devoid of interest to the many, who, even though experienced travellers, may perhaps have failed to visit the out-of-the-way places in the Mediterranean reached by the writer in his little craft, the *Principe Farnese*.

While Commissioner of Labor Statistics for the State of Missouri, I was directed by a resolution adopted by the House of Representatives to investigate the subject of convict labor. My report to the legislature on the Missouri penitentiary is embodied in the thirteenth volume of the Labor Bureau, published by my successor in the office of Labor Commissioner. The interest thus aroused caused me, where opportunity offered, to examine the systems of prison labor in Europe. I also noted the condition of workingmen, and the cost of producing such Mediterranean fruits as are exported to the United States, in competition with the fruits grown there. These questions, though of interest to students of social problems, are scarcely so to the general reader: in the present volume they are touched upon only here and there to serve as ballast to the lighter part of the pages.

LEE MERIWETHER.

St. Louis, September, 1892.

CONTENTS

CHAPTER I
PAGE

Getting Passports — The Cablegram from Vienna — The Voyage — How Miss Detroit upset the Professor's Calculations — We pass the Azores — Coast of Portugal — Mysteries of Italian Cooking on the *Birmania* 1

CHAPTER II

Arrival at Lisbon — Perigarde appears — We find ourselves Millionnaires — The King and Queen — Adventure on Top of a Cathedral — Condition of Portuguese Labor — The Girl, the Maid, and the Garden — Cost of a Trip to Portugal........................ 13

CHAPTER III

A Gloomy Dungeon — Living Men in Coffins and Shrouds — Perpetual Isolation — How a Nunnery was transformed — A Fat Judge, a Squalling Baby, and a Frightened Family — Miss Detroit invites us to the Theatre — A Visit to Portugal's Dead Royalty — Ghastly Appearance of the Kings and Queens.................. 32

CHAPTER IV

Perigarde studies Lotteries — How Portuguese Children disappear through a Wall — The Bull Fight at Torres Vedras — Spanish and Portuguese Bull Fights compared — Two Surprises — The Baroness and the Milkery — The Professor disappears.................. 49

CHAPTER V

The Tobacco Factory of Seville — Six Thousand Girls with Roses and Babies — Spanish and American Tariffs — The Octroi — The Kodak gets us in Trouble — El Sereno — The Civil Guards and the

Englishman — Twelve Years in Africa — Why Mr. W. threatened to cut down his Trees — Mediterranean Fruits.................. 66

CHAPTER VI

A Trip to Xeres — How Sherry is made and why it goes to India — Perigarde, the Baroness, and the Baron — The Mosque of Cordova — Mistaken for Burglars — A Kodak Story — Night Journey to Ronda — Why they robbed us — The Ronda Fair — Signorina Cellini changes her Name.. 82

CHAPTER VII

On Donkey Back to Gibraltar — How we escaped the Muleteers — Scaling the Pyrenees — The Posada de la Paz and the Enchanted Castle — Pastoral Scenes — Don Rodriguez saves us from Prison — Gibraltar — Second Impressions — Curious Sea-Eggs — A Trip to Tangiers — The Cadi's Court — Scene from the Arabian Nights — Moorish Wedding — Mack buys Antiquities.................. 100

CHAPTER VIII

Spanish Prisons in Africa — Remarkable System — Prisoners pay to Work — Convict Life — The Governor of Ceuta — Procession of the Sacred Picture — Off for Malaga — Leviathan Mills — Romantic Notions exploded — Story of the Republicans — Men who die for Freedom — Social Life in Spain........................ 122

CHAPTER IX

Why we missed the train to Granada — Why the Cabman pursued us — And why we fled to the Consul's — The Alhambra — Youthful Illusions — In Prison again — Convicts in Clover — The Cemetery — Rented Graves — At the Opera — Perigarde finds a "Soul's Mate".. 137

CHAPTER X

Along the Spanish Coast — Cartagenian Prisons — Almeria's Remarkable Wall — Peaks and Castles — Alicante and Valencia — Convicts who stay at Home — Roasting Nuts on an Ass's Back — Barcelona — How we were trapped in Jail.................... 151

CHAPTER XI

The Shoemaker, the Anarchist, and the Editor — Labor Unions in Spain — Troubles of May First — What Monarchies have to fear — Barcelona's Rambla — Spanish Politics — The Anarchist Plan — Excursion to Montserrat — The Virgin's Cave — Pilgrims and Penances — What it costs to travel in Spain.................. 163

CHAPTER XII

A Jump to Toulon — Bicycling along the Mediterranean — Nice — Monte Carlo — Facilities for Suicide — The Republic of Andorra — Stopped at the Frontier — Why Windows are Sham in Italy — We run over an Italian — The San Remo Druggist to the Emperor — Wheeling into Genoa............................. 182

CHAPTER XIII

Genoa — Motieri tells a Story — A Day in the Tyrol — Perigarde reappears — Loss of his "Soul's Mate" — Bicycling to Rome — Monte Oliveto — A Thirteenth Century Monastery — Triumphal Entry into San Quirico — Radicafani's Peak — Our Bicycles mistaken for Tram Cars — Excitement of the Peasants — Inglorious Conclusion of the Bicycle Trip............................ 196

CHAPTER XIV

Rome Revisited — Renewing Acquaintances — Visit to the Queen of Heaven — What it costs to live there — House of Correction at Tivoli — San Stefano's Gloomy Ergostola — Terrible Effects of Isolation — Prison Systems compared — Lunatics in Italian Jails.. 212

CHAPTER XV

Changes in Naples — How the Poor are housed — Italian Taxes — We hire a Boat — The *Principe Farnese* — Yachting on the Mediterranean — Capri and Sorrento — A Tramp over the Mountain — Mack wants a Nursery — A Ducking at Scaracatajo — What it costs to run Dr. Kelly's Yacht, and what it costs to run the *Principe Farnese*................................... 233

CHAPTER XVI

Amalfi — Macaroni-Makers — Burden-Bearers on the Via Molini — A Night Cruise to Pæstum — How Mack nearly lost his Ear — Puffed Preservers at Policastro — We take a Passenger — Paranzo's Strange Story — Pursued by his Wife — Reception at Fuscaldo — Mistaken for Princes — The Banquet, the Speech, and the Escape 248

CHAPTER XVII

Curious Asylum at Cosenza — Grave of Alaric the Goth — How Two Rivers guard the Barbarian's Bones and Booty — Life on our Boat — Swimming with the Fish — Midnight View of Stromboli — Volcanoes compared — Ascent of Stromboli — Lipari — Strange Conduct of the People — The Girl and the Deserted Quarry — Arrested on Angelo's Peak — Mistaken for Manutengoli — Two Nights in Jail — The Cave-Dwellers of Volcano — An Island rises in the Sea 267

CHAPTER XVIII

A Sirocco Storm — Running before the Wind — The *Principe Farnese* weathers the Gale — A Tramp in Calabria — Scilla and Charybdis — Messina's Strait — Sicily — Cruising along the Coast — A Town of Nut-Crackers — How St. Agatha saved Catania — Perigarde meets a Fräulein — Syracuse — Perigarde astounds us 287

CHAPTER XIX

Voyage to Greece — Birthplace of Venus — Milo — A Soldier Passenger — Mysterious Disappearance — Our Greek Sailor put in Jail — The Home of Perseus — Cruising 'mid Classic Scenes — Syra — The Shrines of Delos — Storm on the Ægean — Aristotle's Skull and Tomb — We bid Farewell to the *Principe Farnese* — Cost of Yachting 298

CHAPTER XX

Athens — Curious Costume of the Greeks — Their Prison System — The Bay of Salamis and the Hill where Xerxes sat — Rue Byron in Athens — The Corinthian Canal — A Stupendous Work — We climb Pentelicon's Peak — Primitive Ways and Means — How Money is changed 312

CHAPTER XXI

Smyrna — Imprisoned by the Turks — Barbarity of the Moslem — How Taxes are farmed and Peasants robbed — Mr. McNaughton the Missionary — A Good Samaritan — From a Foul Dungeon to the Deck of the *Minerva* — I step on an Austrian — Chios and Rhodes — Through the Ægean Sea — Prison Circles of Rhodes... 320

CHAPTER XXII

Howajani Sulah and the Russian Prince — Fifty Hours' Fast — Marko falls in Love — The Marriage in Cyprus — I receive a Proposal — Russian Jews and Moslem Turks — Horrors of a Deck Passage — Turks capture the Ship — A Day in Syria — First Glimpses of the Nile — Cholera Quarantine at Alexandria — Mr. Abbott proves a Friend 331

CHAPTER XXIII

Naked Alexandrians — "A.D." Sights in Egypt — The Ride to Cairo — Why Abdullah's Ass is losing his Ears — Fantastic Scenes — Fragments of a King — Rameses at the Bulak Museum — Mahmud jerks me up the Pyramids — Memphis — Under the Libyan Desert — Tombs of Sacred Bulls — Crocodile Pits of Maabdeh — Devoured by Vampires — Suez Canal — Paranzo again — Captured by his Wife — Conclusion.................................. 345

LIST OF ILLUSTRATIONS

Forward Deck of the "Principe Farnese" .	*Frontispiece*
	TO FACE PAGE
Market at Alicante	16
Monte Carlo	32
The Trappist Monk	48
An Italian Island Prison	64
Burden Bearer on the Via Dei Molini	80
The "Principe Farnese"; Amalfi in the Distance	96
Sicilian Women threshing Wheat near the Greek Theatre, Syracuse	112
Ruins of the Greek Theatre, Taormina	128
Taormina, from Summit of Greek Theatre	144
Ruins of the Roman Theatre, Syracuse	160
Street in Syra	176
Harbor of Zea	192
Bay of Salamis, from Hill where Xerxes sat	208
Grape Vendor in Athens	224
Athens	240
The Corinthian Canal	256
Deck of the "Minerva"; Smyrna in the Distance	272
Street Scene in Smyrna	284
Scene in Cyprus	296
Abdullah and the Author setting out for the Pyramids	308
Climbing the Giseh Pyramid	320
Scene on the Way to Memphis	332
Egyptian Water Carrier	344

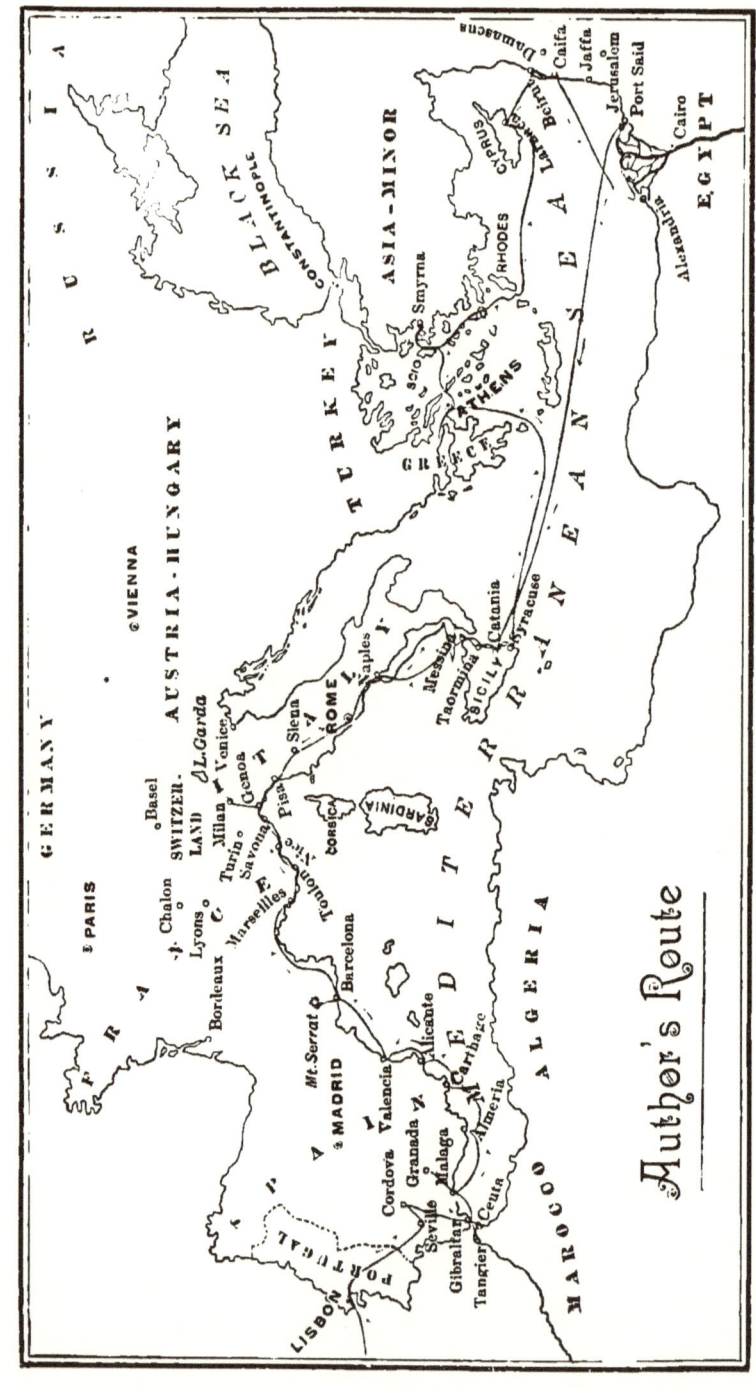

AFLOAT AND ASHORE ON THE MEDITERRANEAN

CHAPTER I

Getting Passports — The Cablegram from Vienna — The Voyage — How Miss Detroit upset the Professor's Calculations — We pass the Azores — Coast of Portugal — Mysteries of Italian Cooking on the *Birmania*

EN ROUTE to New York my friend Mack and I stopped at Washington for passports. On my "Tramp Trip" I neglected this precaution, and many were the occasions when I regretted the lack of some paper to show that I was one of the sixty odd million people who inhabit the "foremost and grandest country on God's green earth." In fact, so many and serious were the difficulties incurred by lack of a passport that finally in Vienna I was obliged to get one from the American Minister, and at greater expense than would have been the case at Washington. I might have felt the need of a passport less had I travelled first class instead of on foot as a Tramp; nevertheless, I saw enough to learn that the traveller in foreign lands can dispose of a dollar to no better advantage than by giving it to the Secretary of State for the sheet of parchment bearing the picture of an eagle with a shield and the stars and stripes clutched in his talons. The Department of State has issued a circular stating that "passports are necessary for the Turkish

Dominions and for some parts of Germany," thus leaving the inference that they are not necessary in other countries. The traveller who acts upon this inference may regret it. My advice is, get a passport whether you are going to Turkey or not. Should you have no occasion to use it in Europe, you will at any rate get value received; the experience gained through a visit to the passport office is worth several times the price of the paper. Mack and I entered the grand building on Pennsylvania Avenue that houses the War, State, and Navy Departments, and finally found a door marked "Passport Division."

The sole occupant of the office beyond this door was a pleasant-looking gentleman sitting at a desk covered with official looking papers and long blue envelopes. When we said we wanted passports he did not make a word of reply, he did not even stop chewing the gum he had in his mouth: he merely opened one of the drawers in the desk, took out a slip of paper, and began deliberately writing. At about every other line he looked up and gave us a sharp glance. Mack thought he was watching to see that we did not walk off with the furniture, but this was not the reason of his sharp and frequent glances. He was, so to speak, taking mental photographs, and the result showed that the pleasant-looking gentleman was thinking more of his chewing-gum than his subjects. His descriptions were neither flattering nor correct. He described me as having a "square level head, an oblong face, a prominent chin, and a pug nose." My head may be level, but I, deny the "square," and disown the prominent chin and oblong face. The pug nose I accepted without demur, but felt it unkind to have that unfortunate feature pulled to the front in so conspicuous a way. When I got a passport from the American Minister at Vienna I had a round head and a respectable nose which was called straight. The American Minister so certified over his signature and over the great seal of the

United States. I have that certificate yet; I also have the nose; yet the pleasant-looking gentleman who chews gum and issues passports in the State Department at Washington condemned me to go about the world with a document declaring that I had a square head, an oblong face, a pug nose, and a prominent chin. It is appalling to contemplate the changes a few passports work in one's outside presentment. The State Department should keep a supply of kodaks on hand and start travellers off with their photographs pasted on their passports, and thus spare them the humiliation of being described as dime museum freaks.

After the publication of my "A Tramp Trip; or, Europe on Fifty Cents a Day" I received a number of letters from young men in different parts of the country, asking for hints additional to those contained in my book. Some requested me, in case of a second trip, to accept the company of the writers as travelling companions. Among these correspondents was a young Creole in New Orleans. Perigarde's letter was so frank, so pleasant, and engaging, that it led to an agreement on my part to invite him to accompany me on my next trip to Europe. The correspondence dropped, but the agreement was not forgotten, and a month or so before the departure of the *Birmania*, I wrote Perigarde an outline of the proposed trip and cordially invited him to join us. As the day of sailing drew near and no reply came from New Orleans, I concluded he had either forgotten me or left the country. But the morning of our departure the bell boy came to my room with a telegram that explained Perigarde's silence.

"Our sailing-boat," I said to Mack, "will be crowded."

"How so?"

"Because there will be three of us. You know that while two are company, three are a crowd."

"But who is the third party? You have never spoken of any one going with us."

I handed Mack the telegram:—

"Vienna, April 15.
"Meet you at Gibraltar.
"PERIGARDE."

"Who the mischief is Perigarde?" asked Mack.

"He is a handsome young fellow if he is like his picture: and if he is like his letters, he is as bright as he is handsome."

Mack thought it hazardous to invite a stranger. "There is no time," said he, "when one's temper is more sorely tried, no time when disagreeable qualities are more apt to develop than when travelling."

I admitted this, and perhaps, generally speaking, it is wiser to travel alone than with one whose congeniality is untried, whose temper is unknown. It did not result so, however, in Perigarde's case; he proved a capital fellow, a trifle sentimental and susceptible to woman's wiles; nevertheless, a jolly companion. I cabled him to meet us at Lisbon, the *Birmania* agents having at the last moment ordered the vessel to call at that port before proceeding to Gibraltar.

The Italian steamers are not built to carry many passengers, but the accommodations for those they do carry are excellent. The state-rooms are large and commodious, the service good, the table excellent if you happen to like Italian cooking. If you do not like *maccaroni al pomi d' oro, arrosto polli con insalata*, etc., do not take a Florio Rubattino steamer, where the traveller is expected to relish things Italian, and is kept on a strictly Italian diet. Two or three sorts of wine are served without extra charge, the captain sits at the head of the table and treats passengers as a host treats guests, laughing, chatting, seeing that every one has as pleasant a trip as possible. This is not possible on the Liverpool steamers with their four hundred or five hundred passengers: on the Florio ships, with a maximum of fifty or sixty, and usually not more than fifteen or twenty passengers, they come to feel like a family party, and a spirit of friendly sociability prevails that is not lessened by the greater length of the voyage.

The *Birmania* was advertised to sail at two o'clock, but anchor was not weighed until nearly three. We spent this extra hour taking a farewell look at the charming panorama around us. So far there were no signs of other passengers, and we had come to the conclusion we were to have the *Birmania* all to ourselves, when there walked up the gangway a short, sandy-haired man with a Gladstone bag in each hand, and on his rather large head a fore-and-aft steamer cap that caused us at once to set him down as an Englishman. After depositing his "grips," the sandy-haired gentleman gave us an inquiring glance.

"We are glad to see that after all we shall have company," said Mack affably.

The sandy-haired man blinked his little red eyes, took off his gold-rimmed spectacles, wiped the glasses methodically, and as he adjusted them to his eyes again, said: —

"You are not going on the *Birmania*, are you?"

"That is our intention," replied Mack sharply. "Have you any objections?"

"No, oh no: only the agent said there were to be no passengers. I selected this route because I wanted to be alone."

This was certainly frank: the man was good enough to add, however, that he did not particularly object to male passengers.

"You see," said he, "I am a professor in a female seminary. The girls — there are two hundred of them — have nearly worried the life out of me, and I feel as if I never want to see a woman again."

We told the professor his explanation was satisfactory, though we secretly felt that it would take more than two hundred girls to disgust us with the sight of a petticoat. We knocked about the ship together, looking at the Brooklyn Bridge and the miles of buildings on both sides of the East River, glad to get this last glimpse of our native land, yet grumbling because the steamer did not leave at the appointed hour. When at length the gang-plank was hauled up and the signal for departure given, the professor heaved a sigh of satisfaction.

"Thank goodness," he murmured, "the Seminary and the two hundred girls are all left behind."

Alas for the poor professor! Not yet were we off, nor was the *Birmania* destined to afford entire relief from the presence of petticoats. A carriage came dashing down the Mediterranean docks, the driver leaped to the ground, two young ladies and an elderly gentleman stepped out of the carriage, and all four, rushing to the edge of the dock, began crying out and waving handkerchiefs. The gang-plank was thrown out again, the two young ladies embraced the elderly man, — their uncle, — cried "Good-bye," and the next moment were aboard the ship with two good-sized trunks that followed quickly after. The professor's face dropped; he went off sadly and sat down at the far end of the steamer, and seemed to feel as badly as if every one of the two hundred had boarded the vessel. The newcomers were passengers to Gibraltar. The lateness of their arrival was explained by the fact that they had originally taken passage on one of the Anchor Line vessels. The sinking of the *Utopia* of that line a short time before had disarranged the sailings of the Anchor boats; hence it was that at the last moment these two young ladies secured passage on the *Birmania*. Both were young, both good-looking, one very pretty. I think their youth and beauty dismayed the professor all the more: it is an admitted fact that woman-haters hate young women more than old women.

"Fate is against me," he groaned, when Mack and I tried to cheer him by saying that we, the masculine portion of the passengers, were in a majority. "It's all the worse for that," he added dismally. "They'll be demanding all kinds of attentions, and we shall have to pay them — it is the way with women."

Mack and I promised to take all that on ourselves; we would martyr ourselves to save the professor.

"We shall keep with them all we can," said Mack, cheerfully; "we shall endure the agony of their society every hour to save you, Professor."

"That's not exactly it," said the professor, wiping his spectacles. "I wanted to rough it — flannel shirt and all that. Of course with girls along that is impossible."

"Not at all. We mean to lounge around and take it easy just as if there were no girls within a thousand miles. If they are sensible, they will think nothing of it; if they are not sensible, we do not care what they think."

"The presence of young ladies," said the professor, solemnly, "necessitates formality. One has to dress for dinner when there are ladies."

The professor pulled from his pocket a little book labelled "Etiquette at Sea," and turning the leaves, finally paused at a passage where, sure enough, was the injunction he mentioned. Mack, however, with the breeziness of the West, declared he would put on no dress suit, etiquette or no etiquette. My dress suit being in St. Louis, a thousand miles away, I was obliged to side with Mack. The result was, that later, as the Jersey coast was fading into a misty outline, when Giovanni announced "pranzo," — dinner, — the professor was resplendent in a full dress suit, spotless shirt, white silk tie, while Mack and I were in sack coats, blue flannel shirts, and no ties at all. As the professor scanned our unfashionable attire, his face assumed a complacent self-satisfaction at his own superiority. He was as pleased as any solemn peacock could be, made the ladies a profound bow, and, on the whole, seemed as desirous to please them as if he had never been tormented by two hundred of the sex. Before dinner was over we were all acquainted. We told each other something of our plans and settled down on a friendly footing. The professor, as he had already told us, was taking a three months' rest from his seminary girls. Mack and I were bound for a cruise around the Mediterranean, while the two young ladies were off for a jaunt through Spain. When the professor heard this, he took off his spectacles, wiped the glasses, adjusted them to his eyes again, and muttered one word: —

"Alone?"

"Oh no," replied Miss Detroit, pleasantly. "We two intend to travel together."

The professor was awestruck. To his English conservatism, the idea of two young and pretty women travelling through Spain without maternal or masculine protection seemed not only highly improper but highly dangerous. Miss Lebanon and Miss Detroit, however, were two wide-awake American girls, not a bit afraid of English conservatism or English professors. They were blissfully unconscious of his disapproval, and chatted gaily of the pleasant times they expected to have in Andalusia. The professor's disgust at the two hundred girls he had left behind had made Mack and me think him a woman-hater: he was nothing of the sort. No man ever tried harder to please ladies than he did. Not only did he get himself up in that dress suit every day for dinner, but he took extra care of his red hair, brought the ladies' chairs on deck, arranged their wraps, read poetry to them — in short, seemed to have completely forgotten the two hundred girls he had fled from. Mack and I saw that the vivacity, the winning smile, and pleasant manners, of Miss Detroit were getting in their work on the professor, and putting to rout every one of the tormenting two hundred. Whenever Miss Detroit took a constitutional on deck, the professor seemed to think one necessary for his digestion too. When Miss Detroit played the piano, — which she did often and well, — the professor was there to turn the music. And if Mack and I happened to go for a walk before turning in at night we were almost sure to find the two ladies leaning over the poop-deck rail, the professor by Miss Detroit's side, gazing at the phosphorescent glow caused by the revolutions of the steamer's screw, and talking poetry — yes, poetry! The two hundred seminary girls had not absorbed *all* the poetry of the professor's soul.

"Mack and I admire your philosophy," I said to the professor one day.

"What do you mean?" retorted the professor, sharply, turning as red as his hair.

"Why, you said you came this route to get out of the way of ladies. You gave us to understand you hated women, yet you bear their society with great fortitude."

"The fact of the matter is," replied the professor, confusedly, "the — the — er unprotected situation of these ladies appeal, you see, to — to er a man's gallantry. You see?"

We assured the professor we saw — saw plainly.

"The case," added the professor, thoughtfully, "is very different from those two hundred seminary girls — very different indeed."

Mack and I readily admitted this and forbore to press the point. Mack went forward one day to photograph the sailors at dinner. They were all eager to have their pictures taken and posed in all sorts of absurd and stiff positions. Fortunately, the kodak works instantaneously, and we had the views before they knew what we wanted. Before starting on the trip we experimented with a number of cameras, and finally settled on the number four kodak as the most compact and convenient for a traveller. It is light, takes an excellent picture cabinet-size, and is loaded with a spool of sensitive film long enough to make one hundred photographs without reloading. Extra spools were in our valises, so that we were prepared to take views *ad libitum*. The illustrations in this book are from photographs taken with our kodak.

Colonel Knox, in his interesting book "How to Travel," says there is little danger of starving on transatlantic steamers. On Italian steamers there is danger of stuffing, not starving. They have five meals a day. At seven every morning Celeste brought to our state-rooms a light repast of coffee, fruit, and crackers. This was followed by another hour or two of sleep, then a walk on deck until the main breakfast at ten, an elaborate, formal affair, more like dinner than breakfast. It begins with soup, followed by half a dozen courses down to fruit and nuts. At one o'clock comes a lunch of beefsteak, potatoes, fruit, and nuts. At five o'clock comes "pranzo"—the great event of the day. An idea of what an Italian "pranzo" is like may be obtained from the following copy of one of the *Birmania's* menu cards:—

Minestrone alla Lombarda.
Antipasto.
Manzo bragiato guarnito.   Fritto misto.
Arrosto: Polli con insalata.   Dolci: Gelato alla crema.
Frutta.   Formaggio.   Cafíë.
Vini: Ordinario, Marsala, Vesuvio.

The unsophisticated reader may imagine that with an Italian dictionary he would be able to understand what he was eating, but he would not. Of course, you may learn that "arrosto: polli" means roast chicken, or that "gelato" means ice cream, but what sort of chicken or cream? Such cooking is never seen in England or America, and to understand the above bill of fare one must consult an Italian restaurant, not an Italian dictionary. Wines are served at each course, and the unwary traveller who fails to heed the Kentucky caution not to mix drinks will be apt to go under the table. Tea at eight o'clock is a light affair; yet light as it is, we could not touch it after the immense "pranzo" at five. Perhaps one reason why fare and service are excellent on the Florio line is because the steamers have a "complaint book" which is examined by an inspector at Genoa on the completion of each voyage. A passenger who has objections to make enters them in this book: if the objections are well founded, the offending servant of the company is summarily dealt with by the inspector at Genoa.

The tenth and eleventh days of the voyage were enlivened by fine views of the Azores and their lofty mountains. On the afternoon of the fifteenth day the blue rim of Saint Roque mountain peeped up out of the sea. Gradually it grew sharper and higher. At its base became visible stretches of a sandy, surf-washed shore; at last we could see trees, houses, and even men — welcome sights after fifteen days of the ocean's wide waste. As we all stood on the captain's bridge, — note that this privilege is not permitted on English steamers, — the professor unburdened himself of much historical knowledge — such and such battles had been fought ten miles south of Saint Roque, Wellington had built his great defences thirty miles in this direction, Nelson had done this and that at the mouth of the Tagus. We rejoiced at receiving so much instruction.

For two hours the *Birmania* skirted close to the coast, in full view of the mountains, of the surf dashing high on the rocks, lighthouses and villages scattered here and there: so lovely were these glimpses of land and life, after the long ocean voyage, when Giovanni announced "pranzo," it was with reluctance that we descended from the captain's bridge to take our places for the last time around the *Birmania's* merry board. It was a hastily eaten dinner, so highly seasoned with excitement that only our youthful and vigorous digestions enabled us to manage its various courses. Every two or three minutes a glimpse through the window of some enchanting bit of landscape brought us to our feet, and only a movement on Giovanni's part to remove the dishes brought us to our seats again. About the fourth course, long before dinner was ended, the vessel entered the Tagus. This was more than we could stand.

"I expect to get dinner once a day during the remainder of my life," said Mack, "but I do not expect to be on the Tagus again. I am going on deck."

We all followed. On both sides of the broad and noble river is a panorama that for picturesqueness, both of people and scenery, has not its superior in Europe. The sun was setting as we cast anchor off Lisbon: as its red glow died away, the lamps in the city were lighted, until finally the tall houses and the streets leading up the steep hills were aglow as with a thousand twinkling stars. The music of a military band floated across the water, we could see the throng of people in the great square that faces the Tagus, and that has in its centre the colossal statue of Don José surrounded by horses and elephants. The boatmen demanded 5000 reis to row us ashore. The proper price for our party of five was 1000 reis: this attempt at extortion, together with the lateness of the hour, decided us to remain one night more on the *Birmania* and not go ashore until morning.

CHAPTER II

Arrival at Lisbon — Perigarde appears — We find ourselves Millionnaires — The King and Queen — Adventure on Top of a Cathedral — Condition of Portuguese Labor — The Girl, the Maid, and the Garden — Cost of a trip to Portgual

THE first thing I heard next morning, was some one calling my name, and then Celeste, the cabin steward, saying, "Si, capisco, il signore dorme — the signore is asleep."

"No he isn't," I cried. "What is wanted?"

The next moment Perigarde was in my room. I recognized him from the photograph he had sent me: but photographs are very misleading; he was by no means a handsome man, though amiable and jolly. I asked Perigarde how he had found us so promptly.

"Very simple," said he: "I received your cablegram at Vienna. You had written you meant to sail on a Florio steamer. I learned that the *Birmania* had arrived, and so got up early this morning to meet you. I have a boat waiting, and your rooms engaged at the hotel; all you have to do is to take possession."

I told Perigarde of the increase in our party: he declared in his jolly, good-natured way that it made no difference; the more the merrier; that the Hotel do Universo could hold the *Birmania's* passengers and crew also. It was not long before he had made the acquaintance of the ladies and of Mack and the professor, and was helping us put our things into the boat. Then we gave three cheers for our trusty ship, waved our handkerchiefs at the crew, which had assembled, from captain Pizzarello to the cook's scullion to bid us good-bye, and off we were for shore — not to return again; for the *Birmania* was to remain so long at Lisbon, we decided to reach Gibraltar by land. The quay was lined two or three deep with small boats and lighters, over which we had to climb before getting ashore. The lighters were filled with sulphur from a ship just arrived from Sicily. The dark Portuguese, yellow with dust from the great sacks of sulphur carried on their heads, tripped lightly up the steep, narrow plank leading from the lighters to the quay. For twelve hours of this hard work the Portuguese stevedore receives from forty to sixty cents. In America, the same labor commands two or three dollars a day. Just beyond the lighters and piles of sulphur sacks were the customs officers — the most inquisitive we ever saw. Not satisfied with searching our baggage, they put their hands in our pockets, and even wanted Mack to open the kodak.

"Photographee — photographee," exclaimed Mack, desperately. The officers, not understanding, or else deeming it a ruse to smuggle cigars into the kingdom, insisted on the box being opened. We showed them the window in the camera and explained as well as we could, that to open the box would destroy its hundred gelatine plates. By dint of much shouting and gesticulating, we persuaded the Portuguese that we were not smugglers, and they finally gave a surly assent to our passing. A danger scarcely less than that at the custom-house arose from Mack's enthusiasm. It was his first trip to Europe, and the streets of Lisbon struck him as so queer and crooked, before I knew it he had taken a dozen pictures. Even the kodak has limitations, and the novice must look to it that he does not exhaust the gelatine roll too rapidly. In the case of Lisbon, it must be admitted, there was reason for Mack's enthusiasm; the streets are as narrow as those in Genoa, as steep as those in Constantinople, as winding and tortuous as those in Naples.

As soon as we were settled in the Hotel do Universo, I set out with Mack and Perigarde to find our banker. Accustomed as I am to finding the way in foreign cities, it was not ten minutes before we were all three lost in the labyrinthian streets of Lisbon. The banker's address was written plainly on a card. The first person to whom we showed the card directed us up a street composed of a flight of steep steps. It was the right street, but somehow the numbers were all wrong, and after going its whole length, or rather height, without seeing our number, we inquired of another passer-by. This one happened to speak English, and explained that numbers in Lisbon streets run up one side and down the other, so that No. 1 is opposite No. 500, or whatever may be the highest number. The system is confusing, and we counted ourselves fortunate in finding an English speaking Portuguese to explain: otherwise we might not have found the banker in a month. When we did find him, I was surprised to find that I was a millionnaire. Little did I dream, on leaving New York with a few dollars in my pocket and a small credit on a foreign bank, that, in fifteen short days, I could count my money by the millions; and little did the people in Lisbon dream, as they saw me walk along their streets in flannel shirt and shabby coat, that a millionnaire had lighted in their midst. My pride of purse received a sudden fall when I found that it required 2,000 reis to pay for one day's board at a hotel; that a plain overcoat of which I stood in need would cost 20,000 reis; that a dress suit, of which I did *not* stand in need, would cost 40,000 reis. It takes about a bucketful of reis to make a dollar. We thought of California Forty-niners with their ten dollars a day wages, flour $50 a barrel, boots $30 a pair, clothing $100 a suit, and appreciated the fact that one may have a bushel of money and yet be poor.

It is not expensive in Lisbon; it only seems so because of the small value of the money. Reduced to American dollars the cost of living is small. At the Hotel do Universo we had pleasant rooms with balconies looking out on the Praça de Dom Pedro: the table was abundant and good, and our bill was only one dollar a day. Similar accommodations would cost three dollars in Paris, and two or two and a half in Florence or Rome. Lisbon is comparatively neglected by tourists; hence prices have not been raised for the benefit of English and Americans, as they have been in most parts of Europe. For a summer vacation combining romantic interest with prosaic economy I recommend a voyage to Lisbon. The figures would stand about thus:—

Round trip, New York to Lisbon............ 30 days, 100 dollars.
Board in Portugal at one dollar per day .... 60 " 60 "
Extras: car fares, etc.......... .... .40 "

Total, three months .... 90 " 200 "

With an extra allowance for railroad fares the sixty days need not be passed entirely in Lisbon and vicinity. For $250 a trip could be taken as above and made to include Seville, Granada, Malaga, and Gibraltar, where the steamer to New York could be taken without returning to Lisbon. The Portuguese capital is worth seeing, not because of monuments and museums, — although it has both, — but because of its unique street life, its picturesque scenery, and still more picturesque people. Among these I made investigations to ascertain their wages and manner of living. In one of the first half dozen houses I visited I made a lucky find. It was in a crooked little street standing on one end and winding around like a spiral staircase — the Beco do Bogio. I was beginning with the usual apologies in broken Italian, — that being the nearest language to Portuguese I could talk. — when the good woman whose house I had entered, said:—

"I think you must be an American, so am I: let us talk in English."

How foolish one feels to find one has been talking broken Italian to an American! How came she, an American, in this outlandish place? She explained that her husband was

MARKET AT ALICANTE

a Portuguese seaman. They married in New York and had once lived there, but now their home is in Lisbon. At this point a bright boy of fifteen or sixteen entered.

"My son John," said the lady. "You need not talk Italian. John talks English as well as I do."

John also spoke Portuguese so I engaged him as interpreter and guide. During the rest of our stay in Lisbon John was my constant companion; as he performed his services so faithfully and well, I give his address for the benefit of the reader who may find himself in Portugal: John M. Celestino, Jr., Beco do Bogio, No. 5, Lisbon.

The unfavorable impression as to the condition of Lisbon labor which my investigations gave me, have since been confirmed by the panic, almost revolution, that took place in the kingdom. It is not that wages are low; for they are not, as wages go in Europe. The trouble is that too often there are no wages at all — too often men, willing, anxious to work, find no work to do. Portugal is blessed with a fertile soil, a glorious climate; her people possess intelligence enough to dig the ground, to bring together the two factors necessary (and sufficient) to supply human necessities, — land and labor; yet it is a cruel fact that many are not able to satisfy the simplest wants of life, notwithstanding land and labor are all that is necessary, and notwithstanding Portugal has an abundance of both. I have sufficient confidence in mankind to believe the time will come when the strangest thing the historian can relate to our descendants will be the fact that there *was* a time when men, willing and able to work, starved for lack of work. Returning one day from the castle of Belem, we saw the king and queen dashing along in a showy carriage, drawn by four horses and preceded by outriders. The queen is an amiable, handsome woman, the king, a manly-looking man; but, as my eyes turned from them to a poor woman bowed down under the weight of an enormous burden on her bended back, we could not help asking what good *they* — the king, and queen, and outriders — did *her* and the thousands like her. It seems the people of Portugal have also been asking this question, and if the recent crisis may be taken as a sign of the times, it will not be long before they awake to the fact that royalty and noble families make no adequate return for the millions the people pay to support them. It is becoming the fashion to deride these views, to attribute them to youth, but as I grow older, I am impressed more and more with the injustice wrought by man's reversal of the Biblical command. Instead of the non-eater being he that doeth no work, the men who work hardest often have least to eat, while those who work not at all have more than they can eat though they live as long as Methuselah.

One night, while John and I were strolling through a narrow, crooked street, we saw a crowd in front of an arched doorway leading through a tunnel into a small court, whence a flight of stairs led into a hall. When we succeeded in wedging a way through the crowd, a man at the foot of the stairs stopped us and demanded the pass-word.

"Tell him I am an American," I said to John. "Explain that I am studying Portugal and the people."

During the next two or three minutes John and the man at the steps indulged in an exchange of pyrotechnical sentences and gestures. The frequent words, "Americano," "Republicano," were all that I understood; then John told me some one had been sent for to determine whether we should be admitted. When this man came and the words, "Americano," "Republicano," were again uttered, apparently with pleased emphasis, the door was opened, my hand seized and warmly shaken, and I was escorted into the hall which was crowded with men and women. On the walls were placards on which were conspicuous the words "Liberty" and "Fraternity." One motto read: "A Emancipacão dos Trabalhadores deve ser obra dos mesmos Trabalhadores" (Labor's emancipation must be accomplished by Labor). After the speeches, which, judging from John's translation, were none too loyal to the established government, the members crowded around me with eager questions as to the way labor organizations are managed in America. What surprised them most was my account of the way in which certain trades limit the number of apprentices, and, in a measure, fix the scale of wages; for instance, certain kinds of iron workers, nailmakers, bricklayers, and carpenters. They were so interested in this account that I had little opportunity to question them. Finally, however, I succeeded, through John, in getting them to talk of their own affairs. They have no unions in the American sense of the word; there is no attempt to limit the number of apprentices, and there is no danger of nine-tenths of the employés striking because the other tenth do not belong to the union. The only organization not political which careful inquiry brought to my knowledge was in no true sense a labor union, the main purpose being insurance. The members pay fifty cents a month, and, in case of sickness, the daily benefit during the first month is forty cents; during the second month, thirty cents; during the third and succeeding months, sixteen cents. No one, however, is paid the benefit unless a member of at least three months' standing.

"This union is a great thing," said a carpenter, as I sat on a bench in his workshop; "but for it many of us would go without bread when sick: wages are too small to save much for rainy days."

I asked if there was no way in which workmen could invest their earnings: prosperity is often as much a matter of saving as of making, and he who devises a *safe* and profitable investment for small earnings will fill a long-felt want. The carpenter said that this question was of no interest to workmen in Portugal, since they rarely have savings to invest.

The Monte Pio Geral on the Rua do Orio, Lisbon, receives small deposits, and pays three per cent interest. "But," said the carpenter, "even skilled workmen seldom have need for the Monte Pio Geral. A cabinet-maker earns only a dollar a day, while ordinary carpenters earn barely seventy-five cents." Pointing to one of the men in his shop carving the head of Christ, the carpenter added: "That man makes the finest Christ heads and images in Lisbon, yet he is lucky when he earns a dollar and a quarter a day, beginning at seven and working until six."

The master carpenter himself was a well-to-do man. His home consisted of seven small rooms in the rear of the shop; in one of these rooms, which overlooked the tops of the houses across the street and the broad Tagus beyond, was a piano, a sofa, and three or four nicely upholstered chairs. The carpenter noticed my look of surprise at these unusual evidences of prosperity.

"You see," said he, "I have not always lived in Portugal. For two years I was in Rio de Janeiro, three years in Valparaiso, and in those places I made such good wages that I brought home enough money to set up this shop."

He showed us in one room a number of stout, iron-bound boxes, each fourteen inches long, nine wide, and six deep, that belonged to the bank of England and Spain. Each box, when it comes from England, contains £5000 in gold sovereigns. The bank has the boxes repaired, and uses them in shipping money to Rio de Janeiro, Montevideo, and other South American ports. The shop and seven small rooms cost $200 per year — much less than would be charged for as favorable a location in an American city as large as Lisbon.

There seem to be few beggars in Lisbon: either the police prohibit begging, or the people prefer to work no matter how small the wages. The narrow *becos* or alleys are honey-combed with hovels in which patient men and women, and even children, toil from early morn until late night for pittances barely enough to keep body and soul together. In strolling through one of these *becos* we heard the buzz and clatter of sewing-machines from almost every door, and, but for the queer streets, the pink and blue houses, the dark, swarthy people, it would have been easy to imagine ourselves in the Third District of New Orleans, where whole streets are occupied by poor sewing-women. John knocked at one of the doors; a voice bade us, in Portuguese, to enter; the next moment we were in the sewing-*man's* home: the operator at the machine was a man, not a woman, and he was working in leather, not cloth.

"There are a great many who do this work," said the operator. "The factories send out the lower part of the shoes, and we sew on the uppers at our homes. Fourteen cents are paid for making the button-holes and sewing the uppers on a pair of low quarter shoes. On high shoes we receive twenty cents a pair. My wife and I earn about eighty cents a day."

"Is living cheap enough for you to get along on eighty cents a day?"

"We must make it cheap enough," replied the sewer of uppers, shrugging his shoulders, and waving his hand at the dingy, squalid surroundings. The room, which was not more than six feet wide and twelve long, served as workshop, dining-room, and kitchen. A ladder in the rear led to a small loft, without light or ventilation, where slept the family of six — husband, wife, wife's sister, and three children. The rent of the hovel with its gloomy loft was $1.50 per month. The shoemaker said that he would have to pay $2 but for the fact that his family has lived there for several generations: his father, his grandfather, and his great-grandfather had lived in that gloomy house. The clothing of the shoemaker was scanty, but his food seemed sufficient both in quantity and quality. The dinner which the wife's sister was preparing consisted of eels, onions, green peas, bread, and wine. Wine and eels are very cheap in Lisbon. The streets fairly swarm with fisher-women bearing on their heads broad, flat baskets, laden with eels and sardines. Even the poorest workmen manage to have the one or the other fish once or twice a week. From replies to my questions, I prepared the following table, showing the earnings and cost of living of the shoemaker's family of six.

Breakfast at eight: Bread and coffee. Dinner at twelve: Fish (sardines, boiled cod, or eels), wine, bread, sometimes potatoes or peas. Supper at six: Rice, bread, wine or coffee.

Cost of living: —

Food, per day, 50 cents; per year		$182.50
Fuel, 1 kilo (2¼ lbs.) per day, 3 cents; per year		10.95
Water, 1 barrel per day, per year		7.30
Rent, $1.50 per month; per year		18.00
Clothing of husband	$17.80	
" wife	9.10	
" sister	10.95	
" children	8.00	
		45.85
Total yearly expenses of family of six		$264.60
Earnings of wife and husband, 80 cents per day, 300 days,	$240.00	
Earnings of wife's sister (19 years old)	18.00	
		258.00
Deficit		$6.60

When the reader bears in mind that this is the condition of a whole class, a class that represents skilled and constant labor, he will realize that, imperfect as is the condition of American labor, it is infinitely superior to that of labor in Europe. True, *some* American laborers live in hovels as bad or worse than that of the Lisbon shoemaker; but nowhere in America will the above description apply to a whole class of skilled mechanics. Sewing-women are excepted; everywhere, and in all times, it seems as if this unfortunate class is doomed to the longest hours, the hardest work, the smallest pay. We visited a seamstress living a few yards from the shoemaker, and despite evidences of grinding poverty, found the woman at the sewing-machine uncomplaining, in fact almost cheerful. Said she: —

"They give me twenty cents for each cap, and I can make five or six a day."

"That is more than a dollar a day," I said, surprised at the amount. But the buxom little woman quickly explained. She furnishes the silk, the thread, and other materials, which consume all but twenty or thirty cents of her day's earnings. Considering that shoemakers, bricklayers, and other skilled mechanics make barely sixty cents a day, the seamstress with her twenty or thirty cents is relatively as well paid as her sisters in America. Her room had absolutely no other furniture than a poor little bed, the chair in which she was sitting, and the sewing-machine, which served also as dining-table: her dinner, a loaf of bread, was lying on the leaf of the machine when we entered.

These rambles through the poor quarters of Lisbon often brought us into strange places. Descending, one day, some steep steps that led into what seemed a dark cave, we came to a door which yielded to pressure, and opened into a long, dark tunnel, twenty feet below the level of the street. We explored this tunnel to the end, and were rewarded by finding another door that admitted us into a gallery seventy-five or a hundred feet long, with an ancient tile roof supported by posts and rafters, that sloped on one side to within five feet of the floor. On the other side the roof was full thirty feet high. The five-foot side was open, looking out on the tops of the neighboring houses, and on a garden in the rear of the house 150 feet below; for, notwithstanding we had descended twenty feet to reach this place, it was high above the street in its rear. The view from the gallery was charming, but it did not hold our attention as did the gallery itself. At one end was a wheel, five feet in diameter. A girl with a perfect profile, dark, expressive eyes, pretty brown arms bare to the shoulders, stood slowly turning the wheel, while a handsome, curly-haired man, also with bare arms, walked backwards from the wheel, manipulating the hemp as it twisted into rope, — a charming picture which, unfortunately, did not last long: our unexpected entrance caused both girl and man to stop short and stare. Of course I returned the stare, especially at that pretty, brown-armed girl with the mild wonder in her dark eyes; but explanations were more in order than staring, so I smiled, doffed my hat, and uttered the words I had so often found of magical power — "Americano, Americano." This may be thought a rather limited explanation, but it goes a long way in Portugal. The Portuguese, who dislike the English on account of the complication in Africa, like Americans, and pardon them for what, in an Englishman, they would look on as an unforgivable offence. During our stay in Lisbon I walked into dozens of private houses, and in no case was the intrusion resented after learning I was an American. I always spoke that word myself, then referred to John for particulars. The password did not fail in the case of the ropemaker. His look of surprise gave way to one of good-natured curiosity, and it was not long before he was telling me all about himself and the sad decline in ropemaking in Lisbon.

"Formerly," said Antonio, "I kept twenty men, and we had to work far into the night to make the rope that was ordered. Now Mendoça [the pretty girl] and I make all and more than we can sell."

There is food for reflection in Antonio's remark. For the moment it made me think of civilization and the march of human progress as a remorseless Juggernaut crushing over working people, grinding them into the earth. Here is Antonio do Souza, the ropemaker, slowly but surely being ground into the hardest poverty between the two millstones of civilization — new inventions on the one hand, importations of machine-made ropes on the other. *Tempora mutantur et nos mutamur in illis* — but what if we do not change with them? "Ah," replies the philosopher, the economist, "as the victim in front of Juggernaut is crushed, so are crushed those who cannot keep up with the times — there is no escape from the inexorable law of the survival of the fittest." As far as present facts go, the philosopher and political economist are right. That Juggernaut of modern times — machinery and division of labor — marches on unpityingly, giving no heed to the thousands of Antonios it grinds under its wheels. I am not unmindful of the vast increase in the sum total of wealth due to machinery and division of labor, but I cannot shut my eyes to the present suffering caused by the changes. The problem to be solved is not the production, but the distribution of wealth, and it seems to me, if the Antonios of the world have not the inherent force, ability, adaptability, or whatever it is that is necessary to enable them to change with the changing times and wring from Nature at least a bare living, political economists should include human feelings in their calculations and cease coldly propounding that cruel doctrine, "survival of the fittest," — a doctrine which, in effect, is to advise a helpless victim to soar upward if he would be saved, well knowing he has no wings to soar. Antonio, who has worked twenty years making rope by hand, has not the capacity, the adaptability, to take up new methods. What is to be done with him? It is of course easier to ask than to answer questions. New methods and new machinery are beneficial in the long run, and the world cannot afford to neglect means by which the production of wealth is cheapened and simplified. It is not right, however, in doing this, to neglect the Antonios who, unable to adapt themselves to new conditions, become lost in the struggle and are crushed as between two millstones by the march of human events. Once a shoemaker could make a shoe. Put him on any spot of the earth, and, with the proper tools and materials, he could fashion you a shoe. The shoemaker of to-day can no more make a shoe than he can make a wagon. If a "pecker," he can make the sole of your shoe; if an "upper" worker, he can make the tops; if a "heeler," he can put on the heels: but do all of these? make a complete shoe? He could as easily construe a passage in Homer.

> "Each morning sees some task begun,
> Each evening sees its close;
> Something attempted, something done,
> Has earned a night's repose."

Can this be said of labor to-day? In years past, the shoemaker, the coat-cutter, the skilled artisan saw his labor take definite shape, saw his work grow into a finished and visible whole. But the artisan of to-day must have a vivid imagination to realize, as did Longfellow's Village Blacksmith, that something is done. He knows he has pressed a lever the past ten hours and seen several thousand shoe soles drop into a basket, but he never sees a shoe. Nor is the coat ever seen by the cutter who runs a razor-like knife through slits in a table, cutting a dozen garments at a time. With the rapid and easy production of wealth I have no quarrel: I only wish to put in a plea for some attention to the problem attendant upon the present division and displacement of labor. To Antonio do Souza on the Rua do Milagre do Santo Antonio No. 4, the improvement in the art of rope-making has brought practical ruin. The only ropes he makes now are ordinary clotheslines seven yards long.

"Mendoça and I," said he, "make seven ropes an hour.

We get the hemp from Russia for sixteen cents a kilo [2.2046 pounds], out of which we make six ropes that sell for forty cents. In a day we spin ten kilos into sixty ropes that sell for $2.40. Deducting $1.60 for the hemp, Mendoça and I have eighty cents a day for our wages."

Of this eighty cents the worthy Antonio keeps the lion's share, the dark-eyed, brown-armed Mendoça receiving only twelve cents for a day's turning of that monotonous wheel. Another acquaintance of mine in Lisbon is a little, dried-up old man who makes handles for paint-brushes. We saw him in passing his shop, a hole in the wall five feet square, and just high enough to sit up in. A lot of round sticks twelve inches long lay before him on the jamb of the door. Stepping over these round sticks and squatting by his side on the floor, I chatted with the handle-maker about his life and work.

"It is not hard," said he, "but very slow. I cut the sticks and scrape them round and smooth, but I eat up the money faster than I can cut the sticks"; with which reflection he picked up his scraper and began rounding the piece of wood he held in hand.

"Stop work," said I, "and let me talk to you. I will pay you for your time. How much do you earn an hour?"

The dried-up little man seemed at a loss what to make of this proposition. Evidently it was the first time any one had appreciated his conversation enough to pay for it. Finally, when his mind had taken in the idea, he began to calculate how much he earned per hour. A bundle of wood weighing thirty-two pounds costs ten cents: out of one bundle are made eight dozen handles which sell for ten cents per dozen: to make eight dozen smooth and round takes ten to twelve hours. This would make the honest fellow's toil worth six or seven cents an hour: I gave him double this sum for the hour I kept him talking about his life and work. In the rear of his shop was a pile of rags that served as a bed: over head, on the black, grimy wall, was a shrine with a figure of the Virgin and the infant Christ. The handle-maker's life was pathetic in its loneliness and monotony. Forty years had he worked in that hole in the wall. Father, mother, friends, one by one had dropped out of his life: some had gone to the great unknown beyond the grave; others to foreign lands, to Africa, and to North and South America; while this withered, bent old man, without a friend to cheer him, still sleeps and prays and scrapes sticks in the dingy den that has housed him since his boyhood half a century ago. His breakfast consists of coffee and bread; dinner, of sardines or eels, bread, oil and vinegar; supper, same as breakfast — total cost about twenty-five cents a day.

"No, it does not cost much," he said, when I figured it out for him. "You see, I am getting old and do not eat much now. Some days my back aches so I cannot work, then I spend all I have saved on other days." He looked reverently up at the shrine and the image standing in it, and I wondered if he had made friends with it and found companionship and comfort in seeing it there always so near him. Although profuse in thanks for what he called my generosity, I fear, after all, the poor little man lost by the operation. My visit was such an event it seemed to unsettle him. When I started away he shut his shop and followed me about, stopping now and then to tell people of the strange American. The next day while I was interviewing the proprietor of a charcoal shop, the little man came in and hung about in a wondering way.

Charcoal shops are numerous in Lisbon, where the stove in common use is a clumsy sort of vase a foot high, five or six inches deep, and about eight inches wide at the top. Cakes of charcoal are put in this shallow bowl, and the pot or cooking-utensil is placed over the charcoal. This primitive arrangement is in almost every house, real stoves being seldom found in the homes of the poor and middle classes. The charcoal cakes are made of a mixture of slack and fuller's earth, pressed in moulds and put on shelves a week or ten days to dry. A dozen cakes four inches in diameter and one inch thick cost three cents. The cakes consume slowly, hence form an economical fuel. Coke costing one cent a kilo is used with the charcoal, and in lighting the fire, instead of kindling wood, dried grass is used costing two cents for a bunch large enough to start twenty fires. The man in the charcoal shop, a black, sooty place, seemed much puzzled at my questions, but he showed no hesitation in replying. He receives as manager $4.50 per month, and bed and board. He explained that he received "good" wages because of the responsibility of his position. He has to weigh the wood and coke, and in making charcoal cakes, must see that they are not too large for the money. His assistant has quite as much work, but no responsibilities, so is paid only $3.50 a month, and board. The following figures given by the charcoal workmen show what laborers' clothes cost in Lisbon:—

Trousers, $1.80; shirts, 60 cents; undershirts, 36 cents; drawers, 44 cents; shoes, $2.50; sandals, 50 cents; hats, $1; overcoats, $3.

Even on $4.50 a month the charcoal man saves a little money, which he sends to his parents in the country. The assistant is unable to save out of his $3.50 salary, so his wife is obliged to support herself.

"She works on a farm," said the poor fellow, "and I see her only once a year," adding that he "might as well have no wife."

With the exception of such very poor men as the paintbrush handle-maker and the charcoal men, the workmen with whom we came in contact in Lisbon seemed self-respecting, neither asking nor expecting money for the information they gave. Only once did we come across a skilled artisan who expected a fee. Previous experience had led us to think it was not the right thing to offer fees, and quite a scene occurred in consequence of our mistake in the matter. It was in a macaroni factory. After watching the swarthy, half-naked men, and the machines grinding out little Niagaras of white paste, we thanked the workman who had explained the process and turned to go. The man accompanied us to the door, and just as we were going out, extended his hand. "How friendly these Portuguese are," I thought, shaking his hand warmly. The fellow looked disappointed; he called to his comrades, and, as we descended the steps that constituted the street, we were followed by the jeers and maledictions of the macaroni-makers. The way we accounted for this, after the uniform courtesy elsewhere extended, was, that the macaroni factory, being central and interesting, is visited by tourists who have accustomed the employés to "tips" for any information extended.

In rambling about looking into the condition of wage-workers, we sometimes stumbled into residences of the wealthy — this from the fact that the exterior of a Lisbon palace is often as dingy as a Lisbon hovel; in fact, the ground floor of a palace may be rented to shoe cobblers, venders of charcoal, grocers, butchers, etc. On one occasion, after passing through a gate, we found ourselves on top of a cathedral; the street from which we entered was a hundred or more feet above the next street on which the cathedral faced; the door we entered opened on the roof. It is not often that, on entering a dingy gate, apparently leading to a workshop, one finds oneself on top of a church; still more seldom will one find a residence and a garden there as we did that morning in Lisbon. There were fig and orange trees, grapevines, rows of beets, cabbages, and peas, a chicken-yard; in short, so rural was the scene we had to go to the side and look down upon the steep streets and the miles of pink and blue houses to realize that we were not in the country. A glance through a stained glass window at one end of the roof showed that we were really on top of the cathedral: we could see the priests, the kneeling people, and the lighted candles on the altar far below. While wondering at the strange place, a woman came out of the house to gather vegetables from the garden. She did not see us at first, and was stooping, putting peas into her apron when I startled her by telling John to say that she had a fine garden. Of course the woman did not need any one to come all the way from America to tell her her garden was fine; still the remark was successful as a "feeler." When John followed it up by saying I was an American and had entered the garden for the charming view, the good woman colored with pleasure.

"It is beautiful here," she said; "but if you will come with me, you shall see a finer view than this."

She led the way into the house, up a pair of steps, into a kind of observatory, whence one could look over nearly all Lisbon and the Tagus with its hundreds of sails from all parts of the world. A young girl of fifteen was in this observatory, reading. At first she looked at us in blank surprise, but when the garden woman said I was an American come to see the view, she smiled, and going to a cabinet got a telescope, which she kindly placed at my disposal. The young girl was niece of the "master"; the woman was servant. She said her wages amounted to only $18 a year, with bed and board. When I said many woman-servants in America make as much in a month, she shook her head: —

"I love my master; I have been with him many years. I have all I wish, and would not leave him and Marcia," looking affectionately at the young girl, "for eighteen dollars a day."

CHAPTER III

A Gloomy Dungeon — Living Men in Coffins and Shrouds — Perpetual Isolation — How a Nunnery was transformed — A Fat Judge, a Squalling Baby, and a Frightened Family — Miss Detroit invites us to the Theatre — A Visit to Portugal's Dead Royalty — Ghastly Appearance of the Kings and Queens

BEING interested not only in free, but also in convict labor, I set out to investigate the condition and policy of the Portuguese penitentiary. The event proved it much easier to "set out" to do this than to actually do it. In America, almost any prison may be visited by any man presenting his visiting-card. In Portugal, the admission of a visitor to the penitentiary is a grave matter which cabinets and ministers debate. Not knowing this at first, I was surprised when the secretary of the Minister of Justice refused even to make known my request.

"It cannot be done," said he in such a gruff, disagreeable way that I was the more anxious to do it. I went to Mr. George S. Batcheller, the American Minister, presented letters of introduction, explained my interest in social studies and my desire to visit the prison. Mr. Batcheller said:—

"It is a pity you are interested in these matters. That alone will be considered excellent reason why you should not be admitted. Nevertheless we can try. I will write you a letter."

Mr. Batcheller kindly wrote a letter, not merely introductory, but requesting as a favor the permission desired. When I returned with this letter to the officer of the Minister of Justice, the supercilious secretary appeared to be more sur-

MONTE CARLO

prised than pleased. But the seal of the United States Minister impressed him, and he condescended to deliver the missive to his superior. It was fortunate for me that the anteroom of the Minister overlooked the handsome Praça do Commercio, else the unreasonably long time it took to consider Mr. Batcheller's letter would have dragged more slowly than it did. I watched the people on the square and under the arcades, looked at the equestrian statue of Dom José and at the statues of the elephants, and did a good deal of strong thinking about official red tape, before the secretary returned with the information that the Minister of Justice was not the proper authority to issue the permit.

"Who is the proper authority?" I inquired.

"His Excellency is of the opinion that you should apply to His Excellency the Procurator General."

"Why will not one Excellency do as well as another?" I asked; but John very sensibly refused to translate this question, and off we started to the Procurator General. The office of this Minister was in another building, on another street, reached through a maze of crooked corridors and up flights of winding stairs. When finally we arrived there, we had only our trouble for our pains. His Excellency assured us courteously, but firmly, that *he* was not the man we wanted. True, he sent persons to the penitentiary, but those he sent went there "for keeps," not as visitors. Who was the person we wanted? Well, really, he could not say; he *had* thought the Minister of Justice the proper authority, but since His Excellency had said he was not, why then he was not.

"But there must be some one who has authority to give permission to inspect the prison?"

The Procurator General, a polite, pudgy little gentleman, twirled the ends of his mustache a moment in profound reflection; then, as if suddenly inspired, said: —

"Perhaps the man you want is the Minister of Religion."

"Where is he to be found?"

"In the office of the Minister of Justice. The fact is," added the Procurator General, smiling suavely, "the portfolios of Justice and Religion are held by the same individual. When His Excellency said it was not in his province to issue this permit, possibly he meant as Minister of Justice. Try him as Minister of Religion."

This was charming: we went back on our winding way through the maze of corridors, down the steep steps, and in half an hour were again confronting the supercilious secretary of the Minister of Justice and Religion. I told John to say that the American Minister would feel trifled with if his letter were not given attention. If the Portuguese government wished to refuse the permit requested by the American Minister, it could of course do so, but an answer one way or the other was due to the dignity of our government. This sounded very important and exerted a visible effect on the secretary. When he came back from the Minister's office, it was with a message to the effect that, if we would call at four o'clock on the third day, an official reply would be made.

"Hadn't His Excellency better take more time? Say a month or a year? He should not hurry in a weighty matter like this."

But John's good sense came again to the rescue; he refused to translate, and there was nothing left but to wait until the appointed day and hour. When it came, I was gratified to learn that, as "Ministro dos Negocios Ecclesiasticos," he had issued the permit which he had refused as "Ministro de Justiça." The document was addressed to the governor of the prison, and read as follows: —

"*Ministerio dos Negocios Ecclesiasticos e da Justiça:*

"Encarrega-me o Ex.mo Sñr Ministro da Justiça de rogar a V. Ex.a que se digne de permetter que o Exmo Sñr Ministro dos Estados Unidos em Portugal veja essa Cadeia Geral Penitenciaria. Deus Guarde á V. Ex.ª

" SECRETARIA D'ESTADOS DOS NEGOCIOS
ECCLESIASTICOS E DA JUSTIÇA."[1]

"Why," said John, as he read this letter, after descending the steps to the Praço do Commercio, "this is an order to admit His Excellency the American Minister. The governor of the prison will not admit you upon this order."

It was out of the question to try the circumlocution office again: I did not expect to remain an eternity in Lisbon; I resolved to call on Mr. Batcheller and ask him to go with me to the prison. Fortunately, circumstances did not require this exhibition of assurance.

"Take my card with you," said Mr. Batcheller. "They do not know me at the prison, and ten to one no questions will be asked. If they do ask questions, you need only shrug your shoulders and intimate that you do not speak the language."

This plan was adopted, and when I presented the letter of the Minister of Justice, acccompanied by Mr. Batcheller's card, the governor of the penitentiary took it for granted I was the American Minister and ordered the guards to show every attention and answer every question. Mack, Perigarde, the professor, and John were with me, and it was soon whispered around that the American "Ambassador" and suite were visiting the prison. Though rather uncomfortable at finding ourselves in so false a position, like Macbeth we felt we had gone too far to retreat; going back would be as bad as going

---

[1] *Ministry of Ecclesiastical Affairs and of Justice:*

I am deputed by His Excellency the Minister of Justice to request Your Excellency to graciously permit His Excellency the Minister of the United States in Portugal to visit the general prisons of the penitentiaries. God guard Your Excellency.

SECRETARY OF THE STATE'S ECCLESIASTICAL
AFFAIRS AND OF JUSTICE.

forward. So we nerved ourselves for the ordeal, resolving to do credit to the high position thrust upon us.

The prison is one of the costliest, yet one of the gloomiest, most soul-oppressing places I ever saw. The system is that of complete isolation. The convicts are confined in separate cells which open into a number of long corridors radiating from a common centre. The centre of the Dodecagon is like the hub of a wheel, and the twelve corridors are like twelve enormous spokes. Spiral iron stairs wind up to a second floor of the "hub": the guards stationed there and on the third floor can look down each of the twelve corridors and see the door of every cell in the prison. Five of the corridors are not long empty galleries leading to the cells, but are honeycombed with curious, sentry-like boxes arranged in tiers, one row above the other, the first row on the ground floor, the last — at the end of the corridor — touching the roof fifty or sixty feet above the first row. In these boxes, which look like coffins stood on end, the prisoners stand for an hour every Sunday while the chaplain performs mass before an altar on the second platform of the hub, or central point of the Dodecagon. The gilded altar, with its marble figure of Christ, and with its lighted candles, is visible to each and every prisoner in the coffin-boxes; so, too, is the chaplain; but no one prisoner can see another. When they file from their cells into the chapel corridors, they are enveloped in shroud-like sheets that conceal their bodies from head to foot: as each prisoner steps into his box, the door is fastened with a spring lock. The side looking toward the chaplain and altar is closed to within a foot of the top, so that only the head of the prisoner is visible. The chaplain has the appearance of a man addressing several hundred phantoms in coffins standing on end, the eyes of the prisoners flashing through the two little holes in their masks adding to the uncanniness of the scene.

The first gallery has 142 of these repulsive sentry-boxes; the second gallery has 109; the third, 78; the fourth, 109; the fifth, 95: in all, 533, or two more than the total number of prisoners in the building on the day of our visit. Every day, from 8.30 A.M. to 3.30 P.M., a professor occupies a platform at the centre of the Dodecagon and instructs different classes in the rudiments of reading, writing, and arithmetic. He illustrates the lessons on a blackboard. Through the peepholes in their masks, the convicts can see and hear the professor, but they are not allowed to ask questions. The professor must take it for granted that his ghost-like pupils understand all that he says. From the time a man enters the Portuguese penitentiary, until the day he leaves, he is made as much like a dead man as possible; he is kept speechless and noiseless. On his feet are felt slippers which make no sound on the few occasions when he is permitted to leave his cell. On his body is a white uniform that extends in a peaked hood covering the entire head and face, with the exception of three little holes for the eyes and nose. The first glimpse of these miserable beings makes one shudder — they are like phantoms as they glide silently along. The only glimpse one prisoner gets of another is through the two little eyelet holes in the mask, and even this is not often gained; for, except when *en route* to and from the chapel and the exercise triangles, each man is locked alone in his cell. The exercise triangles are at the ends of each of the spokes of the huge wheel; that is, at the ends of each of the long corridors radiating from the common hub or centre. The triangles, each side thirty feet long, are ranged about a tower. The guard on this tower can look down into each triangle, and each prisoner can look up and see the guard; but no one prisoner can see the other. The walls of the triangles are ten feet high, so as to keep the wretched creatures perfectly isolated even during the one hour out of the twenty-four they are allowed to exercise. We ascended one of the watch towers, whence we saw the poor prisoners pacing to and fro like unhappy spirits of the dead. The exercise triangles are so few in comparison with the number of prisoners, that no sooner is one set of men through with their hour's pacing to and fro than another set takes their places, the first set returning to the cells. Though alone in his cell, the convict is never sure that the eye of a guard is not upon him. In each cell door is a peep hole an inch in diameter. Covering this peep hole is a brass shutter that can be lifted only from the outside: guards move about in noiseless, felt slippers, lifting now this shutter, now that, reporting for punishment any prisoner not at work. The poor fellow may swear that he was resting only that particular moment, that he had worked hard the rest of the day — no excuse is accepted. He is forthwith taken to a dark cell, where his bed is the stone floor, and his food the piece of bread and the cup of water which is thrust once a day through a trap in the door.

One good thing may be mentioned: the cell where the prisoner remains solitary, twenty-three hours out of every twenty-four, is roomy and well ventilated: being his workshop as well as his sleeping room, this is necessarily so. Some have carpenter's benches and tools; others, machinery for book-binding; others have old-fashioned hand weaving looms, hand machines for making shoes, etc. After peeping through the hole in the door of one of the shoe cells, we asked the guard to let us enter. The door unlocked with a big key, and the next moment we were in the cell, facing the phantom prisoner, who had arisen upon our entrance and stood silently by his machine, awaiting the guard's commands. His eyes burned like two coals through the two holes in the ghastly mask.

"We should like to see this man's face," I said. "Can he not remove the mask for a few minutes?"

The guard looked grave at this request, but finally, after

carefully closing the cell door, ordered the convict to uncover
— the face was scarcely less uncanny than the mask. Shrunken
and pallid cheeks, hollow eyes, livid complexion, showed the
effects of solitary confinement in a cell and a white shroud.

"How long has this man been here?" I asked.

"Two years."

Only two years? A short time as we count it, but an eternity to that poor convict shoemaker. The hours, the days, the weeks, go by slower than snails creep, and each one more dark and despairing than the other: for his sentence is a life one. No. 113 had been in the prison five years, but seemed to have borne the ordeal better than the shoemaker had borne his two years. No. 113 was a maker of walking-sticks and umbrellas. No. 476 was an intelligent man and seemed grateful when the guard gave him permission to remove his mask. His cell was ornamented with a number of trinkets which showed both taste and ingenuity. There was a windmill, a tramcar with horses, figures of men and women, all made of papier-maché. He was eager to show these things, and as pleased as a child at the compliments I bestowed. Not yet had this man's spirit been broken, not yet has he been made to feel like the shrouded corpse he so closely resembles: but there is time, ample time; for only six months of his eight years' sentence have passed. Should he survive eight years of this living tomb, he will then go to the African penal settlement for twenty years more. Such horror does the solitary cell, the coffin-like box in the chapel, the triangle-exercise cage inspire, that going to Africa is regarded as a great boon. No masks are worn in Africa, no upright coffins to stand in on Sunday, no solitary cell; prisoners in Africa have the blessed privilege of seeing human beings, of realizing that they themselves are human, that all the world is not composed of white, soundless phantoms. Hope dies hard in the human breast: doubtless, even these unhappy creatures in the Lisbon prison dream of the possibility of escape, or of semi-freedom in Africa.

"It is strange they do not go mad," said the professor to the guard.

"Or do not commit suicide," added Mack.

"They do both," replied the guard, "though we take every precaution to prevent. Every night the tools are removed from their cells, guards patrol the corridors constantly, often peeping in to see that all is right. At five in the morning the danger is over, for at that hour the prisoners arise and begin work. At exactly six, the traps in the doors are opened and a piece of bread and a bowl of coffee is thrust into each cell. This disposed of, the prisoners work on until eleven, when the traps in the doors are again opened, this time to admit their dinner of beans or macaroni, rice with meat or codfish, and potatoes. Dinner over, work goes on again until the exercise hour. Supper is at six; at 9.30, bed. Such is the convict's daily life."

Each man is paid for his work, the amount varying from ten to fifty cents a day. Three out of the five hundred and thirty-one prisoners earn eighty cents a day — two blacksmiths and one bookkeeper. The average earnings do not exceed twenty cents, of which one fourth is paid weekly, the balance, when the prisoner finishes his sentence. The fourth received weekly may be expended for tobacco, stamps, and writing material, though not for newspapers. The tobacco may be smoked during the exercise hour, the writing material used on Sunday, after mass.

The foregoing description, imperfect as it is, is yet sufficient to render superfluous the statement that the prison is not self-sustaining, that in fact it is not meant to be. The one hundred and eleven convicts working at shoes made only eight hundred and sixty-five pairs in the month of April, 1891. The same number of convicts in an American penitentiary, having machinery and division of labor, would make more shoes in three days. The solitary system is maintained even in the hospital: it was a pitiful sight, those disease-racked wretches with never the sound of a human voice in their ears, never the sight of a human face for their eyes. On the shutters covering the peep holes we noticed different colored tags.

"Each color," explained the guard, "has a different meaning. A red tag signifies an extra allowance of food of all sorts. A white tag means an extra one-fourth pound of bread, etc., etc. The steward observes these tags, and in delivering the food into the sick man's cell, acts accordingly."

When, finally, the twelfth and last of the Dodecagon corridors had been traversed, our inspection came to a close, and we emerged again into the open air, with that feeling of painful pity which always comes at the sight of suffering one is powerless to relieve.

I had seen other prisons of the solitary system, but none which carry out the principle as rigidly as this, and therein lies a great difference. For instance, the penitentiary at Nuremberg, in Bavaria, is on the isolation system, but the Nuremberg masks are not quite so dreadful as the Lisbon. The Nuremberg mask comes a little below the nose: even this mask they do not always wear. I saw many in the yards and corridors, their masks thrown back on the tops of their heads, engaged in work that even permitted occasional opportunities to speak. One prisoner in the Nuremberg penitentiary was a gray-bearded man, seventy-two years old, — an honest man, until, in his old age, a temptation was placed in his way that he could not resist.

"He was a miller in a Bavarian village," said the prison director, "and his temptation came about thus: the schoolmaster of the village, who was about to take the first trip of his life, had accumulated, during his thirty years of toil, 3000 marks, and this sum he put in a jug and buried in a field, for safe keeping, during his trip to Nuremberg. He thought no one observed him while burying the jug, but he was mistaken. The daughter of the miller saw him, and no sooner was the simple schoolmaster gone, than the jug of money was gone too. The girl kept 2000 marks for herself and gave her father, the old miller, 1000. In addition to the theft, when the frantic schoolmaster discovered his loss and had the matter investigated, they committed perjury, so both father and daughter are in prison, — the father here, the daughter in the separate prison for women."

The way to the Lisbon penitentiary is through a field brilliant with red and yellow wild flowers. As we retraced this way to the city after three hours in the gloomy prison, we congratulated ourselves that the difficulty had been to get in, not out. It would be interesting to note what effect this terrible system has upon crime; whether the years following its adoption showed a material decrease in crime over the years preceding its adoption; whether there are as many "second termers" under the present as under the old system; or whether the mask and solitary cell inspire the convict with enough horror to make him careful not to deserve second imprisonment, — these, and similar points, I attempted to cover, but either the Portuguese authorities have no statistics, or are unwilling to disclose them. The idea in Pennsylvania, where the isolation system originated, was that solitariness would give prisoners more time to reflect upon the error of their ways, and insure speedier reform. The solitary cells, the coffins in the chapels, the lonely triangular cages, certainly afford time for reflection, but it is to be doubted if they are promotive of reform, speedy or slow: rather would they seem to induce melancholy — despair — lunacy.

The Lisbon prison for boys and young men seemed quite cheerful in comparison with the Lisbon penitentiary. As we entered, a boy nine years old was standing in the centre of a large court blowing a horn, in response to which summons speedily appeared one hundred and fifty boys in blue cotton breeches and white cotton shirts. The boys stood in a row while being counted, then filed into their dining-room — a lofty, vaulted chamber which had served during three hundred years as a place of prayer for nuns: the Lisbon house of correction is an ancient nunnery. As the years rolled into centuries, the religious order grew smaller and smaller: one by one the sisters died, until thirty years ago, but one solitary nun was left — "Just like the ten little Injuns — and 'then there were nun,'" remarked Mack irreverently. What were the thoughts of that last remaining nun, as she wandered alone in the cloisters and chapels, the sole survivor of an order hundreds of years old? No one can tell, for she died without relating her experiences during the three years she remained alone. The government forthwith appropriated the building and converted it into a house of correction. The life of the present inmates is doubtless as rigid and hard as that of its former occupants, the nuns. The boys have for breakfast at eight o'clock, bread, potatoes, and beans; dinner at 3.30 consists of beans with tripe or potatoes, sometimes codfish, and once a month a pint of wine. At 7.30 there is a supper of black bread and black coffee. The cost of this food per boy per day is $15\frac{1}{2}$ cents; the pint of wine costs $4\frac{1}{2}$ cents; so that on one day of each month the cost is increased to twenty cents. Four cents of the daily allowance is for the bread, of which each boy is allowed 700 grammes ($1\frac{1}{2}$ pounds). Although this menu is neither as good nor abundant as the menu in American prisons, the cost is greater. The daily per capita cost of food in the Jefferson City, Missouri, penitentiary is only 10.01 cents, and the convict lives sumptuously compared with the convicts in even the best European prisons.

The total daily cost to the State of Missouri for each prisoner is as follows: —

Food, 10.01 cents; fuel, 4.03 cents; clothing, 2.37 cents; ordinary repairs, 1.02 cents; salaries of officers and employés, 11.75 cents; miscellaneous, 4.60 cents: total, 33.78 cents.

While costing more, the Portuguese prisoners produce less. In the St. Louis house of correction, eighty-five boys make 120,000 pairs of shoes per year. In the old nunnery at Lisbon, beyond making a few helmets and straw mats, the boys do little or nothing. During certain hours they are allowed to play in the cloisters and courts; then those places, once devoted to the pious service of holy women, ring with shouts and laughter, and rough words of rude boys.

"The next place to visit," I thought, after finishing the prisons, "is the place which sends these gloomy buildings their occupants," and off we started for the Law Courts. At the foot of a flight of stone steps stood a sentry. These steps led to a large square with cloisters on each side of its four sides; the different courts open out from the cloisters. Entering one of these courts, we witnessed the way in which Portuguese justice is dispensed.

Some twenty or thirty benches without backs were in the further part of the hall, for the benefit of spectators. Then came a railing, beyond which were the lawyers, officials, and, finally, on a high platform, His Honor the Judge, a ponderous man, with a face so fat from high living and little exercise, that the eyes were almost closed. Over his shoulders was a long, black gown that fell in folds on the platform, over his feet. To the left of the judge sat his secretary, a sallow man, also begowned, one end of the gown tossed over his left shoulder. A little to one side sat the prisoners, — a family, husband, wife, and five children, the latter ranging in age from twelve years down to twelve months, an infant in the mother's arms. The family were accused of the heinous crime of attempting to emigrate from Portugal without the government's permission. Their guilt was plain; they had been found on a steamer about to sail for Brazil, and the sallow secretary looked stony and severe as he read aloud the indictment. Every time the baby gave a squall, the secretary gave a vicious twirl to his moustache and a severe glance at the unhappy mother of the little squaller. It must be admitted, the little beggar was extremely audacious to open its mouth in that sacred place right under the eyes of the representative of Law's Majesty. True, the little criminal was brought there against his own will; but was that any excuse? Evidently not, thought the secretary. The lawyers began. John translated: one of them wanted the whole family executed, or, at least, imprisoned for life; unless they were made an example, what might not the country expect? How long would it be before Portugal would be depopulated? The law was plain; the guilt of this family was plain; let them be so dealt with as to prove a warning to future offenders! etc., etc. When the lawyers were through, the secretary tapped the ponderous judge on the shoulder, awoke him from his doze, and said the case was ready for decision. The fat covered eyes of the judge peered out sternly at the frightened family as if he meant to sentence them to instant death; then, leaning to the side of mercy, he merely delivered a lecture on the folly and wickedness of leaving a land like Portugal for a land like Brazil.

"The present offence will be condoned," said he, in conclusion, "but, as a reminder of your crime in attempting to leave without a passport, your application will now be denied. Portugal is good enough for Portuguese."

On returning to the hotel after the visit to the court, Miss Detroit and Miss Lebanon presented a joint memorial, setting forth the folly of travellers spending their time in jails and workshops, and invited us to visit some of the "tourist" sights of the city.

"Perhaps, after your jails and things," said Miss Detroit,

"you do not think there are any sights in Lisbon, but there are, and you must see them. Let us begin by going to the theatre; 'Donna Juanita' is to be given to-night at the Colyseu dos Recreios, on the Rua Nova da Oalma."

Of course, such an invitation was not to be declined; Miss Detroit and I went for the tickets and learned the peculiar way in which one reserves theatre seats in Portugal. After we laid down $2.40, the price of six tickets, the box-office agent raised his voice in a regular Indian war-whoop. We thought him suddenly insane, but he was not. He was simply calling a man some hundred yards away in another part of the building. This man, when he appeared, carried a paste-pot and a brush with a long handle.

"Follow him," said the ticket agent; and we followed him into the auditorium of the theatre. The man with the paste-pot waved his hand at the seats, told us to make our selection, and, when we had done so, he pasted numbered strips of blue paper on the backs of the chairs. Then he left us to look around the theatre. The scene-painters were at work on the stage; the purchasers of tickets came in every few minutes with the paste-pot man to reserve their seats. That evening, we saw things quite as odd as the method of reserving seats. In the first place, the programme was unceremoniously changed from an opera to a sleight-of-hand performance. In the second place, every man in the audience put on his hat the moment the curtain went down. The performance lasted so late that next morning none of us felt inclined for early rising. It was ten o'clock before we met in the "Universo" parlor, eleven o'clock before breakfast was over, and nearly noon before we found ourselves on the street, bound for the church of Sao Vincente de Fóra.

"And it will be night before we get there," said Mack, noting the leisurely manner in which the three tramcar mules proceeded.

There was ground for this remark, since the Lisbon street cars run on a unique and original plan — a plan more picturesque than rapid. There are tracks, but they exist only as a concession to modern ideas, not really for the use of the cars. The cars are not expected to remain on the track, and the driver frequently takes short cuts down narrow lanes that have no track at all. After rattling through such a lane five or ten minutes, the car gets back on the track again, and you ride smoothly (comparatively) until another short cut is made. While off on one of these side trips, we got into a street so narrow that the wheels of the car collided with the paniers of a donkey which was trying to squeeze through. The owner of the ass was so indignant when he saw the contents of his paniers scattered on the street, that he began beating, not our driver, but the three mules, the astonished and innocent cause of his disaster. Our driver, being a brave fellow, answered this challenge without a tremor. He picked up his whip and, running back, *began beating the poor donkey!* The passengers in the car looked quietly on, making not a word of protest at the delay or the cruelty to the poor beasts chastised for the sins of their masters. Finally, the owner of the ass returned to pick up the contents of his paniers, the driver returned to his car, and all proceeded merrily as before.

The Sao Vincente de Fóra is an unusually interesting cathedral. Its massive walls, though injured by the great earthquake of 1755, did not fall; they yet remain to attest the skill of their builder. Although mass was over when we entered, fully a thousand worshippers still knelt on the marble floor, not in a compact body, but scattered here and there over the vast edifice: a man in a red cloak was going around with a long pole, snuffing out candles. We asked him to show us the crypt where repose the bodies of Portugal's royal family. The man in the red cloak, sniffing American fees in the air, stopped snuffing candles, and conducted us through a long corridor at the further end of which was a massive door opening into the crypt, a gloomy place, dimly lighted, and filled with coffins. The recent dead are in modern caskets, but those of past centuries lie in long boxes with round tops, precisely like so many travelling-trunks. These trunks are stowed away two or three deep on shelves that line the four walls of the crypt; so small is the space, and so ever increasing the number of the dead, that, unless additional space is provided, it will not be long before they will have to stand the coffins on end. In the centre of the crypt is a catafalque, draped in black and decorated with wreaths of artificial flowers. This catafalque is reserved for the last king: at present, Dom Luis, the late king (died 1889), rests here; but when the present king dies he will be placed under the catafalque, and Dom Luis will have to take a back shelf. Our guide with the red cloak and the bunch of iron keys tripped nimbly about, pointing out the inscriptions on the different coffins. To cap the climax, he got a step-ladder, placed it near one of the shelves, and bade us ascend. We did so, and shall never forget the ghastly sight that met our gaze. There, separated from us by only a thin, transparent sheet of glass, was the mouldering corpse of Dom Fernando II. Pushing the step-ladder further along the shelf to the next coffin, we saw the late empress of Brazil, wife of Dom Pedro. The empress's hands were crossed on her breast, her eyes were sunken, her face was splotched and mildewed: drops of water had formed, and were standing suspended from the under side of the glass — sights that made us shudder. The red-cloaked man offered to show us more kings and queens and empresses without extra charge, but we had had enough. We paid him his fee and hurried from the royal charnel house. When in the fresh, pure sunlight again, we felt relieved, and Miss Detroit said she thought Sao Vincente de Fóra quite as bad as my jails and workshops, and requested the professor to consult the guide book and see if

there were no pleasant sights in Lisbon. The professor's
attentions had not relaxed since coming ashore, and he did
his best to find the information Miss Detroit wanted. But he
did not find it, whereupon, Miss Detroit and Miss Lebanon
saying they were sleepy, and a vote being taken, it was
unanimously decided to postpone further sight-seeing until
the morrow.

CHAPTER IV

Perigarde studies Lotteries — How Portuguese Children disappear through a Wall — The Bull Fight at Torres Vedras — Spanish and Portuguese Bull Fights compared — Two Surprises — The Baroness and the Milkery — The Professor disappears

THE next day Perigarde left the hotel early in the morning and, to our surprise, did not return until late at night. Our surprise increased when he explained by saying he had been studying statistics. We knew Perigarde hated statistics.

"Everybody," said he, "buys lottery tickets, and everybody, or *nearly* everybody, sells them. I've been studying the lottery business. An old woman stopped me on the street and sold me a ticket for three cents. The tickets are so cheap, and the drawings so frequent, even the poorest people are constantly wasting their little pittances in the government gambling shops. Printed lists of the winning numbers are hung in all the tobacco stores. I saw a poor woman with a bundle of work under her arm eagerly scanning the numbers and comparing them with the ticket in her hand. At her side was a young girl with a broad tray of fish on her head. Next to the fish girl was a dandy with silk hat and kid gloves. The lottery is a democratic leveller. The fish girl, the old woman, and the dandy were on common ground in their desire to see *their* tickets among the winners. When they got to the bottom of the long columns of figures without finding their numbers there, the sewing-woman heaved a sigh, tightened her grasp on the bundle of work, and walked sadly away; the fish girl walked off, crying her wares in shriller tones than before; the dandy gave a vicious twirl to his ticket, dashed the crumpled pieces on the ground, and walked into the tobacco shop to buy a new one and try his luck again."[1]

"All this is very interesting," observed Mack, as Perigarde paused, "but what else have you done? Surely you have not missed lunch and dinner, and staid out until eleven o'clock, watching people buy lottery tickets?"

"Well, no; that is, not exactly," stammered Perigarde, with a sort of sheepishness we had never seen him exhibit before. "After looking into the lottery question I investigated some of its results. It seems the lotteries are all under the government control, and the proceeds are for the benefit of asylums like the Santa Casa da Misericordia, an interesting place with a very convenient arrangement for mothers who wish to abandon their children. There is a hole in the wall with a revolving cradle. A mother puts her babe in this cradle, gives it a turn, and the little one passes from her sight forever. Even should she repent and wish to reclaim the infant, it is impossible; the attendant who takes the child from the cradle after it is swung within the walls, puts it along with hundreds of others, and in a week the mother herself could not identify it."

"That idea is borrowed from the French," remarked the professor, who, no matter what the topic, always had some additional light to throw upon it. "'There is a similar wheel

---

[1] State lotteries are not uncommon in Europe. In 1890 the Italian government received from sales of lottery tickets 73,988,591.44 francs, or 2.56 francs for each man, woman, and child in Italy. In Naples the amount spent for lottery tickets was 15.34 francs per capita. In Rome it was 7.41 — less than half the amount spent by the pleasure-loving Neapolitans.

or 'tour' as it is called, at Bordeaux, founded in 1619, by an old maid named Tanzia. Over the wheel she inscribed the words: 'Mon père et ma mère m'ont abandoné, mais le Seigneur a pris soin de moi' — my father and mother abandoned me, but the Lord has taken me in His care. France spends 12,000,000 francs a year on foundling asylums, and the number of children taken care of is something like 70,000 per year. Out of 25,000 children abandoned by French mothers in 1889, only 343 were afterwards reclaimed. This can now be done in France, as a mother wishing to abandon her child can no longer put it in the chair, give it a whirl, and have it disappear as by magic. The authorities now require the mother to submit to an examination. Her address is recorded, and if she expresses an intention to reclaim the infant, a colored ivory necklace with an identification tab is placed around the neck. The wheels were found too convenient. When their use was prohibited, the number of abandoned children rapidly decreased. The chair at Antwerp was suppressed a few years ago, and the number of foundlings fell off twenty-five per cent in a single year."

"All very interesting," observed Mack again, as the professor paused in his discourse, "but *cui bono?* We are here to learn something new: this foundling asylum business is decidely *not* new. The Sisters of Charity established one in New York twenty years ago. They place a crib in the vestibule every night, and so easy is this method, that they received the first year more than a thousand infants under three weeks old. To my notion, this poking around foundling asylums is as ridiculous as Meriwether's prisons and workshops. It is late: if we want to catch that six o'clock train in the morning, we had better be off to bed."

"I am ready for bed," said Perigarde, "but I do not think I shall be ready for any six o'clock train in the morning. In fact, I have determined not to go to the bull fight at Torres Vedras."

We forgot all about foundling asylums in the surprise this announcement created. Perigarde's face reddened; he had a guilty look we could not understand. Hitherto he had been the energetic member of the party, never tired, ever ready to go. What had wrought this change? We let him off for the time being, and turned in at once to get as much sleep as possible before our early start in the morning. A six o'clock train means a five o'clock breakfast, and a five o'clock breakfast means getting up at 4.30, so that we seemed scarcely in bed before Miguelles, the Universo porter, knocked on our doors to arouse us. Immediately on leaving the station, the train plunged into a long tunnel: as it emerged at the other end, there was a clatter of hobnailed boots on the roof of the car, and presently a man reached down through a hole in the top and gave the lamp a twist to put out the light. That is the way they do in Portugal,— as indeed, in most European countries,— no porter walking through the car and climbing up on your seat to put out the lights, as they do in America. The lamps are attended to from the roof by a brakeman who has a sort of nest on top of one of the cars of the train.

The trip to Torres Vedras, three hours from Lisbon, afforded an interesting glimpse of Portugal's land and people. The stations were thronged with men, women, and children of every grade and kind. There were peasants with peaked Phrygian caps, long quince-wood staffs, short jackets that barely reached to the top of the broad sash worn around the waist; there were beggars in rags, women with bundles and babies, soldiers in gay uniforms, dandies and aristocrats in gloves and silk hats — all eager to see the bull fight. In Portugal and Spain the bull arena is common ground, where prince, peasant, and pauper jostle elbows and vie with each other in applauding the daring and skill of the toreadores.

We saw from our window the massive walls and arches of the ancient aqueduct. For miles, the train follows nearly the same course as the aqueduct, which spans the valleys on lofty arches and pierces the hills through long tunnels. At short intervals square towers stand near the aqueduct, fortresses formerly used for its protection and repair.

When our train — a special, to enable Lisbonians to attend the fight — drew up at the Torres Vedras station, it was received with almost royal honors. A line of soldiers stood on the platform with arms presented; a military band greeted us with martial strains. Scores of carriages, driven days before from Lisbon, lined the square in front of the station: there were omnibuses, stage coaches, asses, mules, two-wheeled gigs, and every other kind of conveyance heard of or unheard of. We were fortunate enough to secure seats on top of one of the stages, which elevation afforded an excellent view of the scene around us. The approach to the town is through a long avenue lined on both sides with shady trees, from the branches of which, on this occasion, hung hundreds of Japanese lanterns, flags, and banners. For some time all was confusion, a mere surging mass of men, women, soldiers, children, musicians, asses, donkeys, and carts. But finally order was evolved out of chaos, and the procession, headed by the band and the soldiers, followed by the vehicles, then by the equestrians (if the riders of asses may be so called), lastly, by the pedestrians, started down the long avenue, passed through the crooked streets of the city and on to the bull ring, a quarter of a mile away.

The fight was not to take place until four o'clock, but the ceremony of introducing the bulls was about to commence; we went to see this while John secured our tickets. Several thousand people were already in the enclosure when the procession formed by the passengers on the Lisbon special arrived: the whole formed a curious scene. Such a combination of picturesque people, all wild with excitement, could only be found at a bull fight in Spain or Portugal.

The ring at Torres Vedras had just been built; this was the opening or dedicating fight, which fact added to the interest and excitement. The ceremony of introducing the bulls was short. The keeper of the door leading into the den opens the door with a jerk, at the same moment quickly leaping into a slit in the wall, so narrow that the bull cannot enter. The bull comes leaping and careering into the ring; a sky rocket goes up with a loud "bang" to announce to the multitude without that the bull has entered. For a few minutes the beast is left alone, pawing the earth, bellowing, and making desperate charges at the doorkeeper secure in his narrow slit in the solid stone wall; then the door is opened again, a second bull rushes in, a second rocket shoots up in the air, and there is a second short pause to enable the spectators to observe the fine points of the beast; then the door is opened again, and so on until all the bulls — on this occasion there were twelve — have entered the ring. The ceremony is then concluded: a band of tame oxen with clanking bells dangling from their necks is introduced through a wide gate, and by a little skilful manœuvring, the wild bulls are induced to follow the oxen through the gate back to their den. For witnessing the introduction ceremony, only five cents was charged: "sombra" (shade) tickets to the fight itself cost eighty cents. The crush in front of the ticket office was so great that John had not yet secured our seats, but we felt confidence in his ability to get them, and telling him to rejoin us at the castle, set out for that famous height there to eat luncheon and rest until time to go to the fight.

Torres Vedras is not only very picturesque, it is also historically interesting; for during the Peninsular War this town, with its three thousand inhabitants, was the centre of Wellington's operations against the French under Masséna: history does not afford instances of more stupendous fortifications than those then constructed. The first line of defence reaches from Alhandra on the Tagus to the mouth of the Sizandro on the seacoast, twenty-nine miles away. From five to ten miles within this line was a second one twenty-four miles long, and within this was still a third, which Wellington designed to cover the embarkation of his troops in case the French succeeded in carrying the first two lines of defence. We climbed the lofty height just back of the town, and there, under the shade of the castle's walls, shattered by Masséna's shells, we ate lunch, and while gazing at the long stretch of country, over hill and dale, where Wellington built his three great lines of defence, preparing for the awful tragedy of battle, the babble of voices from the town and valley came up to us — the voices of the rabble seemingly as unthinking as the bulls they had come to see. Yet were these same careless men called to the ranks, they would doubtless fight as bravely as the men who crossed the ocean in the old time and conquered Mexico and Peru.

Two hours before the fight was to begin the amphitheatre was packed. Every inch of space was occupied, yet crowds still surged in, overflowing into the strip between the seats and the ring, and finally into the ring itself. Those in the ring made desperate efforts to clamber up into the benches, but the peasants in the front seats repelled the invaders vigorously, bringing their long quince staffs down on the enemy's heads with resounding whacks. The military had to clear the ring before the performance could begin.

Portuguese bull fights are very different from Spanish. We afterwards saw a Spanish fight at Barcelona. The Portuguese fight, though not so brutal and revolting, affords the same opportunity for exhibitions of daring and skill. In some respects it surpasses the Spanish fight. In Spain, the long, sharp horns of the bull are uncovered, and it seldom happens that less than a dozen horses are cruelly gored to death in a single fight. One of the bulls we saw at Barcelona killed, in rapid succession, eight horses, and badly wounded one of the toreadores, who had to be carried away, bleeding and faint, on a litter. One or two of the horses which had been gored and gashed were, nevertheless, still alive; but each time they attempted to stagger to their feet the bull made a rush, goring them again and again, until they dropped quite dead, a shocking sight, their entrails and blood running out on the ground. It is a mystery how any human being can like such horrors. As the butchery of horses is expected, only poor hacks are offered as a sacrifice. The unfortunate animals are blindfolded, their riders' legs are cased in iron, and when the bull charges, no effort is made to escape, the death of the horse being expected and desired. If less than fifteen or twenty horses are killed, the administration is hissed and accused of niggardliness. At the Barcelona fight twenty-five horses were killed. There is nothing of this in Portugal. There, the bulls' horns are sheathed with blunt iron covers, and the horses are the most beautiful and agile that can be found. After the banderilheros (those who spear the bull) and the moços de força (those who seize the bull by the horns) had entered and stood in line before the box of the president, a wide door was opened and a cavalheiro came prancing in on a magnificent black stallion. There was no blindfold on the horse, no iron armor on his rider; on the contrary, the rider was dressed in the style of a French gentleman of the time of Louis XIV. — silk knee-breeches, lace ruffles, cocked three-cornered hat, with black ostrich plume, and white gloves. Riding across the ring, and making a way through the crowd of moços and banderilheros, the cavalheiro paused under the box of the president, made a profound obeisance, then, with a twist of the rein, caused his handsome steed to sidle round the ring, not once turning his face away from the people, who shouted, and beat their staffs on the benches, and threw their hats into the ring as evidence of their appreciation of the cavalheiro's masterly horsemanship. When the entire circuit of the ring had been made, a trumpeter gave the signal, the doorkeeper opened the door, then leaped back into his niche in the wall, just in time to escape the mad beast that came rushing in, bellowing, and pawing the ground. In Spain, the picador sits stolidly on his blindfolded nag and waits for the bull to hoist both horse and rider into the air; not so with the Portuguese cavalheiro, who gives a deft twist to the rein, leaving the infuriated bull to dash on two feet or so to the right of him. Sometimes this is repeated, the bull lowering his massive head and plunging at his enemy, who each time wheels lightly and swiftly out of danger. This done two or three times, the Louis XIV. gentleman in silk knee-breeches and lace cuffs and white kid gloves gives another exhibition of his skill. One of the banderilheros hands him a javelin four feet long, barbed with steel at one end, decorated with light-colored ribbons at the other. The next time the savage bull makes a lunge, the cavalheiro wheels his stallion aside as before, but as he wheels by he leans far out of the saddle and with a sharp strong stroke plants the barbed javelin deep in the bull's neck. Then, while the frantic beast leaps into the air, paws the earth, writhes and twists to dislodge the spear, the cavalheiro canters round the ring, pauses to bow before the president's box, and makes his exit amid thunderous applause.

It is now the banderilheros' turn. One of them swings two of the gaudily trimmed farpas, or javelins, before the bull's eyes: the furious beast forgets the cruel barb in his neck and plunges at this new tormentor. The banderilhero leaps nimbly aside, planting, as he leaps, the two javelins in the bull's neck. Again, while the poor brute writhes and twists with pain, the audience thunders its applause, the men hurl their hats into the ring, and frequently follow them with cigars and leather bottles of wine. Then another banderilhero plants *his* darts in the bull's neck, and so on until the blood streams from the many wounds, and the light trimmed javelins stick in his neck as numerous as needles in a pin-cushion. In Spain, the performance of the banderilhero is followed by that of the espada, who displays marvellous skill and courage in avoiding the bull's sharp horns, sometimes by scarcely more than the breadth of a hair. The Spanish espada, when tired of this sport, awaits the bull's charge, sword in hand, and when the charge is made, with a single thrust buries the shining blade to the hilt in the animal's neck, causing almost immediate death. The Portuguese substitute for the espada's act, though requiring far less skill, is equally exciting. When the last banderilhero has planted his javelin, the vast audience cries, "Á unha — Á unha!"—which means, "seize him — seize him!" The moços de forçado, a dozen or more sturdy, determined-looking fellows, dressed in red jackets and leather breeches, who hitherto have been lounging to one side, leap to the front at the cry of "Á unha!" their leader, or captain, plants himself squarely in front of the bull, all the fiercer because of the javelins in his neck, and when the charge is made, instead of leaping lightly aside, the captain of the moços stands firm, extends his hands, and clutches the iron covered horns just in time to escape being dashed to the ground. The bull pitches and tosses, but the moço's grip is like the grip of death: the other moços rush to the rescue, some grab the bull by the tail, others leap on his back, on his neck, turn and twist the javelins planted there, until at last the savage brute is conquered, and admits his defeat by standing still with no further effort to attack his captors. At this *denouement*, hats come flying into the ring; the smiling moços, many covered with wounds and blood, toss the hats back to their owners, who then throw cigars and money. Ten or a dozen tame steers are driven into the ring, they rush around a minute or two, clanking the tin horns around their necks, then rush out followed by the bull, whose wounds are filled with salt and vinegar that they may heal ready for another fight in the near future. As soon as the arena is cleared, the trumpeter gives a signal, the cavalheiro comes prancing in, this time on another horse, the door of the pen is opened, a second bull rushes in, and a performance precisely like the first begins. To see one is to see all: one is enough for a lifetime. We squeezed our way through the crowd, and spent the rest of the afternoon rambling through the streets of quaint Torres Vedras.

On our return to Lisbon that evening we received two surprises. . First, from the professor, who announced his intention of going on to Seville; second, from Perigarde, who announced his intention of *not* going to Seville.

"You see," said the professor, "there is no telling when the *Birmania* will leave. I can wait just as well at Seville, and when the steamer leaves Lisbon, I can run down to Gibraltar and catch it there."

"There's no need of saying we are delighted," said Mack; "our whole party will rejoice. We only wish you were going all the way."

"You really think it is all right?" said the poor professor. "I mean, you do not think my change of plan will look — er — will look marked — that is, er — I mean, it won't appear bad form?"

Since Miss Detroit and Miss Lebanon were going to Seville, it was easy to understand the professor's change of plan, but Perigarde's puzzled us. When pushed to the wall he confessed that there was a woman in the case. We had not failed to observe that Perigarde was peculiarly susceptible to the wiles of women; it seemed impossible to get it into his head that there are sharpers of the gentle sex as well as of the sterner, so Mack and I constituted ourselves mentors to keep him safe from the insidious senhoritas who might seek to fascinate him. After a little persuasion, he made a clean breast of the adventure that had befallen him.

"On the day you lent me John," said he, "we got hungry in the middle of the day, and to appease our appetites as well as to get statistics for you, we stopped in one of the numerous milkeries that abound in the Portuguese capital. The cows are kept in well-cleaned stalls, the name of each cow overhead, in big, gilt letters on the wall, and attendants ready to milk any cow you select. Some customers take a fancy to a certain cow, and will drink the milk of no other. There were eight cows in the milkery where we went — a room thirty-five feet deep by sixteen wide. In the rear a ladder leads to a loft where the attendants sleep, and where is kept the hay and grass. The salary of the head milker is $15 a month; that of his assistant, only $13. The average value of the sleek, well-kept cows varies from $90 to $100."

"How kind to take all that trouble for Meriwether," remarked Mack, dryly.

"I owe you a thousand thanks, Perigarde," I said.

"Give me your attention," said Perigarde, in a burst of confidence, "but not your thanks. I do not deserve them. My sudden love for statistics was inspired through the fact that asking a lot of questions gave me an excuse to remain a long time in the milkery, and I wanted to remain because a very beautiful woman came in while we were there sipping warm milk. As she sat there at one of the little round tables, she looked so charming I could not hold in.

"'By Jove,' I said to John, in English, 'by Jove, that woman is pretty.' Then I asked John if it was the warm milk or the Portuguese climate that makes such dazzling complexions.

"John thought it was a little of both. I went on jotting down notes as an excuse for remaining. Presently I said, partly to myself, partly to John: —

"'I wonder if she is as bright as she is pretty. I wish these lovely girls could talk English.'

"'This one does,' said my beauty, in pure English, and I

wanted to sink through the earth and come out on the other side. With a merry look, she added, 'Do you mind my asking why you are counting cows?'

"This question made me more anxious to make that trip to the antipodes. I tried to apologize. I said I had no idea she was English.

"'I am not English,' she laughed; 'I am an American. But you have not told me why you are counting cows.'

"'I am getting statistics.'

"'Statistics? What is that?' asked the lovely creature.

"I explained, told her the government sends out men to take notes regarding the condition of the people.

"'And cows?' she quickly added.

"'Yes; you see cows belong to the people.'

"'I see; and you came here to get notes about the cows. They are interesting, aren't they? That is mine,—Corlina. I won't drink any milk but Corlina's.'

"I vowed from that moment Corlina should also be my cow, that I would drink no milk but Corlina's. The beautiful woman became very friendly. She was as glad to see a countryman as I was to see a pretty woman. She perceived I was a gentleman who would not abuse her confidence and told me all about herself. She is from New York. By persuasion of her mother she married a wealthy Portuguese baron. She respects, but does not love the baron. They live in Lisbon, but she hates this country; she is a true patriot and is sometimes tempted to run away back to America. All this and much more she told me as we took a ride on a tramcar to Belem — you see, I had to keep up my statistical business, and told her I was going to Belem to look at the school for orphan boys kept there in the old monastery. She thought I had to count the boys as well as the cows; women are so ignorant, they never understand business of a statistical nature. The boys were at play, romping around in the old cloisters where the monks used to walk and pray: they ran so fast, round and about, the baroness thought there were two thousand of them, but I could not make out half that number — of course, though, I was not looking as much at the boys as I was at the baroness. The warden of the school showed us everything. He took us to the dormitories where are hundreds of narrow iron bedsteads, to the kitchen with its lofty Gothic ceiling, and three cooks busy at a huge range; then to the refectory where are four rows of tables one hundred feet long. By each plate was a cup, a knife, and a spoon. Aren't these statistics useful, Meriwether?"

"They are invaluable, Perigarde, my dear fellow; but your baroness interests us just now more than knives and spoons. Go on with the baroness."

"The warden told us that spoons meant rice for dinner," continued Perigarde, gravely. "When there is meat, a fork is placed by the side of the plate instead of a spoon. I know that will interest you."

"Yes, of course it does. I hope you found out how often the boys have meat?"

"I did," he replied, solemnly. "I made strict inquiries on that matter just to please you. The boys have meat twice a week. For breakfast they have chocolate and bread; for dinner, bean or macaroni soup, cabbage and bread. On Sundays they have a dessert of some sort of pudding, and once a month each boy has a cup of wine. Supper is the same as breakfast, — bread and chocolate."

"But the baroness," interrupted Mack. "Confound your statistics. It's bad enough for one member of the party to run on that. What of the baroness?"

"'The warden told us," proceeded Perigarde, taking not the slightest notice of Mack's interruption, "how the orphan school at Belem is supported by private subscriptions, and how no boy is admitted who is not a good Catholic with

papers to show that his parents were properly married. We
— that is, the baroness and I — listened to all these things,
and I made notes of them for you, Meriwether. I thought
they would be good statistics for you."

"My dear Perigarde, you are thoughtfulness itself. I'll
make a note of the facts and figures; in the meantime, do tell
us what you did with the baroness, or rather, what the baroness
did with you!"

"I am coming to that; don't hurry a fellow so. I begin to
believe you are jealous because a lovely woman has fallen to
my share of the trip. When we returned to the city we had
supper, then strolled on the Avenida da Liberdada until
10.30. You see now why I did not get back to the hotel last
night until eleven."

"Where was the baron all this while?"

"Oh, the baron? Well, he is not at home just now; he's
gone to Madrid."

Mack and I used all our eloquence to dissuade Perigarde
from further acquaintance with the American baroness. We
hinted our belief that she was a sharper. Perigarde was indignant; we had to retreat from that position, or he would have
fought us on the spot. Then we appealed to his honor. Was
it right for him to compromise an innocent lady, probably
arouse her husband's jealous anger? What troubles might not
his visits bring to this beautiful baroness? Perigarde was
scornful; she was a lady of superior mind, he said; she
knew what she was about: she knew her own husband: if he
was a jealous fool, she would tell him she was simply glad to
see her own countryman, glad to talk her own language. He,
Perigarde, would certainly be a churl, and a coward in the
bargain, if he were afraid to call on a lady when invited to
her house.

The upshot was that Perigarde remained in Lisbon, while
we started at seven in the evening for Seville. The next

morning at six the train reached Badajoz, where Spanish customs officials overhauled our baggage, and pried into our lunch basket. Badajoz is a curious frontier town reached from the railway station by a long bridge and entered through a lofty and massive gate. The train made a two hours' halt, and we availed ourselves of the opportunity to stretch our limbs, cramped after the night in the coupé: when we came to the big gate at the end of the bridge, Mack and I wanted to explore what seemed a tunnel in the massive wall. But scarce did we enter the tunnel, than a young girl, half dressed, sprang out from a room in the interior, and began scolding us in the liveliest way; at least, we thought it scolding from her flashing eyes and angry gestures. She talked so fast we did not understand a word she said; nevertheless, we beat a rapid retreat. Spaniards, we remembered, are famous for fierce jealousy. What if the girl's husband or father or brother should catch us in her presence at that early hour in the morning, and she half dressed? The vision of sharp stilettos hastened our steps quite as much as the girl's sharp tongue. Holding her gown close about her person, she followed us, scolding till we were out of sight.

At seven o'clock in the evening, when still thirty miles from Seville, our train was side-tracked to permit the passage of the express from Seville to Lisbon. There was a great crowd and bustle on the platform. While we were strolling about, listening to the babel of tongues, the express from Seville arrived. Then a curious thing happened: the moment the express came to a stop, out sprang from one of the coupés a young and handsome man. Darting keen glances up and down the platform, his eyes lighted on our party, and his face fairly beamed with joy. The next moment he was greeting Miss Detroit in a way which no doubt sent cold shivers up and down the professor's spine. There should be a law compelling pretty young women to wear an engagement badge of

AN INDIAN ISLAND PRISON

some sort, a red or yellow ribbon on the right arm, or pinned in a knot on their left shoulders — *some* way should be devised to save susceptible hearts like the professor's from useless pangs.

When Miss Detroit's blushes and excitement abated enough to permit her to remember ordinary mortals, she introduced us to her *fiancé;* but the professor — where was he? He and his travelling-bag had both disappeared: the climax was too much for him. We saw his sad but sandy-colored face in the window of one of the coupés of the express, as it flew by on the way to Lisbon.

"I am so sorry, George," said Miss Detroit, sweetly, "the professor is such a dear little man."

Have women no pity for such wounds? Did she know how hard he was hit? These were the questions that bothered Mack and me as we took our seats in the coupé and resumed our journey to Seville. We had come to like the professor, and to have him drop out of our party so suddenly made us feel badly: conscience gave us pricks as we remembered our jests and jokes about him; we now thought only of his solid, good qualities, his truth, and delicacy of feeling, — not a bad thing to have even if a little strained according to our free and large Western ideas. Miss Detroit and Miss Lebanon left us at Seville, so that Mack and I were now alone.

CHAPTER V

The Tobacco Factory of Seville — Six Thousand Girls with Roses and Babies — Spanish and American Tariffs — The Octroi — The Kodak gets us in Trouble — El Sereno — The Civil Guards and the Englishman — Twelve Years in Africa — Why Mr. W. threatened to cut down his Trees — Mediterranean Fruits

I FOUND Seville rather disappointing. It cannot be compared with Lisbon. There is little to interest the stranger except the cathedral, the alcázar, Pilate's House, and a few "patios." Even the cathedral is not in a condition to be seen; it is filled with scaffolds, ropes, pulleys, and workmen repairing the damage caused a few years ago by the sudden collapse of one of the great roof-supporting pillars. The art museum, though a small collection, contains some celebrated paintings by Murillo and other masters. It is interesting to observe the spirit of the Spanish painters: their subject is invariably either war or religion. A curious specimen of the latter kind is a picture called "The Day of Judgment," by Merthen de Vos. On the left of the canvas is a group of angels at work pulling the quickened dead out of their graves, and hoisting them up to heaven; the devils, who occupy the right-hand side of the picture, are equally as busy with pitchforks, thrusting the doomed into the fiery red mouth of a prodigious lion, which symbolizes hell. One by Valdés Leal is an odd conception of the temptation of St. Jerome. The saint is represented in the conventional style, with skull, and cross, and book. But behind him are not the usual beautiful women with scant clothing. The tempters of St. Jerome, according to Valdés Leal, were a number of uncommonly plain, not to say ugly, women, dressed in gaudy red and yellow gowns, with long feathers in hideous bonnets.

Seville's reputation with tourists rests mainly on its romantic and historical interest; it is, however, not without objects of modern interest, as, for example, its tobacco factory, the largest in the world, also a large iron foundry, one of the few to be found in Andalusia. We spent a day there watching the methods of work and inquiring into the life and hours of the men. Iron moulders, boilermakers, fitters, and mechanics work fifty-four hours a week. They begin at seven in the morning, stop half an hour at 8.30 to eat breakfast, and three-quarters of an hour at one o'clock for dinner; they go home at 5.30. During the dinner hour, we saw many of the workmen sprawled out fast asleep under the trees of the neighboring "plaza," or square. Spanish mechanics receive ninety-five cents a day; the mechanics brought from England to instruct the Spaniards, get as much as $16 a week; the foreman receives $25. The tobacco works, from a tourist's point of view, are more interesting than the foundry. The government in Spain has a monopoly in tobacco, and farms out the privilege of manufacturing it for an immense sum per year. The factory at Alicante employs 4000 girls, that at Madrid, 6500, at Valencia, 3500. The factory at Seville, built in 1757, is the largest of all, having 6500 female and 200 male employees. The huge building that shelters this industrial army looks like a soldiers' barracks. The entrance is through a lofty arch, guarded, on both sides, by uniformed officials who charge twenty cents admission, the contractors having been authorized by the government to collect that amount to help restore the cathedral to the condition it was in before the roof fell down. The tobacco monopoly has still some years to run and, notwithstanding the enormous amount paid the government, the contractors make much money if one may judge from the number of employees, and from the universal smoke habit that prevails in Spain. A glimpse at the thousands of girls at work in the Fabrica de Tabacos is well worth the peseta charged for admission. The long workhalls and corridors stretch out a quarter of a mile, and in each hall are great numbers of women, girls, and babies. Every girl has a rose in her hair, and almost every one has a baby in her arms or in a cradle. The work benches are low, and while with deft fingers the cigarette girl rolls the tobacco, with equally deft feet does she rock the cradle and put her baby to sleep. Down some of the aisles we saw women with baskets of roses and cans of milk, selling the roses for the cigarette girls' hair, and the milk for their babies. These girls are as bold as the number of their children would lead one to expect. It was with difficulty that we could keep out of their clutches. Mack, on one occasion, had to take refuge up a ladder. The girls saw him sketching and a score or more jumped up from their benches and insisted on seeing the picture. Mack, knowing their tobacco-stained hands would spoil the paper, refused, whereupon they boldly made a grab for his sketch-book. Mack rapidly retreated up a ladder which had been placed against the wall to reach a high shelf. The girls as quickly climbed after him. Mack sprang on the high shelf; quick as squirrels the girls jumped to the floor, removed the ladder, and left poor Mack perched up under the ceiling, his long legs dangling twelve or fifteen feet above our heads. The girls shouted with laughter; in fact, every one laughed, even Mack, though in a rather sickly way. The forewoman, hearing the commotion, ran up to restore quiet, but it was some time before she could succeed in getting the rude girls to release their victim.

The wages of Spanish cigarreras, tobacco girls, are regulated by the work performed. For three thousand cigarettes, selling twenty-five for five cents, a girl is paid two and one-half pesetas (forty-five cents). The same amount is paid for making two hundred cigars, and we were told that in four months a bright girl can learn to make two hundred per day.

Each girl keeps a book by her side and notes the amount of her work. When she leaves the building at six o'clock, she is carefully searched, and punished if found trying to smuggle out cigars or cigarettes. There is a kitchen where the girls may prepare their lunches and make coffee or chocolate. A number of shrines are also provided, that the girls may not forget religious duties. The girls' toilet rooms are separate from those of the men — a thing which cannot always be said of tobacco factories in America. The male employees are separated from the women even while at work, though it must be said the great number of illegitimate children indicate that these measures add little to the sum total of morality. Complaints are lodged with an inspector, whose judgment is usually, though not always, final. Once, in Madrid, a complaint was not decided to the satisfaction of the girls, who thereupon marched in a body of four thousand and literally drove the inspector out of the building. Whether the management thought the girls in the right or not no one knows; they saw four thousand infuriated women on one side, and a pelted and detested inspector on the other, and so, prudently, let the matter drop, and for once women had their own way.

In addition to the kitchen provided by the company within its huge barracks-like building, there is a laborer's kitchen on the outside a few blocks away, where fairly good food can be had at very low prices. A pint bowl of lettuce costs one cent; a plate of bean or macaroni soup with bread, two cents; a plate of beans and potatoes with a small piece of meat, two cents; coffee with sugar but no milk, one cent. When it is remembered that every article of food is doubly taxed, once at the frontier by the government tariff, and again at the city gates by the "octroi," the reader will be as surprised as we were at the cheapness of these prices. At the frontier, wheat is taxed $1.60, and wheat flour, $2.64 per hundred kilograms (220 pounds). Pork, lard, beans, and hams are taxed

$10, rice, $2.12 per one hundred kilos; on cattle, $8 per head must be paid. Almost everything else is taxed by a similar high tariff, but onerous as is this tariff levied at the frontier by the general government, it is not so onerous as the tax exacted at city gates, called "octroi." The following specimens will suffice to show the nature and extent of the Spanish octroi. I select the figures for Xerez, of 1891, as a fair sample of Spanish cities.

ARTICLE.		AMOUNT OF OCTROI TAX.
Fresh meat..................	4⅔	cents per kilogram (2⅕ lbs.).
Salt........................	7	" " "
Wine of all kinds...........	$4	" 100 litros.[1]
Vinegar.....................	80	" " "
Bread.......................	53	" " 100 kilos.
Fish, from sea or river.....	2⅔	" " kilo.
Wood........................	12	" " 100 litros.
Coke........................	6	" " "
Common Salt.................	1¾	" " kilo.
Tea, natural or artificial..	$1.73	" 100 kilograms.
Chickens....................	44	" " piece.
Milk........................	1	" " 100 kilograms.
Butter......................	1¼	" " "
Honey.......................	2	" " kilogram.

The reader who will glance over the foregoing figures will see that bread, for instance, is first taxed $2.64 per 220 pounds by the general government, and then fifty-three cents per 220 pounds by the city, or a total of $3.17 per 220 pounds; in other words, the tax on bread, in Spain, exceeds one cent per pound. All city expenses are borne by the octroi; than which, no more unjust and oppressive system of taxation was ever invented. The millionnaire may have a dozen palaces, and may receive from the government a hundred times as much protection as the day laborer, but he eats no more, possibly

---

[1] 100 litros = about 110 quarts.

not so much, — he may have dyspepsia or indigestion, — in which case the day laborer pays actually more octroi taxes than his millionnaire employer. When one reflects upon the tariff, and its oppressive and unjust nature, it is surprising that it is continued by any civilized nation as a system of raising revenue; when its iniquity is focused, as it is in the case of a city octroi, when its injustice is made so glaringly apparent as it is there, it is amazing that it is allowed to survive a single moment. Yet it *is* allowed; soldiers stand at the gates of Spanish cities, and every parcel is closely scrutinized and examined. Whenever I returned after a day's ramble with the kodak, an officer stopped me at the gate and insisted on prying into the camera. They have long rapiers which they plunge into carts of hay, sand, etc., to see if dutiable articles are concealed. The workman who eats a kilogram (two and one-fifth pounds) of salt meat must pay seven cents octroi tax, which goes to furnish police, fire departments, etc., to protect the property of the titled and untitled rich man, who perhaps lives in villas out of town, and so pays no octroi tax at all. Were it not that I have become accustomed in America to seeing the masses taxed for the benefit of the few favored classes, I should be more surprised at the Spanish people tamely submitting to so odious an oppression, which amounts to legalized robbery.

There are no waiters in the Seville workmen's kitchens. Each customer walks up to the counter, receives his food, after paying for it, then takes a seat at one of the zinc-covered tables — that is, if he can; generally there are more customers than seats, fully two thousand dinners being served every day. There are three such kitchens in Seville, and each is crowded with from two to three thousand persons per day.

Hotels in Seville are rather expensive, but the economical traveller is not obliged to go to a hotel if willing to put up at a pension, comfortable as any hotel, though lacking the pretension and style. For $1.45 per day we obtained excellent quarters at the pension of Mme. Bjorkman — an English lady, in spite of the name, — at No. 1 Calle Jernan Espino. Our window at this comfortable, homelike place looked out on the famous Giralda tower in the distance, while nearer, in fact immediately across the narrow street, it overlooked a house in course of erection. The bricks, much longer and narrower than American bricks, were carried to the fourth floor of the new building in baskets made of a coarse, strong grass. These grass baskets do not hold more than ten bricks; accordingly the bricklayers are half the time without brick; they seem to enjoy it, however, whistling, gazing down at the people, or in the distance at scenery to while away the time. During our stay I tried to help them in their efforts to kill time, by sitting out on our balcony and asking all sorts of questions. From what I saw, as well as from what the bricklayers said, it is evident that Spaniards build solidly, if slowly. No houses in Spain fall down before they are finished. The house I watched was designed for an ordinary dwelling, but the walls were nearly as thick as the walls of a seven-story building in America. The front walls were twenty inches, the partition walls twelve inches thick. The men who carry the brick up in grass baskets receive forty cents per day, which is within twenty cents as much as the bricklayers earn. No ordinary skill is required to build a Spanish house, where even the floors rest not on iron or wooden sleepers, but on brick arches, and it is odd that the bricklayer should receive only sixty cents a day when the hod-carrier receives forty cents. An American bricklayer receives $5 per day, an American hod-carrier not more than $1.50 or $2 — perhaps only $1.25 — that is, the proportion is less than a third instead of two-thirds, as in Spain. The foreman on the Spanish building, who received ten cents a day more than the bricklayer (seventy cents a day), said that an intelligent workman could learn to lay brick within a year; that a very good man can lay as many as one thousand brick in a day. The brick, twelve inches long, by six wide, by two thick, cost $4 a thousand, and $1 a thousand for delivering. These figures — low as they are — at least as regards the price of labor — did not prepare me for the unusually cheap rents which are charged in Seville. A Spanish gentleman with whom we became acquainted, said that the rent of his residence was eighty cents a day. His house was in a pleasant, respectable part of the city, had sixteen large, comfortable rooms, and would cost at least $75 a month in any American city of 150,000 inhabitants.

Another object of interest often visible from our balcony, was one of the comical Sevillian policeman in long coat, with a spear like an alpenstock. At night he carried a lantern suspended from his belt, and promptly at twelve o'clock began calling the hours. Midnight is about the time most people are ready to go to bed who are not already there, and one would think it would be more serviceable to have the hours called before instead of after midnight. In Seville this has not been thought of, hence "El sereno" does not begin with his "Ave Maria purisima, se von las doze" — "it is gone twelve, it is gone twelve, and all is well" — until exactly the time when people want to sleep, and don't care whether "it is gone twelve" or twelve hundred. If it happens to be raining, that fact is mentioned without extra charge to the taxpayer. The "sereno" receives forty-five cents a day — not a large sum, and one which I am sure travellers would willingly double if thereby they could stop his doleful howls and sleep in peace. These local police with their long coats, alpenstocks, and nocturnal howls, are laughed at even by the Spaniards. There is another kind of policeman, however, to whom is paid a respect amounting to awe. These are the civil guards, 25,000 of whom are scattered throughout the kingdom. The minimum punishment for resisting a civil guard is twelve years' imprisonment, besides which, the civil guard is authorized to shoot without ceremony any one who offers resistance, no matter what the circumstances or provocation. An American resident of Malaga related an incident that occurred in that city shortly before we met him in Seville.

"It happened at a fire some nights ago," said Mr. X. "There was a big crowd in the street, and an Englishman, anxious to see Spanish fire police at work, tried to push his way to the front. One of the civil guards put his hand on the Englishman's shoulder and shoved him back. The English traveller said something sharp to the civil guard, who promptly gave him a second and more vigorous shove than before. The Englishman whipped out his revolver, the civil guard as quickly knocked him down with the butt of his musket, and locked chains on his hands and feet. The procurator declared that an example must be made, that the civil guard must be held sacred even by foreigners, and nothing saved the Englishman a long sojourn in Africa but the untiring efforts of influential friends, who finally induced the governor of the province to shut his eyes while the charge on the magistrate's book was changed from 'assaulting a civil guard' to 'drunkenness and disorderly conduct.'"

"Does not this 'sacredness' with which the civil guards are invested make them despotic and overbearing?" I asked.

"Possibly, to some extent; yet in Spain it is necessary. Were there no civil guards I would not venture out of my house after dark, and would not dare to go from one city to another without an armed escort."

"Do not the city police afford protection?"

"The city police — Bah! They are good to call the hours and keep people awake, but they are neither feared nor respected, whereas the most hardened malefactor stands in awe of the civil guards. He knows they are invested with power to play both judge and executioner, and instantly, on the spot.

This insures order wherever the civil guards are, which is to say, in all parts of Spain. They patrol the highroads as well as the cities, they are at every railway station, and on every train, always in couples at least twelve feet apart, to avoid being surprised together. Spanish juries are often too lenient in sentencing homicides, and this undue leniency is sometimes counteracted by the civil guards."

This statement seemed so curious we asked for explanation.

"Why," replied Mr. X., "I mean that the civil guards in escorting their prisoners to the penal settlement in Africa are frequently compelled to shoot them in order to prevent escape. A civil guard has only to make a declaration that his prisoner attempted to escape, and he is held justified in shooting him. A few days ago, Lawrens, a very popular man, the mayor-elect of Malaga, was killed in a peculiarly cold-blooded manner. His assassin will probably get a short sentence from the jury, but it is equally probable the civil guards will receive a hint from high sources, and on the way to Ceuta will find it necessary to shoot the assassin to prevent his escape."

This statement was hardly credible, yet it was made in all seriousness by Mr. X., a resident twenty years in Spain; it was afterwards corroborated by other Americans living in Spain. As an instance of the *esprit de corps* maintained among the civil guards, Mr. X. related an incident that occurred in Madrid a few years ago. A son of General Prim, then the practical dictator of Spanish affairs, was arrested while on a drunken spree, and imprisoned by a civil guard. General Prim ordered the civil guard punished. The officers of the civil guards, from the general commanding, down to the lowest lieutenant, handed in their resignations. "The civil guards," they declared, "must be inviolable," and they carried their point. General Prim was obliged to restore to his rank, with honor instead of punishment, the man who had had the courage to arrest the son of the commander of all the Spanish armies. Although Mr. X.'s long residence gives his opinions weight, it is difficult to believe that any body of men can be invested with such power without engendering tyranny. Even in America, with commissioners and boards of revision, it not infrequently happens that police officers are guilty of most outrageous oppression. A case in point occurred recently to two friends of mine in New York. As they were strolling down Broadway after the opera, they stopped for a moment to look at an address under the light of a corner lamp. A policeman ordered them to move on. My friend L. is an inoffensive gentleman, but has an immense amount of dignity. At this gruff and uncalled-for command, he replied quietly that he would move on when ready, not before. In this, he reckoned without his policeman, for no sooner had he spoken than the officer seized him by the collar and began marching him away.

"Hello, there, officer," cried Mr. McC., my other friend, who had been looking up the address under the lamp-post, "where are you taking that man?"

"To jail, and if you don't look sharp I'll take you, too."

"I'd like to see you do it," replied Mr. McC., hotly.

His wish was instantly gratified. The burly Broadway policeman grabbed him by the collar, and threatened to club them both out of their senses if they made the slightest resistance.

There was nothing but to obey, and in half an hour my two friends found themselves in a cell along with a lot of the lowest wretches from the slums of a great city. In vain they protested their innocence of any crime, in vain they offered money as bail for appearing in the morning; the officer at the station said he had no jurisdiction, that they had been brought there under a charge of disorderly conduct and obstructing the pavement, and there they must remain until court convened and they paid their fine or were acquitted. During the night drunken people were brought in from time to time, and, as may be imagined, their oaths, their vile talk, the bad odors they exhaled, kept my two fastidious friends from sleeping. When court convened at ten o'clock, L. and McC. were ushered in along with the other prisoners, and for some time were obliged to sit in their malodorous company in full view of the spectators and lawyers. When, finally, their case was heard, they were almost immediately dismissed, as even the policeman who arrested them made out a very weak case. They consulted a lawyer as to whether there was any redress. The disciple of Blackstone said: —

"You might possibly get the policeman removed, but you would have to convince the commissioners, and if you attempt to do that, you must make up your mind to stay in New York at least two months."

Business required them to return much sooner to their homes in the West, so they were compelled to content themselves with merely anathematizing the arbitrary power of what has been called America's standing army. When we asked Mr. X. whether the arbitrary power vested in the civil guards of Spain effected such security as to render unnecessary the carrying of arms, he replied: —

"No force, however large or well organized, can entirely prevent disorder; the claim made for the civil guards is that they have brought the proportion of crime from its former high figures down to something more reasonable. Acknowledging then that crime, though lessened, still exists, the question is whether it is advisable to carry arms. That question is difficult to answer; for while a revolver may save your life in an emergency, it is, on the other hand apt, sooner or later, to bring you into trouble with the authorities. The penalty for carrying weapons is severe, and one had better submit to being robbed than run the risk of going to a Spanish prison for carrying a weapon. Not long ago an English doctor, while descending the Tower of Cordova, shot and killed the guide accompanying him. The Englishman said, that, as they were descending, the guide planted himself in the way and demanded his money, and that he did not shoot until it was evident his liberty could not otherwise be restored. The courts finally justified the Englishman and set him free, but his expenses in the trial, not to speak of worry and loss of time, amounted to much more than would have satisfied the guide. As a mere matter of business, therefore, it is wiser to submit to being occasionally victimized than to draw or attempt to use a revolver."

As a matter of business, yes; but the average human being has an innate repugnance to being swindled, which causes resistance, even where resistance is more costly than submission. This question is one the traveller is frequently called upon to decide. Once, when boarding a Russian steamer at Constantinople, a villainous-looking Turk brought the matter up for my consideration. I made a distinct bargain as to the fee for rowing me to the steamer, yet half-way out he doubled his demand, and refused to row one way or the other until the demand was paid. I tried diplomacy, promised to do what was right on reaching the boat; but the Turk knew, once aboard the steamer, he would be in my power instead of having me in his power, so he insisted on being paid on the spot. Then it was I abandoned diplomacy, seized the club I always carry when travelling, and standing over the thieving rascal, threatened to hammer his head if he made a motion to rise, or ceased rowing direct for the Russian steamer. When we got there, and when my effects were safe aboard, I paid the fee originally promised. This course may occasionally make trouble for the individual, but it pays in the long run. The English, for instance, are famous as sticklers for their rights even in small matters, and have gained a reputation for not submitting to imposition, consequently impositions are less frequently attempted upon the English than upon Americans, who are known to put up with extortion and annoyance rather than take the time and trouble to repel them.

I regret to have to record the fact that during our stay in Seville, a coolness arose between Mack and me. We entered a tailor shop to have my measure taken for a suit. Unluckily the tailor's boy was out, and Mack was requested to note the numbers as the tailor called them. The way Mack did this was unkind indeed. He did not have the candor to admit his deep and dense ignorance of Spanish; hence when the tailor called thirty-five, Mack put down sixty or seventy, or any other number that came in his head. When the suit was delivered, it was a wonder to behold. Mack tried to console me by saying that in such a suit I could make a fortune as a curiosity; but this was poor consolation for my wasted pesetas, and, as the papers say, our relations for the while were "strained."

The fourth day of our stay at Seville, a telegram came from Perigarde, saying he would join us at the end of a week. We decided to remain a few days longer, anxious to hear the sequel of his adventure with the lovely baroness. In the meantime we made some inquiries into the question of producing fruit, its cost, and profit. Some years ago, when in the famous and beautiful Santa Clara Valley of California, a gentleman drove me out to see his orchard of peach, prune, and apricot trees. Mr. W. pointed with pride to the delicious fruit which hung from the trees in such profusion that the boughs had to be supported by props.

"Look," he cried, "look at that prune tree; I took $37 worth of prunes last year from that one tree. Sometimes the San Francisco buyers pay $200 or $300 per acre for my fruit while on the trees, the buyer bearing the expense of picking."

I expressed the anticipated wonder at these figures, but shortly afterwards referred to them in a way which made Mr. W. wish they had never been mentioned. The conversation happened to turn upon Mr. Cleveland's so-called free trade message, then just before the American people.

"It is outrageous," said Mr. W., vehemently, "perfectly outrageous that an American President should work in the interest of foreigners."

"Of foreigners? How is Mr. Cleveland working in the interest of foreigners?"

"By that free trade message. If Congress listens to such doctrines, I shall take an axe and chop down every tree in my orchard: they would be worthless except for kindling-wood."

"Even that prune tree with its $37 worth of prunes a year?"

"Well, maybe that tree might stand, but I'd cut the rest down; yes, sir, every one of 'em."

"So then it is not your beneficent climate, your fertile soil, your warm sun, that is responsible for this delicious fruit worth $300 an acre on the trees?"

"Of course we *have* the finest climate in the world," said Mr. W., a little less vehemently; "still, we cannot compete with the pauper labor of Europe, and free trade means an axe at the root of California vines and fruit trees."

It seems to me the millions of farmers who are glad to clear $10 an acre, and the millions of workmen earning barely a dollar a day, ought not to be forced by a protectionist government to pay a large bonus to Florida and California orchard-owners who clear $300 an acre: this bounty they are forced to pay; hence it is interesting to know how much truth there is in Mr. W.'s claim that free trade would strike an axe at the root of every American fruit tree — the claim that, without the aid of government, American orchards could not compete with orchards in Europe. After investigating this subject both at home and abroad, I am of the opinion that, excepting certain tropical fruits, there is no reason why American fruit-growers need fear the "pauper" fruit of Europe. No country in the world can produce a better or cheaper

Burden Bearer on the Via dei Molini

orange than Florida, nor, with their balmy climate and pauper labor combined, can either Spain or Italy injure California prunes, peaches, pears, and grapes. A fair average yield of California vines is two tons per acre at two years, three tons at three years, five tons at four years, seven tons at five years. The average value of the grapes is $20 per ton on the vine; that is, a vineyard set out from cuttings will yield, in the fifth year, $140 per acre. Nowhere in the Mediterranean countries did I find this yield exceeded or even equalled. In Spain and Italy, six thousand pounds of grapes per acre are considered a good yield, and the sales per acre rarely exceed $60 to $75. In the Riverside district of California, eighty to one hundred orange trees are planted to the acre, and when full bearing, these trees, as I was informed by Mr. E. W. Holmes, editor of the Riverside *Daily Press*, net, above all freight and commissions, from $200 to $1000 per acre, according to variety and condition of market. Charles Dudley Warner says that "there are young groves at Riverside five years old that are paying ten per cent net upon $3000 to $5000 per acre"; that is, the owners of those orchards receive from $300 to $500 per acre for their oranges. Can this showing be equalled in any other country? The nearest approach to the Riverside orchards that I know of in any Mediterranean country is at Boufarik, Algeria. Messrs. Holden and Cox have there an estate of 585 acres. Last year they sold the produce of thirty-seven acres of full-bearing orange trees for three years in advance, for the sum of £1000 per year; that is, for $131 per acre, or less than half the amount Mr. Warner says is realized by Riverside groves five years old.

CHAPTER VI

A Trip to Xeres — How Sherry is made and why it goes to India — Perigarde, the Baroness, and the Baron — The Mosque of Cordova — Mistaken for Burglars — A Kodak Story — Night Journey to Ronda — Why they robbed us — The Ronda Fair — Signorina Cellini changes her Name.

XERES, three hours from Seville, is the centre of a great grape-growing district, and the home of the wine which derives its name from that of the city, — sherry. The railroad, protected on either side, not by wire or wooden fences as in America, but by formidable cacti hedges, traverses a vast rolling plain on which graze herds of fierce Andalusian bulls. In the distance are mountains white with snow; all else is tropical, — lemon and orange trees and a burning sun that makes one quite willing to pay the two cents charged at stations for a glass of water. In our coupé was a well-dressed lady who ever and anon lifted a bottle she carried and applied its contents to her eyes. At first we thought she mistook her eyes for her mouth; afterwards we learned that her sight was failing, and that the bottle contained holy water, with which she was endeavoring to restore it.

Xeres has an English colony engaged in the sherry business. During our stay we were guests of an English gentleman, Mr. Alexander Williams, owner of a large bodega, to whom I am indebted for many of the facts given in this chapter. The bodegas of Xeres are worth seeing: the 150-gallon casks, piled up almost to the very roof of the lofty halls, contain sherries of different grades and ages. The "taster" of the bodega goes through the long halls with a rod at the end of which is a cup holding half a gill. This rod he plunges through the bung hole, bringing out upon its withdrawal a sample of the beautiful liquor within. The visitor to a bodega must beware how he dallies with the taster's cup. The courteous attendant will offer a sample from each of the two thousand casks, and, needless to say, if you do not politely but firmly decline, you will soon be unable to determine whether you are on your head or your heels. The staves of the casks are imported from America. Before the butts are filled with sherry, they are given a day's bath in boiling water to destroy the taste of the oak. Even after this boiling, only sherry of the poorest grade is put in the cask: good sherry is not put in a cask less than six months old. The coopers who make the casks out of the American staves seem to have imbibed a little of the American workingman's ways. They alone have a labor union, and through that union they have succeeded in raising wages to ninety-five cents a day. In 1886 they received only eighty cents. The union was formed, a strike took place, and for five months not a cask was made in Xeres. Coopers were brought from other districts, but were speedily persuaded, sometimes at the ends of clubs or stilettos, that Xeres was bad for their health. The result was that in the sixth month of the strike the increase to ninety-five cents was conceded. As it requires from two to three years to learn the cooper's trade, it cannot be said that even the present rate is exorbitant. It is so considered in Spain, however, and the Xeres coopers are about the only workmen who have an opportunity to use the savings bank instituted for the benefit of workmen and paying three per cent on deposits of fifty cents and over.

The oldest and best sherry is that belonging to Spanish estates. This is not thrown on the market except in case of family disputes or reverses which necessitate selling out everything, including the wines. The commercial sherry is the result of the careful treatment of the grape juice by the managers of the bodegas. When ripe, the grapes are picked and laid in the sun for a few hours. Then they are brought to the bodegas in paniers on the backs of mules and asses. The owners of asses flock to the grape districts in the fall, and from three in the morning until late at night are busy transporting the luscious fruit to the bodegas. For bringing grapes from the vineyards to the bodegas in Xeres, the ass-owners receive $1.25 per 260 arrobas (about 6500 pounds). One donkey carries 250 pounds; one man can drive half a dozen donkeys, and make three or four trips a day, so that the fortunate owner of six asses makes, during the harvest season, as much as ninety-five cents a day. The *trabajadores de viña*, laborers of the vineyard, who prune vines and gather grapes, receive forty-eight cents a day, in spite of which modest wage they fancy themselves superior to other laborers. During at least seven months in the year the only person required on a vineyard is an overseer or manager, so that the *trabajadores de viña* are employed not more than five months out of twelve. They consider it beneath their dignity to work at anything outside of the "profession," and in winter and spring may be seen loafing about the Spanish towns and cities, lean and hungry, but proud as hidalgos.

On reaching the bodega, the grapes are put in a press and about eight quarts of juice extracted from every arroba (twenty-five pounds). The refuse of the grapes, which is sold for a small sum (usually eight cents per 1500 pounds) forms, when mixed with water, a juice used in adulterating brandy. The purchasers of this refuse are usually poor men with rude presses of their own. They receive one and one-half cents per quart for the juice they make out of the refuse, provided it contains not less than six per cent of alcohol. The first and best juice of the grapes, after being extracted in September and October, is placed in butts and kept until March or April of the following year. Fermentation being then complete, it is drawn from the butts, leaving the lees; brandy is added in varying proportions according to the quality of the wine; it is then placed in the cellars to remain until sold — that is, for three, possibly thirty, years. Sherry less than three years old is not considered fit to drink. Mr. Williams said that the cost of producing sherry beginning with the weighing of the grapes and including pressing, placing in the casks, etc., is about $65 per butt of 470 litres. A cask costs $9; but as the same cask does service for a lifetime, its cost is not included, though it is added to the price of the sherry when sold. Some sherry is sent on voyages around the world to perfect its flavor, the ocean voyage being supposed to have a great effect. A cask that has made a trip or two to India commands fancy prices.

The Spanish have a proverb: "La viña y el potro, que lo crie otro" — "The vineyard and colt let others raise." As slow as is the vineyard in making return, it is quick compared with the date orchard, which does not begin to pay until the seventieth year. It is surprising how any one can be induced to embark in a business whereof the profits cannot possibly be reaped until one's grandchildren come on the scene. Few Spanish owners live at their vineyards more than six or eight weeks in the year: the rest of the time they live in cities, and the vineyard is deserted except by the overseer. The result of this system is that the house on a Spanish vineyard is usually dilapidated and uninviting. No attempt is made to plant shade trees or gardens; the visitor sees only a house, the whitewashed walls of which glare in the sun. On returning from a horseback ride to one of these cheerless places, a pleasant contrast to the sunbaked plain was afforded by the shady avenue leading into Xeres. As we rode down this broad street, fragrant with the scent of two long rows of orange and lemon trees, the *élite* of the quaint old Spanish town were out for their evening airing. That extremes meet was illustrated by the view, often side by side, of fashionable equipages with liveried coachmen and footmen, and donkeys with paniers and carts patterned after models of the fourteenth century.

In 1890 the exports of sherry from the Cadiz district amounted to 56,000 butts worth £16 per butt ($4,345,600). Twenty years ago, the average value per butt was fully fifty per cent more than now. The decrease is owing to the ever smaller demand in Europe. Were not sherry growing in favor in America, prices would show an even greater decline, and many of the big bodegas in Xeres would be obliged to close their doors.

The day of our return to Seville happened to be Sunday, the infant king's birthday. At the end of the celebrated Plaza of Seville was an oil portrait of His Majesty, by the side of which stood two soldiers with guns presented, as if even the counterfeit presentment of royalty needed protection. At night, the beautiful palm trees of the Plaza were strung with lights, a military band discoursed music from a stand, and the cavaliers and dark-eyed señoritas promenaded back and forth, looking at the portrait of the baby king, framed in lights, casting amorous glances at each other and probably regretting the rigid Spanish etiquette that prevents the sexes walking side by side. The morning after this celebration of the king's birthday, Perigarde put in an appearance, looking rather crestfallen, not to say positively woe-begone.

"I am a fool," he said, when we got him to his room at Madame Bjorkman's, "I am a fool, and I admit it — so let us say no more about it."

"All right to the first part of your proposition," said Mack, cheerfully, "but curiosity forbids acquiescence in the latter. We want to know how you got on with the baroness. And the baron — we are deeply interested in the baron."

"Confound the baron!" burst out Perigarde, indignantly.

"With all our hearts, double confound him; but what did he do?"

"My acquaintance with the baroness was of the most innocent and platonic character: instead of rejoicing that his wife had met a congenial countryman, one with whom she could speak in her native tongue, that beastly baron made a scene when he saw us promenading on the Avenida da Liberdada. I thought he was in Madrid. Confound him! such brutes always turn up when least expected. He pretended to think I was interfering with his — his — er marital rights and — and demanded — money. Yes, I had to pay that brute every cent I had."

"And the baroness?"

"That's where the worst comes in," said poor Perigarde, "to think that lovely creature has such a brute of a master. She fainted, actually fainted, when she saw me get out my pocket-book. Of course I paid rather than have a scandal on her fair name."

We told Perigarde he had better let us look after him in the future; we would keep brutal barons at a distance, and pretty baronesses —

"Not a word about her," cried the loyal Perigarde; "she is an angel, an unfortunate angel. We'll drop the subject."

We did drop the subject, but secretly resolved to keep a sharp eye on our friend, who was too unsuspecting to travel alone in this tricky world. It took four hours to go from Seville to Cordova, the train running the entire distance between two hedges of aloe plants. When we reached Cordova, it required only four minutes to see why the guide books call it a decayed city. Mack had wondered that Cordova should be thus particularized, since so many Spanish cities are decayed — at least, as far as one can judge from the unpleasant odors which so often assail the traveller's nose. We found that Cordova is called a "decayed" city, not because of the variety and intensity of odors indicative of dead things, but because of the apathy of its citizens and the downfall of its fortunes. It would be hard to find another city of fifty thousand inhabitants so quiet, so slow, so dull and lifeless. It rivals Pompeii, although in going to sleep Pompeii got the start by nearly two thousand years. The only thing that brings visitors to Cordova is the mosque, and were it not heretical to say it, I should say that they are brought there under false pretences. Not that the mosque is not worth seeing. Once in Cordova, spend an hour or two under its cool arches if you like. But unless you are particularly interested in mosques, or are only trying to kill time, you are apt to feel disappointed at going out of the way to get there. When I uttered these sentiments to Mack, he looked as if I had expressed the rankest heresy.

"The remarkable thing about this mosque," said Mack, "is, that it differs from all others. It is the only one of its kind in the world. True, St. Sophia is now a mosque, but it has not always been. St. Sophia is a specimen of Byzantine, this of Moorish, architecture. You do not see a thousand columns in St. Sophia. *You* don't appreciate a thing unless it is gigantic," he concluded scornfully.

Mack is a true artist and has a perception of the beautiful even though it be microscopic. He said the Cordova mosque has another advantage, that of being low; to see Byzantine and Gothic architecture, one's neck is always strained through having to look upwards at the lofty ceilings. In the Cordova mosque the effect is gained by detail and by horizontal distances. No doubt this is all true; Mack is an authority on art subjects whom I seldom presume to contradict.

I left Mack and Perigarde at the mosque, and went off to take views of the town. It was late when I returned to the hotel, and Mack and Perigarde had gone to bed. I roused them up to get their help in reloading the kodak, the spool of which was exhausted. While Mack arranged the new spool of gelatine films, Perigarde told a kodak story.

"You know," said he, "they always send you a picture as a sample of the work the kodak can do."

"Yes; they sent me the picture of a horse."

"They do not always send the picture of a horse, as a young Southerner I know found to his sorrow. This Louisianian received with his kodak the photograph of a beautiful girl. He fell in love with that picture, and wrote the kodak people begging the name and address of the original. No attention was paid to this letter, and the kodak people forgot all about the matter, when one fine day the romantic young man from Louisiana turned up at the factory at Rochester, showed the picture, and renewed his request for the name and address of the original. He was so earnest the kodak people consented to introduce him to the original — an easy matter, for she was an employee in the factory, a remarkably handsome woman, and, perhaps on that account, used as a subject in sending out specimen photographs."

"And they got married and lived happily ever after?" said Mack.

"Nothing of the sort: she was already married and had two children. The romantic swain had to be carried back to the railway station on a shutter."

Just as Mack was about to unwrap the new spool, having carefully closed the door and windows to exclude all light, we noticed a ray of light through a crevice under the door. That would never do; actinic light would destroy the new films. Mack stole out into the hall, put out the lamp, then returned, closed the door, and began unwrapping the spool. Scarcely had he taken the black paper off when the door burst open and half a dozen servants of the hotel fell headlong into the room.

"What the d—— do you mean?" cried Mack, concealing the kodak under his gown, and rushing out on the balcony in the dark to protect it from the light.

The servants, already amazed at the sight of three men in the middle of the night, squatting in the middle of the floor, pawing about in the dark in a way utterly incomprehensible to people unfamiliar with the kodak business, thought Mack was making off with stolen property and raised a terrible hubbub. Not until the lamps were brought and they saw who we were, did their fears dissipate; then they explained that one had seen Mack's long, lank form stealing through the hall to put out the light, and had given the alarm, thinking burglars were at work. When matters quieted down and perfect darkness was restored, we resumed our seats on the floor and pawed around some more until the old spool was out and the new one in.[1]

The journey to Ronda can be made only partly by rail. At Gobantes, a small station at the base of a ridge of rugged rocks, the stage ride begins. It was the day before the annual Ronda fair, and we feared it would be difficult to get good seats in the stage. In most countries where stages are run, the outside seats are preferred and cost more money. It is exactly the reverse in Spain. The inside seats are preferred and cost more than those on the outside. While the inside of the Gobantes stage was crowded with jolly peasants and dancing-girls from Malaga, all going to the fair, we had the outside to ourselves with the exception of two civil guards. The driver cracked his whip with a report like that of a pistol, and off the four mules galloped over the smooth road — one of the few Spanish roads, be it remarked, concerning which compliments can truthfully be made. The jingling bells on the mules reminded us of sleigh bells in winter; there was no

---

[1] Recently the kodak manufacturers have perfected a sensitive film that is not injured by exposure to light. Travellers should be careful to select this improved film, as it is often difficult to find a dark room in which to reload the kodak. The incident at Cordova would not have occurred had we been provided with the new films.

other reminder of winter. The sun which beat down on our unprotected heads was a drawback to the pleasure of our outside seats, but the free open air, and the chance we had of seeing, on the road, the peasants in their picturesque costumes more than compensated for the heat of the sun. The men wore knee-breeches, red sashes, and funny little jackets, so short they did not quite meet the sash worn around the waist. The women had short skirts and red or blue bodices like corsets laced up over a white shirt or jacket, no bonnet on their heads, only gay-colored kerchiefs. At the first stop to change mules, we got down and walked ahead. The time required to make the change was very long, or else the new mules were very slow: we walked four miles before the stage overtook us. When at last it did catch up, the driver was in a merry mood. As he approached, he whipped up his mules and dashed by at a gallop. Not knowing but the fellow really meant to leave us, we set out on a run as fast as our legs could carry us, to the great amusement of the peasant passengers, who poked their heads out through the doors and windows, and shouted and laughed, and waved their handkerchiefs in great glee: they seemed to think it rare sport to see three Americans running after a Spanish stage. When the facetious driver had run us a quarter of a mile, he stopped the mules until we caught up, panting and puffing, and resumed our places by his side. After that, we did not try walking.

As night drew on, and the road ascended higher and higher, the air grew colder. At first we shivered in our thin summer clothing, then we felt as if freezing to the marrow. At ten o'clock the stage dashed down the white pike into the one long street of a village, whitewashed, and glistening in the moonlight, and while the driver changed mules, we opened our valises and put on every garment they contained — two suits of underclothing, two pairs of trousers, two pairs of socks, etc., etc. The peasant girls laughed immoderately as they saw us on top of the stage, putting on layer after layer of clothes, until from slim youths we were transformed into so many Falstaffs. Thus equipped, we defied the cold, and enjoyed the wild scenery, which looked all the wilder in the silent moonlight. Gardens and cultivated fields had given way to rugged cliffs, to bleak mountain peaks; the soft air of Andalusia was gone, and in its place icy winds from mountain tops. At one point we saw a solitary individual awaiting our approach on the road. We thought the stage would stop for him, but it did not. He was the post-office agent, to whom the driver tossed a bundle of mail without stopping or even slackening the mules. Looking back, we saw the agent untie the package, and there on the roadside begin sorting the letters and papers by the light of the moon.

"No wonder," we said, when we saw this, "no wonder we don't get letters in Spain."

In no country is the post-office perfect, but Spain is the only country I know of which finds out the way a thing ought *not* to be done, and then does it that way. You cannot buy a stamp at a Spanish post-office: you have to look around for a tobacco shop; and if, when you find the shop, it does not happen to have the sort of stamp desired, you must either take a larger stamp or go without. Frequently I was told there were no five-centimo postal cards, and so had to buy ten centimo cards, although the five would have answered my purpose. The tobacconist makes more profit on the ten than on the five-centimo stamp, hence the difficulty of finding the latter. As for finding letters addressed *poste restante*, the guileless traveller who attempts that feat in Spain or Portugal will secure much experience, but little mail. A number of friends wrote me at Malaga, yet on inquiring there at the post-office, the clerk, after a desultory examination, said there was nothing.

"But there must be something; be so good as to look again."

The servant of the people or the crown intimated that he needed no instruction in his business, and closed his window with a bang. Going to the nearest tobacco shop, I asked for a five-centimo postal card, could not get one, so took a ten-center, wrote myself a note and dropped it in the letter-box. The next day but one I went again to the post-office window and was again told there was nothing for me.

"If that is true," said I, "your mails travel marvellously slow. I dropped a postal in the letter-box not fifty yards from the window. The postal was addressed to myself, Malaga, *poste restante*, and although two days have passed, that postal has not yet travelled the fifty yards to this window."

This made the clerk mad, but it also made him look in his pigeon holes again; when finally the postal card he had overlooked was produced, I showed him a telegram from Gibraltar saying that a large packet of letters had been forwarded to me two weeks ago.

"Why didn't you say that before?" said the clerk. "You ought to have told me the letters had been here two weeks."

"But you declared there were none here."

Going to a corner of the room, he rummaged around among some parcels on the floor, and finally returned with my package and long-expected letters. As another illustration of post-office amenities in the Iberian peninsula, I may mention that in Lisbon the *poste restante* clerk told me day after day that there was no mail for me. On arriving at Gibraltar, the postmistress gave me a detailed list showing dates on which a number of telegrams had been sent me at Lisbon. I sent this list to the American Minister to Portugal with the request that he would cause an inquiry to be made at the post-office. The result of this inquiry was the production of several letters which bore the Lisbon postmark and dates prior to the time I had called at the Lisbon post-office and been told there was nothing there. As I always presented my name printed on a card, there was no excuse on the score of not understanding the name.

These post-office grumbles, which Mack, Perigarde, and I indulged in while rattling along in the moonlight, on the top of the Gobantes stage, were at last brought to a period by the glimpse we got in the distance of the lights of Ronda, and by the stream of peasants we overtook trudging along the pike on their way to the fair. The traveller in many Spanish and Portuguese cities has at night to stumble about narrow streets in the darkness; but not so in Ronda: that town, remote as it is from tourists' haunts, distant from railways,[1] stuck way off in the "jumping off" corner of Europe, is all ablaze at night with electric incandescent lights. As the stage drove up the long, steep hill leading to the town, the electric lights at the gates and on the walls shone on us like little suns, paling the light of the silver moon.

Ronda is often accused of being unfriendly to strangers — Ronda boys are said to have a playful habit of throwing stones from heights down on the heads of unwary travellers. Murray's Guide, even in its edition for 1890, warns the reader against this danger, and many travellers are thereby deterred from visiting one of the most interesting places in Spain. During the week we rambled through Ronda's nooks and corners, neither Mack, Perigarde, nor I experienced any of these disagreeable things; the people were friendly enough, and not a boy threw stones at us, or down on us from dangerous heights. These reports come from English tourists; no doubt Gibraltar is a thorn in the Spanish side, as once was Calais in the French, and the small boy gets even, so far as he can, by dumping boulders on Englishmen's heads. The Ronda boys like Americans.

The morning after our arrival we met one of the stage passengers who had been quite frigid towards us the night before,

---

[1] A railroad now (September, 1892) runs from Gobantes to Ronda.

but who was now very cordial because he had learned we were not English, but Americans. This man, as he was walking along, with his broad sombrero and his staff six feet long, spied us in the crowd, and came to us beaming with smiles, and anxious to "make a communication."

"The English — *that* for the English," he said, snapping his fingers to express his contempt. "But you are Americans, and I shall communicate to you that you were cheated by the stage agent at Gobantes."

"You don't say so?" The now friendly Spaniard insisted that he did say so.

"I saw you when you paid your fare," he said; "you gave twelve pesetas each, but you should have given only eight."

"Did you pay only eight?"

"That is all, and that is what the others paid for inside seats. You had outside seats and should have paid even less."

"Why were we charged more?"

"The agent thought you were Ingleses."

The stage office was opposite our hotel, the Fonda Rondeña. Before going to dinner, we stopped there to ventilate our opinion of the Gobantes agent. But first, to see whether the Spaniard had spoken correctly, we inquired the price of passage to Gibraltar. "Ten pesetas," replied the agent, promptly. This was neither twelve, the amount we had paid, nor eight, the amount the Spaniard said ought to have been paid. Possibly the agent had misunderstood us, but a repetition of the question elicited the same reply. Whereupon we said the price from Gobantes to Ronda was only eight pesetas.

"Of course," said the agent, blandly, "the fare from Gobantes to Ronda is eight pesetas, but it is ten from Ronda to Gobantes."

Admiring the agent's oily falsehoods, we wondered what he would say when we informed him the Gobantes agent had charged us twelve pesetas instead of eight, the amount the

Ronda agent had himself just admitted was the proper fare. When we told him, his smile did not lose an iota of its oily smoothness.

"Of course you paid twelve," he said. "You had first class. When I said eight pesetas, I meant second class."

"What part of the stage is first class?"

"What seats did you have?"

"Never mind that. Tell us what part is first class."

The oily agent avoided answering this question until he went to the stables and learned from the driver what seats we occupied on the coach. Then he returned, and said smoothly, "You paid twelve pesetas, Señores, because you had first-class on top of the coach. Here is the invoice of our Gobantes agent — 'three Ingleses, twelve pesetas each.'"

This invoice exonerated the Gobantes agent from robbing his company, but it did not exonerate the company from robbing us; for it is well known that, in Spain, the first-class seats of stages are on the inside, not on the outside, where we sat along with the driver and the two civil guards.

Ronda is worth seeing because of its remarkable position on both sides of a deep and narrow gorge through which the Guardairo rushes, a foaming torrent; from the 20th to the 22d of May each year, the town is especially interesting because of the fair which attracts crowds of people from all parts of Andalusia. During this fair, the long, narrow street of the town is lined with temporary booths, refreshment stands, and "fake shows." In front of one of the latter was the picture of a wild Arab mounted on a camel, his gun levelled at an enormous snake coiled around a palm-tree. Beneath this exciting scene was the inscription: —

"GRAN COLLECION DE FIERAS!"

The entrance fee was only four cents; in we went, and learned that human trickery is not entirely confined to our

THE "PRINCIPE FARNESE", AMALFI IN THE DISTANCE.

own countrymen. The "grand collection of wild beasts" consisted of a sad-eyed camel and a stuffed snake that lay stretched on a shelf at the end of the tent. When I pulled out my notebook to make a few notes, the visitors in the tent crowded around me wonderingly. They could not understand how the ink kept flowing from my fountain pen, and the notes, which were written in shorthand, they mistook for Arabic. One fellow, who had been to Morocco, began speaking to me in that language. When he found I did not understand a word, he expressed surprise at my ability to write a language which I could not speak. With him, it was just the reverse; he could speak Arabic, but could not write it; "in fact," he added, naively, "I can't even write Spanish."

Following the long street of the town to its termination in an open space on the top of a five-hundred-foot, perpendicular cliff we found ourselves in the midst of the Ronda fair; that is to say, in the midst of a vast concourse of men, women, children, pigs, goats, asses, chickens, and other farmyard animals. So lank and lean were most of the brutes, that Perigarde said they were brought to the fair by mistake, being really on the way to the boneyard. This hypothesis was incorrect; for we saw two men examining and buying razor-backed hogs, emaciated goats, and asses weary and worn, and often with sore backs. There is so little water in Spain, even on the mountain tops, and the pastures are so scanty and poor, Spanish cattle can hardly be other than razor-backed. We strolled about through the crowd, admiring the skilful manner in which each herdsman kept his own flock of goats or pigs from mingling with his neighbor's flock. On going back to the town, flaming posters announced that a troop of American acrobats would give a performance. Patriotism demanded that we should patronize our country-people. We felt proud of their acrobatic powers as we read the poster.

"Gran Aconticemiento artistico — Funcion brillante y extraordinaria para hoy Miercoles 20 de Mayo 1891 " — " debut of a notable and numerous company gymnastic, acrobatic, and pantomimic, composed of thirty artists of both sexes from America. Under the direction of Mr. Georges Brocquinn and the celebrated, and without rival, Mis Scot." No. 1. Symphony by the band. No. 2. Tumblin Americano. No. 3. Another symphony by the band. No. 4. More "tumblin Americano." A "nota bene" in the corner informed us it was not possible to give even an approximate idea of the "Extraordinary conglomeration of wonders" in this performance, and that therefore no attempt was made to itemize the marvellous feats witnessed by those fortunate enough to see "Mis Scot," "Mis Clara," and the other members of the troop ("No pudiendo dar una idea approximada de lo grandioso de este espactaculo," etc., etc.). Of course we went in a quiver of expectation, but we shall not be so mean as to describe what we saw. Each traveller must judge for himself. We advise Americans in Europe, if they have a chance, to see "Mis Scot" and "Mis Clara," the unrivalled American acrobats — though from what part of America they came not even a mind-reader could tell.

After the performance was over, we made our way to the dressing-room to pay our respects to "Mis Scot" and "Mis Clara," our fair, or rather very dark, countrywomen. When those athletic young women came forward, we found, to our surprise, they did not understand a word of English. The manager assured us, though, that they spoke "American" like natives, that if we would only talk "American," the ladies would be happy to converse. As we obstinately refused to speak anything except English and Italian, we got on quite well in the latter language, and discovered that these ladies had changed their pretty Italian names for the prosaic "Mis Scot" and "Mis Clara."

Three bridges span the deep gorge that divides the old from

the new part of the town of Ronda. One of the three bridges has a single arch of more than one hundred feet, looking down fully three hundred feet on the Guardairo rushing on its way to the valley. The bridge is lined with pedlars and peasants; but, for once, scenery proved more attractive than people, and our time on the bridge was spent gazing down into the fearful gulf below, at the fig trees clinging to the side of the precipice as if growing out of the living rock, and at the foaming torrent that sends the wind and spray whistling through the narrow defile with such noise as to completely drown our voices on the bridge above. On a ledge of the cliff, almost at the bottom of the cañon, is a miserable house, the home of a woman who earns her living by gathering and selling manure. On the way into the gorge, we stopped to see this house, a filthy place, half filled with manure which the woman brings in large baskets, and stores until there is enough to sell. Perigarde marvelled at the wrinkles, the yellow skin, the ugliness, of this poor creature, who could not stand upright, her back had so long bent under heavy burdens.

"You need not marvel," said I. "A Venus would bend, and shrivel, and wrinkle under the loads this woman carries. Think of the steps she daily takes, the steep cliffs she climbs with that heavy ill-smelling burden on her back! The wonder is, not that she is old and wrinkled, and looks as if tottering on the brink of her grave, but that she has not tumbled in it long ago — poor creature! such work God never intended women to do, yet all over Europe women do cruel work like this."

The bottom of the cavern is only twenty or thirty feet wide: at the top it is about one hundred and fifty, so that, even at midday, the sun scarce reaches its bottom depth. In that deep rift between the rocks it is ever cool, ever shaded. We climbed along the ledges above the foaming torrent, now crawling through dark tunnels, then emerging again, and gazing up at the three bridges hundreds of feet overhead, seemingly suspended in the air. At one point far above us, we saw a ruined castle covered with ivy; some hundreds of feet below, clinging to ledges on the almost perpendicular cliff, was a flock of goats that had escaped from the herdsman, who was on a shelf just below, trying to dislodge them by throwing stones and shouting. The stones did not reach, nor did the shouting stir them. Finally, a boy appeared on the scene: the youngster, nimble as any goat, scaled the precipice, and drove the animals back to their master. It was a daring deed: it made our heads swim to see a human being climb a height so steep and dizzy.

It has been said that there is but one Ronda: certainly, there is no other city in Europe so strangely situated on both sides of a deep gorge, on a thousand-foot precipice commanding so wide and grand a view. Travellers in Spain will make a mistake if they allow foolish talk about small boys and big stones to deter them from visiting Ronda.

CHAPTER VII

On Donkey Back to Gibraltar — How we escaped the Muleteers — Scaling the Sierras. — The Posada de la Paz and the Enchanted Castle — Pastoral Scenes — Don Rodriguez saves us from Prison — Gibraltar — Second Impressions — Curious Sea-Eggs — A Trip to Tangiers — The Cadi's Court — Scene from the Arabian Nights — Moorish Wedding — Mack buys Antiquities

WHEN we inquired about going to Gibraltar, we encountered an unexpected difficulty: it was difficult to make the Spaniards understand our pronunciation of the word "Gibraltar." We called it "Gibel-terra," "Gibraltoe," and a dozen other ways, but in vain: finally Mack drew a sketch map, Perigarde said "dove Inglesi in Spagna" (where English in Spain), and the fellow with whom we were negotiating for horses said he understood. But though he understood, and agreed to be at the Fonda Rondeña by six o'clock the next morning, he did not appear, the reason being, according to the innkeeper of the fonda, that he had made a better bargain with other travellers. Ronda is undoubtedly an interesting place, but we had already been there a week, and had no desire to remain longer. We threw out a drag-net, so to speak; that is, during that day's ramble, each of us, separately and singly, engaged every horse, mule, and donkey that we saw to hire. Perigarde even engaged a little four-dollar ass, thinking if all else failed, this homely beast might carry the luggage while we would walk. The result of these engagements insured ample facilities for getting away from Ronda, but it did not insure getting away with whole skins. The quadrupeds with their masters began to assemble at four o'clock in the morning, in front of the Fonda Rondeña. An observer, had there been one at that early hour, would have thought a caravan was being organized for an expedition into Central Africa. At five o'clock the posadero of the fonda hammered on our door with an energy born of deep indignation.

"At least twenty men with horses and mules are waiting outside," he shouted. "I have told them only three travellers go to Gibraltar, but every man of them declares he is engaged and refuses to leave."

"Say we shall be down directly," we said, with calm dignity; but when the innkeeper was gone, our dignity wilted. What to do, how to face these much-wronged muleteers, was the question. Perigarde took a cheerful view of the matter, said it was all right, that out of the twenty mules we should at least get three. A duchess preparing for the queen's reception could not have taken more time to make her toilet than we took that morning, as we cudgelled our brains trying to find a way out of our dilemma. Again the innkeeper pounded on the door to announce the arrival of more horses and more men. Then Perigarde was for going back to bed, sending word we were violently ill, and waiting until night, when we could make a safe retreat; but Mack and I were impatient to be off. Taking the posadero into our confidence, we primed him what to say, seized our stout walking-sticks, and all four marched down stairs prepared to meet the foe. They were assembled in the court of the fonda: at the first glimpse of us coming down the steps, every man of them made a rush, and began gesticulating and jabbering, while their asses and mules set up a loud braying. Our hearts quailed, but we contracted our brows into a stern frown and put on a resolute air.

"You engaged me, Señores: I am ready," shouted one.

"But I am he you engaged," shouted another.

"He has no horses, Señores: only mules. Look at my beautiful horses," cried a third; and so forth.

We knew we were in the wrong, and, after the way of wrongdoers, we tried to throw blame on the innocent; so frowning sternly, we yelled at the poor fellows that if they did not stop the noise we would return to our rooms and not go to Gibraltar at all. Then we gave the innkeeper his cue and the terms he was to offer for peace. He told them of the fellow who had deceived us, how that disappointment had shaken our faith in Ronda muleteers; "And now," said the innkeeper, "their Excellencies are going to choose one of you; to the rest they will give ten pesetas for your trouble and to drink their Excellencies' health. But mind, you don't get one *real* if you make a noise and disturb their Excellencies."

This speech and the ten pesetas settled the war to the satisfaction of all parties. We selected, as guide, a man who said his horses were fresh and strong, just bought at the fair. One of the "horses" was a mule, and on this patient beast was placed the burden of the baggage as well as a rider. The possession of this animal was decided by lot, and the lot — bad luck to it! — fell to me. The panniers bulged out so that it was out of the question to ride astride. When not walking, I sat perched on a small mountain of goods and chattels, cross-legged, like the unspeakable Turk. Our worthy muleteer, who rejoiced in the name Guajun Lama, — he lives in Ronda, No. 51 Calle Molino, — regarded his selection among so many competitors as a high personal tribute. It put him in an amiable mood. As we crossed the gloomy gorge for the last time, wound through the streets of old Ronda, and began descending into the valley under the very shadow of the ancient Moorish castle, Guajun proudly pointed out the attractions of his animals. The horse Mack rode cost as much as $60, and seemed, in Guajun's eyes, the perfection of the equine species. Everything is relative in this world. In comparison with my mule, Mack's $60 horse might be called a Maude S., but in any American city the Humane Society would order it sent to a pasture for its health. In the interest of the poor beast, we told Guajun his horse would be magnificent if he would only fatten it up a bit.

The scenery between Ronda and Gibraltar is wild and rugged. The road soon leaves the valley, and becomes a narrow bridle-path as it winds up and among mountains so high that, although in the southern extremity of Europe, even in summer time the air is chill and cold. Occasionally from those bleak and barren heights we saw, thousands of feet below, vineyards planted in terraces on the mountain's side. There are no farmhouses on those vineyards, the "Bauerdorf" (peasant village) system prevailing in Spain as well as in Germany. Every five or ten miles, a turn in the path revealed one of these peasant villages, nestled far below in some cosy valley, the white houses and the church steeples gleaming in the sun and looking like mere toys in comparison with the gigantic crags that overhang them. The first glimpse of Gibraltar is magnificent: there are mountains yet to climb, valleys to traverse, but the traveller from Ronda crosses a mountain pass higher than most of the peaks, and from this pass sees Gibraltar, the Mediterranean, and even the mountains of Africa, beyond. The great rock of Gibraltar, with its fifteen hundred feet of cliff, rises perpendicularly from the water. Nearer at hand, and about two thousand feet below, lay the town of Gaucin, where we intended passing the night. It was not pleasant riding down that steep trail without saddle or bridle; it seemed so easy to slide over the head of the mule. As such a slide would not terminate short of the valley at the bottom of the precipice down which we were winding, I did not ride, but walked, leaving the mule to stumble along with the baggage as best it could. My progress was much more rapid than that of the mule — a fact which led to an exciting adventure. Stopping at the first posada in the town of Gaucin, I inquired the price of accommodations. The posadero, seeing me on foot, worn and dusty, thought I was a tramp Italian pedlar (I spoke to him in Italian), and did not charge more than twenty or thirty per cent above his regular prices. A bargain for our party was made, and twenty minutes later, when Mack and Perigarde appeared with Guajun and the horses, the posadero of the Posada de la Paz was the maddest man in Spain. Guajun lost no time whispering to him we were American "Milords" running over with money. However, a bargain had already been made, so we did not worry over the matter.

The posada was a typical Spanish inn — the arched doorway led from the stony street into a large, cobble-paved, barn-like room, at one end of which was a brick stove and a long table. At the other end were troughs and food for cattle, while the sleeping-rooms opened out from the remaining side of the square. Depositing our luggage in two of these rooms, entered through the uninviting medley of peasants, garlic, and cattle, and leaving Guajun behind to expatiate still further upon the grandeur and wealth of his three American excellencies, we set out for the castle, hoping to reach the summit in time to see the sun set. The castle of Gaucin is romantically curious and picturesque. Gaucin itself is two thousand feet above the Mediterranean; its castle is still higher, being situated on a ridge of rock five hundred or six hundred feet above the town. This rock, distinct from the other mountains, rises solitary and alone, a huge mass that is visible for miles around. Portions of its perpendicular sides are serrated; other portions present the appearance of natural turrets and towers. Steps cut into the living rock lead to the summit, where a massive door admits the traveller to the ancient castle, one of the first the Moors built in Spain. The dangerous and subterranean caverns where the Moors once buried Christian knights are still there. Mack kindly offered to lower me down if I cared to explore, but as the stones we dropped went rattling seemingly to bottomless depths, his offer was politely declined. It is said that these caverns lead to some secret outlet, and were used by the Moors in olden times when besieged by enemies. We remained in this ruin, with its magnificent view of mountain, and valley, and sea, until the golden glow of the sun faded into the softer light of the moon; the whitewashed houses of Gaucin at the base of the precipice, six hundred feet below, glistened as brightly as did the snow-capped peaks. On the very summit of the castle is a fig-tree, the roots of which subsist on soil accumulated in the course of ages.

Perigarde, always romantic, thought he would like to remain all night viewing the enchanting scenery, — doubly enchanting in the light of the moon, — but Mack and I vetoed this suggestion. We said, "With a hard day's ride behind us, and another one in store for to-morrow, it won't do to take on so much romance at one time." So we descended at nine o'clock. This, however, did not mean going to bed at that reasonable hour; for while on the way back to the posada, the sound of tinkling guitars floated out from one of the houses on the narrow street we were traversing. When we peeped through the door, we saw a sight as charming as it was simple and graceful — a company of peasants and villagers entertaining themselves with songs and dances. Unspoiled by contact with tourists, as soon as they saw us they invited us to enter with a cordiality to which travellers in beaten ruts are little accustomed. In Granada the guides arrange dances for visitors; needless to say, those artificial affairs are not to be compared with the pleasant and spontaneous dances of the peasants, such as we saw at Gaucin. The young men sat in a row on one side of the room; on the other side sat the girls, their olive cheeks glowing with health, dark, dreamy eyes, red roses in their black hair. Lamps suspended from the wooden rafters and the wood fire in the huge fireplace lighted up the scene. The dancing was lively and graceful. The dancers approach to within a few inches of each other, then, just as the man appears about to grasp his pretty partner around the waist, she gives a swift, coquettish twirl, and pirouettes to the other side of the room. This is performed again and again, and the pleasure and applause of the spectators is measured by the adroitness with which the girl escapes the eager hands of her partner.

The pleasant impression made by this pastoral scene was rudely effaced by an incident next morning. Washington Irving somewhere speaks of Spain as "a country where the most miserable inn is as full of adventure as an enchanted castle, and every meal is an achievement." Washington Irving must have been in the Posada de la Paz of Gaucin. Certainly it was an achievement — a very disagreeable one — to eat its meals, and, as for adventure, we had, in that dingy, dirty old posada, as exciting an adventure as one could possibly have in enchanted castles. The padrone felt that his mistaking me for an Italian, and the consequently smaller charges than he would have made had he known we were Americans, was my fault, and determined our bargain should not bind him. Next morning, when I handed him the amount agreed on, he shook his head and demanded more.

"Why do you ask for more?" He said something about our being more trouble than expected, whereupon Mack committed the mistake of asking how much the extra trouble was worth. The sum mentioned was so extortionate, we saw he simply meant to rob us. While the innkeeper was jabbering excitedly, our muleteer stood complacently by with an air that plainly showed he was at the bottom of the whole business: we had reason to believe that he was to receive part of the expected booty on his return from Gibraltar. Mack and Perigarde were already on their horses, though they had not yet passed through the arched doorway into the stony street.

"*Anda*, let us go," I said to Guajun. "We have paid what was bargained — the posadero shall not have a single *real* more." But Guajun did not budge. He shrugged his shoulders, pointed at the posadero, and said it would be necessary to first settle with him.

"All right," said I. "You stay here and settle if you like. *We* are going," and seizing the bridle of my mule, I called to Mack and Perigarde to follow, and started for the door. But we were reckoning without our host; that rascally fellow, anticipating our move, planted himself in the door and declared we should not go until he was paid. A crowd of twenty or thirty onlookers were now assembled, — rough, dark Spaniards who evidently sympathized with the innkeeper in his efforts to rob the "Ingleses." Mack and Perigarde jumped down from their horses, and while they prevented attack from the rear, I brandished my club and marched straight to the door. Then came a crisis. The posadero did not give way as I expected, but, dodging the blow I aimed with my club, he made a rush, and with his superior physical strength would doubtless have done me up, had I not leaped to one side and, at the same instant, whipped out my self-cocking revolver and levelled the shining barrel square in the fellow's face.

"Move and I fire!" I said in English, which, of course, he did not understand, but he understood the pointed American of the Smith and Wesson five-shooter, and displayed an agility in getting away that would have done credit to a professional acrobat. The coast was clear, the padrone was out of sight, the crowd of onlookers scattered into remote parts of the court of the innkeeper, but we were not willing to leave under such circumstances. Mack and Perigarde agreed to remain while I went off to find the alcalde, and have the matter set straight according to law. As I started off, the warnings of the American resident in Malaga came back to my memory. Visions of imprisonment in Africa rose before my mind's eye; the minimum punishment for drawing a pistol was two years. An idea came to me that it might be wiser not to return to that misnamed posada (de la Paz — of Peace!), but to flee as quickly as possible to Gibraltar, and throw myself under British protection. Looking back, I saw a file of soldiers entering the inn; this increased my uneasiness, and also made me think an attempt to flee would be futile — a bold course was the only course, after all. I found the alcalde, Don Eugenio Rodriguez, on the Plazuela Botica, Gaucin, province of Cadiz, Spain, and explained the situation at the Posada de la Paz; Don Rodriguez gravely put on his hat, and ordered me to follow him to the seat of war. As we walked along, men, women, and children trooped after us. The whole town was excited; my heart thumped wildly; I did not know but that was the way Spanish alcaldes marched offending foreigners to prison. Looking back on that procession from the vantage ground of safety, I see it as a triumphal march. First came the alcalde; second, the American, who did his best to look undaunted; then a hundred or two hundred men, women, children, and babies. Mack and Perigarde were as badly scared as I; the innkeeper had gone out and brought in that file of stern soldiers. But all is well that ends well. The alcalde proved himself a second Daniel come to judgment; I stated my case, the posadero stated his — telling the lie that we would not pay the amount agreed upon. The alcalde sublimely swept aside the posadero's lie.

"Never mind what you made them promise — cuanto vale? — what is it worth?" demanded this second Daniel.

"But, Señor Alcalde, they promised — "

"Never mind that — cuanto vale?"

"But they are Ingleses; they can pay more; they — "

"Never mind that — cuanto vale?"

And this was all the alcalde said, but it was enough. The poor pasadero was beaten; he glowered at us, but he dared not tell the alcalde his miserable accommodations were worth one tenth the sum he demanded. When, finally, he admitted we had paid him ten pesetas, — Spaniards would not have been charged five, — the alcalde told us we had paid enough and were free to go. Should the eyes of Don Eugenio Rodriguez ever meet these words, he will understand that his sense of justice and right evinced to foreigners certainly received the respect and gratitude of the three Americans who found so little peace in the posada of that name in Gaucin.

The rock of Gibraltar has a city of twenty-five thousand inhabitants, yet is regarded merely as a fortress, and is held under strictest military rule. No one can leave or enter after sunset, nor can one enter at all without a permit from the governor. This, however, is but a form. There is a little room near the gate, where you have only to ask for a ticket to receive it. When we approached the window of this little room, the officer asked: —

"Are you British subjects?"

"We are not subjects of any country," replied Perigarde, proudly. "We are American citizens."

"That's all right," returned the officer, pleasantly; "you are first cousins, and it is only a matter of a short time when we all shall be of one country."

"Do you mean," said I, "that the two countries will become one big monarchy, or will England become a republic?"

"Oh, England will become a republic — all English-speaking countries must, sooner or later, become a grand federation of republics."

It is curious to note the difference between first and second impressions. When I first landed in Gibraltar, five years ago, direct from New York, it seemed a wonderfully strange and outlandish place. When I arrived there in 1891, on the back of a mule, direct from Gaucin, Ronda, and a dozen other towns quainter than towns of an artist's imagination, by comparison, Gibraltar was plain and prosaic. The streets, when fresh from New York, seemed crooked and narrow; after Lisbon, and towns in Spain, Gibraltar streets were wide boulevards. Nor did the Arabs excite the interest and surprise which they had done before a trip into Turkey deprived them of the advantage of novelty.

I had a letter of introduction to Major H. of the Royal Engineers, and through his kindness obtained an insight into garrison life and manners. The existence of both officers and men is dreary enough, — a monotonous round of drilling and changing watches. With the exception of a small stretch called the Alameda, the rock is treeless and barren. The soldiers spend their time off duty in drink shops and dance halls. The Spanish dance, in these latter, is an odd mixture of dance, guitars, and castanets. It is not graceful, and though not modest, as a Frenchman said of it, "it has not the merit of being vulgar." To see it once as a curiosity may do, but we felt sorry for the Gibraltar soldiers dependent upon the inane Spanish music-hall dance as their staple amusement. The officers have their club and their library with fifty thousand or sixty thousand volumes and the leading periodicals of Europe and America. Some better amusement ought to be provided for the private soldier.

It is no longer permitted to go to the summit of the Rock, on account of certain secret experiments being there conducted. Sentries are stationed on the paths leading to the top, and for neither love nor gold is the traveller permitted to ascend. However, an excellent view of the tremendous precipice on the Mediterranean side of the Rock can be obtained by walking around the north end, hiring a fisher's boat, and rowing to Europa Point. We spent half a day floating along the base of the Rock, landing here and there to explore curious caverns and to bathe in the cool, blue water. Should the reader ever follow our example as to the bathing, he must look out for what are called "sea-eggs"—small, black briars of a substance resembling slate, sharp and painful. These sea-eggs cover some of the rocks, and if the swimmer puts his hands or feet on them ever so lightly, he will be apt to spend the next day or two digging the detestable things out with a lancet. We afterwards saw these sea-eggs off the coast of Greece and Sicily, and, until warned by unpleasant experience, suffered considerably from the way they buried themselves in the flesh the moment we touched a rock or ledge where they were deposited. As we paddled about in the Mediterranean, the goats far up on the perpendicular heights appeared no larger than mice or rats. Some of the caves extend long distances in the rock, and in these we had great sport firing our revolvers and listening to the reverberations as they thundered through the dark passages, finally dying away in the mysterious depths of the Rock. Returning from this boating and swimming trip, we were lucky enough to see a sight that occurs in Gibraltar only once a year, — the celebration of the Queen's birthday. It was four o'clock, and we had scarcely reached the large, open space north of the Rock before the soldiers appeared at the end of the bridge leading from the fortress, their banners flying, their bands sending forth martial music. Column after column filed across the bridge, until finally some five thousand sturdy Englishmen and fierce-looking Scots in Highland kilts were in the field at the base of the precipice, fifteen hundred feet high. While the English and Scots were forming a square a quarter of a mile long each side, we heard the tramp of troops from the mainland, and, turning, saw the Spanish, small and swarthy in comparison with the soldierly British, approaching, to participate in the celebration of Queen Victoria's natal day.

"What a strange thing is humanity," we thought. "Here are five thousand human beings reduced to mere automata. One man in Downing Street a thousand miles away has only to give a scratch with his pen, and the five thousand fellow-beings go this way or that, fire their guns in the air as they are going to do now, or into the breasts of fellow-beings as they have done before and may do again. What a wonderful machine is an army!"

When the firing began, the effect was striking. The guns discharged by companies, and so nicely did one follow the other, that it was as if one had set fire to a long train of powder. The crash and roar of the musketry swept, like a flash, round the long sides of the square. When it reached the point whence it started, the hundred cannon in the galleries took up the refrain. The face of the grand precipice, to its very summit, fifteen hundred feet above the sea, is pierced with winding galleries, from whose port holes protrude the black mouths of cannon. At one moment, this tremendous cliff was silent and dark: the next moment a mass of flame and smoke issued from its hundred cannon holes, and

SICILIAN WOMEN THRESHING WHEAT NEAR THE GREEK THEATRE, SYRACUSE

there was a roar and reverberation louder than thunder. The sudden change was wonderful. After this monster salute, the troops went through a series of manœuvres, then marched back into the fortress. It was a fine sight, one that would have repaid photographing, but sketching and photographing are strictly forbidden in Gibraltar. A tourist, ignorant of this rule, took several views of the streets and of the hundred-ton guns. He was hauled up before the authorities, given a severe lecture, and deprived, not only of the Gibraltar views, but of all the other views that were on the same spool. Kodak readers will do well to make a note of this military rule of Gibraltar.

An interesting and cheap excursion is that from Gibraltar to Tangiers. Before crossing the straits, the little steamer skims close along the Spanish shore, passing within a hundred yards of Tarifa. As we gazed on its white walls and towers, relics of the early Middle Ages, when the Moors levied tribute on passing vessels, we wondered at the sublime audacity which in the United States calls "American" a policy originated a thousand years ago by the barbarous Moors of Tarifa.

In Gibraltar streets are commonplace after Spanish and Portuguese; the same cannot be said of Tangiers. The dusky Arabs dress in a kind of meal-bag, a conical hood over the head, no sleeves and no breeches, their legs being naked below the knee where the sack leaves off. They look queer enough by day; by night they are weird. The night after our arrival we took a stroll through the dark and silent streets. Here and there lay men asleep on the cobble-stones. They did not seem disturbed by the rats which scampered about in droves. It was so dark we stumbled over them: they (the men, not the rats) never swore at us, but would rise up, and, like spooks, silently glide away. While rambling along, sometimes almost falling over these sleeping phantoms and wondering why so large a city could not afford a single street lamp, we saw a light approaching. Presently a pair of baggy white breeches appeared behind the light. When within a few feet, we saw a coffee-colored man dressed in white from the turban on his head to the sandals on his feet.

"How you do, gentlemen? Your health good?"

Such were the polite inquiries of the coffee-colored man with the white robes and lantern. We said our health was fairly good, whereupon the coffee-colored man kindly informed us it would not continue so if we strolled around Tangiers in the dark. Not knowing what to reply to this, we said nothing. Our coffee-colored man continued:—

"Me your guide make, me Ben Belassen, the guide."

Belassen's English was so good, not to speak of his lantern, that we engaged him on the spot, and a lucky investment he was: for Ben forthwith took us to see a sight we should not have seen but for him and his lantern. This was a Moorish wedding.

"You no can go in," said Ben Belassen, pausing before an arched tunnel that led into the court of a curious house. "You stay here. You can see here."

We followed this injunction, taking up positions against the wall opposite the entrance of the tunnel. Soon there was a great noise of groans and shouts accompanied by the twanging of stringed instruments. This was hardly well under way before the darkness in the tunnel changed to light, and there issued a procession of men in meal-bags and conical hoods, boys with lanterns and tapers, and an ass bearing a top-heavy sort of cage held on by ropes and by men walking along at the ass's side.

"That's the bride," said Ben Belassen, in a whisper.

"Where?" we questioned, eagerly, wishing to see the beauty of a Moorish bride. Ben Belassen gravely pointed to the cage on the ass's back. The bride was in the cage; we could not see even the tip of her nose. The procession wound through the tortuous streets, the boys with the lanterns shouting at the top of their voices, the men in meal-bags beating tambourine-like instruments, and creating a din that would do credit to Bedlam. After making night hideous with their howls, the procession halted in front of the groom's house, the groom himself appeared at the door, and the cage containing his bride was lowered from the ass's back and carried into the house, out of sight of the gaping crowd that had assembled. When the meal-sacks had dispersed, Ben Belassen conducted us to a café where we heard some Moorish music that smote on our Christian ears more painfully than that of the bridal procession. The rooms of the café opened on a small court. The whitewashed walls and floors were covered with mats. The guests, after leaving their sandals and lanterns outside in the court, squatted cross-legged on the mats, drank coffee, thumped on tambourines, squalled, and did other things which, to the Arabic mind, passed for music. One group on the floor consisted of half a dozen graybeards playing with a Spanish deck of forty cards. They were excitable old chaps, shook their fists in each other's faces, knocked their turbans awry, and shrieked at each other in discordant tones that sounded above the din of the singers and tambourine-players. Why they continued to play when each, to judge from their angry tones and fierce gestures, deemed the others robbers and cheats, was a mystery to us. Our guide listened to the discordant din in a sort of ecstasy.

"America no music like that?" he said.

"No, Ben Belassen," replied Mack, feelingly, "there is no music in all America like that."

"Except in Chinatown, San Francisco," I added. "There, Americans can listen to dulcet sounds like these, Ben Belassen."

This nice sarcasm was lost on Ben Belassen; but the compliment it seemed to convey highly pleased him.

Our hotel, the Ville de France, stands just outside the city, in a garden, upon a high terrace that overlooks the white tops of Tangiers' houses glistening in the hot, southern sun, and beyond over the dark rolling ocean. At the base of this terrace is the "Soko" (market), where, on Thursdays and Sundays, congregate a motley crowd of wild and strange-looking peasants from the hills and plains of Morocco. Hundreds come on camels: we saw a herd of those homely beasts lying on the ground, their legs curled up under their bodies, all of them chained together, to prevent them from rising and straying away. Among the many curious vocations carried on in the Soko, none seemed more curious than that of the restaurant-keepers. The Moor's cooking-stove consists of a block of stone four feet long with a six-inch trough hollowed out on the top. A lot of needles, eight or ten inches long, are strung with bits of liver, fat, and beef chopped into pieces the size of a walnut. The cook plays on the hundred or so needles before him something as a musician plays on a piano, touching first one key then another. That is, he keeps turning the different needles until the bits of meat have all been exposed to the glow of the coals underneath. His hands must be as tough and callous as leather, for he never winces as he picks up the hot needles and turns them, one after another, in rapid succession. These bits of roasted liver and fat are regarded as delicacies: crowds surround the cook, each man waiting his turn to buy one of the needles. No matter what the time of day, the cooks and the crowd are there. They seem to eat all day.

In some of the booths we saw men hammering plates of brass. Ben Belassen said they were working figures of mosques on the brass, and that a good workman could make as much as ninety cents on Fair day. In other booths we saw how the long Moorish guns are made. A boy sits perched on a box, working a pair of rude bellows, while the gunsmith manipulates a long tube that looks like a section of gas-pipe; this is the embryo gun-barrel. The bellows boy gets four cents a day for blowing the smith's fire, while the smith gets whatever he can for his guns. These guns are rarely seen out of Morocco, their export having been prohibited by the Sultan. In a barber shop we saw a row of dejected men sitting on a shelf while a barber earned four cents from each by shaving the tops of their heads. Ben Belassen said living was expensive for these people: coffee costs one cent a cup; eggs, ten cents a dozen; a small mule costs $4; one of the meal-sacks which constitutes the Arab's suit of clothes costs from $1 to $1.50. Everything is relative: one cent for a cup of coffee would not be considered dear in New York, yet it is dear in Tangiers, where the best mechanics earn only half a dollar a day. The gun-maker told us, through our interpreter, that the sale of his guns scarcely nets him more than $2 a week. He begins work at six o'clock, after a breakfast of dry bread. At noon he stops to eat some more bread, and on Thursdays and Sundays, — Fair days, — one of the needles of meat is added to the bill of fare. At half-past six he eats more bread, this time with a cup of coffee. The weavers of the coarse cloth, out of which the conical hooded bags are made, have about the same hours and the same meagre diet. They make, with their rude machines, about four yards of cloth per day. While watching a weaver at work, we noticed he frequently stopped the loom in order to inhale something from an egg-shaped object that dangled from a chain around his neck. Most of the workmen wear these egg-shaped things, which Ben Belassen said were hollow and contained fine powdered snuff. A jewelry workshop we saw was a mere hole in the wall five feet square. The jeweller sat cross-legged on the floor, a little skin bellows at one side, a few antiquated watches at the other, and in front, two eggs, bread, and a bunch of onions, from which he was making his midday meal.

These illustrations suffice as samples of the scenes witnessed in the Tangiers Soko every Thursday and Sunday: they also indicate how much is left of the refinement, the skill, the grace, and intelligence that once made the Moors a daring, ambitious, and powerful people.

But more interesting than the workshops and booths are the jugglers and snake-charmers, who take advantage of the fair at Tangiers to display their skill, and reap a copper harvest — copper, for of course the Moors do not give either gold or silver. A snake-charmer whom we watched was a wild-looking fellow; the front part of his head was shaved, but from the back fell a long mass of thick, matted hair. At one side of the circle was the leather bag containing the snakes; near by squatted three assistants with instruments as noisy and musical as Indian tom-toms. The charmer himself had a kind of flute which he blew vigorously. As he blew out wheezy squeaks, the mouth of the leather bag slowly opened, and there wriggled forth some four or five slimy snakes. The crowd drew back, while the beating of the tom-toms became louder and wilder, the wheezy flute shriller and shriller; the charmer, with wonderful dexterity, fixed the reptiles' tails between his toes and held them down fast, while their long bodies writhed and their forked tongues darted out from their mouths. Again and again they struck at their captor's legs, endeavored to stick their fangs in his flesh; but the charmer whacked them on the head with his flute and made them wriggle and writhe in another direction. Unlike Orpheus, he charmed not with music, but with a musical instrument.

Mack thought the scene worth photographing; exciting as was the wild snake-charmer's performance, it did not stir the onlookers as did the kodak. The benighted Moors must have thought the square leather box some sort of an infernal machine; for no sooner did Mack get it levelled than the crowd gave a yell, and broke and ran in every direction. The place was cleared as suddenly as if cannons and guns were aimed at it. If the rest of the Arabs may be judged by those we saw surrounding the snake-charmer, the cheapest and easiest way to conquer the country would be, not to carry guns and cannons there, but to fit out a squad of amateur photographers with a supply of kodaks. The first day or two in Tangiers Mack succeeded in getting some good snap shots, but the news soon spread, and thereafter he had only to take out the kodak to clear a street or square.

One day, while strolling in the upper part of the city, we suddenly came across a chapter out of the Arabian Nights. The second governor of Tangiers was holding court on a broad logia or portico supported by marble columns, and looking out on an open square. Soldiers in white gowns with guns eight feet long guarded the entrance to this portico. On a raised platform at the rear reclined the cadi and his scribe, the former, a handsome, coffee-colored Moor, not over forty, clear-cut features, snow-white turban, and a manner denoting languor and ennui. The scribe, a patriarchal old chap, also with snow-white turban and gown, sat near his master, surrounded by parchments, inkbottles, and curious, sharp-pointed sticks that served as pens. For an hour we stood there watching the proceedings of this curious court, and we agreed that if it could only be transplanted "verbatim" to an American theatre, the manager would make a fortune. A case of attempt to murder was being tried. The cadi, as he reclined on the cool matting, languidly examined the antique blunderbuss with which the shot was fired. Outside of the portico was a lot of strange-looking people, some in rags and tatters, all in the national dress; that is, in meal-bags, with conical hoods. These people were the witnesses; one by one they removed their sandals and were admitted into the portico to give their testimony.

Each witness prostrated himself before the cadi, received permission to rise, then began shouting and gesticulating in a way that would secure a witness from a European court a life sentence. But the cadi seemed to think it all right; he preserved a languid, tired air as if hardly giving a thought to what the witnesses were so wildly talking about. He lazily turned the blunderbuss around as if examining its make from idle curiosity. After eight or ten wild-looking men had gone through this ceremony of prostrating themselves before the cadi, bumping their heads on the floor, and talking loudly in Arabic, the cadi gave a last gentle glance at the blunderbuss, motioned the soldiers to admit no more witnesses, and muttered something in a low tone to the patriarchal scribe, who forthwith jabbed one of the sharp sticks into a bottle of ink, made some hieroglyphics on a piece of parchment, then shouted in his heathen tongue to the soldiers. Up to this time, so interesting were the proceedings, we had not observed a poor fellow sitting on the stone floor at the end of the portico. We noticed him now because two soldiers went up to him, seized him by the collar, and marched him off to the prison, the door of which was only some forty steps away. By offering a small fee to the jailer, we were permitted to enter and see the miserable results of the cadi's justice — men with heavy leg chains that clanked and clattered as they hobbled from one end of the stone-paved court to the other. Some were chained to the wall like wild beasts, others had iron spurs welded around their ankles, spurs projecting a foot on each side of the leg preventing the wearer from walking at more than a snail's gait. The prisoners depend entirely upon their own resources for existence. The government provides neither food nor clothing, and the convict, unable to make grass baskets, or lacking friends to supply food and money, soon makes his escape through those grim doors into the grave. Indeed, even those who have money, and so do not die of starvation, cannot long endure the damp dungeons with their horrible filth and foulness.

While inspecting this place, we heard a series of piercing shrieks, followed by a loud volley of musketry which caused us to hurry back into the square. Fifteen minutes before, the square had been silent and empty; now, it was filled with hundreds of men with long guns which they fired in the most reckless manner. The guns looked like gas-pipes, and the volleys they fired made us think of the time the gas works exploded. Ben Belassen said it was not an insurrection, as we fancied, but a troop of hill tribe men arrived to pay honor to the cadi, and to make him an offering of a bullock. The two-year-old animal, half frightened to death at the shouts of the men and the noise of the guns, was conducted to the steps leading up to the portico. The cadi was reclining in exactly the same place, and wore the same look of ennui which we had noticed during the trial. The uproar and confusion did not in the least disturb his tranquillity.

The chief of the hill tribe, after hurling his gun high in the air and catching it, then twirling it about dexterously to show his skill, made a profound salaam, and presented the bullock to the cadi, who nodded his head indifferently and ordered the soldiers to take the offering to his palace; then the crowd dispersed, firing their guns, and yelling and shouting as they went.

The round trip from Gibraltar cost us $3 each: Ben Belassen charged a dollar a day for himself, lantern included; good hotel accommodations in Tangiers cost from two to three dollars a day. We paid the former price at the Ville de France, and not only had a good table and comfortable rooms, but a magnificent view of the market below the terrace, and of Tangiers and the Atlantic Ocean.

Even antiquities are cheap in Tangiers: Mack bought, for $2, an old knife with the blood stain of a noble Spanish knight slain by the Moors. Mack thought the blood stain of a noble Spanish knight cheap at $2: the knife itself he did not count, it was rusty and jagged; still, it will have an honored place in Mack's collection of antiquities on account of the blood of the noble Spanish knight.

CHAPTER VIII

Spanish Prisons in Africa — Remarkable System — Prisoners pay to Work — Convict Life — The Governor of Ceuta — Procession of the Sacred Picture — Off for Malaga — Leviathan Mills — Romantic Notions exploded — Story of the Republicans — Men who die for Freedom — Social Life in Spain

OUR visit to Ceuta was on account of the Spanish prisons located there. The question of convict labor occupies so large a place in the studies of political economists and in the thoughts of American workingmen, that I desired to study it in foreign lands. In Spain and Portugal, workingmen seem as opposed to convict labor as are the workingmen in America; after careful inspection of the chief prisons of the two countries, it is difficult to see how Spanish or Portuguese labor is injured by convict labor. Especially is this true of Spain, where the system, or rather lack of system, is so peculiar as to appear almost incredible. The days of weary waiting in the anteroom of the Portuguese Minister of Justice had taught us a lesson, and access to the Spanish prisons was gained, not by application to high officials, but by good, fat fees to turnkeys and jailers. One of the Ceuta turnkeys who had been to Gibraltar and spoke English accepted a fee and showed us through the seven prisons, containing upwards of three thousand convicts.

The most striking feature of the Spanish system is the liberty permitted prisoners. In the penitentiaries of most countries, hard labor is the rule, and conversation, even in the lowest whispers, is forbidden. In the Missouri penitentiary, the eighteen hundred convicts are given the liberty of the prison court two days a year, — July Fourth and Christmas. On those days, looked forward to with longing and joy, the

Missouri convicts are permitted to mingle with each other in the big court, to play games and talk as much as they please until two o'clock; then they go back to their cells, and work and silence reign another six months. The reader has seen how the Portuguese convict is put into a white shroud, and while yet alive, is made to appear as corpse-like as possible. The Spanish prisoner knows nothing of Portuguese living tombs, nor does he have to look forward six months for an opportunity to see and speak with his fellow-prisoners. The liberties which the Missouri convicts enjoy only two days a year, and which the Portuguese convict never enjoys, Spanish prisoners have every day; besides other liberties which the American felon does not possess at all. On entering the huge court at Ceuta, we saw hundreds of convicts lounging about, some playing cards, some patching their clothes, some sprawled on the ground asleep, others reading and smoking, — all seeming to do just what their feelings prompted. From the top of the high walls, patrolling sentries looked down upon the motley scene. The sleeping-places of the prisoners consist of long, cobble-paved halls with a window at their further end; on each side, extending from the door to the window, runs a sort of brick shelf, on which the convicts spread their mats and sleep. There are no closets, no arrangements for washing; the filth of their surroundings is the main hardship the prisoners have to bear.

So far from having to work, the Ceuta prisoner is not permitted to work, except upon paying the government $3 a month for the privilege. Spaniards are not so wildly fond of labor as to be willing to pay for the privilege, hence the workers are few in comparison with the idlers. We saw a thousand men lounging about, some dozing, some playing games; the workers did not number more than a few hundred. Some work in spite of the $3 month tax, because their work affords an excuse for leaving the prison; as, for example, bricklayers and carpenters. A good bricklayer in Ceuta earns sixty cents a day or $18 a month. This leaves the convict $15 net after paying the government tax. The prison governor requires but two things of a convict plying his trade outside the walls: first, that the $3 tax be promptly paid; second, that the prisoner returns to the penitentiary by sunset. Being subject to no supervision outside the prison, it is not unusual to see convicts at cafés, drinking and enjoying themselves as if they were quite free. Sometimes a convict gets boozy and fails to return by sunset. In such cases the governor does not leave him long in doubt as to his being really a prisoner. He is locked up in a dark dungeon, and fed on bread and water for from ten to thirty days, according to the length of time he was absent after sunset. When we visited the dark dungeons we saw a wreath of smoke issuing from a crevice at the far end of the passage-way leading to the doors of the cells. This smoke came through a narrow slit in one of the doors. When we approached with the turnkey, the latter put his mouth to the slit in the door and passed the compliments of the day with the prisoner. This familiarity between prisoner and guard is one of the striking features of the Spanish system. While we were in a room looking at the different kinds of chains used in shackling prisoners, a jolly sort of convict pushed through the door, and snatching the chain which the turnkey was exhibiting, said: —

"Oh, you don't talk good English; let me explain to the gentlemen."

The turnkey, instead of sending him to the dark cells, which would be the punishment for such familiarity in an American prison, merely laughed, and replied: —

"Well, you ought to speak better English, since you are an Englishman."

"Yes, and I know more about the chains than you do. You

see," he added, turning to us, "I had them on myself last week, so I know all about them."

"What had you done to be chained?" we asked.

"Nothing at all; they just put them on. I 'adn't done a thing."

"Come, come," remonstrated the turnkey, "don't tell the gentlemen that. You know you were not chained for nothing. Tell what you did."

"Well, I should not call it anything. They were putting irons on Antonio Perez. Tony 'adn't done nothin', so I chinned the guard and told him it was a bloomin' shame to iron poor Tony. Then the guard ups and irons me."

"Served you right," said the turnkey, pleasantly. "You should not interfere with the guards."

Imagine a Missouri convict arguing with Captain Bradbury, the disciplinarian who, for thirty years, has been the terror of turbulent prisoners at Jefferson City. The conversation above is given verbatim. Before we finished our inspection of Spanish prisons we witnessed other incidents showing the same extraordinary free and easy ways of prisoners, and the good-natured tolerance of their jailers. The English prisoner was undergoing a thirty-year sentence for murdering a fellow-sailor at Cadiz. His fate did not seem to impair his cheerfulness; he was as jolly as a cricket, accompanied us during the rest of our inspection, and when finally we started away, he pushed out through the gate. The guard took him by the arm and endeavored to shove him back, whereupon the English convict looked at him reproachfully.

"You won't let me see my English friends out? It's a bloody shame. I merely wish to tell 'em good-bye."

The guard relented and made no further opposition; the convict followed us out on the street, wished us a pleasant voyage back to "Hold Hengland," and stood waving his handkerchief until a turn in the road took us out of sight.

Occasionally the government makes convicts work on fortifications. Those so engaged, if without private means, must live on the short prison rations consisting of two daily meals, one at nine in the morning, and one at six in the evening — both times merely bread and a bowl of bean broth. This, of course, is a slim allowance for an able-bodied man: those forced to live on it can be readily known by their sunken eyes and hollow cheeks. The majority get money from friends, and occasionally jobs of work, and buy extra food, also extra clothing. The government allows but one suit in three years; those without private means are, therefore, not only half starved, but half clothed, covered by rags and tatters. Those who buy their own clothing are permitted to exercise their own taste, hence there is no uniform dress among Spanish convicts. Despite this lack of a distinctive garb, escapes seldom occur. Ceuta is on a mountainous neck of land projecting into the sea. Guarded on three sides by the ocean, the fourth side, where it looks upon the inhospitable desert of Morocco, is barricaded and patrolled by soldiers. There are instances where convicts scale the barricade and elude the soldiers, but they are almost always captured and returned by the Moors, who are zealous in the chase for the double reason that they wish to curry favor with Spain, also that they want the reward paid by the governor of Ceuta.

These prisons are not self-supporting nor intended to be. When we started back into the city the turnkey accompanied us. Passing a well-dressed man inspecting a house in course of erection, the turnkey said: —

"That man is in for forty years."

"In where?" said I.

"In prison. He is a convict."

"Do you mean that gentleman in the Prince Albert coat?"

"Yes. He is having those houses built. He has a number of houses in Ceuta, all well rented except the one he lives in."

"The one he lives in? Did you not say that he was a convict?"

"Yes, he is a convict, but he only sleeps in the prison. During the day, he stays with his family or attends to his buildings."

This is a pleasant, and, it must be admitted, an extraordinary, side of Spanish prison life. Of the other side we could learn nothing at the prison itself, but outside much was darkly hinted. An American resident in Spain said that a prison guard can be bribed to practically murder a convict.

"There was a man," said he, "who was sent to Ceuta for attempt to murder. X, his victim, recovered, and towards the end of his would-be murderer's sentence, went to Ceuta and had an interview with one of the guards. There was no witness to that interview. From that day, however, the criminal, Z, was most harshly treated. Guards have the power to punish prisoners for violating prison rules. After the guard's consultation with X, it seems Z did nothing but violate rules. He was whipped every day, imprisoned in the dark dungeons and kept all the time on half rations of bread and water. X boasted, in Malaga, that Z would never live to complete his sentence, and he did not. He was literally whipped and starved to death."

If this American resident of Spain does not exaggerate, many of the prison guards ought themselves to be in dark dungeons.

Travellers are not permitted to enter or leave Ceuta without passports. The passport is surrendered on landing. When ready to leave, you go to the governor and receive the document back. When we went for ours, His Excellency was not in, and as there were no seats in the anteroom, we told the sentry we would stroll about and return in half an hour. During the half-hour we were gone, we saw a curious sight, — a sacred image on its way from one church to another followed by a long line of pretty girls with flowers in their hair, and lighted candles three feet long in their hands. A regiment of soldiers headed by a brass band followed the pretty girls. Every few yards the cavalcade halted to permit the dense crowd lining both sides the street to pay homage to the image. Many fell on their knees as it passed, all uncovered their heads and muttered prayers. Among the spectators were two or three convicts. When we saw them, we said to the turnkey:—

"How is it they are here? The sunset gun has been fired."

"Yes, but they will be excused. They have remained out to pray to the Holy Image."

When we returned to the governor's office the anteroom was filled with people, but His Excellency had not put in his appearance. Finally he sent word that he was sick and could not come, so we did not see the African governor. But we got our passports from his secretary, and took the first steamer to Spain, and thence to Gibraltar. In leaving Gibraltar for the last time, we had unusual difficulty with the boatman. The traveller on the Mediterranean becomes accustomed to difficulties with boatmen; he expects them, and even gets so that he is disappointed if the boatman does not try to cheat.

Although we had long since reached this stage, we were surprised at this Gibraltar row, because we had employed the same boatman a number of times in making short trips along the coast and had always been fairly treated. But the rascal knew that we were now going away, that he would no more get our custom, therefore he would cheat us all he could. After our baggage was brought aboard the steamer, we handed him the regular fare. He looked at the money with an air of contempt and demanded more. A number of passengers were standing about, among them several pretty girls, which made Perigarde ashamed to have a squabble.

"Give it to him; what are a few pesetas?" whispered Perigarde. "Don't you see that girl looking at us?"

Ruins of the Greek Theatre, Taormina

The eyes of a pretty woman always fluttered Perigarde. Mack and I were more hardened and went our way, leaving the boatman to grumble and the girls to look as much as they pleased. No matter how deep the water is in a Mediterranean port, the steamer does not anchor so that passengers may walk ashore. At Barcelona, our steamer's prow touched the dock, but the steps were lowered thirty yards away, and the small boat had to be hired as usual. No matter how much you bargain with a boatman, he will try to extort more when you land. We made a distinct bargain with the Malaga boatman, yet, on shore, he demanded an extra peseta, and even attempted to seize the luggage, until a demonstration with our clubs convinced him that three Americans were not the kind of travellers to impose upon.

In Spain, the land of romance and beautiful women, of Don Quixote and chivalry, we did not expect to find so realistic a thing as one of the largest manufactories in the world. The Don Carlos and Don Emanuel mills in Malaga employ 4500 persons, and cover acres of ground — enough to contain any three factories of New England. The engines indicate 2300 horse power; the one item of repairs and renewing machinery amounts to $50,000 per year; the yearly expenditure for coal is $250,000. Mr. Crenshaw, the English manager, when asked if the combination of English machinery and Spanish cheap labor does not enable the company to undersell the English, said: —

"No, for the reason that Spanish labor is *not* cheap; that is, it is not cheap measured according to productiveness. For instance, drawing and slubbing machines, which make the cotton into the first bobbin, require here two girls and a man; in England, only one man or woman is necessary. In England, one man and boy is allowed to each pair of mules; here, there are two men and a boy, and still the output is twenty-five per cent less than in England. The reason of this is, Spaniards are not ambitious, and, although working by the piece, they work slowly, being content if they make enough to barely exist. Were it not for the Spanish high tariff, England could undersell us in Malaga itself, despite the distance and so-called cheap labor."

Infant industries in America, although big enough to wear No. 10 shoes, and kick into poor-houses workmen ungrateful enough to ask for better wages, still plead infancy, still cry for "protection" against the pauper labor of Europe; while in Spain, the pauper labor cries for protection against the better paid and unprotected labor of England. Another reason why the Spanish mills cannot compete with England is the high price of machinery and coal, both of which come from England, and both of which are enhanced in price because of the tariff and cost of transportation. The coal used by the Don Emanuel mills of Malaga, although bought by the ship-load, costs $5 to $7 per ton. As we walked through floor after floor of the vast factory, the only visible signs of one's ideal Spain were the roses in the girls' hair — there were none on their cheeks; life amidst that clatter and roar of machinery, breathing impure air, is as destructive to rosy cheeks in Spain as in New England. But the operatives wear roses in their hair and in their corsages, which lends a little Spanish gaiety to the scene.

"They are all 'rachone' workers," said Mr. Crenshaw; "that is, their day is from sun-up to sunset. In that time, a spinner earns from forty to fifty cents. Women weavers earn from fifty to sixty cents; winders, thirty-five cents. The girls and boys who help the spinners and weavers make ten or fifteen cents a day."

It is pitiful to see seven-year-old children working fourteen hours a day for the wretched pittance of ten cents. We were glad to learn that the Spanish Cortez is likely to pass a bill prohibiting the employment of children under thirteen. In connection with the Don Emanuel mills are extensive boiler and machine shops; in Spain there are few facilities for procuring such outfits, and mill-owners are obliged to do a hundred things which, in England and America, are done by outside firms. Even skilled Spanish machinists receive only sixty cents a day. When asked if they were satisfied with such wages, Mr. Crenshaw said: —

"No, of course not, but they cannot help themselves. Last year [1890] they got up some sort of a union and struck for shorter hours and more pay. At the Don Carlos mills, the men were told they would be given whatever our men got, so the Don Carlos employés continued work and gave part of their wages to our men to help them keep the strike up. But even with this aid the strike was a fizzle. In six weeks the strikers were nearly starved, and gladly returned to work on the old terms. Soldiers were barricaded around the mills, and the first attempt at disorder was so promptly and severely quelled that it was not followed by another."

"Did not the managers think the men right, at least in the matter of hours? Fourteen hours is a long day."

"Yes, it is long; but the managers did not argue the question. No one is obliged to work for the company: those who wish to work must do so on terms dictated by employer, not employé."

What a cruel circle have Spaniards — indeed, the majority of mankind — allowed themselves to enter! First, the priests have instilled into their minds that rulers reign by the grace of God; then, that there must be soldiers to uphold the rulers; then come monopolies of land, grants, and privileges, to bribe the few who have intelligence and power; then come the masses, hewers of wood and drawers of water, too crushed by toil to give much thought to the causes of their oppression. Suppose there were no kings or politicians to support, no standing army would be necessary, no monopolists nor special privileges would be granted a favored few; natural opportunities would be open to all who chose to labor; work would not be considered, at the same time, a boon and a disgrace, and Mr. Crenshaw would not be able to make such a remark as that quoted above. The Don Emanuel directors would find themselves obliged to discuss the question, and either shorten their hours or close altogether, as otherwise labor could exert itself on adjacent fields now idle, but appropriated by favored persons, and capable of supporting the thousands of employés in the cotton mills. One reason given for Don Emanuel's disinclination to listen to the strikers was their alleged lack of appreciation for past kindnesses shown by the company. Said Mr. Crenshaw: —

"At the time of the cholera, in 1885, we established a penny kitchen in the mill. Good cooks were employed, every facility provided, and wholesome food dealt out at cost price. A plate of soup, with vegetables and beef, was sold for two cents; a ration of bread, one cent, etc. Payment was made in brass checks which the employés bought at the office. The food was so good and cheap that they began buying checks, not only for themselves, but for their friends. It was a common sight to see an employé making his way to the gate, loaded with several rations of soup, coffee, and bread for friends and relatives. The result was, that, when pay day arrived, a good part of their wages had already been drawn; the numerous dinners, however, were forgotten. They only remembered that they had worked all the week and now received but a fraction of what they earned. Don Emanuel was so indignant at the accusations of fraud and cheating, that he telegraphed from Madrid, ordering the kitchen closed, the cooks discharged, and the pots, pans, and kettles sent to the junk shop. Our thousands of employés must now eat cold dinners, instead of the cheap and hot ones served from the kitchen."

We observed, however, that many continued to have warm dinners, despite the abandonment of the kitchen. In the bottom of the four or five story can in which they bring their food is a charcoal compartment. At noon the charcoal is lighted, and the dishes above are quickly heated. Most of the employees occupy houses owned by the company, the rent being twenty-five cents per room per week — rather less than is charged by other landlords in Malaga. In passing out through the office, we saw a pretty girl at a table covered with stacks of money. The pay-roll amounts to thousands of dollars a week, and this pretty girl is kept busy twelve hours a day weighing money into packages of twenty cents each. I say weighing, because she does not count it, but shoves it into a pair of delicately adjusted scales, which tip at exactly the right amount. To pay the thousands of employees, a ton and a quarter of copper coins is used each month, in addition to silver and paper.

Malaga, a decidedly republican city, possesses several monuments to men who lost their lives fighting against the Madrid government. Perhaps the most striking evidence of this is the shaft on the Plaza de Riego, trimmed with black marble and erected to the memory of forty-nine republicans executed in 1831. It was not three years before these men, who were starved, shot, and their bodies robbed and insulted, were revered as martyrs and patriots. On December 11, 1834, the third anniversary of the butchery, solemn high mass was held in honor of the republicans, in the chapel where they had been starved and imprisoned. In 1842, the government, no longer able to resist the popular clamor, acquiesced in the erection of the monument in the Plaza de Riego, and the king, as faithless and brutal as his tool, treated General Moreno, who had starved and shot the republicans, with such coolness that he joined the Carlist movement, and was subsequently executed by his own soldiers.

An American lady who has lived many years in Spain gave us notes regarding Spanish social life. Said Mrs. C.: —

"Social intercourse does not exist in the American sense. Young ladies do not receive visits from gentlemen, nor is there visiting among married people, as there is in America, where your friends are apt to drop in any evening after dinner, for a chat or a game of whist, or perhaps for a little music. In all the years we have lived here, we have not received half a dozen evening calls from Spaniards and their wives. At first, I tried giving card parties, musicales, and light entertainments. The Spaniards came, but everything was stiff, dull, and formal. The men got off by themselves, the women seemed to have nothing to say, and it was so solemn, so funereal, that the experiment was soon abandoned."

"What does the Spaniard do with himself if he never calls with his wife? Does he call alone?"

"No, he does not call at all, nor does he expect you to call. The Spaniard only sleeps and eats at home: he drinks and *lives* at the cafés; it is there he meets his friends, and talks of women, business, or whatever else amuses the Spanish mind."

"Where, in the meantime, is his wife?"

"At home, or gossipping with the neighbors in the flat below or above. Women see and talk with women; they rarely do so, however, in the presence of men. This is natural when you consider the Spanish system of courtship. There is no opportunity for a Spaniard to learn anything of his prospective wife's mental fitness, so he contents himself with learning her financial condition. This is easily done. A child cannot be disinherited except for sufficient cause: the courts are slow to find causes sufficient, hence, the 'lover' has but to find out how much the father is worth, and divide the sum by the number of children. The marriage is purely a matter of business. The man neither expects nor asks for mental companionship. The ceremony that binds them being over, he introduces himself to his wife's banker, draws her money, then resumes his life in the cafés as before. You will understand, of course, that I am speaking of 'society' people.

"The lower classes have no bankers, the women who work have necessarily to give up habits of seclusion, the sexes see each other, and love, not money, is the spring that makes their marriages. A woman in the upper classes is a veritable slave; she dare not cross the street alone for fear of being molested. A crowd of so-called gentlemen may see a woman insulted in broad daylight, but they would not come to the rescue. They would ask her why she came on the street alone. Men are called women's protectors: from whom do they protect her? Why, from men, so that woman is protected from her protector."

Mrs. C. gave the following, as the routine life of a Spaniard engaged in business or practising a profession: Coffee, 7 A.M.; office, 8 A.M.; home for breakfast ten to twelve; office until 6 P.M.; at home for dinner, 7 to 8.30; café until midnight.

"This being the routine nine days out of ten," said Mrs. C., "you see how much, or rather how little, the Spaniard knows and cultivates his family. He never invites a friend to dinner, nor does he himself expect to be invited. Only at the café does he see his friends."

This system produces a host of cafés, and it is there one can best observe male Spanish life and character. From nine o'clock until midnight the cafés are crowded with men of every grade and kind. A marquis and a merchant may jostle each other at one table, a bearded soldier and a juvenile swain at another. All are drinking black coffee, all jabbering, all gesticulating. It is a lively sight and one that we witnessed every night we were in Spain; but all its noise and gaiety do not make up for the cosy library, the student lamp, the bright fire, the family, mother, sister, wife, around the table, that make life worth living in America.

Frequently, during our strolls, we saw specimens of courtship among the middle and upper classes — girls at iron-barred windows looking down on sighing swains pacing the cobble-paved street below. On one occasion, while walking with the American consul at Barcelona, he called our attention to a pretty girl in a third story window, and to an officer with a picturesque cloak draped over his shoulder, leaning against the wall, and gazing intently at the girl in the window.

"I close my office precisely at five," said the consul, "and my evening constitutional brings me to this point at precisely this hour six days out of every week in the year. Every day for the past six months I have seen that girl in the window, and that officer leaning against the wall. The girl pulls down the blinds after about ten minutes; then the officer goes away until the same hour next day."

"Is he in love with her?"

"It may be and may be not. He has learned that her father has a suitable 'dot,' possibly he thinks she is pretty, and so thinks he is in love, but he does not know her. How could he? He has never spoken a word to her. When this silent courtship tires him, he will go to her father, ask for the daughter's hand, and the story ends in marriage. She goes to her new home, where she sees little of her husband, and gossips with servants and neighbors, whilst he goes to cafés and gossips with his friends. Such is Spanish life."

"How long does the courtship usually last?" asked Mack, who was thinking of the figure he would cut were he obliged to stand out in front of a certain Chicago house instead of being admitted, and given a seat on the sofa beside the prettiest girl in Illinois. The consul said there is no rule as to the length of the courtship. It may last a year, or, if the man has many debts and the girl much money, and the girl's father does not oppose, it may not last six weeks. But whether short or long, they learn nothing of each other until too late to avoid a life of unloving dulness. The American system certainly affords a little better opportunity of studying character, of looking before leaping; yet even in America, where young men and women so freely mingle in social life, both parties too often take great care to keep out of sight unlovable and ignoble traits before marriage and too little care to conceal them after, so that the same misery and disappointment result. Obtaining money under false pretences is a penal offence and covers the offender with disgrace; yet every day men and women obtain mates for life by deceit and deception. Neither law nor society condemns, yet the offence is baser, and a thousand times more injurious to the persons interested than if the dross of worldly goods were concerned.

It is this species of social deception which causes the numerous divorces, and the still more numerous cases of mismated misery as great as that disclosed by the divorce courts, but unheard of because pride induces the victims to suffer in silence rather than admit to the world their mistakes and misery.

CHAPTER IX

Why we missed the train to Granada — Why the Cabman pursued us — And why we fled to the Consul's — The Alhambra — Youthful Illusions — In Prison again — Convicts in Clover — The Cemetery — Rented Graves — At the Opera — Perigarde finds a "Soul's Mate"

THE fare from Malaga to Granada, second class, is twenty pesetas (about $3.80). The round trip costs only 23.80 pesetas ($4.70), so we determined to take a return trip and see the Alhambra before continuing east. We left all except our hand-satchels at the Hotel de Paris, No. 2 Calle Marquis de Larios, intending to walk to the station; but just as we reached the sidewalk in front of the hotel, Mack was unlucky enough to see a cab across the street, and suggested that we ride instead of walk. Perigarde seconded the suggestion and motioned the cabman to come over. When he came he demanded so exorbitant a fare that we told him to "go to," and started off to walk. To our surprise, the cabman whipped up his horses until the cab was alongside us, then jumped down from his box, and demanded two pesetas. This was less than he had asked at first, but we were determined now to walk, and were about to push on when he planted himself in the way and declared we should not proceed until he had his fare. We had no desire to get into a difficulty, at the same time we did not propose to be victimized. We stepped off the sidewalk, intending to go around the cabman, but again did he plant himself in the way, and when we endeavored to push by, he laid his hand on my shoulder. This was too much. In a moment my heavy walking-staff was in the air, and the next instant would have cracked his head had he not leaped aside. He jumped back on his box, turned his horses, and started down the street as fast as he could drive. We thought the matter ended and hurried on to catch the Granada train. In about five minutes, however, we heard voices shouting, and wheels rattling; turning, we saw the cabman driving up at a great rate accompanied by two soldiers. On overtaking us, the carriage stopped, the cabman and two soldiers leaped out, and the latter ordered us at once to pay out two pesetas.

"For what?"

"For ordering this cab."

"But we did not order it."

"You caused it to cross the street."

"Yes, but we did not ride in it: we did not even get in it."

"No matter; you ordered it, and you must pay."

We thought it most decidedly did matter, and said we would not pay, whereupon the soldiers placed us under arrest to the extent of not letting us move on, yet not to the extent of taking us to jail. A great crowd collected; the cabman and soldiers jabbered away excitedly. Mack happened to look up and saw the American stars and stripes — we were right under the American Consulate, and pushed our way to the door. When we reached it, we all three made a rush up the steps, hotly pursued by the soldiers, the cabman, and the howling mob. The hubbub gave warning of our approach, and Major T. M. Newson, the Malaga consul, met us at the door. The Spaniards did not dare pursue us beyond the Consulate's sacred line. They stood in the hall, eying us sharply while we explained the cause of the trouble.

"Young men," said Major Newson, "the law is against you. If the cabman left his stand, you must pay."

On the whole, we had reason to be grateful to the cabman, since the incident was the means of introducing us to the consul. It was too late for the Granada train, and Major Newson was kind enough to show us the sights of Malaga. We had not imagined that the old city contained as many objects of interest as he showed us in that one afternoon. After seeing the city, he drove us to one of its beautiful suburbs. The road ascended until our carriage stood on top of a mountain commanding a noble view of Malaga, of the Mediterranean, and of the mountains. From the city, which lay right at out feet, came floating up the voices of the fishermen, and venders crying their wares. To the right, we saw on the summit of a spur of the mountain a chapel with three large crosses, the Mecca of thousands of devout pilgrims.

"Once a year," said the consul, "crowds of pilgrims visit this chapel, climbing the mountain, and remaining for hours at the foot of each of the three crosses."

Descending the mountain by another side, we drove several miles along a road with the Mediterranean on the one side, and on the other a succession of charming villas with gardens of tropical plants and flowers. As we sat in a restaurant garden at the further end of the picturesque drive, eating dinner under an orange tree, the blue waves of the sea breaking on the beach not twenty yards away, we felt quite thankful to the cabman.

The next day we made another start for Granada, and this time we got there after passing through deep cañons and gorges, and at the base of one-thousand-foot precipices that reminded us of the magnificent scenery just west of Manitou and Leadville. In Granada, most tourists go to the Washington Irving Hotel, because of its name, also because they have the idea that there is nothing to see in Granada itself, and so wish to be on the hill, as near as possible to the Alhambra. This is a mistake. The traveller located on the hill finds himself at a disadvantage. It is easier to go up the hill by day, when the Alhambra is open, than it is to go down to the city, then back up the hill at night — the time when one wishes to see the theatres, the cafés, and the street life. We weighed these considerations, and stopped in the city, at the Victoria Hotel, opposite the principal cafés, and looking on a square always filled with people, always lively, always animated. It was a pleasure simply to sit on our balcony and watch the peasant women milking goats, to hear the street venders crying their wares, and to see the stages from mountain towns dash up, with flourishes, and cracking whips, and jingling bells, and stop in the square to let out a lot of picturesque peasants from remote mountain districts. Another advantage we enjoyed, was our comparative freedom from beggars and pedlars. The Hotel Washington Irving is so frequented by tourists that the beggars and pedlars for miles around come there, and make it the centre of their operations. We were unfortunate enough to sit once in its garden; soon a whole tribe were upon us. We escaped their importunities only by retaining one of their number to drive the rest away.

Emanuel Alvares did this with such vigor and success, that we concluded it a good investment to employ him during our whole stay. Every morning he descended from his height on the hill and awaited us at the door of the Hotel Victoria. When other guides who had seen us on our visits to the Alhambra attempted to waylay us, Alvares repelled them with a club, thus obtaining a freedom and relief worth double the daily wage of fifty cents which we paid him. In the cafés, flower girls and beggars always hover about foreigners. It is disagreeable when one is eating an ice or sipping coffee, to have a pair of socks or a fine-tooth comb thrust in one's face, accompanied by a beseeching voice imploring one to buy. We were spared all this by the invaluable Alvares. He asked the flower girls why they did not importune the Spaniards.

"Because the Spaniards will not buy."

"Neither will the Señores Ingleses," Alvares would reply; "get out, leave us alone," — and off he would send them. We could not but admire his lordly way of saying "us," and his air of *hauteur* as he sat at a neighboring table sipping the coffee we ordered for him. Spanish guide-books have a great deal of nonsense about the proper way to dismiss beggars. Murray says, when you do not wish to bestow the solicited alms, you must say, in Spanish: "Pardon me, brother, for the love of God." Mack and I repeated this time and again, to no purpose — they would not leave us; but when Alvares cried out with emphasis: "Anda — vamos; clear out, or I'll break your necks," it acted like a charm. A critical reader cannot fail to observe in this a difference from the formula prescribed by Murray.

The Darro and Genil rivers, of which one reads so much in the history of the siege of Granada, are so small they would be called little creeks in America. The two put together are not seventy-five feet wide. Washington Irving, on one occasion, refers to a ramble in "remote parts of the Alhambra."

Such chance expressions make lasting impressions on youthful minds. We go to places with preconceived notions, which, nine times out of ten, are wide of the facts. From general reading on the subject, I had gathered the impression that the Alhambra was a large, rambling sort of a place, in which one could wander about for hours. In reality, it is a small palace; there are no "remote" parts about it, and Irving must have rambled at a snail's pace, if he did not reach its furthest limit in ten minutes. You can, of course, spend hours studying the marvellous details of a single room, or beauties of a single court; what I mean, is, that the palace covers a small area, and there is disappointment in store for the reader of Washington Irving's delightful book, if he expects to find a palace with winding galleries, passage-ways, and courts, and "remote" parts, where one can lose one's self as Washington Irving did. The visitor who should try now to ramble to "remote" parts of the Alhambra would be obliged to ramble clear off the hill.

During our stay in Granada we had another opportunity to observe the Spanish prison system. The ancient convent De Belen has been converted by the government into a penitentiary with an average of more than one thousand prisoners. The general features of the prison are the same as at Ceuta. The prisoner is not allowed to work unless he pays for the privilege; he is not allowed to work at all outside the prison walls. The cloisters and chapels of the old convent are filled with convicts; a few make rope, sandals, and mats; one or two blacksmiths hammer on anvils; the majority sit around gambling, or doing nothing. In what was once a small chapel we saw thirty-five shoemakers, who said they earned, on an average, twenty-five cents a day each. To earn this amount, they work from six in the morning until six at night. By their work-benches were pots of coffee and loaves of bread. No officer watches them, no one cares whether they work or idle, and it is seldom that half a dozen or more may not be seen sprawled out asleep on the floor instead of sitting up at work, at their benches. The convicts in the De Belen penitentiary do not believe in the theory of "honor among thieves." They never trust their few belongings out of sight. In the morning, on leaving the dormitories to come down into the court, each man brings his bundle or box of clothing and personal effects, and keeps them under his eye until night comes, then he takes it back to the dormitory and sleeps with it by his side.

One of the most interesting shops was that under the dome of the old convent. There, under those ancient frescoes, blackened and begrimed with age, a gang of men make baskets and panniers out of a tough sort of grass. Near by is a solitary weaving loom, the owner of which does a thriving business, since the government allowance is only one suit in three years, and the convict usually wears out two or three. The system of letting the prisoners do what they please, while it fills the courts with hundreds of idlers and gamblers, has also the effect of developing certain talents that could scarcely be developed under any other than the Spanish system. Certain convicts with shrewd trading instincts manage to make a good living, buying and selling. Others of executive ability become employers and manufacturers. The weaver who makes the cloth under the old convent dome is merely an employé of a convict, who bought the loom as an investment and who has made it so profitable that he now, without working, has a good income, and a good dinner from a neighboring restaurant every day. We saw one man who has an ingenious knack of making papier-maché walking-canes. He buys the paper, the steel rods which form the backbone or centre of the cane, and keeps half a dozen men employed as assistants. He has to pay the government sixty cents a month for each assistant employed; still he makes a good profit. Señor Josef Mota, chief barber of the prison, also does a fine business. Señor Mota, whose present retirement from the world is due to the fact that he ran a stiletto too far through the ribs of a friend, was formerly a bull-fighter, and for that reason is looked upon with affectionate reverence by his fellow-convicts. The walls of his barber shop are covered with pictures illustrating exciting scenes in the arena. Señor Mota, who does not personally shave his customers, merely directing his corps of assistants, has hands as soft and white as any woman's. He told us that, while a matador, he earned several hundred dollars a fight. His account of former triumphs was interrupted by the loud blast of a trumpet. The twenty or thirty convicts, who had been sitting around listening to our conversation, jumped up, and darted out of the door.

"Only the call for rations," explained Señor Mota.

"And do you not get any?"

"I? *prison* rations?" Señor Mota looked wounded. "I cannot eat the filthy stuff. My dinner comes from the hotel."

We went out into the court to see what this dainty bull-fighter called filthy stuff. The rations were dealt out in tubs, each tub holding food for five or six men. The majority of the thousand or so prisoners were squatting around the huge court in squads of six, their tub of food before them, each eating with voracious haste lest he should not get as much as his companions. When we examined the contents of the food tubs, we were obliged to admit the term "filthy stuff" was deserved. The food consisted of hunks of black bread, and a watery sort of bean and potato broth. In strong contrast to this disgusting compound were the dinners of such of the convicts as were able to buy food from the outside. We saw one fellow with green lettuce and roast beef; another was eating a baked pigeon, with onions and tomatoes. The unfortunates dependent upon the prison diet hung around these beef and pigeon eaters, waiting on them, and performing other services in return for the scraps of the feast.

TAORMINA, FROM SUMMIT OF THE GREEK THEATRE

One small chapel of the convent is still used for religious purposes on Sundays. On week days it is used as a school by those of the convicts who choose to avail themselves of the services of Señor Antonio Orosco, a young prisoner who teaches, without pay, all who care to learn. While talking with this intelligent young man, a fine-looking old gentleman passed by with a silk hat on his head and a rose in the buttonhole of his Prince Albert coat. We took him to be the governor of the penitentiary, or possibly a director; but Señor Orosco said he was an ex-notary serving a twelve-year sentence for forgery. He has his meals sent him from a caterer, books and papers are supplied him; his only hardship is at night. During the day he can retire to some distant and unfrequented part of the extensive building, read his papers and smoke his cigars in quiet; but at night he has to sleep in the long dormitory along with the other felons. The only prisoners who do not sleep in the dirty dormitories are the half dozen men who serve as book-keepers and clerks. These occupy cots in the office where they work.

The chief of the office force is Don Antonio Perez, a gentleman of birth, who, like Señor Josef Mota, was unfortunate enough to kill a "friend." Judging from the number of prisoners who assigned killing friends as the reason of their imprisonment, we thought killing friends must be a favorite pastime in Spain. I suspect, however, that other crimes are concealed under this name, since the average Spaniard thinks it far more respectable to murder than to steal. Don Antonio was like the chief barber in another respect,— admiration for the bull ring. He has never performed, but he informed us that he intends to enter the ring as soon as his twelve-year sentence ends. On his desk were bound copies of "La Lidia," the Madrid illustrated paper devoted to the bull-ring; that Don Antonio had studied its reports was attested by the dirty and well-thumbed pages. He said he expected to be pardoned in a year or two, and showed a sword with which he practises lunging at an imaginary bull, so as to be ready to enter the arena the moment he leaves prison.

One of the numerous small courts of the penitentiary is reserved for prisoners to receive visits from their families. Women bring their children and sewing and spend the day in this visiting court, chatting with their captive husbands, and seemingly as jolly as if at home instead of in prison. The convicts dandle the babies on their knees, kiss their wives, eat the good things brought them, and have a good time generally. When the convict is sick, his fate is not so comfortable. He is put into a cheerless corridor and left pretty much to himself on the swim or sink principle. If he does not pull through, it is his own fault; the government does not seem to feel responsible for his fate. The sick man may have raving maniacs for companions, for all are put in the same corridor. Big rings are fastened in the wall, and the more violent maniacs are chained to these rings. Clanking chains and gibbering lunatics are not conducive to an invalid's recovery, but in Spain who cares?

The bread, beans, and potatoes served twice a day to the thousand or so convicts in De Belen cost thirty-nine centissimos (about seven cents) per convict. This amount is less than the allowance for food in most prisons — just half that allowed in Portuguese penitentiaries, and three cents less than the daily per capita allowance in the Missouri penitentiary at Jefferson City. But small as is the amount, it is enough to purchase far better food than that actually provided. The Missouri penitentiary provides meat once a day, bread, potatoes, coffee, and occasionally stewed fruit, in abundance. If this can be secured for ten cents a day, surely seven cents in Spain ought to buy more than two meagre rations of bread, beans, and potatoes. We visited other Spanish prisons in other cities, but as the system of all is practically the same, I shall spare the reader further details, and take leave of this unpleasant topic after merely mentioning that, although the prisons are graded according to the length of the sentences, a prisoner with money can select his own prison. This is a great privilege, as some prisons are much cleaner and more laxly governed than others. Prisons of the first grade, for sentences varying from one to twelve years, are at Granada, Burgos, and Valencia. Prisons of the second grade, for twelve to twenty years sentences, are at Cartegena, Valencia, San Toña. Ceuta has seven prisons of the third grade; that is, for sentences from twenty years to life. The prison for women is at Alcalá. The system of commutation of sentences for good behavior is not practised at any of the penitentiaries in Spain.

From the prison of De Belen we took a walk beyond the city to the hills where the gypsies live in huts and caves, and on the way passed the cemetery gate, in front of which was a very solemn, not so say ghastly, spectacle. Fifty or sixty persons were standing around the dead body of a man which lay on a board on the ground. There was no covering, there were no sides on the board to keep the body from rolling off. When the officiating priest was through, two men picked up the ends of the board and slowly bore their burden to the grave. We followed the little procession and saw the corpse thrown into the ditch, without coffin, and covered with quicklime. A few rods away was a trench, ten feet wide, ten feet deep, and about thirty long. In this trench bodies are buried by wholesale. Skulls and bones protruded from the thin covering of earth that had been spread over recently buried bodies. Graves are rented, not sold. The corpse we saw buried will have to vacate its grave in a few years; its bones will then be placed in the long trench. As we passed out of the cemetery, a man entered with a bundle under his arm. This bundle was laid down near the gate while the man went in to see the sexton. Presently the man, accompanied by the sexton, came back to the gate and uncovered the bundle, showing the body of a dead child. For some minutes the two haggled about the rent of the grave; when it was settled, the man picked up the child and entered the cemetery to bury it. To Americans, this way of dealing with poor, dead mortality is shocking.

We went one night to see "L'Africaine" at the Granada opera house. Three seats in a box cost sixty reals ($2.95); the government collected a tax of two cents on each seat, so that the total price for three was $3.01. Granada's beauty and fashion were there. The dark-eyed señoritas were in full dress. Some of the cavaliers were in swallow-tail black coats, others were in the more picturesque Spanish costume, — short jackets, sashes, knee-breeches, and broad brimmed sombreros which were doffed only when the curtain was up. The moment the curtain fell, each man put on his sombrero again and kept it on until the curtain went up and a new act began.

Meyerbeer's opera was well represented. There were thirty-one pieces in the orchestra, the chorus was both large and good, the leading rôles were taken by Italian singers of merit and reputation. In the second act, Selika and Nelusko and the thirty-one instruments made enough noise to stir the dead, but Vasco Da Gama paid not the slightest attention, sleeping through it all. After the first act we went out into the lobby, where were promenading those of the señores who were not visiting the dark-eyed beauties in the boxes. Many of the men were reading letters in the lobby. Perigarde, ready to find love and romance in Spain, said these letters were love missives from señoritas. When we laughed at this, saying we thought they were business letters, or duns from tailors and bootmakers, Perigarde indignantly asked if we supposed a man would read business letters in such a place.

"The opera," he said, "is a kind of underground post-office, the result of penning girls up and not letting them see the masculine sex," — with which the impressionable fellow took himself off to where he could get a better view of the beauties in the boxes. By this time he had entirely forgotten his misadventure with the American baroness, and was ready for another. Much to our dismay, the poor fellow returned to us even more madly in love than he had been with the baroness. Neither jests nor arguments weighed a feather against feelings and fancies when they took possession of poor Perigarde; or rather, when the beauty of some woman took possession of him.

"But you know nothing of this woman," we said.

"The mischief I don't. I know she's the most beautiful creature on earth; isn't that enough to know until I get acquainted with her and her family? That's what I mean to do before I leave this city."

"The customs of the country will not let you get acquainted with your beauty; you may possibly come to know her father, but what good will that do?"

"*Good?* what flints you are! You go through Europe blind as bats to the beauty of its women. Mack is wedded to his art, while I — I, my dear boys, adore beautiful women. To me, happiness means to find my other self. It exists; of all the millions of women on earth, there is one meant for me. She is somewhere; why not here?"

"Your notions are certainly romantic," said Mack, "but they are hardly original. Aristophanes got off the same sort of stuff three thousand years ago. He believed that man was originally round and was cut in halves by the gods. 'Each of us,' he says, 'when separated, is but the indenture of a man having one side only, like a flat fish, and he is always looking for his other half.' Come to think of it, Perigarde, you are not even romantic; at least, there is nothing romantic in being like a flat fish, and that is what you are like, according to Aristophanes."

"Aristophanes be blessed!" exclaimed Perigarde; "*he* didn't know what it was to love. I feel strangely drawn toward this girl. I must see her, must know her, must see if she is that other half. Look at her and you will understand my feelings."

We did look, long and lingeringly; she was a beauty even for Spain where beauty is so plentiful. A wreath of roses reached from her shoulders to her waist, a simple blue ribbon encircled her throat, in her hair was a rose. Without jewels, without so much as a ring, this Spanish girl made a picture which we secretly felt was lovely enough to warrant Perigarde's enthusiasm. We did not think, though, that it warranted his remaining in Granada to meet her, yet this is what Perigarde said he meant to do. When at length the curtain fell on the last act, Perigarde jumped to his feet and hastened to the corridor in the rear of the boxes. When we rejoined him, he was watching the door through which his divinity was to pass.

"What of Malaga?" we said. "Have you forgotten that we leave at six?"

At this moment there was a noise at the end of the corridor, the door of box No. 1 opened, and the party passed out.

"Hush!" whispered Perigarde, motioning us back into the shadow; "*she* is coming. I shall try to learn her name. Meet me at the Café Suizo in half an hour."

Before we could remonstrate, the box party had passed, and Perigarde was lost in the crowd behind them.

We went to the Café Suizo, almost deserted at that hour, and ordered a couple of ices, then sat down to await Perigarde. He came before the thirty minutes were over, red and out of breath from running.

"*Helados de limon* — lemon ice," he cried to the waiter, dropping into a seat and mopping his face. Then he related what had happened. He had followed the carriage, had been out-distanced, but would find the house where the beautiful Spaniard lived, and intended calling on her the next day. We tried to dissuade him, said that even acquaintances and friends were not permitted to meet Spanish girls, that he would not be allowed to see her — our words were useless. Perigarde felt in the secret depths of his soul that this girl was the long-sought-for mate of his being, etc., etc. It was like lunacy, and we had to leave the poor fellow in Granada. We left the Café Suizo for our hotel, slept what little was left of the night, and at six o'clock, as the train started for Malaga, from our car window we bade farewell to the last city of the Moors in Spain.

CHAPTER X

Along the Spanish Coast — Cartagenian Prisons — Almeria's Remarkable Wall — Peaks and Castles — Alicante and Valencia — Convicts who stay at Home — Roasting Nuts on an Ass's Back — Barcelona — How we were trapped in Jail

WE had intended hiring a boat at Malaga, but finding nothing that suited us at the price we were able to pay, we took one of the Spanish coasting steamers, and saw in that way about as much as we should have seen with a private yacht. The Spanish steamers go only a few hours at night and stop during the day at some city or town. It was nine o'clock at night when we left Malaga; by six next morning we were in Almeria, one of the strangest places in Spain. The town lies on a snug bay at the base of two bleak and lofty peaks. An old Moorish castle stands on the summit of one of these peaks, a ruined fort stands on the other, and a remarkable wall follows the steep sides of the mountain down into the valley and up the slope again, connecting the two ancient ruins. We ascended Alcazaba, the Moorish castle, for the view, then

began the descent on the top of that wonderful wall. This
expedition nearly cost us our lives, for at places the top was
scaly and crumbling; extreme care was necessary to avoid a
fall that would have ended only at the edge of the sea, five
hundred feet below. As the ravine or valley which the wall
crosses is thick with bristling cacti, a fall would have been
fatal even had it extended no further than to the base of the
wall, which varies from fifty to a hundred feet in height. At
intervals arise battlements, square towers, where in old times
soldiers peeped through narrow port-holes and dealt death
to the enemy hardy enough to attack that mass of lofty
masonry. Following this old wall down its winding way into
the ravine, then up the mountain to the ruined fort, we finally
returned safely to the steamer.

Next morning we were at Cartagena, where there was another
old castle on a high peak overlooking the blue sea, and the
white, flat roofs of the oriental-looking town. It seems as if
the first thing people did in old times was to look for an
isolated, lofty peak; when one was found, the next thing was
to build a castle. We spent half the day at the old Roman
castle of Cartagena, the other half in the penitentiary and at
the government docks. The prison presented no new features.
There was the usual court with its hundreds of idle convicts,
and only a few rooms occupied by shoe and basket makers;
not many men seemed anxious enough for work to pay for the
privilege. In the centre of the court was a marble fountain
where the prisoners take an annual bath. The fountain also
serves for washing clothes; being the only water provided, it
is filthy beyond description. Many of the sixteen hundred
convicts never wash at all, probably thinking that the dirt on
their bodies would only be increased by dabbling in such
water. When we mentioned our visit to the prison to an intelligent English-speaking Spaniard, and asked why the convicts are given neither clothes nor the means of making them,
the señor replied with the question: —

"To do one or the other would be logical, would it not?"

"Certainly; that is why we ask the question."

"And that is why the government does not do it. The Spanish official finds out what is logical, then does the opposite."

This reply was pithy, but it was not satisfactory.

"What would the Minister of Justice say were we to ask him that question? Surely he would not reply that the convicts are treated as they are, because to treat them otherwise would be sensible and humane?"

"No, he would say he did not believe the conditions you describe exist."

"But if we proved it to him, if we took him to Ceuta and showed him five thousand convicts lounging about, nothing to do, idle, yet naked and half starved, what would he say to a suggestion that they be given looms for weaving cloth to hide their nakedness, and work to get food to fill their empty stomachs?"

"In the first place," replied the señor, "the Minister would not go with you; in the second place, he would say that if the conditions are as you describe, there must be good reasons therefor, — that old customs are not to be changed lightly."

That such a reply could be made by a minister in the last decade of the nineteenth century seems incredible, yet the señor's contemptuous opinion of the Spanish Minister of Justice is borne out by the fact that the prisoners, not only in Cartagena, Ceuta, and Granada, but in all Spanish prisons, have hands and muscles, and ability to work to supply the necessities of their being, yet are kept idle, starved, and naked.

"But with money," said the señor, "you can accomplish everything, even getting work in a Spanish prison. Some prisons are better than others, cleaner and drier. By a judicious bribe, a condemned man can select his prison; indeed, he can sometimes elect not to go to prison at all. A friend of mine was sentenced six months for seditious oratory. The prison happened to be full, — it was just after the first of May, — and the jailer was exceedingly distressed because, when my friend offered money for private quarters, there were no more private quarters to be had. Then my friend said, 'Look here, there is no use in your losing this money. I will stay at home and pay you four pesetas a day, just the same as if you gave me a private room in the jail.' The matter was arranged accordingly, and my friend remained at home the entire period of his sentence."

The most skilled of the three thousand men who work in the government arsenal at Cartagena, the mechanics who put the finishing touches on the delicate machinery of the engines of torpedo boats, receive five pesetas (ninety-five cents) a day. The average mechanic's wages is not more than three and one-half pesetas, while many get only two pesetas. We wondered how such cheap labor can fancy it needs "protection" against the much higher paid labor of England; we also wondered at our being permitted to walk about inspecting the machinery, the manufacture of the war-vessels, and of the torpedo boats. Some governments maintain a great deal of mystery about such things, and admission to arsenal works can be had only by permit from high authority. Spain, however, is as free and easy in this respect as in that of her prisons, and we inspected the huge arsenal at Cartagena quite at our leisure. On the way back to the city we stopped to rest in the cool nave of the cathedral, and while there saw a characteristic Spanish scene. A mother and daughter entered and dropped on their knees to pray; at least, that was the mother's motive. The daughter knelt a few feet behind her mother, and while the latter was absorbed in religious devotions, a man brushed by the daughter, snatched a note she extended, and a moment later was devouring its contents behind one of the big, roof-supporting columns. Twice he kissed the paper fervently, then pulled out pencil and paper, wrote a hurried note, and soon the dark-eyed señorita had the precious missive hidden away in her dress, while her face looked up at the Madonna with as rapt and innocent expression as if heavenly, not earthly, love agitated her young heart.

At Alicante the following morning there was the usual peak and castle. Peaks and castles had become a trifle monotonous, still we made the ascent for the sake of the view. We got a view of about twenty feet in diameter, no more, because the road winding to the summit is shut in by high walls and houses, and because a sentinel at the top end of the road presented a bayonet and a request to lose no time getting back whence we came. Of course we acceded to his request, not because we did not wish to see the view, but because that sentinel was so earnest and pressing in his invitation. We never learned what the Spanish were doing on top of that peak. It was the only one we were not allowed to see, and so, of course, was the very one we most wanted to see. At Valencia we received a surprise by seeing a Spanish city on the Mediterranean without either castle or peak. The surprise was heightened by the further fact that the surrounding country, instead of being bleak, and burned, and yellow, was bright green, and dotted with trees. A street car runs from the quay to the city three miles away, down a broad boulevard shaded by four rows of tall trees. So luxuriant is the foliage of these trees that we found our perch on top of the street car too high, and escaped the branches only by ducking our heads. It was Sunday when we entered Valencia, and the first thing we did was to go to the cathedral. While listening to the droning of the priests, in Latin, and to the responses of the hundreds of kneeling figures, the faint sound of bugles and drums reached us: the sound grew louder and clearer, then came the heavy tramp, tramp, of marching feet: in a few minutes, a column of soldiers swept down the narrow street in front of the cathedral door. The effect was dramatic; first the dim, religious light, the praying priests and peasants, then the faint sounds of martial music and men, coming nearer and nearer, until the tramp, tramp of the hundreds of soldiers and the burst of military music passed the very door, drowning the droning of the priests and the responses of the people, then disappearing as it had come, slowly dying away.

Spanish markets are specially interesting on Sundays; the crowd is larger and there are more varieties of peasants. At the Valencia market, one pedlar had an ass loaded with nuts and with a lighted stove. The nuts were similar to American peanuts, and the fire was there to parch them. It was an odd sight, that donkey with a smoking stove on its back, though neither donkey nor people seemed to think it odd. The stove was strapped on the donkey's back. I do not know that the donkey's back was burned, though it must have been unpleasantly hot. In Spain, the anti-cruelty to animals societies have not yet been formed, though they are needed there, as, indeed, they are needed in all Europe, England excepted. I saw no cruelty to animals in England. Supplies are sold at the market in very small quantities. For instance, instead of buying a whole chicken, the average purchaser never dreams of getting more than a leg or a wing. One bright-eyed girl had a cow, and for two cents offered to milk us a glass "fresh from the cow." A calf was tied to the cow's tail, and from the lusty young brute's efforts to escape, we feared the unlucky cow's caudal appendage would snap asunder. Good apricots were selling for two cents a pound. The leg of a chicken cost ten cents; a wing, five cents. Eggs were sorted in boxes, according to age, those of greater antiquity selling much cheaper than younger and fresher ones. We filled our market basket and returned to the steamer. Marketing was a regular practice with us, for we did not eat at the steamer table.

Every morning when we sallied forth, it was with a market basket, which we filled with fruit, bread, cold mutton, beef or ham. On returning in the afternoon, we took a swim around the vessel, then spread our lunch out on deck in regular picnic fashion. It is a delightful way to travel; one enjoys the delights of picnicking, of sea-bathing, of seeing strange people and places all combined. Our swims around the *Nueva Valencia* made us acquainted with her every screw and pin as few passengers know their steamer. Often when we were sailing along in the moonlight, Mack and I leaned over the poop deck rail and watched the water come boiling from the steamer's screw, from the fans of which we had dived only a few hours before.

At length, on the morning of the fifth day, our lazy voyage came to an end. The captain told us we should reach Barcelona by eight o'clock; so Mack and I were up at six to get a view as the vessel entered the harbor. The sight of the rugged mountains with their villages and castles, and the calm blue water of the Mediterranean dotted with hundreds of fishing-boats, well repaid early rising. Barcelona sets back from the sea in a sort of natural amphitheatre, with lofty mountains for walls, so that the traveller approaching from the Mediterranean does not see the city until a sudden turn brings it all into view at once. It is a surprise one will never forget: one moment high mountains, bleak and bare, the next moment, a city stretching out in semicircular form along the bay, and extending in terraces up the mountain's side like the tiers of a gigantic theatre. In fifteen minutes from the moment the vessel rounded the southern horn of the crescent bay, we were in the harbor and along the dock. But though alongside the dock, we had to land as usual in a small boat. It would break a Mediterranean steamship company's heart really to land a passenger at the point contracted for; so when they strike a port like Barcelona, where the water is deep enough to anchor alongside the docks, they get around the difficulty by letting the steps down on the *opposite* side of the steamer and compelling passengers to disembark there. This is what they made us do, and of course there was the usual row with the boatman. After that came a row with the customs officer. As we had arrived on a Spanish vessel, from a Spanish port, neither Mack nor I anticipated any trouble at the Custom House. We were not unaware that customs officials are often, like Poo Bah, amenable to "insults," so they be heavy ones. But in Barcelona alone did we meet a customs official who asked outright for a fee, and who, when refused, made a vigorous and vindictive search of our luggage. The porter we employed said it would be better to give the examiner a peseta. Mack thought the trouble of packing his valise worth twenty cents, and was for administering the bribe. It was against my grain to submit to swindlers, so I told the brass-buttoned official to proceed with the show. He did so. In five minutes our few worldly goods and chattels lay spread on the floor in the wildest confusion.

"Is there anything else you wish to examine?" I cheerfully inquired of the official, who searched as closely as if he expected to find anarchist bombs, and seemed disappointed and mad at not finding them.

Barcelona is the centre of the labor movement in Spain. The leaders live there, the plan of campaign originates there, the organizations are formed there, and it is there, if at all, that one obtains information concerning the nature and extent of the labor movement in the Iberian peninsula. I was aware of this fact, and as soon as we had coffee, sent for the interpreter of the hotel and told him I wished to meet the labor leaders, and to visit the workshops and factories. The interpreter looked at me as if doubting his senses.

"Whom do you wish to meet?"

"The labor leaders, the heads of the unions in Barcelona. I wish to talk with them and to employ you as interpreter."

The interpreter gave me a haughty look as he proudly said that he was not acquainted with people in that walk of life.

"I associate only with gentlemen. If you wish to visit the cathedral and objects of interest in Barcelona, I can show them to you, but I know nothing of anarchists and agitators."

As I did not wish to see the cathedral just then, and did wish to see the persons so unfortunate as not to possess the good opinion of this haughty Spanish guide, I declined his services, and sent for the interpreter of the Four Nations Hotel. That individual, while not so haughty, was equally ignorant of the class I wished to visit. He had many calls for cathedrals, but none for workshops. As for labor leaders and labor unions, there were such things, but *he* knew nothing of them; *he* had too much to do to run around after anarchists and agitators. It was now nine o'clock, and as two professional interpreters had failed us, we thought of the American consul. That gentleman was very courteous and very willing, but he too knew nothing of the men we wished to meet. Doubtless I should have failed in my purpose, had not a singular incident thrown me into the very midst of the labor leaders, and afforded an insight into their methods and character. It happened thus: —

While strolling along the Rambla, after our fruitless visit to the consul's, our attention was drawn to a crowd crossing the Rambla at right angles to the course we were pursuing. The head and front of this crowd were two civil guards, their guns cocked in readiness to fire in case the four prisoners they were escorting attempted to escape. In St. Louis or New York we should not dream of joining the rabble which collects on such occasions. In Spain, however, one does many things one does not do at home, so we turned and joined the crowd that was following the civil guards and prisoners. As we penetrated further into the labyrinth of narrow streets, the crowd thinned, until finally the entire party, including guards, prisoners, and onlookers, numbered not more than a dozen. Three of the onlookers, friends of the prisoners, remained close by their sides, engaged in animated conversation. When at last the civil guards turned into an arched way leading to a dark, gloomy, court, the few remaining spectators stayed outside, while the three friends of the prisoners entered along with the party. They were so interested among themselves that they did not observe us. The guard at the door took us for members of the party, and after being searched and deprived of our penknives and canes, we were admitted like the rest. The four prisoners were hustled through a second iron door, and were soon lost to view. Their three friends at the same time hurried in the opposite direction down a long corridor, up a flight of steep steps, and into another corridor, where was a noise worse than any Bedlam.

Following closely in the wake of the three, as they wedged themselves through the crowd of shouting, jabbering people in that upper corridor, we at length found ourselves near an iron grating; behind us was a yelling, shouting mob; before us, on the other side of the grating, a pale, nervous-looking guard; beyond him, another grating; beyond that grating, another mob, as shouting and noisy as that behind us. Of all officials, the most unfortunate are certainly the Spanish guards, who have to sit ten hours a day in the little space between the two gratings which separate the prisoners from their friends. Both visitors and prisoners thrust their hands through the bars in an effort to pass cigars backward and forward, they yell and shout, laugh, cry — in short, a pandemonium which the guard seems not to notice, and certainly does not check. Scarce had we pressed through the ill-smelling crowd and reached the grating, before we saw, beyond the other grating, the four prisoners we had followed through the street. As soon as they appeared, the four prisoners on their side, and the three

RUINS OF THE ROMAN THEATRE, SYRACUSE.

friends on our side, began rattling away in the most excited manner, thrusting their arms through the gratings, and gesticulating so violently that the guard had to edge off to a corner to keep his head from being thumped.

"The people on this side are friends of the prisoners?" we asked of a man in the crowd. Our Spanish was very poor, and mystified the man, so we volunteered the information that we were Americans. "Oh, entiendo," said the man; then shouted something to a prisoner on the other side, who in turn began crying out in shrill tones for the "friends of the Americanos." Of course, when he returned from his hunt, it was with the information that the "friends" of the Americanos had not responded. Our command of Spanish was too limited to make our real meaning understood, and to this day that crowd thinks, if it thinks at all on the matter, that we were there to visit imprisoned friends. Half an hour sufficed to satisfy our curiosity. We made our way out of the crowd, down the steps, and along the corridor to the door first entered. There a surprise awaited us as unpleasant as it was unexpected. The jailer who had first searched and admitted us was on the other side of the grated door. We told him in our best Spanish that we had seen all we wished and were ready to go. There is no doubt that our Spanish, bad as it was, was good enough to make that jailer understand that we wished to get out. But instead of opening the door, the turnkey jabbered something, shook his fist, and motioned us to go away and let him alone.

"But look here, señor, we want to get out. We are not prisoners."

I said this in a mixture of English, Spanish, and Italian. Possibly the turnkey did not understand a word, but he understood that we were still at the gate, and it threw him into a rage. Opening the door with one of his huge iron keys, he glowered so darkly, shook his fist so fiercely, we quite understood he did not intend to open the gate, and so retreated down the corridor; then the jailer went back through the iron door, locked it, and composedly sat down. It was a singular proceeding: we reflected, however, that our imprisonment could not last very long. No doubt the friends of the prisoners would be let out at *some* hour; we were supposed to be friends, and so would surely be let out too. As long as we kept away from the barred gate, there was no let or hindrance to our movements, and like the four hundred or five hundred other voluntary prisoners there, we were at liberty to move about at will. At a landing half-way up one of the flights of steps was a window overlooking a court in which were a hundred or so real prisoners, some sprawled out on the cobble pavement fast asleep, others mending and patching their garments, others gambling, others playing handball. While on the landing looking down on this strange scene, a sad-faced woman with a baby in her arms came up the steps, and stopping on the landing, reached her hand out of the window, and began waving her handkerchief. For a while there was no response; finally, however, there was a cry below, and the woman's face lighted up as she saw one of the men stop his clothes-mending, look up, and wave his hand towards the window. For half an hour we watched that woman as she stood there talking, occasionally holding the baby up and pressing the little face against the bars, while the prisoner below clapped his hands, chuckled, whistled, and performed all the other arts known to the amusers of infants. The little one seemed to appreciate these efforts: it laughed and shook its chubby fists, while the faces of the father and mother glowed with pleasure.

The people about us had bread and sausages, some had brought lunch baskets, bread, fruit, and wine, and between twelve and one o'clock the corridors of the gloomy place presented the spectacle of some five hundred men, women, and children sitting around on the floors, eating and drinking. We had had no breakfast to speak of, merely a cup of coffee, and were famished; needless to say, the sight of the others eating and drinking did not abate the keenness of our appetites. Having finished their dinners, the five hundred friends of the prisoners returned to their places behind the gratings, the prisoners, being also through eating, returned to their places, the guard resumed his seat in the narrow space between the two gratings, and the yelling and gesticulating began again as in the morning.

We had made two attempts to induce the doorkeeper to let us out, we had inspected every nook and corner of the rambling prison, had asked several persons why we were detained, without succeeding in making ourselves understood, and felt quite uncomfortable as we asked ourselves: —

When are we to get something to eat?
Why are we kept prisoners?
When shall we be freed?

CHAPTER XI

The Shoemaker, the Anarchist, and the Editor — Labor Unions in Spain — Troubles of May First — What Monarchies have to Fear — Barcelona's Rambla — Spanish Politics — The Anarchist Plan — Excursion to Montserrat — The Virgin's Cave — Pilgrims and Penances — What it costs to travel in Spain

CHANCE led us to speak, in Italian, to a man who understood that language. We asked why we were detained.

"I do not know why," said the man. "In Spain, nobody knows the why or wherefore of anything: it is the rule to let no visitor depart before five o'clock. You can visit your friends in prison any morning you like, but when you come you must stay all day — either a long visit or no visit is the rule. That is why every one brings lunch."

"If we ever come again," said Mack, ruefully, "we shall bring a dozen lunches."

The man looked at his watch.

"Four thirty," he said. "In exactly half an hour you can go out and get your dinner."

This Italian-speaking Spaniard was a shoemaker, but much better dressed than the average of his class, also more intelligent. When he learned we were Americans, he wanted to know how it happened we had friends in a Spanish prison. We told him of our interest in labor matters, how we had followed the civil guards, and entered along with a party of prisoners and their friends simply to see Spanish life and law. This led to a discussion of labor: he was curious to learn the condition of workmen in America, and discanted freely on the industrial situation in Spain. Pointing to a batch of prisoners beyond the grating, he said: —

"Do you see those men there? Those are the men I came to visit. They are agitators, anarchists."

We went up close to the grating and had a good look at Spanish anarchists. They were the most honest-looking men in the prison. We said as much.

"Do you think a man is dishonest because he is an anarchist?"

"But why are they in prison?"

"Because they are agitators, not because they are dishonest. There are more rogues in the cabinet at Madrid than there are in that crowd of men. The government denies us the right of free speech. If more than nineteen men gather at a meeting, the government sends soldiers, disperses the meeting, arrests the speakers. The men you see there are the leaders of the labor movement in Barcelona. They were arrested, not for having done anything illegal, but for fear they *would* do something. They have been here since a few days before the first of May."

"How long will they remain?"

"As long as the government chooses. There were great strikes and demonstrations on May 1, 1890. The government feared the movement would be serious this year, and, beside massing thousands of soldiers here, it also collected in the harbor a number of gunboats and men-of-war to shell the city. Not satisfied with these precautions, in the last week of April, the leaders were suddenly and without warning dragged from their beds and thrown into prison, where, as you see, they still are."

A few minutes before five, the five hundred friends of the prisoners began to press their way to the grated door; promptly at five the door was unlocked, and all made a rush for freedom. Our shoemaker invited us to accompany him to a place where we would meet men who could give any information we desired regarding the status of labor in Spain. We gladly accepted this offer after taking a hurried lunch at a neighboring café. No. 2 San Olegario is the office of "El Productor," the anarchist organ of Catalonia, which, judging from appearances, is in a prosperous condition. An arched doorway and a pair of zigzag steps brought us to the editorial room, crowded with newspapers, waste-baskets, paste-pots, and other paraphernalia of the sanctum. On the walls were portraits of Parsons, Spies, and the other Chicago Anarchists. Opening from this sanctum was a large hall provided with chairs, a speaker's desk, the walls decked with flags and with portraits of agitators and anarchists of all countries and times. Conspicuous among them were the seven Chicago "martyrs," with a legend underneath, draped in black, bearing the words "11th November, 1887," and the names of the seven. In the library we noticed the works of Henry George, and the speeches of Hugh O. Pentecost (editor of the New York

"Twentieth Century"). The editor of "El Productor" is also a lithographer, and was at the lithograph establishment, not at the newspaper office, when we called. The friendly shoemaker volunteered to conduct us to the lithograph establishment. We soon found ourselves in the presence of Señor Esteve, a bloused workman, yet a man one would instantly pronounce a thinker of force and education. When the shoemaker explained how he had met us, and our interest in the labor situation in Barcelona, Señor Esteve's thoughtful face lighted with a smile.

He said he could not stop his work to talk, but that if we would come to him at night, he would gladly give all the information in his power; in the meantime he would give us a note to a gentleman who speaks English, and whom it would interest us to know. It is not often that a day in jail leads to acquaintance with scientists and savants, yet that is what our visit to the Barcelona jail did. The gentleman to whom the editor of "El Productor" gave us a note of introduction, is a remarkable man. It seems to me that when the condition of the masses of men in any country are such as to produce men like Señor T., it is time the rulers of that country should seriously consider the danger of the situation. We were informed that these men represent hundreds of thousands of workingmen in Spain. Señor T. is a man of letters, member of the Section of Sciences of the Barcelona Athenæum, and known in Spain as a scientist of originality and ability. When ushered into his library, we found the señor surrounded by microscopes, writing materials, books of science, history, etc. His aspect showed him to be a man not of the times, not serving the times, but devoted to an ideal. He is perfect master of all the modern languages of Europe, including Greek, Turkish, and Russian.

"You are right," he said, "in supposing Barcelona the centre of the industrial movement in Spain, but to understand the existing situation you must look back a few years and see the causes of the feeling which now exists. Prior to the death of Alfonso XII. in 1885, the Conservatives were in power. After Alfonso's death, the Liberals gained a majority in the Cortes which they held until the summer of 1890. When you know how they lost control, you will not wonder that anarchists now advise workmen not to vote. The government counts in its own candidates no matter how the people vote. In the last election, of forty thousand qualified electors, only eight thousand voted."

"If the Government candidates are known to have fewer votes than the Liberal, is there no remedy?"

"The Cortes, like your American Congress, decides such cases, and decides as the government wishes. It has the power and uses it arbitrarily."

Remembering the way the ruling party in Congress has more than once unseated members of the opposite party although elected, as in one case, by seventeen thousand majority, we could well believe what the señor said of the Spanish Cortes.

"The Liberals were in power up to the summer of 1890," I said. "How did they lose it?"

"By treachery of the Prime Minister. Universal suffrage and the right to trial by jury, secured by the Liberal party, had won that party the affection and confidence of the nation. The Conservative party was on the high road to destruction. General Martinez Campos, who overthrew the Republic in 1875, and is called the Dry Nurse of the Monarchy, because of his influence over the Queen, grasped the situation, and resorted to bold measures to stem the rising tide of democracy. He told the Austrian princess, mother of the infant king, that if the Liberals continued in power, the Conservative party would die, and with it the Monarchy. The Queen, alarmed, sent for Sagasta, the Liberal Prime Minister, and commanded him to let the Conservatives form a ministry. A large majority of the Cortes were Liberals, the Spanish people were Liberals, yet the Prime Minister was told by the Queen that he must turn over the government to the Conservatives. The Queen's arguments must have been powerful, for Sagasta eagerly set out to accomplish the traitorous task. As soon as the session adjourned, he handed in his portfolio. The Cortes was not to convene until January, 1891, six months later. This gave the Queen time to form a Conservative Ministry. Knowing the Cortes, when it convened, would repudiate the new Ministry, she, on the last day of December, 1890, a few days before the old Cortes was to convene, exercised her power of declaring it dissolved, and ordered a new election. A ministry can dissolve a Cortes and call an election at any time. In this case, the Ministry was subservient to the Queen and controlled the election in favor of the Monarchy. Had Mateo Sagasta not been a traitor, he would have retained his portfolio; the Queen might have dissolved the Cortes, but the Liberal Ministry would have controlled the election and been returned to power. By his resignation the Queen was enabled to form a subservient Ministry which counted out Liberals and counted in Conservative members in a most shameful manner."

"Did not this treachery prove the political death of the Prime Minister?"

"What does he care? He has the estates and treasures which rewarded his treachery. It is baseness of this sort which has caused the ballot to be abandoned by workingmen, and which bands them together as anarchists. Oppression makes rebels. There never was and never can be rebellion against freedom. Our people are now oppressed in a way that rasps their souls. They are not allowed freedom of speech. Officers of the law may send a commissioner to any public gathering, who has power to disperse the people; he may even call the civil guards and arrest the speakers and leaders.

Under Señor Antonez, civil governor while the Liberals were in power, gatherings of workingmen were permitted and liberty of speech prevailed. Upon the downfall of the Liberal Ministry in July, 1890, Señor Antonez had, of course, to resign: under General Gonzales, the present civil governor, one can never be sure one's words will not be construed as seditious and dangerous to the common welfare. The commissioners acting under General Gonzales, who is himself only acting in accordance with the Conservative·Ministry at Madrid, avail themselves of the slightest pretext to declare a meeting dissolved. In former times it often happened that a commissioner would arise at a meeting and suggest to the orator a more moderate tone. This is not done now. The Conservative commissioners are only anxious to catch people napping, only anxious for a pretext to throw them into prison. The government is afraid of discussion. There was a general strike on May 1, 1890, the force of which the government broke as far as it could, ordering the soldiers to take the place of the strikers. Soldiers filled the bakeries and workshops and drove the street cars. The civil governor resigned; martial law was declared. Fortunately, General Blanco was a man of moderation as well as firmness. The tramcar drivers had worked eighteen hours a day. General Blanco told the employers these hours must be reduced. A crisis was at hand, the soldiers threatened to withdraw, and the employers reluctantly reduced the hours of labor to eleven. The other trade strikes were settled in the same way by General Blanco's firmness and decision, and in eight days civil government was restored. On the first of May, 1891, the movements of the people were anticipated by General Solesio. Ships of the line were anchored in the harbor, troops were massed in the city, the labor leaders were thrown into prison in April, and soldiers patrolled the large factories and streets. Thus was peace and quiet secured — a peace much like that which reigned at Warsaw. In a few of the trades the men struck this year, either to gain new concessions, or to hold those gained in 1890. The stevedores, who last year reduced their hours from ten to eight, struck this year for recognition of their union. The stonemasons and carpenters struck for the same principle. You may have noticed walls five or six feet high around buildings now in course of construction. These, and the soldiers who patrol about them, are for the protection of the 'scab' carpenters and masons."

Señor T. was already well posted as to the general movement of labor in the United States, but of some of the wrongs which prevail with us he had never heard,— of the "Pluck-me" or truck store system in Pennsylvania, Missouri, and other mining states, and the fight being made to abolish it.

The Villaroel, one of those new quarters which have recently been opened in Barcelona, reminds the American traveller of the uptown tenements of New York — only they are handsomer, cleaner, and the rents much cheaper. The building in which Señor Esteve lives is plain but respectable-looking; the broad street is planted with shade trees. For his flat of six rooms on the third floor, Señor Esteve pays but thirty pesetas ($6) a month. A similar flat would cost $40 in New York, and at least $25 in St. Louis or Chicago.

Señor Esteve, like Señor T., had a library, though not so large nor embracing so many languages. As he sat at his desk, surrounded by books and papers, it was difficult to realize that he was the same man I had seen the day before in workman's blouse, sleeves rolled up, hands and arms stained with ink and paint. In reply to my inquiry as to what trades in Spain were most thoroughly organized, Señor Esteve said: —

"'There are no stable or permanent organizations in Spain. A trade organizes for some specific purpose; that accomplished or defeated, the organization languishes and dies. In 1881 the Workman's Congress in Barcelona was attended by delegates representing 15,000 organized laborers. This Congress gave an impetus which was evidenced the following year by the fact that there came to the Seville Congress delegates representing 100,000 workmen, and 'La Revista Social,' the organ published at Madrid, reached a circulation of 22,000. The movement, however, has never since reached the height it attained in 1880. In 1883 the Congress at Valencia represented only 20,000 organized laborers. This great falling off was largely due to the severity of the government. Several cases of brigandage had occurred in Andalusia. The government pretended to believe this due to the labor unions, and instituted persecutions against them such as was never known before. Thousands were imprisoned, so that our succeeding Congresses have been held in secret. Secrecy is one of the first results of tyranny; craft comes to cope with power. Government oppression and internal dissensions in our own ranks are the main causes of the decline in three years from 100,000 to 20,000 members."

In reply to my question as to the nature and origin of this dissension, Señor Esteve said: —

"The spread of trades-unionism. The first Congresses at Barcelona and Seville declared their main principle to be anarchy and collectivism; that is, a grand union of labor of all kinds and nations. They did not ignore strikes and trades-unions as a method of raising wages and reducing hours; but they regarded these as only a means to an end,— the grand end of Universal Brotherhood among men. Unfortunately, the masses were unable to grasp this grand aim. The organizations began to weaken, to lose cohesion, until finally, in 1889, a radical change of plan was adopted. The attempt to combine trades-unionism with anarchy was abandoned. The trades-unions took up the local work, that is, dealing with questions of wages and hours, while to the anarchist section was delegated the work of propagation and education. The effect of our propaganda was first seen in the strikes of May 1, 1890 and 1891. In the beginning the trades-union wing was lethargic, but the success of the anarchists' efforts aroused them to action, and it is not improbable that, despite government opposition, we shall be able to accomplish something definite ere long. The dyers of woollens and calicoes have so strong a union that they have succeeded in raising their wages to four pesetas a day, and in forcing the employers to recognize their organization. Trades not large enough in membership to form a separate union combine in the 'Seccion Varia,' composed of many trades. This union is gaining strength and taking up new questions from time to time. That of limiting the number of apprentices and forcing recognition of unions are the questions now at the front. The dyers' union is the only one that has secured recognition, by which is meant the employment only of members of the union. In no trade is there any limitation as to the number of apprentices which masters may employ. Organizations are strongest in Barcelona, hence it is here that the best wages are paid. For instance, stevedores here receive seven pesetas for a day of eight hours. In Bilbao and other ports lacking organization, one to two pesetas is the rule. Moreover, in those places, one frequently sees women carrying sacks and burdens on their backs from the ships to the lighters and docks. In the Barcelona organizations women take equal rank with men. Often they participate in the discussions and make speeches that for vigor and force surpass those of their brothers."

Señor Esteve smiled when I expressed surprise at this, mentioning the romantic notions which the average American has as to the "dark-eyed señoritas" of Spain.

"'Those notions," said he, "may be true as to the few daughters of wealth, but for the masses of womankind in Spain,— as, indeed, for the masses everywhere,— there is only hard work and scanty pay. Labor recognizes this fact, and while the Spanish Don's daughter is kept in seclusion and taught only to coquette with her fan, the workman's daughter sets about making a living the best way she can, first by joining in union with her fellow-toilers, then by keeping her eyes open, speaking when necessary, and examining all measures likely to better her condition."

Anarchism, as I understood it, and as Señor Esteve defined it, means no government whatever. I ventured to question him.

"When all mankind is sufficiently unselfish to be able to distinguish between *meum* and *tuum* there will be no need for government to protect the weak and punish the wrong. But as mankind is *not* yet thus civilized, can we afford to abolish government?"

"We think we can," replied Señor Esteve. "We believe government does not prevent, but creates crime. The governments of every people in every age have committed more crime than all the criminals they ever condemned, punished, or tortured. I refer you to the history of the Roman Empire, and of every kingdom in Europe since that Empire was broken up into kingdoms. The history of our own Spain is a fair sample of the criminality of government. Look at our Inquisition — but why go back to the past? The newspapers of to-day give evidence of some of the crimes committed by the governments of to-day. What is more monstrous than Russia's treatment of Jews? or Spain's treatment of Liberals? suppression of free speech, arrest, and imprisonment for exercising the God-given right of discussion? When justice rules, when equality of rights prevails, and labor has its just dues, every man and woman will have enough, want and starvation will disappear, and with them, crime."

Señor T. seemed practical enough on all other matters; he was a close and critical observer and reasoner in scientific questions; on the subject of anarchy he seemed to me an impractical dreamer. I said: —

"An American living in Malaga told me that some years ago, before the establishment of the civil guards, he dared not go from one city to another without an armed escort, that at night he dared not go about even in Malaga. The civil guards have restored tranquillity, and it is now as safe to travel in Spain as in other countries of Europe. Would not your anarchist programme bring things back to the condition existing when my friend first went to Malaga?"

"Not at all: besides, even with the civil guards there are murders and crimes."

"But not so many as there were before. Do not statistics show that there are fewer crimes now than thirty years ago?"

"Bah, who makes the statistics? The government; and it takes care that they show what it wants shown."

I ventured a little Darwinism on this dreamer — yet reasoner.

"It has taken Nature thousands of years to evolve the best of humanity, to develop the faculty of reason, of justice. You must admit that in our midst are large numbers of men and women in whom these higher faculties are yet dormant, in whom only the brutal instincts rule — the appetites for food, the passion to propagate. Take from these lower specimens of our race the fear of physical punishment for wrongdoing, — that is, take government away, — and what will prevent such men and women from preying upon society?"

"There are two complete answers to your proposition," replied Señor T., promptly. "In the first place, it is not true that Nature has made man as you describe. Men are vicious and devoid of moral sense because of man's injustice and inhumanity to man — "

"But since he *is* thus devoid of moral sense, no matter how he became so, must not these deficient if unfortunate beings be restrained by government?"

"I was coming to that," said the señor. "By restoring

justice, anarchists will remove the cause of crime. When each person does his just share of work, the average day's labor will not exceed three hours. The laziest will be willing to work three hours, if, by so doing, the necessities of his being can be supplied: this fact will surely abolish crime. It is not natural for man to prey on man. The savage carnivora do not prey on their own kind — lions do not eat lions, or tigers, tigers. The unjust inequalities of society are the cause of all crime on earth. Remove the cause of an evil, and the evil ceases; hence, to abolish crime, we must first abolish social inequalities."

While still regarding the anarchist scheme as an impracticable dream, my respect for the men who harbor this dream was increased after meeting Señores Esteve and T., animated as they are by that spirit which makes men suffer persecution, even death, in the cause they believe represents the Highest Truth. Señor Esteve's paper, "El Productor," devoted to the propagation of his opinions, is sent forth every week to educate the people in anarchism. I read to him my notes of our conversation, and he fearlessly desired they might be given the widest publicity. He said it is only necessary to see the truth to embrace it.

Sculpture and paintings, as well as books and newspapers, show the trend of a people's thoughts. In the shop windows of Barcelona are cheap chromos which show the incoming tide of public opinion. These chromos are powerful object lessons for the crowds of common people who stand before the windows and study them. One of the chromos represents an arch, the keystone of which is a king in robes of purple. From the mouth of the king come the words: "Os gobierno a todos" (I govern all). Beneath the king is a gay cavalier, with sword, and plume, and jaunty cap. The cavalier is saying: "Os mando a todos" (I command all). Beneath the cavalier is a shovel-hat priest, prayer-book in hand, saying:

"Rezo por todos vosotros" (I pray for you all). Then comes the judge, pompous and well fed: "Hago mi negocio con todos vosotros" (I live upon you all). Then the beggar, one legged, hat in hand: "Os pido limosna a todos" (I beg from all). Then, last of all, with brawny shoulders, and straining muscles, standing like two columns, supporting the arch, are two men representing Labor: "Sostenemos a todos" (We support all).

The fact that such lithographs are published and scattered broadcast is a sign of the times which crowned heads should ponder. The king still governs all, the cavalier still lords it over all, the workman still pays for all; but the workman is beginning to realize the fact, and this is a great step, one that portends great change in the future.

The people in Barcelona have a spring and alertness about them that makes it difficult to believe they are of the same country and race as the slow-going, sleepy Andalusians. Even Paris cannot boast a livelier or more charming Boulevard than Barcelona's Rambla. Wider than Pennsylvania Avenue in Washington, the Rambla contains a broad walk in the centre for pedestrians, with a row of shade trees and a wide driveway on either side of the broad walk, then two more "trottoirs," or sidewalks, on both sides of the driveways. The majority of pedestrians frequent the broad walk between the two rows of shade trees. In the forenoon, flower-girls bring their wares to the Rambla, and for two or three hours it is brilliant with hundreds of stands on which bloom the loveliest tropical flowers. No matter what the hour, day or night, this beautiful boulevard is animated with life. Up to midnight, it is packed and thronged with people.

An interesting excursion from Barcelona is that to Montserrat. The round trip, second class, costs only two dollars, and can easily be made in two days. You go to Monistrol by rail, whence a lumbering old-fashioned stage-coach

Street in Syra

with six mules conveys you in three hours up the zigzag mountain road to the ancient monastery. In addition to the magnificent scenery and the unkempt pilgrims toiling up the mountain to perform penances before the sacred Black Virgin, Mack and I had to interest us on the journey a Spanish bridal couple. They sat beside us on the first seat behind the driver, holding each other's hands, and looking so happy that the happiness was reflected on the rest of the passengers, and put all in good humor. The young husband, in the excess of his contentment, felt so kindly to the world at large and to his fellow-passengers in particular that he insisted on making us share his lunch. When I complimented the bit of sausage which I accepted, he thrust at me all he had,—a piece about two feet long,—and insisted on my eating every inch of it. When I made him understand it was impossible to eat more than an inch or so at one time, he cried warmly:—

"Take it, take it with you to America. It may be you will not get such sausage there."

Montserrat is a remarkable mountain, not because of its height—it is only four thousand feet above the sea: it is remarkable because of its peculiar formation, and because of the fact that it rises abruptly from a level plain, a single and solitary mass of rock with a tremendous rift in the centre three thousand feet deep. On the edge of the top of this cañon stands a monastery more than a thousand years old. On reaching this lofty ledge, two thousand feet above the plain, yet still a thousand feet below the overhanging cliffs and crags, we descended from the stage and entered the office of the monastery to secure quarters for the night. Sometimes a thousand or fifteen hundred pilgrims visit the place at one time: the huge building, however, accommodates all who come. A bare but neat cell is given to each one. For this no charge is made, although a donation is expected. The attendant who assigns you your cell reminds you of the donation should you happen to forget it. A Barcelona author has written a three-volume book called "Three Days in Montserrat." It is fortunate the monks permit no visitor to remain longer than three days. There is no telling how many volumes that Barcelona author would have written had he been allowed to extend his visit.

The most interesting place on Montserrat is the Virgin's cave, reached by a path that winds a few hundred feet downwards from the monastery, along the brink of a stupendous precipice. The natural cave in the prodigious rock has been converted into a chapel where pilgrims, especially women, perform devotions. We saw a number of bright-faced peasant girls kneeling before the altar, a rapt look on their faces as they gazed at the image of the Virgin. It was in this cave that the sacred Black Virgin, carved by the Apostle Luke, was buried a thousand years ago when the Moors invaded Spain. In the year 880 A.D., some shepherds were attracted to the spot by "heavenly lights and sweet odors." They found the black image in the centre of these lights and odors, and forthwith set out with the image for Manresa. Although His Holiness the Bishop of Vich was along, the image stopped halfway and positively refused to go farther. A chapel was erected to protect her from the weather, and for one hundred and sixty years the sacred image remained on the spot where it had first halted on the journey to Manresa. The cross which now marks the spot bears the inscription: " Se hizo inmovil la Santa Imagen." A nunnery was founded near the spot, but in 976 the Benedictine monks took and held possession until the sacrilegious French blew up the convent with gunpowder in the beginning of the present century. Fortunately, the Black Virgin was not injured: it now occupies the most sacred spot in the chapel of the monastery at Montserrat. It is this image, black as tar, which draws thousands of pilgrims up the mountain; for it is the most sacred of all images, and works miraculous cures. It was a solemn scene, even for my Protestant eyes — the vast chapel, the thousand kneeling pilgrims, their forms shadowy and indistinct in the dim light, the deep notes of the organ swelling forth. The image stands high above the altar, framed in gold and precious stones, and thus has stood ten centuries. Every year during those ten centuries, thousands of believing pilgrims have knelt and prayed before that Black Image, which looks down on the kneeling figures of to-day as silent and inscrutable as it looked on its first group of worshippers a thousand years ago.

The ascent to San Geronimo, the topmost peak of the singular and prodigious mass of rock, is through a delightfully shaded gorge. Shade is so rare in Spain, even on mountain tops, that when it is encountered it must be noted. Near the summit of San Geronimo is a house where the traveller, fatigued and hungry from the climb, can obtain rest and food at prices wonderfully cheap considering the loneliness and height of the place. For one peseta (18½ cents) we got an omelette, a bottle of wine, and all the bread we could eat. On the top of Pike's Peak I paid a dollar for a cup of coffee and a ham sandwich. That is one difference between Pike's Peak and San Geronimo. Another difference is, that on Pike's Peak there is a prosaic signal officer, while the person we found in charge of San Geronimo was one of the prettiest of all the pretty girls we saw in Spain. Mack was so smitten he ordered a second omelette, not because he was hungry, but because he wanted an excuse to stay longer, and talk more with that beautiful girl. Mack thought he would never weary looking at her dark eyes and long lashes: his purse, however, could not endure the strain of ordering more omelettes, so he was forced to bring his homage to an end at the second one.

The view from San Geronimo embraces the plain as far as Barcelona, the blue Mediterranean, and even the faint outline of the Balearic Islands. When we descended the mountain on the way back to Barcelona, the road was literally thronged with the swarms of pilgrims toiling up the steep, zigzag path on their way to the shrine of the Black Virgin. There were peasant women staggering under bundles of bread and clothing. Some had flat loaves of bread three feet in diameter which they carried in front like a shield, or else thrust a pike through the centre and swung it over the shoulder. The men carried their own extra clothing; the women had to carry the provisions as well as their extra clothing. Sprinkled here and there in the dense throng were fine ladies with lace mantillas, quite as picturesque, but not quite so gaily dressed as the peasantry. The only place I ever saw to compare with this is the Pilgrim Church at Kiev, Russia: there, the pilgrims are as numerous and as strangely costumed, but the Russian scenery lacks the wild grandeur and massiveness which characterizes Montserrat.

The evening of our return to Barcelona, while at the table d'hôte of the Hotel Del Oriente, a surprise met us in the person of our head-waiter from Lisbon. He was no longer the awe-inspiring individual he had seemed in Lisbon. His swallow tail coat was gone, his spotless expanse of shirt front no longer aggressively stared at us, his demeanor was no longer pompous and overpowering; in short, our head-waiter was now a mere mortal like ourselves. He was on the way to Italy to visit his mother. During the several days he remained at the hotel waiting for his steamer, he sat next us at dinner, and, so far from being proud and haughty, he was meek and modest. Thus do the grand and mighty fall — even head-waiters. We noticed that when Pallavicini went away, the Hotel Oriente did not charge him for his stay, expecting by this hospitality to win the head-waiter's recommendation when he returns to his post in Lisbon. Another feature of interest at the table d'hôte, on our return from Montserrat, was a South American family consisting of father, mother, and daughter. Our Lisbon head-waiter said that the father had made money in Brazil, and had come to Barcelona to marry off his daughter. She was a beauty and an heiress, a combination that, no doubt, will speedily gain her a husband despite her table manners, very unlike the polite standard of Europe.

Mr. Lathrop in his book on Spain tells his reader that a journey in the Iberian Peninsula *may* be made on $60 a week, but that $100 had better be allowed. The guide books all speak of the "dear" Spanish hotels. This may be true of some fine hotels. We met an American lady who said she paid $10 a day at her Madrid hotel. Of course, we gave ten-dollar-a-day hotels a wide berth, and by seeking more modest quarters found travelling in Spain and Portugal as cheap as in any country of Europe. The best season for a trip to the Iberian Peninsula is, undoubtedly, early spring, though the seaport cities can be visited, without suffering from heat, in June or even July. Autumn and early winter, October and November, are also favorable seasons. The traveller will not see the glorious green, the flowers, the budding vines of March and April; but the rains will have cooled the parched earth, the grass will have lifted its blades, and he will have the pleasure of seeing a burned, parched country transformed into a verdant garden. If London be made the starting-point, Lisbon should be visited by steamer. The fare by steamer is $30, $10 less than second class railroad fare *via* Paris. Some steamers charge only $20. The Forwood steamers charge only £5 10s. first-class London to Gibraltar. From America, a Spanish trip can be best commenced from Gibraltar. The round trip from New York to Gibraltar costs $100.

CHAPTER XII

A Jump to Toulon — Bicycling along the Mediterranean — Nice — Monte Carlo — Facilities for Suicide — The Republic of Andorra — Stopped at the Frontier — Why Windows are Sham in Italy — We run over an Italian — The San Remo Druggist to the Emperor — Wheeling into Genoa

AT Port Bou, on the way from Barcelona to Toulon, the train entered a tunnel; when it came out again, the change was as great and as sudden as though made by an enchanter's wand. At one end of the tunnel there was nothing but Spanish; at the other end French was the language: there were French soldiers, French signs on the station walls; even the aspect of the land was different from that in Spain. To Americans, accustomed in their own land to travelling thousands of miles and finding ever the same language and people, nothing is more surprising than the complete change often effected by a five-minute ride in a European tunnel. Eighteen hours brought us to Marseilles, and two more to Toulon.

The exquisite beauties of the Riviera, beauties of nature heightened by the art of man, cannot be half appreciated by the railroad traveller, since the trains go so fast and are half the time in one or the other of the many tunnels that pierce the mountains lining this part of the Mediterranean. This fact had decided us to go by rail only as far as Toulon, thence, over the Corniche road on bicycles ordered from London. While waiting for the station master to find and unpack our machines which had arrived several days in advance, we donned bicycle suits, and sallied forth for a glimpse of the place where Napoleon planted his batteries and shelled the English, and where a bursting bomb scattered sand on Junot's letter and helped turn an innkeeper's son into a duke. Our knee-breeches and stocking-covered legs caused the Toulonese to stare and follow us about, which we thought odd, inasmuch as ours were by no means the only knickerbockers in town. The costumes of the peasants in the market were as comical in our eyes as we were in theirs. The Toulon market is on a narrow lane so crooked that the vendor of frogs' legs cannot see the vendor of mushrooms though their booths may be only a few yards apart. At the time of our visit, the lane was thronged with gaily dressed market-women and vivacious madames and mademoiselles who seemed to attach as much importance to the purchase of frogs' legs and Brussels sprouts as a minister of war attaches to the purchase of Krupp cannon — and why not ? The stomach is man's most vulnerable point ; when the stomach is wrong, all is wrong, — dyspepsia, melancholy, perhaps suicide. The French realize this, and look out as much for the stomach as they do for the Prussians. There were young misses with dancing eyes accompanying portly mammas to learn the art of marketing ; there were sour-visaged dyspeptics, and men and women fat and round, the result of too generous living — all with little baskets, all with sharp eyes, examining the stalls of the peasants, selecting the articles that go to make up a French dinner.

At one end of the crooked lane that is used as a market-place is France's greatest maritime arsenal. We tried to visit it, but were refused admission, which, in a small way, served to show how sensitive are the French since the German invasion. We had no difficulty in visiting Spain's chief arsenal at Cartegena, and subsequently were allowed to visit arsenals in Italy and England ; but in France we were obliged to take on faith the statement that the Toulon arsenal is one of the largest in the world.

When one takes a bicycle into the United States, it is good policy to first leave the machine out in the rain and get it muddy and rusty, since the forty-five per cent duty is levied ad valorem, and a dilapidated appearance secures a low valuation. This plan does not work in taking a bicycle into France, where the duty is higher the cheaper, poorer, muddier, your wheel is. The tax on a fine new machine, light and strong, is much less than that on a cheap machine, made of iron instead of steel, and worn and muddy instead of new and clean. This is because the French duty on bicycles is 1.20 francs per kilo (about twelve cents a pound) regardless of fineness or value. Our "Singer" safeties were of light steel, so that the duty on each amounted to only twenty-eight francs ($5.60). This we paid, taking a receipt to secure its return on passing out of France; then, having packed our bicycle bags with articles necessary for the journey, we shipped the rest of our luggage by rail to the Italian frontier, and set out on the high road for Nice and Monte Carlo.

French roads are famous the world over, and of all French roads the smoothest and best is that along the Mediterranean. There are hills, but the labor of climbing them is well repaid by the long and delightful coasts in descending them. The streets of Nice are broad and well paved. We rode through the Piazza Garibaldi early in the morning, and began the journey to Monte Carlo before the sun was high enough to make it hot. The first two kilometres were up a hill. On reaching the summit, we sat on the parapet, our feet dangling over the wall, the Mediterranean dashing against the rocks several hundred feet below, and Nice in the distance embowered in groves of tropical trees. The road, sometimes a shelf hewn out of the solid rock, sometimes a tunnel through the rock, is always near the sea; as we sped along, the roar of the surf was constantly in our ears. A bicycler whom we passed had a gun, and in a basket fastened in front on the luggage-carrier stood a dog that looked as if he enjoyed whisking along the Corniche road quite as much as his master. French roads are so smooth that bicycles are used by sportsmen, scouts, and couriers in the army.

We hurried on this portion of the trip because it was Saturday, and we wished to reach Monte Carlo before Sunday, supposing the Casino would be closed on the Sabbath. This was a mistake. The Casino is not closed on Sunday; on the contrary, the crowd is larger, the gambling more spirited on Sunday than on any other day of the week. Amateur gamblers flee from the little principality on the approach of summer; but the inveterates, the men and women to whom gambling is not a pastime, but a business — these are there summer and winter. It was a pitiful sight to see old ladies, their gray hair hanging down in long corkscrew curls, fingering stacks of napoleons, eying anxiously every movement of the man at the wheel which makes or mars their fortune. There were fat, coarse Russians, excitable French and Italians, imperturbable, phlegmatic Germans; there were two young women dressed as fine as duchesses; near them were kitchen maids from a Nice hotel. Monte Carlo is a democratic leveller — prince and peasant jostle elbows at the green covered table. The chambermaid of our hotel at Nice was there, occasionally playing, but usually merely looking on, for the reason that one turn of the wheel was enough, as a rule, to transfer her little pile from her side of the table to that of the croupier. The smallest sum played is five francs.

As a general thing the stakes are small, not more than the minimum of five francs. We saw one man, however, who never played less than 1000 francs. Sometimes he staked as much as 5000. During the half-hour we watched him he lost 75,000 francs. He did this by placing several 5000-franc stakes in rapid succession on the same square or number. Had the wheel favored him, he would have won thirty-six times the amount risked. But it did not favor him, so he lost a fortune in less than an hour. Each time his stack of glittering gold disappeared behind the croupier's rake, the player took from a big pocket-book five 1000-franc notes, changed them into gold napoleons, and put them on the same number without a word, without a sign, except that, as his losses became larger and larger, beads of perspiration broke out on his forehead. When the wheel went slower and slower, he would look away as if the strain of watching was painful. His losses were made known to him by the impassive voice of the croupier calling the winning number. Then the heavy player would mop the beads of sweat from his brow, pull out the pocket-book with the 1000-franc notes, and go on losing.

The entire Principality of Monte Carlo can be explored in an hour. The high rock juts out into the sea, a promontory with cliffs whence one can easily take a leap of from one to two hundred feet. This is so neat a method of self-extinction it is strange that suicides do not select it in preference to the commoner method of the revolver, which scatters blood and brains over the beautiful garden.

Monaco's history is not uninteresting. After the upheavals of the French Revolution it was annexed to France, but the Allies in 1814 re-established the principality, and Honoré IV., detained in Paris by illness, sent his son to take possession. The Prince had proceeded as far as Cannes when Napoleon's grenadiers, just landed from Elba, stopped his carriage and announced that the Emperor thought Monaco could manage to worry along as a part of France. It did during the Hundred Days; then Napoleon went to St. Helena, and once more the rock called Monaco set up in business for itself. The natural scenery was as beautiful then as now, but all the world did not flock to it then as now. There was no chance in those days for people to lose a fortune in half an hour and commit suicide as there has been since that day thirty years ago when M. Blanc arrived from Nice with 1,700,000 francs in a black satchel. M. Blanc pointed to the satchel, then to his watch.

"'The train returns to Nice at three,' said he, 'and I must return with it.'"

It was a short time for determining so large a matter, but M. Blanc declared he could not wait; it must be yes or no by three o'clock. The 1,700,000 francs were too tempting. When M. Blanc had finished his lunch and returned for his answer it was "Yes." The black satchel with its precious contents was left in Monaco; in its place M. Blanc carried back to Nice the franchise to establish and conduct a gambling Casino at Monte Carlo. M. Blanc's amazing success has stimulated other gamblers to seek places in which to establish gilded Casinos, but thus far Monte Carlo has no rival. In a lonely but picturesque part of the Pyrenees between the confines of France and Spain is the little republic of Andorra. At present no railroad penetrates to this remote and primitive place; it is reached by days of climbing along rugged mountain paths. There is no post, no telegraph, no stage. The people are poor and completely cut off from the world, but they are contented, and when a second M. Blanc appeared with offers of wealth and railroads and telegraphs in exchange for the privilege of establishing a gambling Casino, the senators of the little republic declined the offers after only an hour's reflection. To them gold could not replace peace and quiet and contented consciences as it has done in Monte Carlo, the inhabitants of which pay no taxes, yet receive the benefits of gardens, free concerts, entertainments, and public improvements on a scale unsurpassed even in Paris, where citizens pay handsomely for the improvements around them.

We left Monte Carlo at seven in the morning; twenty-five minutes down hill at the rate of twenty miles an hour brought us to Mentone. There is not much to see in Mentone, and we did not intend to stop there, but on a bicycle trip one often does things one does not intend or wish to do. We not only stopped at Mentone; we stayed a day there. We had passed through the town and were half way up the winding slope beyond when we saw soldiers skulking in the bushes both above and below the road.

"Queer place for soldiers to be loafing," said Mack. "What are they doing?"

"Nothing, unless eying us be called something."

Half a mile further at the summit of the hill, just as we were getting ready for a grand coast, a man stepped out of a small house on the road-side and ordered us to halt. The man was a soldier, but not uniformed like those we had passed. He was an Italian, and his hut was on the boundary line between France and Italy. We were told that before stepping across that line, or rather before wheeling across it, 168 lire ($33.60) must be paid as duty on the two bicycles. This was unpleasant, it was still more unpleasant when the officers said they knew nothing of the 56 francs that were to be refunded on taking the wheels out of France. That, they said, must be attended to by the French officers at Mentone. It is odd how much more careful nations are to keep wealth out than to let it in. Bicycles are things which people desire, yet the government which let us take our two bicycles out of France without a word gave a great deal of trouble when we attempted to take them back again. The soldiers we had seen skulking in the bushes, when they saw us returning from the Italian line, stepped out on the road, halted us, and demanded payment of duty.

"But we have already paid for bringing these machines into France. That is why we are returning. We want our money back."

The soldiers said that we might or might not have just left France; that did not concern them; they were there to prevent bicycles entering France until the duty was paid.

"It strikes me," said I, "that we are between the devil and the deep sea. The Italians stop us at the top of the hill, the French halt us at the bottom. The quickest and cheapest way out of the trouble will be to dump our bicycles over the parapet into the sea."

Mack refused to adopt this plan; he argued with the

soldiers, showed our French customs receipt, and finally induced them to permit us to cross the line and proceed, escorted by a soldier, to Mentone. In this inglorious fashion, on foot and under guard, did we re-enter the town we had left with flying colors one short hour before. Arrived at the custom house, the chief refused to refund the duty because the amount was not specified. Our receipt showed that we had introduced into France 48⅓ kilos of bicycle at the rate of 1.20 francs per kilo. It was not difficult to calculate the amount thus paid; we even offered to make the calculation, but the chief smilingly insinuated that, though figures will not lie, liars will figure. It might be easy to multiply 48⅓ by 1.20, and the result might be 58; it was not for him, the chief, to deny arithmetic; all *he* knew was that our receipt said, not that we had paid 58 francs but that we had paid 1.20 francs on 48⅓ kilos, which to his official mind was a very different thing. He further intimated that inasmuch as we had gone up the hill as far as the Italian hut, which was across the frontier, we ought to be thankful that another 58 francs had not been exacted on re-entering France. We did not feel at all thankful; on the contrary, we used some emphatic language and started off to find Mr. Clericy, the American Consul. The rest of the day was spent between that gentleman's office and the Custom House; finally after a world of words, after telegraphing to Paris, after more time and trouble than the matter was worth, we received the 58 francs and set out again for Italy. The Italian duty on a bicycle is 84 lire ($16.80), regardless of weight or value. We paid this amount at the little hut at the top of the hill, then mounted our wheels and coasted almost the entire way to Ventimiglia.

Ventimiglia (Italian for twenty miles), so named because it is twenty miles from any point that distance away, is where the traveller by train enters Italy, and where he not only has to submit to an inspection of luggage, but where he must begin paying for every pound not carried in the hand. The result of this system is that people carry in the coupés the greater part of their luggage; the result of this is a class of "facchini" (porters), because, when you carry so many boxes and bundles, assistance is necessary in getting in and out of the cars. The facchino is at every train, and for a trifle carries your valise to the station door, but no further; his "territory" ends with the railroad station, and if you want your luggage carried to a hotel, a city facchino takes it from the door of the depot. Another study in cause and effect is afforded by the sham windows so often seen in Italy; some of these shams have figures of persons painted in them as though looking out of the window or reading a book. The sham window results from the heavy tax on real windows. The more windows you have in Italy, the more tax; hence in Italy people try to make painted imitations of light and air do for the real article.

The examination and re-shipment of our luggage to Genoa detained us at Ventimiglia until nine o'clock, nevertheless we pushed on to San Remo the same night. The stretch of road along the surf-washed beach is perfectly level, the moon was bright, the air cool, we sped along swiftly, silently as phantoms; the villagers who sat in their doorways started up with cries of astonishment, but on we flew through Bordighera, through several small towns to San Remo. In winter San Remo is thronged with tourists and invalids from all parts of the world; the Emperor Frederic stopped here, and a druggist from whom Frederic's valet bought a bottle of hair oil has this sign on his window: "Apothecary to his Imperial and Royal Majesty the German Emperor and Prussian King." In summer there are no emperors, no invalids, no tourists, hence the hotels are closed; when Mack and I rolled into the quaint old place at ten o'clock at night we had trouble finding quarters.

We were surprised at one thing demonstrated by our bicycle trip; though the Riviera is thronged every winter by thousands of tourists the effect is not apparent beyond the centres where travellers stop. There is nothing primitive about Nice, Monte Carlo, Cannes, and the score of other places on the Riviera frequented by the pleasure-seekers of the world; but within five miles of any of those places may be seen as simple and unsophisticated a folk as can be found in the heart of Italy.

In Riva Ligue, a village only a few miles from San Remo, the people stared at us as if they had never seen a bicycle or as though we were wild men from Borneo. They blocked the street in front of the little café where we stopped, and asked questions that evinced the most extravagant ideas of the capabilities of the bicycle; one wanted to know if it could make fifty miles an hour. Before we could reply another villager answered, "Of course it could. A man had gone to Paris on one in a day, beating the fastest train." As the distance to Paris was some six hundred miles, this not only beat the fastest train, but the "records" which bicycle manufacturers advertise for their machines — a thing that cannot be done except in the imagination of an Italian peasant. In Italian cities reading appears to be well-nigh universal. The cab and omnibus drivers read between trips, the baker has his newspaper in his pocket and reads while the bread is baking. Shop girls, servant girls in hotels, clerks in stores, may be seen devouring papers and romances. In the country and small villages one seldom sees signs of this fondness for reading.

Every few miles the Riviera road passes through a village, and we usually stopped in each one to see the people and satisfy the thirst hard riding created. The wine was cheap, only fourteen cents a fiasco of three-fourths of a gallon, and being so new it was not at all intoxicating. Later, after returning from Egypt, we passed again through this district and drank the new wine as it flowed from the press. Wine connoisseurs would refuse to drink this unfermented grape juice, but we found it cool and refreshing and preferred it to more costly Bordeaux. The next halt after San Remo was Albenga, a village of five thousand inhabitants, like the other Riviera towns, hemmed in by mountains on one side and by the Mediterranean on the other.

Genoa was to be our next station, and as the distance was ninety kilometers, we left Albenga at four in the morning. A few miles out from the town we saw a smoke rising from a thicket a little to one side of the road; on seeking the cause, we discovered an organ-grinder and his family. The wife was peeling potatoes, the husband was on his knees blowing the fire; the rest of the family was in an old shawl on which Mack came near sitting, supposing it a mere bundle of rags. The woman dropped her potatoes with a shriek and made a desperate grab for her *bambino*, which by lusty yells forthwith made clear that it belonged to the order of animate, not inanimate, things. It was an interesting group, so we tarried even though not allowed to sit on the baby. While the wife stirred her stew of potatoes, cabbage, and garlic, the husband narrated his nomadic life in pretty plain English.

"You see," said he, "I make four years in England and ten in America. I like America, but it not good for my business. England pretty good. Inglese not give much, but every time you come they give. In New Yorka you come once, very good; you come second time, make you move on or calla policeman. Roads in America bad. You leave town, you get deep mud."

"How long since you left America?" we asked.

"Oh, long time. I go away year after Henry George made President."

Further questioning failed to shake this statement; he was positive the great land-reformer had been elected President. He had never heard of Benjamin Harrison (yet had been naturalized and voted), he knew Henry George was President and established in the White House because he had seen him come out of that historic mansion, had seen him pause before his

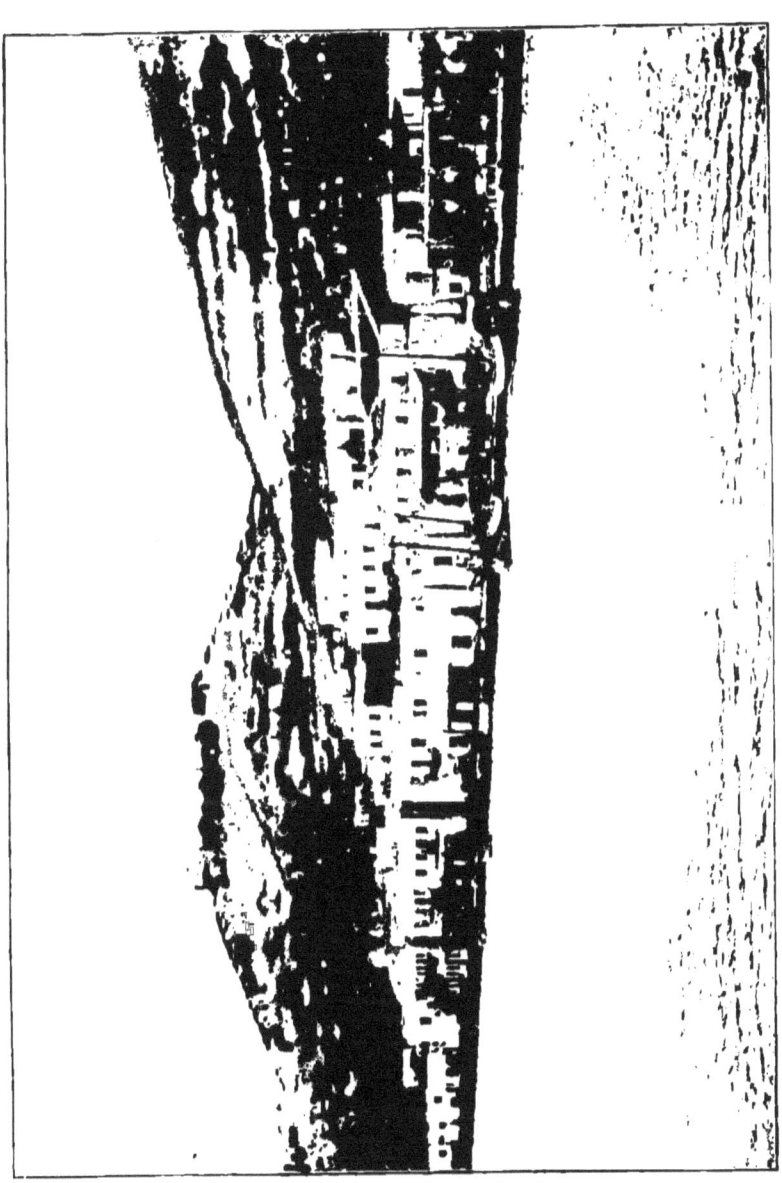

HARBOR OF ZEA

organ, and after listening to a tune, the great man had thrown him a dollar. Who but a big man, a high man like the President, would give a dollar, a whole dollar, only to hear one tune? "Common man," said the organ-grinder, "giva five centa, maybe only two centa, but President giva whole dollar." Of course this argument was convincing, and we yielded the point, especially when it was corroborated by the organ-grinder's giving us a fairly accurate description of Mr. George's personal appearance, as he came out of the White House, as he stood before the organ, as he threw the dollar; it was the only time a dollar was ever given him, and the organ-grinder remembered every detail connected with that great event. The organ-grinder said he liked his Bohemian life, which leaves him free to go whither he will. A sort of hammock underneath the cart holds his baby and clothing and provisions. Wife and baby are his world; the three stroll about the earth, sleeping on the ground in summer, in hay-lofts in winter, with never a care or thought except to get centimes enough to furnish food and raiment, both of the cheapest quality; never a thought of the world's agitation, of the oppressions which all over America as well as Europe have filled the heart of Labor with discontent, disquiet, and in too many cases a bitter desire to wreak revenge, to make a chaos out of which labor shall rise and reap its just reward. This man was happy; I have never seen a happy anarchist.

When the breakfast of bread sopped in the potato and garlic stew was over, this Italian disciple of Henry George ground out all the tunes on his organ, while Mack and I lay stretched on the grass, looking at the blue Italian sky, wondering if, after all, this fellow's idea of happiness was not wiser than that of the politician, the millionnaire, the speculator who schemes and worries — for what? To gain power that is brief, to accumulate millions for spendthrift heirs to dissipate! This incident on the Riviera reminded me of another organ-grinder whom I once met in London. A woman was turning the crank of an organ on which in large letters was this sign : —

> "I AM THE VISCOUNT HINTON, SON OF THE EARL OF PERTH; DISINHERITED FOR NO FAULT OF MINE, I TAKE THIS METHOD OF EARNING A LIVELIHOOD."

"It is not possible," said I to my companion, "that that woman is the viscount?"

"No," said a well-dressed man standing near, "I am the viscount," with which he lifted his hat, made us a courtly bow, and extended a silver saucer. A notice on the organ stated that donations of less than sixpence were not expected. Nevertheless we each ventured to give the noble mendicant a penny, and he made an obeisance which could not have been more graceful had we given a pound instead of a penny apiece.

In one of the villages we passed on the Riviera was a tablet on a wall in memory of some of the villagers who had belonged to Garibaldi's "Thousand," and who lost their lives fighting for the independence of Italy. We stopped to take a note of the inscription, which action seemed highly gratifying to the crowd that collected. They construed it as evidence that we appreciated their patriot townsmen, and were eager to be of service. One insisted on holding the bicycles; another, an old, gray-haired man, wanted us to wait until he got a large sheet of paper so we could copy all the names.

"They were heroes," he said, pointing to the names carved on the tablet. "I knew them all; we were boys together in this very village; but they died, died years ago with Garibaldi."

An incident half an hour later in the next village was not so pleasant. We were bowling along at a rather rapid rate through the one long and narrow street, ringing our bells to warn pedestrians out of the way, when suddenly one of the numerous idlers, standing in the doorways watching us, took it in his head to see if he could stop a bicycle and stepped into the middle of the road too late for us to stop or turn aside.

The front wheel of my machine knocked him flat. Fearing he was badly hurt, we turned to see what we could do to assist. To our joy, we saw the fellow was not injured; he jumped up, shook his fist angrily, and started after us. Several others joined in the pursuit, hurling threats, and shaking their fists. A few vigorous strokes on the pedals got the wheels revolving rapidly, and in five minutes the fleetest of our pursuers were left breathless and out of sight.

Although the road along the Riviera is smooth and solid, bicyclers cannot make "fancy" speed because of the hills and curves. Some of the latter are so sharp coasting is possible only with a firm hand on the brake and at not more than a fivemile gait. Lose control of the brake, and you may be hurled five hundred feet into the sea. Threading along this shelf of a road, towering mountains above, dizzy depths below, gives a zest to the trip, but it makes it a trifle slow. Nine o'clock at night found us still ten miles from Genoa. While speeding along in the dark, the moon not yet up, we saw in the distance a fiery glow which grew more and more lurid and from which came a loud rumbling and roaring. Diverging from the road to investigate, we found the light came through the open doors and windows of an enormous rail mill. The noise was that of the steel bars as they were forced hissing and hot through the rollers that pressed them into shape. When we rolled up out of the darkness and stopped before the door of the great foundry, the workmen seemed as surprised as if two gnomes had sprung from the earth. The bar mill rollers said they earn only a dollar a day. If to protection, not to natural resources, greater scarcity of labor, greater supply of land, strong labor unions, is due the higher wages of iron workers in America, why has not the same cause produced the same effect in Italy? Why are bar mill rollers paid three times more in England where they are *not* protected than in Italy where they *are*?

These were the conundrums suggested by that Italian rolling mill on the last hour's ride to Genoa.

CHAPTER XIII

Genoa — Motieri tells a story — A Day in the Tyrol — Perigarde reappears — Loss of his "Soul's Mate" — Bicycling to Rome — Monte Oliveto — A Thirteenth Century Monastery — Triumphal Entry into San Quirico — Radicafani's Peak — Our Bicycles mistaken for Tram Cars — Excitement of the Peasants — Inglorious Conclusion of the Bicycle Trip

IN Genoa we had pleasant quarters at the Hotel Smith. The proprietor, an Englishman born in Genoa, is a member of the city council, and as thoroughly identified with the place as any Italian. His hotel looks on the sea; from our windows we could see the bay with its ships from all parts of the world, and a little to the left the building now used as a custom house, but which centuries ago was the office of the first bank known to the world, the bank to which Columbus sent his son with the notice that he meant to give one-tenth of his income to the poor. At night the view of the bay with its hundreds of ship lights twinkling like so many stars made a scene not easily forgotten. One day we heard a loud talking and shouting in front of the hotel; looking out of the window, we saw a man surrounded by a crowd of vociferous Italians shouting "Viva Imbriani," — "Down with the Government!" The man was Imbriani, a radical member of the Italian Congress, and the yelling people were some of his enthusiastic supporters. What would be done in Germany should any man cry out "Down with the Government?"

Each morning we hired a small boat and spent an hour rowing on the water. Our boatman told us of the prison at Onegli, where the prisoners must pump water day and night to keep from drowning.

"How is that possible? They must sleep some time."

"Maybe a few minutes; but if they sleep long, the waters come up and drown them."

Motieri said only the worst criminals are sent to Onegli; such, for instance, as those who pour kerosene on their wives and children, then put them in a hot stove to burn.

Our boat trips always wound up with a swim, which invariably brought us in conflict with the officers of the octroi. Our bundle of wet towels was examined; had it contained a loaf of bread or a dozen eggs, duty would have been exacted. Think of a country where one cannot come back from a swim without an officious fellow going through one's pockets and bundles! Our kodak always caused trouble. Often has an octroi guard stopped a tram car and kept twenty passengers waiting while we explained that our black leather case contained a photographic apparatus which could not be opened without being ruined.

At Genoa a telegram came from Perigarde, telling us to await him: we decided to do so at Riva, a little town in the Austrian Tyrol. Nowhere on Como are there such tremendous precipices as line the western side of Lake Garda. At places the bluffs rise almost perpendicularly three thousand feet above the water's level; on the summits of these lofty cliffs hang little towns and villages. At other places water-falls dash down narrow gorges, occasionally disappearing through subterranean passages, then reappearing and leaping hundreds of feet over the cliffs into the cold, blue water of the lake. For three hours the steamer glided along within a stone's-throw of the base of this gigantic precipice, the lake becoming narrower as we advanced, until finally it came to a point at the town of Riva. We did not have long to wait for Perigarde. The next day's steamer brought him, looking quite forlorn.

"How good of you to wait for me," he said. "I did not expect it; I do not deserve it."

Perigarde's appearance appealed to us; he was thinner, his

vivacity was subdued. Always open and candid as a child when questioned he let out his trouble — not at that minute, but that evening in the garden in front of our hotel. The dear fellow admitted he had played the fool. Said he:

"From the moment you left me at the Café Suizo, Granada, at one o'clock that Sunday morning until I telegraphed you at Genoa, I was in a foolish dream. From the Café Suizo I went to my room, but not to sleep. I could not sleep; I had but one thought, one hope — to find *her*. Her face was before me, not six inches from mine — how could I sleep? You cold-blooded fellows can't understand this; you grin and deride — don't deny it; you *do*. No matter, it is all true, all real. I walked the streets, looked at every window — *her* face was at none. I went to the opera, but *she* did not appear again. I lost all appetite. Am I not wasted? [The poor fellow really was wasted.] Do not my clothes hang on my bones? [They really did.] Fate has been very unkind to me; she gave me a glimpse of heaven only to snatch me away to darkness and despair. This went on days and weeks, yet I never gave up, never ceased to seek the one woman I knew ought to be mine."

"My dear boy," said Mack, with tender sympathy, "none of us find the woman who ought to be ours."

"But I did find her," broke out poor Perigarde; "I found her, yes, I found her, I saw her face to face, I talked with her, I looked into her eyes, — it was like looking into Heaven, — but alas, she is lost to me forever!"

We did not press him, we gave him time to recover; and after a while he let out the whole story. While forlornly wandering in the gardens of the Alhambra, he was suddenly confronted with the "mate of his soul" — she was sitting on a bench composedly reading a novel. A cherub of a child and its nurse were playing near by; a word from her lips in purest English emboldened him to address her. She was affable, charming, radiant, everything a "soul's mate" ought to be until — until a big, tawny-bearded fellow in a red coat came up, whom she called William and mentioned as her husband Captain B. of the British army. The cherub child was called to mamma, and the bold captain, the cherub child, the nurse, and the "soul's mate" disappeared forever from Perigarde's sight.

After the excursion to Riva, we returned to Genoa, and there Perigarde separated from us again; not being a bicycler, he took the train to Rome, while Mack and I resumed our journey on the machines. It was not long, however, before we also took the train, as the road was too rocky and the ascent too continuous and steep to make bicycling pleasant. The next day at Pisa, after visiting the baptistery and cathedral and climbing the leaning tower where five years before an American lady mistook me for an Italian brigand, we made another bicycle start and came to another inglorious conclusion. We had not proceeded a hundred yards from the leaning tower when a policeman made us dismount because it is against the law to ride bicycles in Pisa. We had to push our wheels through the city to the eastern gate, — a distance of a mile. No policeman interfered with us outside the gate; cycling, however, was as impossible outside as inside the gate, because of a new layer of cobble-stones that had just been spread on the Florence road. We were disgusted at the outlook and jumped on the first train for Sienna, from which point I was acquainted with the road all the way to Rome, having once made the journey on foot.[1]

On the whole, it was well we took the train. Sienna is thirteen hundred feet above the sea, and even with good roads the climb would be irksome. As it was, we landed there from the cars fresh and strong, ready to enjoy the glorious coast down the other side of the mountain. Almost the entire distance to Buonconvento was made with our feet on the rests, the bicycles propelling themselves by their own momentum and

[1] See Chapter VII., "A Tramp Trip."

gravity. Such a ride, perched upon the top of an airy machine, speeding along without moving hand or foot, is almost as exhilarating as I imagine flying to be. It was a very different matter after Buonconvento, when the ascent of Monte Oliveto began. Despite the good road, we had to walk most of the way, so steep and winding was the grade.

There is a proverb that " Italia e il giardino del mondo, e Toscania e il giardino d' Italia " — " Italy is the garden of the world, and Tuscany is the garden of Italy." The latter would never be inferred from a visit to Monte Oliveto; the surrounding country looks bleak and sterile, the mountain itself is seamed with great rifts and ravines. The huge monastery, erected six centuries ago by the Benedictine monks, stands on an isolated ridge of the mountain; the sides of this ridge tumble precipitously into deep and gloomy cañons. A drawbridge spans one of the cañons at its narrowest part, and it is here, and here alone, that one can reach the monastery. Few forts or castles are so inaccessible, so adapted for resisting hostile approach. It was some time — long after the vast pile was visible — before we found the drawbridge, and threaded our way through the maze of courts and passages to the immense door upon which we hammered and pounded, trying to arouse the inmates. It was now night, and besides being fatigued and hungry, at that lofty elevation we shivered with cold. By dint of much exercise on the door, our presence was made known, there was a rattling of bolts and bars, the big iron key turned in the lock, and we were admitted into what proved to be the kitchen — a huge room with pots and kettles once used in preparing the food of hundreds of monks, but now hanging idly against the walls and from the blackened rafters, of no use to the one solitary priest who remains since the suppression of the monastery a few years ago. The fireplace is as big as an ordinary room; on each of its sides, and well under the chimney, was a bench. We sat on one of those benches, enjoying the grateful warmth of a brush fire, while the servant went off for the "Abate." When the Abate came, he lowered our spirits to zero by saying we could not stay in the monastery; the rule was rigid that no one could remain without a permit from Sienna, and we would have to go.

"But whither are we to go?" said Mack, despairingly. "It is night, and we are nearly dead with fatigue and cold."

"It is painful, distressing," said the venerable Abate, "but the rule is —"

"Father, rules are made for men, not men for rules. Besides, there is no other place on this mountain to which we can go."

The Abate Gaetano Negro is a good man. He has dwelt on top of Monte Oliveto fifty years, and no doubt in all that time has striven to tread the narrow path of right and duty. The rules said, "Turn these young men away." Humanity said, "Take them in." Humanity won the day. A supper of eggs, bread, and wine was served; then the Abate conducted us to one of the hundreds of rooms in the rambling pile, and left us to dreams and slumber. Next morning the Abate informed us that a two days' stay was no greater violation of the rules than a one day's stay, hence we were welcome to remain another night; in the meantime, he would show us the old monastery, and then we could roam about the mountain. This invitation was gladly accepted. It was like spending a couple of days in the thirteenth century; for on Monte Oliveto, rambling through the courts and halls of that ancient monastery, it is easy to imagine oneself transported back to the Middle Ages. In the cellars the Abate pointed with pride to casks of olive oil that had been pressed the winter before in the monastery.

"Stick your finger in — so," he said, suiting the action to the word, then withdrawing his finger and thrusting it in his mouth as if it were delicious. We followed his example, and though neither of us liked the taste of raw oil, the Abate so evidently expected favorable criticism, that we smiled and tried to look as pleased as if he had given us sugar candy. Then he took us to another cask; this time we stuck our fingers in very gingerly, only the tip ends, and tried to get as little as possible. After the third cask, we could not maintain even this pretence, and begged the good Abate to excuse us. I think from that moment he concluded we were western barbarians. The Abate takes a personal and professional pride in his olive oil; it seems to him as if something is wanting, something wrong, when a man is unable to enthuse over it as some do over fine wines. After the visit to the cellars, and after viewing the celebrated frescos in the cloisters, we started for a climb to the village of Chiusure, the Roman Clusurium, on the very summit of the mountain, on a peak overlooking the ancient monastery. A red-cheeked peasant girl whom we overtook on the way was driving an ass loaded with brushwood and faggots.

"I suppose on this mountain you need fires even in summer," said Mack, trying to be agreeable. The red-cheeked girl made no reply, but redoubled her attention to the ass and the faggots. "Is it always as cold as this?" essayed Mack again; this time the girl's whole face grew red, she cast her eyes down, but answered not a word. "It is singular," said Mack in English to me; "why can't this girl understand my Italian — first time I have made a complete failure. Let us see where she lives."

Entering an ancient gate, we followed the girl with the donkey and the brushwood through a narrow alley to the door of a dingy hovel. The donkey and the girl entered the hovel; so did we, and found ourselves in the presence of a pleasant-faced woman, who as soon as we explained matters laughed, and told us why the girl would not speak.

"'Teresa," said she, "has a lover in the army. The last thing he said to her before he left was never to speak to any young man. Teresa loves Gerati and does what he tells her. But you needn't count them," added the woman to the red-cheeked girl; "they are not the sort of young men Gerati meant. They are not Italians. You may speak."

Although the embargo was thus raised by her liberal mamma the red-cheeked Teresa continued tongue-tied, and we departed to pay other visits. In the next house was a withered old woman sitting with her feet over a small bowl of hot ashes; in her hand was a bunch of hemp which she was twisting into twine. The poor woman said that her husband earns only fifty centesimi a day working in the fields; the woman does not make even that pittance, and the two are in part dependent on the town. We gave her two lire (about thirty-eight cents), which so upset her that she put up her twine and hemp and started out to tell the town of the good fortune that had befallen her and of the two "Milords" in knee breeches who gave away lire as others gave away centesimi. The result of this was that the rest of our visit to Chiusure was in the nature of an ovation. The villagers turned out *en masse*, we were invited into the houses, and bonfires of brushwood were burned in our honor. We dispensed smiles to the women, coppers to the children, and salutes to the men, and for one brief hour realized what it was to feel like nabobs. At the end of the hour we were ready enough to come down from that high estate, not because the elation was unpleasant, but because it was expensive, even when paid for in coins of as little value as the Italian centesimo. There were altogether too many children in Chiusure for us successfully to continue the role of English Milords or American Vanderbilts.

On returning to the monastery, the Abate Negro proved himself not unlike the friar who at first refused Ivanhoe entertainment, but who finally admitted him to a sumptuous repast. The good Abate had already admitted us within the monastery; on our return from Chiusure we found he had also prepared a sumptuous supper. There were eggs, a fiasco of wine, lettuce salad, and two roasted pigeons. As we disposed of this appetizing supper, the Abate laughed, told stories, and even perpetrated two puns, one on my name, which he said should be Winter Weather (not "Amenotempo," merry weather), since I had brought such extraordinary weather considering the season; the other pun was on Napoleon, who, said the Abate, should have been called "Mala-parte," instead of Buonaparte. These puns the good Abate enjoyed fully as much as we did. Next morning, on visiting the library, the reason of the "Mala-parte" pun became apparent; Napoleon had despoiled the library of its choicest books. Only a few thousand unimportant volumes now remain. In the chapel we saw a rude image of Christ carved in the eleventh century by a soldier of Barbarossa. It was hung in its present position in 1320. The Abate said that this image is the most sacred in the monastery. The scene in the church after viewing the relics in the chapel seemed to us pathetic — of all the hundreds of monks who once inhabited the place, only the venerable Abate remains. As we sat in the rear of the dimly lighted nave, looking at the old man going through the ceremonies of the mass attended by his one solitary servitor, his cook, valet, waiter, acolyte, all in one, he seemed more like a spirit, a vision of the past, than a living reality. On bidding the old man good-bye, I said we were so delighted with the monastery that we should undoubtedly pay it another visit and see him again.

"You may revisit the monastery," replied the venerable Abate with a smile, "but you will not see me again unless it be in Paradise. I am old, and my end is near at hand."

Twelve of the eighteen miles to San Quirico were covered in less than an hour; the remaining six miles took more than two hours, because instead of having a down grade that we could fly over like a breeze it was mostly up hill; also because half-way up a long slope we encountered a drove of long-horned, fierce cattle. The road was narrow and at that point walled in on both sides; leaping to the ground, we lifted the bicycles, turned them around, and were in the saddles again scarcely a moment too soon to escape the bulls as they came pawing and bellowing down the hill. As soon as they saw us, they lowered their heads and made a rush, but vigorous pedalling and a steep downgrade sent us forward like a shot ; in five minutes we were at the bottom of the hill, and in a few minutes more had reached a roadside blacksmith shop, where we took refuge and watched the herd of bulls as they dashed by, their drivers galloping frantically about, shouting and cracking their whips. This episode might have proved serious had we been going down instead of up hill. The bicycles could not have been stopped and reversed so quickly, nor could we have retreated up the hill fast enough to escape the long horns of our pursuers. During the remainder of the trip, we kept a sharp lookout for droves of cattle, and when a cloud of dust indicated their approach, we dismounted and sought a refuge until the danger was over.

When the bulls had passed, we set out again for San Quirico, and arrived there tired enough after the wild and exciting ride and the double trip up the hill — mountain one may say ; for, like many of the towns in Italy, San Quirico is situated on a lofty height overlooking the plain for twenty miles around. A group of loungers outside the walls, who saw us toiling up the steep ascent, spread the news that two " Inglesi " were coming on " tram-cars," and by the time we reached the gate, a curious crowd was there to receive us. Our entry was in the nature of a triumphal procession. A body of men and women went in advance to spread the news, another surrounded us staring at the machines, while still another brought up the rear. The narrow street was thronged ; women hearing the noise, rushed to the doors and windows and joined the procession, which thus grew larger and larger. When finally we reached the albergo and disappeared within its friendly doors, the crowd still lingered in front of the hotel to discuss the " mad Inglesi " and if possible catch another glimpse of their wonderful " tram-cars."

While sitting on the bench under the hotel's big chimney — our usual resort to avoid too rapid checking of perspiration — I observed that the old woman who was preparing our dinner over the brush fire before us, eyed me closely. Presently she said: —

"Questa non e la prima volta che siete stato qui?" (This is not the first time you have been here?)

"No, signora."

"Siete venuto a piedi — you have come here before on foot, a pack on your back?"

"Si, signora."

"I knew it was you," she cried, dropping the ladle with which she was stirring our soup, "I knew it was you; you stopped here, you sat in that very spot, in this very fireplace," and the good woman grasped my hand and shook it warmly. An American pedestrian is no common sight in Italy; although five years had elapsed, my visit was not forgotten. The fact that one of the "mad Inglesi" was the Signor americano who had walked into San Quirico on his way from Rome to Florence heightened their interest. A young carpenter who was among the dozen or so who had ventured to follow us into the village albergo begged us to go with him after dinner to his brother's café. The shrewd carpenter knew our drawing powers and was not disappointed. The crowd that followed us into his brother's café spent enough money to a dozen times repay the padrone for the coffee and liqueurs which he insisted on our taking gratuitously. One of the men pointed to me and said to his companion: —

"That's the one who walked here from Rome. Old Mariana recognized him. He stopped at her albergo before."

"Then," replied the companion, "he must be madder than the other. It is madder to walk than to ride on a tram-car."

The crowd eyed us and discussed our knee breeches and legs in the same artless, candid way in which visitors at the circus comment on the deformities of the fat man and the living skeleton. This ovation at San Quirico beguiled us into remaining longer than was wise; for although the distance to Radicofani, where we were to spend the night, was only eighteen miles, it was a six-hour ride, owing to the steepness and ruggedness of the road. Radicofani, one of the quaintest villages in Italy, is perched on a barren rock three thousand feet high. We saw it the moment we passed through San Quirico's southern gate; under the clear Italian sky it appeared only a short way off, but night came and found us still pushing slowly up the dizzy height. When at last we reached the summit and passed through the gate, the town was wrapped in darkness and slumber. There is no regular "albergo" in Radicofani, but one of the villagers has a spare room and entertains the few strangers who chance to stop in the town. To find this house unaided is difficult in the daytime, at night it is impossible, so there was nothing for us to do but to pound on the first door we came to and ask for a guide to the Hotel Dante — that is the high-sounding name which the villager gives his house, though no sign informs the traveller. I had learned it on my first visit five years before.

It is difficult to understand how a living can be earned in such a town as Radicofani. The peak is too rocky and barren to grow even weeds, and the labor of descending to the valley in the morning and ascending to the village at night is hard enough of itself to form a day's work. The Radicofanites, however, make this fatiguing climb and work all day in the fields besides. One family we visited lived in a cellar, the rent of which was seventy-five cents a month. The wife gathers brushwood in the valley, the husband works in the fields for one lire (nineteen cents) a day. Their replies to my questions enabled me to make the following table showing

Condition of Family living in Italian Peasant Village.

Family consists of father, mother, three children, two, three, and six years old; six-year-old child cares for two babies during day when the mother and father are in the valley:—

Earnings of father, field labor, six months in year........	$29.64
" " " odd jobs, estimated...............	14.82
	$44.46
" " mother, cutting brushwood...............	40.56
Total yearly income...........................	$85.02
Cost of living:—	
Rent	$ 9.48
Food (bread, macaroni, garlic, occasionally a little cheese, and wine).....................................	64.90
Other expenses, including clothing..................	10.64
	$85.02

Eighteen cents is a small amount with which to buy a day's food-supply for five persons, yet even that pitiful amount is more than many families have. One cannot get terrapin soup or fried frog legs in Radicofani; in fact, one cannot get much of anything. When we asked the padrone of the Albergo Dante for milk, he went out and brought back about a thimbleful, apologizing for the smallness of the amount, on the ground that there was only one cow on the mountain, and the milk had to be kept for the babies. Observations made in our morning's ramble led us to believe there were several hundred youngsters and infants in the town,— they rushed to the doors of every house as we passed, — and we readily excused the padrone for obliging us to drink black coffee. The milk of one cow is certainly a modest allowance for a town of twenty-three hundred inhabitants.

The most enthusiastic cycler does not enthuse when climbing a mountain; amateurs freely admit the performance is pure work without the shadow of sport about it. On that

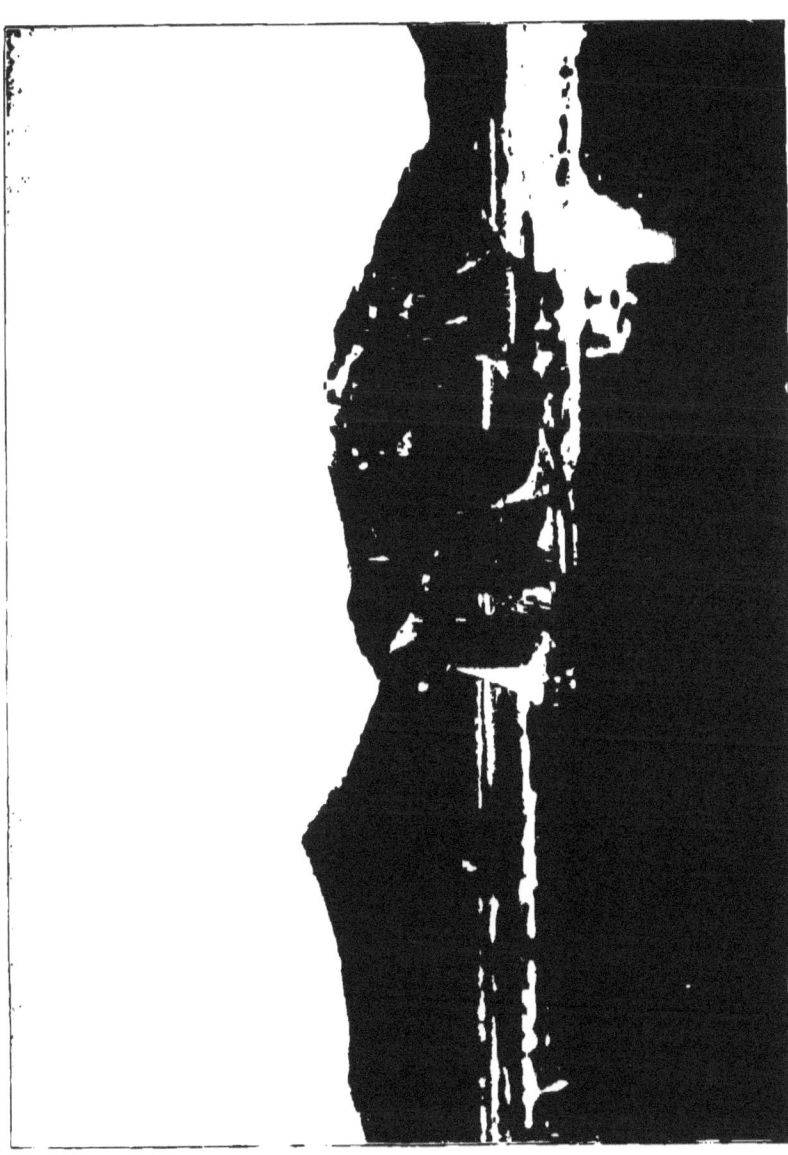

BAY OF SALAMIS, FROM HILL WHERE XERXES SAT

long and fatiguing climb to Radicofani, the only thing Mack and I had to buoy our flagging spirits was the thought that every foot of toilsome ascent added a foot to the smooth coast we would have on the morrow. Imagine, then, our disappointment on setting forth from Radicofani to find a newly made road covered with stones, which not only prevented rapid riding, but in many places compelled us to walk! Nor was our disappointment abated when the rough cobbles gave the bicycles such a severe shaking that early in the afternoon, not long after leaving Acquapendente, where we dined, the tires on the hind wheels loosened, first obliging us to ride slowly, and finally getting so bad we had to walk. In this fashion did we enter Bolsena, an ancient town with a labyrinth of narrow, hilly streets, situated on the banks of the lake now existing in what was once the crater of a prodigious volcano. A rock in the centre of Lake Bolsena served in the sixth century as a prison for Amalasuntha, daughter of Theodoric, and Queen of the Goths. Another island in the lake possesses a handsome cathedral.

The lake, islands, mountains, and antique town present a charming picture upon which, under ordinary circumstances, we should have delighted to dwell; but the disabled bicycles had to be looked to. We searched the town for a coil of flexible wire, and having found one, laid our wheels on the floor of the village albergo and spent the evening wrapping wire around the loosened tires. These efforts interested the hotel loungers, and they lost no time telling the rest of the town that the wonderful machines of the " Inglesi " were being repaired and would be in working order in time for a departure for Rome in the morning. This advertisement brought the usual crowd of curious people around the Porta Romana to see the start. Besides many of the dignitaries and notables of the town, there were a number of peasants on their way to the fields, and ass-drivers going into the campagna to gather twigs and brushwood. We waved our handkerchiefs at these as we flew swiftly by. Four German "Handwerksburschen" (strolling journeymen) called out to us: "Tell the Romans to keep their beards on until we come. We are barbers and want the job of shaving them." The sight of these plodding pedestrians made us quite proud and boastful.

"There they go," said Mack, "one mile while we make half a dozen."

To increase our grandeur, we put on extra pressure and made, during a short spurt, the rate of eighteen or twenty miles an hour; but too soon we realized the truth of the adage, Pride goes before a fall. There was a sharp snap, first on Mack's bicycle, then on mine. The wire binding the tires was cut by the rocks, and in less than two hours after leaving Bolsena, our wheels were absolutely useless. The tires would not stay on, and we could not stay on without the tires. We felt cut to the heart as, one by one, the peasants, the ass-drivers, and the German Handwerksburschen came up, paused for a moment to watch our struggles with the unruly machines, then walked on with smiles and good-natured contempt for the lunatics who risked their lives on uncertain pieces of rubber and steel. The accident occurred just without the town of Montefiascone, home of the celebrated Est-Est wine which so delighted the Canon Johannes Fugger that he never got any further. He cut short his journey to Montefiascone, drank Est-Est wine until he died, and after that sad event had his grave saturated with the delicious beverage once a year, money for that purpose having been left in his will. We came near imitating the Canon Fugger in one respect, that of getting no further, for the sudden snapping of the wire gave us a severe fall. The accident rather disgusted us with bicycling; we hired a cart, dumped the machines in, drove to the nearest railway station, luckily only a few miles away, and finished the journey to Rome by rail.

A year or so ago, at the request of a number of readers, I inserted in a new edition of my " Tramp Trip " a chapter on the comparative merits of bicycling and pedestrianism. My advice then was " Don't try to see Europe on a bicycle." Our trip from Toulon, despite its unpleasant termination at Montefiascone, induces me to modify that advice. Considering the greater ground covered, bicycling is not as fatiguing as walking, and it possesses a zest and exhilaration entirely lacking in any other means of locomotion. On the other hand, this last experience confirmed the opinion expressed in the fifth edition of " A Tramp Trip," that the bicycler must have a deeper and a longer purse than the pedestrian. Not only is he charged more at hotels, the possession of so wonderful a machine stamping the traveller as a man of wealth, able to pay any bills, but wherever transportation by rail is necessary, the expense is considerable. It cost $8 to get our two bicycles from London to Toulon; when we shipped them from Rome to London, the crating and freight cost $11 apiece. The 168 francs' duty paid on entering Italy was refunded upon presenting the railroad receipt and through bill of lading, showing that the wheels were billed through to London.

One disagreeable feature of cycling in Europe remains to be noted. In many towns and cities it is forbidden. As towns are close together, the wheelman often finds himself a footman, carrying his wheel, instead of the wheel carrying him. Where the streets were smooth, Mack and I bowled along, pretending not to hear the policemen when they shouted to us to get down and walk. When the streets were rough, this plan was not feasible, because the policemen would overtake us and compel us to dismount. The streets of Rome are excellent for bicycling, but the sport is not allowed, and we had to visit the sights of the Eternal City on foot.

CHAPTER XIV

Rome revisited — Renewing Acquaintances — Visit to the Queen of Heaven — What it costs to live there — House of Correction at Tivoli — San Stefano's Gloomy Ergostola — Terrible Effects of Isolation — Prison Systems compared — Lunatics in Italian Jails

WHILE waiting in Rome for a permit to inspect the Italian prisons we visited many of the sights of the Eternal City. Nothing so impresses one with the transitoriness of human life as revisiting after the lapse of years the edifices and ruins of antiquity. It was the Coliseum that inspired Gibbon to write his History and to remark on the insignificance of fame and power — a sentence in history covers a king's lifetime, a few pages the life of a nation.

Five years had passed since I stood in front of the Pantheon, gazing upon its massive columns or deciphering its half-effaced inscriptions — five years! what changes, what joys (alas, too few), what sorrows, oft too many, five years bring to man! The great dome still let in the sun and the rain; and through its uncovered top I saw, as of old, the deep blue sky flecked with fleecy clouds, a picture of the heavens more beautiful than painter ever drew. Perhaps that is why the Pantheon's dome has not been frescoed or ornamented. The opening in the top shows the sky and clouds by day and the starry firmament by night. Once a year, on the anniversary of Victor Emmanuel's death, the dome of the Pantheon is covered. I attended these anniversary ceremonies the following January, after returning from Egypt, and was glad to find the dome covered. There was a pouring rain, and had the top been open as usual the King and Queen and the thousand or two people who were in the Pantheon would have been drenched.

On page 52 of "A Tramp Trip," I mention an Italian hat-presser in a little shop back of the Pantheon.

"'Yes, signore,' he said after I had stopped before his shop every day for a week or more to gaze at the walls of that venerable building. 'Yes, signore, it seems strange to me. People come from every land, they stop before my shop, they stare, they talk, they write in little books. Sometimes two or three years go by, then I see the same people again. They look and stare just the same. Ah, I know them, I know *you* when you come back maybe ten years from now. I see so many — they waste so much time. The wall is old? Santa Maria, it is old, very old — what then? I not understand; it seem to me Americans, Inglesi, wrong here,' and the mystified Italian tapped his forehead and resumed his ironing."

The presser was right; he was still in his shop and recognized me the moment I entered.

"Ah, I knew you would come," he said, laughing and shaking my hand. "They all come back. Changed? *Dio mio*, yes, two more *bambini* since you were here, and some gray hairs in my head. But the Pantheon has not changed. It was the same the day I was born; it will always be the same. The good God lets it stand because it is a holy church and has been blessed."

We thought the Pantheon owed its preservation to the massiveness of its construction, but we did not say this to the hat-presser. He lives on the spot, and so, of course, knows more about it than barbarians from a world unknown when the Romans erected it.

When I visited the Catacombs of St. Calistus five years ago, the good priest who showed me around had seen few travellers and was childishly ignorant of the great world beyond his monastery walls. He then thought America a town or village somewhere in Europe. In 1891, after five years' experience with tourists, he was more worldly wise — knew not only of America, but also of her cities, and was especially interested in Chicago and the World's Fair. Evidently Chicago tourists had been to the Catacombs and had not failed to tell of their new and magnificent city. The monk said he liked America, that he would like to be transferred to the Trappist monastery in Kentucky, so as to see something of the land Columbus discovered. How much of our grand country would a man see from behind those monastery walls on the lonely Kentucky hills? In the Catacombs he showed us the niche where St. Cecilia was discovered, and on returning to the city we visited the church to which her body was removed in the ninth century. This church is built on the spot where St. Cecilia lived: portions of her original house still stand. The sexton shows the bathroom where she was asphyxiated after the unsuccessful efforts of pagans to cut her head off. The pipes which supplied the bath-room with steam stand to day just as they stood when St. Cecilia lived fifteen hundred years ago. The marble slab on which her head was placed by the executioner is also preserved. One sees the gashes in the marble made by the pagan executioner's axe. The sexton said that although the axe went so deep through the flesh as to make these gashes in the marble, a miracle prevented the saint's head from being entirely severed. St. Cecilia was finally put to death by asphyxiation. The sexton also informed us that when her body was exposed to view in the sixteenth century, it was perfectly preserved and exactly like the marble image that rests over her grave in the church.

The first Italian prison we visited was the Regina Coeli in Roma, — the Queen of Heaven in Rome, — a pretty name, which, however, does not reconcile the unfortunates to a life within its walls. No one wishes to remain with the Queen of Heaven a moment longer than necessary. Although in the Regina Coeli the condition and discipline of the condemned are mildness itself compared with that of the terrible Ergostola prisons mentioned hereafter, in some respects the Queen of Heaven prison in Rome resembles the penitentiary of Portugal. Five corridors, with four tiers of cells to the corridor, radiate from a central point, whence one guard can see every cell door in the building. The resemblance to the Lisbon system ceases here. There are no masks, no absolute isolation, no chapels so ingeniously arranged that the unhappy wretches are cut off from sight of fellow-beings even during the one hour that they are together on Sunday.

In the Roman prison convicts work in common, and though against the rule to speak, their eyes are uncovered, they see each other, they have the blessed privilege of exchanging glances, of feeling the nearness of fellow-creatures — blessings denied Portuguese prisoners, immured as they are in cells and covered from head to foot in white shrouds. At twelve o'clock we took positions on one of the upper balconies in the hub or central point of the Regina Coeli; each convict was searched before entering his cell for dinner. A dozen guards stood around the focal point of the five corridors. The prisoners entered in double file, no lock-step, but in a slipshod sort of a shuffle. As they entered, twelve stepped forward at a time and extended their arms in the air while the guards searched their pockets, felt their clothing from head to foot, looked in their shoes, peered in their snuff-boxes, and even broke the loaves of bread they carried, to see that no files or weapons were concealed. The search over, the prisoner puts on his shoes, returns his handkerchief, snuff-box, and other belongings to his pockets and shuffles off to his cell, in which he is locked until he eats his dinner. The examination is so thorough and minute that much time is consumed, and the 424 prisoners are kept standing three-quarters of an hour. When all have been searched and locked up, enormous kettles of bean soup are passed down the various corridors, and a quart can-ful handed through the trap in the door of each cell. Six hundred grammes of bread (1¼ lbs.) and a quart of soup constitute the daily food allowance furnished by the government. If he has money, a prisoner may buy extras at a fixed price up to the amount of forty centesimi per day. He is not permitted to spend more than this amount in any one day, no matter how much money may be to his credit on the prison books. Thus a convict who spends but twenty centesimi to-day will not be permitted to spend sixty to-morrow. Nor is he allowed to expend money except for the articles and at the prices on the prison tariff. The door of each cell is provided with a bell, which the prisoner has the right to ring when he wishes to see the tariff card and make an order. The following extract from the tariff card will give an idea of what a prisoner in the Queen of Heaven may have in addition to the bread and bean soup received once a day from the government. The convict may order on

Mondays — Potatoes cooked with oil and vinegar, 15 centesimi.[1]
Tuesdays — 100 grammes[2] of beef, 40 cmi.; or two boiled eggs, 15 cmi.
Wednesdays — Beef steak, 40 cmi.; or fried eggs, 25 cmi.
Thursdays — Beef, 40 cmi.; or 300 grammes of rice with sauce, 30 cmi.
Fridays — Fried fish, 75 grammes, 22 cmi.; sardines, 150 grammes, 17 cmi.
Saturdays — 100 grammes of beef, 40 cmi.
Sundays — 300 grammes potatoes, 35 cmi.
All Days — Various cheeses 60 grammes, from 13 to 17 cmi.; 60 grammes salami, 17 cmi.; half litre milk, 20 cmi.; cup coffee, 10 cmi. Cherries, 300 grammes, 12 cmi.; 300 grammes strawberries, 22 cmi.; 300 grammes plums, 12 cmi.; one lemon, 7 cmi.; 500 grammes white bread, 23 cmi.; black bread, 18 cmi.; half a litre red or white wine, 22 cmi.; one candle, 13 cmi.; 25 grammes snuff (price varies).

If a prisoner does not spend his daily allowance, it is kept by the director until the end of his sentence. Few, however, can live on the one slim meal a day furnished by the govern-

---

[1] A centesimo is a fraction less than the fifth of a cent.
[2] 1000 grammes = 2⅕ pounds.

ment, hence they spend their allowance to the last centesimo. An account is kept with each prisoner. One liberated the day of our visit had earned 158.01 lire in the nine months of his stay. Of this sum he had spent 89 lire for food and 22.15 lire for clothing, so that when he walked out of prison, it was with 46.96 lire, about $9, as the net result of his nine months' labor. In America penitentiary convicts are not paid for their labor. Occasionally, contractors who have fixed a certain task as a day's labor pay a trifle for work performed in excess of the fixed task. In general, however, it may be said that the American convict leaves prison with nothing to show for his, perhaps, twenty or thirty years' labor, except the $5 and the suit of citizen's clothes with which he is presented by the State. Nor is the American prisoner permitted to buy extra food, as has been seen is the case in Spain and Italy. When General McDonald, the friend of President Grant, was sent to Jefferson City for his share in the celebrated whiskey ring frauds, he had to eat the same bread and drink the same black coffee that was furnished the poorest convict in the prison. It was hard on the man fresh from champagne suppers with the President, but the warden refused to let the general import a single outside luxury. In a Spanish prison his money would have secured every luxury; in the Roman Regina Coeli he could have at least had milk for his coffee, a thing which was refused General McDonald in the Missouri penitentiary, of which he made bitter complaint.

The Italian government furnishes prisoners one suit of clothes every five years. If worn out before the end of the five years the prisoner must buy a new suit. If he has no money and if his clothing is worn out, not through the nature of the work, but through viciousness or carelessness, he is punished with the dark cell and the substitution of water instead of soup for his one daily meal. A handkerchief must last six months; shoes from six to twelve months, according to the work. Tailors and shoemakers, who sit most of the time, must make one pair of shoes last a year. There is a regular schedule, and each article of clothing must wear in each trade the time specified in the schedule. The stripes of the uniform are up and down, not horizontal, as in American prisons, nor are the colors a dull brown and white. The legs of the Italian convict's trousers are of different colors, the right leg striped blue and white, the left leg blue and red. The jacket and cap are striped blue and white.

The cells are provided with iron bedsteads which are turned up and locked against the wall during the day, so that the prisoners cannot lie down except at night. On Sunday, he does not go to chapel; he must get on with what religion he can absorb in his cell. To aid in this, the door of each cell is provided with a "tramp" lock; that is, a lock by which the door can be fastened while open six or eight inches. As the far ends of the corridors are two hundred feet away from the focal point where the priest says mass, it is evident that many of the prisoners cannot see or hear, even though their cell doors be ajar. In addition to the search made daily at noon, guards visit each prisoner three times a night, at 9 P.M., at midnight, and at five in the morning. At each visitation, the face of the sleeping prisoner is uncovered and scrutinized for identification. A recording clock is kept for each guard. If this clock does not show a registration for each half-hour in the night, the director knows the guard has been asleep or neglectful and acts accordingly.

These examinations are far more frequent and thorough than in American prisons, and require more guards and are more expensive. The director of the Queen of Heaven prison said the origin of their strict examinations was an escape made by a convict who secreted a file in a loaf of bread and cut the bars of his window. Since that time each loaf of bread is broken into pieces before it enters the prisoner's cell.

The cost to the government for its daily allowance of six hundred grammes of bread and one quart of bean soup is forty centesimi. This is less in amount than the allowance in the average American prison, but in proportion to what the prisoner receives food is much more expensive to the Italian than to the American prison director. In Jefferson City the daily food of each prisoner costs 10.01 cents, for which he lives like a king compared with the Italian prisoner. Instead of one meal he has three, and at each, instead of a meagre allowance of bread and soup, he is given all he can eat of bread and coffee at breakfast, of meat, bread, potatoes, cabbage, etc., at dinner, and of bread, coffee, and sometimes dried fruit at supper. The earnings of American convicts are also larger: those in Missouri bring the State from forty to fifty cents a day per man, while in the Queen of Heaven few convicts earn more than 1.30 lire (thirty cents). The majority make only eighty-five centesimi (seventeen cents). Seven of the seventeen cents are kept by the government, and ten cents are placed to the credit of the prisoner, who usually spends eight for food, so that his net savings amount to two cents for each day that he works. This does not mean every work-day in the year, for in addition to the numerous Italian fast and feast days much time is lost owing to lack of work. These are the gloomiest periods of the convict's life: he must then bear not only the horror of sitting in his cell with nothing to do, but also the pangs of semi-starvation, the extra food allowance being limited to thirty centesimi per day when work is lacking. In the case of a prisoner without work and depending on work for money there are, of course, no extra rations at all. In reply to the question as to whether it is the policy of the government to make the prisons self-supporting the director replied that the government does not hold that object in view. Prisoners are kept for the most part on public works, manufacturing for the army. In the Regina Coeli di Roma 100 men work in the printing and lithographing department where statistical and official reports are printed. The main purpose of the government is stated to be punishment and reform, and the system in vogue reduces to the minimum the productiveness of each criminal, so that an immense amount must be subscribed in taxes by the honest men of the kingdom for the support of the cut-throats and thieves. When a criminal is sentenced as a "Reclusione," he is often provided with no work at all, but is compelled to sit alone in his cell doing absolutely nothing for his own support, thus adding so much to the burdens of honest labor without the prison walls.

The jail system of Italy offers some features as novel as its system of penitentiaries. For instance, prisoners awaiting trial are often given work. The government retains one-third of the proceeds until the guilt or innocence of the accused is determined. If acquitted, the one-third is refunded; if found guilty, the government keeps the money. In one of the Carceri Giudiziere built in 1665 by Pope Innocent X. and used as a jail ever since, we saw twenty-five shoemakers who make one-hundred and thirty pairs of twelve-lire shoes per month. A prisoner is paid 1.75 lire for each pair of shoes. Allowing twenty and a half work-days to the month, the product of these twenty-five men is six pairs of shoes per day, or 10.50 lire — $2.00 — to be divided daily among the twenty-five. Of this beggarly pittance, eighty-four centesimi per man, the government retains one-third, hence the actual cash left in the luckless shoemaker's hand is less than six cents per day. In the face of this fact it is adding insult to injury to say to the prisoner, "You are not limited here as in the Queen of Heaven. There you are allowed to spend only forty centesimi a day. Here you may spend all you want." Which, of course, means all you can, or, as shown above, less than six cents a day. The tariff in the Carceri Giudiziere is moderate enough; a few francs would buy everything on the bill of fare, and the prisoner is at liberty to do this if he can only provide the necessary francs. We saw many first of May men — that is, men arrested on the first of May as " Labor Agitators." The visitor to prisons finds all over Europe these significant evidences of the wide-spread discontent among the people, — a discontent which will not long confine itself to first of May demonstrations if the gross abuses and injustices of the present social system be not speedily and radically mended.

There are two rooms of inquisition in the jail where prisoners are pumped and confessions extorted. When we first entered one of these rooms there were no prisoners present, and the chief inquisitor was pleasant and polite. The walls of his room were frescoed, windows looked out on a pretty view, and altogether it seemed a cheerful place. How different when the inquisition began! The trembling suspect stands before the desk, nervously fumbling his hat, the brows of the inquisitor contract, his eyes grow stern, his voice harsh, as he puts question after question to the confused prisoner. Usually the suspect maintains his innocence: he is then locked up and given a few days to reflect. If a second examination fails to elicit a confession of guilt, he is locked up again. Sometimes weeks, if not months, pass in these alternate inquisitions and cell confinements. When finally a confession of guilt is made, or, failing in that, when the inquisitor thinks he has learned all that is possible from the accused, he is taken from the cell, and either put in the workshop or given a bed in a large room along with a dozen others. Instead of assuming a man innocent until found guilty, Italian criminal law adopts exactly the opposite maxim, and assumes each man guilty until proved innocent. The same principle holds in France. In neither the Regina Coeli nor the Carceri Giudiziere of Rome are prisoners provided with baths. In the latter prison, a contractor furnishes food and clothing at the rate of fifty-three centesimi (ten cents) per day per man. The one meal per day consists of seven hundred and fifty grammes of bread, and soup made of beans, rice, or macaroni. Clothing is furnished only to those who have neither money nor clothes of their own.

Far better managed than either prisons or jails is the house of correction at Tivoli. Few travellers who go to that beautiful spot where Hadrian had his villa, and where waterfalls, glens, and grottos afford the most picturesque scenery in Italy, care to visit the large prison just without the walls on a height commanding a view of Rome and of the Campagna for thirty miles around. Yet to one interested in prison reform, the Istituto di Correzione Paterna in Tivoli is worth visiting. The inmates range in age from thirteen to twenty-one, and live well compared with the inmates of other European prisons. Breakfast at 7.45 consists of bread, milk or cheese, and dried figs. Dinner at noon comprises bean soup and bread, also meat on Thursdays and Sundays, and one-fifth of a litre of wine three times a week. At seven comes supper of bread, potatoes, and, on Thursdays and Sundays, the meat left over from dinner. The cells are solid on three sides; the fourth side, looking on the corridor, consists of a light iron grating from floor to ceiling. The boys can see their neighbors on the opposite side of the corridors, and though the rules forbid speaking, we were told the prisoners are allowed to chat with each other until bedtime. During the day they are kept partly in workshops, partly in school, and partly in the prison courts, exercising. The thirty boys in the shoeshop make two hundred pairs of five-lire shoes per month. In other shops are taught other trades, — blacksmithing, iron bedstead making, carpentering, etc. Many fathers voluntarily send vicious sons to this institution, hoping that the discipline and instruction will make them well-behaved, industrious mechanics. Such fathers, if able, must pay one lira per day. In case of the very poor, the government does not exact this payment, but defrays the entire expense, amounting to 450.80 lire per boy per year — about $87.

The youngsters, who had a bright, contented look, appeared to take an interest in their work, much of which, such as bedsteads, toilet-sets, and carved chairs, was skilfully and neatly done. It is almost certain that if there were more of these institutions of "Paternal Correction," there would be fewer prisons and Ergostolas.

Chance made us acquainted with a man who had been a convict in the Ergostola of San Stefano. He had tried to kill a Neapolitan, and in consequence spent nine months in one of San Stefano's dungeons.

"They chained me to a wall in a solitary cell," he said, "and at first I did nothing but cry, cry, all the time cry. Then they gave me a rat to play with, and I was a little happy. I had only one meal a day, and often the soup was made of meat so bad I could not eat it — that is, not at first; but in San Stefano when you not eat, they keep the same soup and give it to you next day. You never get new soup until you eat all the old soup, so I eat the bad soup though my stomach turn so. I was hungry, all the time hungry, and nothing to do — nothing. I sit and think and think until I most go crazy."

This man's story made me desirous of visiting San Stefano, and the Minister of Justice courteously gave me a letter to the director. Robinson Crusoe's fate is generally supposed to have been a hard one: it is bad enough to be cast away on a desolate, uninhabited island. But Crusoe had light and air and could walk about and look at the sea and the land and drink in the fresh, pure air. The wretches of San Stefano can do none of these things. They are literally buried alive on that gloomy, sea-girt rock. We were lucky enough to find in Naples a steamer bound for the island with a troop of Caribinieri escorting prisoners. For six hours we steamed directly out to sea: the stern, forbidding rock was visible for miles before we reached it. The bluffs rise almost perpendicularly three hundred feet out of the water: steps have been hewn to the summit of the precipice, and it is up these steps prisoners climb, seldom to return. In rough weather the waves beat angrily against the huge rock, making it impossible to land. In winter, communication with the outer world is thus cut off for weeks and months at a time. Even with the calm sea of summer it is no easy matter to get ashore. Our steamer anchored two hundred yards from the foot of the stony steps while the prisoners and soldiers were taken off in small boats. These had to bide their time before landing: the boatmen rowed within ten feet of the bluff, then turned broadside to the sea, and the men sprang on the rocky ledge one at a time as the swell of the waves brought the boat aloft and near the shore. This feat was difficult even for the soldiers: for the prisoners fettered with chains, it was dangerous as well as difficult. No accident happened, however, and soon we were toiling up the rocky height. The scene was inexpressibly dreary and desolate. Water used in the prison is brought in ships from Naples. A few cacti bristle here and there on a bare rock: all else is barren waste. The top of the rock is about two acres in extent. The Ergostola stands on one edge, looking over a three-hundred-foot bluff. Opposite is the residence of the director, the commissary department, filled with stores brought from Naples, and the barracks for the soldiers who patrol the edge of the bluff. There seems no possible chance for a prisoner to get out of the Ergostola; even if he gets out, he cannot escape without a boat. No one is permitted to bring a boat within six hundred feet of San Stefano. One who does so is likely to receive a gunshot reception from the guards above.

The Ergostola is in the shape of a circle measuring six hundred feet in circumference. In the centre of the circle stands a tower whence radiate forty triangular exercise spaces. A walk six feet wide circumscribes the bases of these forty triangles, then come the inner tier of cells, which look out on the tower and the exercise triangle as the boxes in an amphitheatre

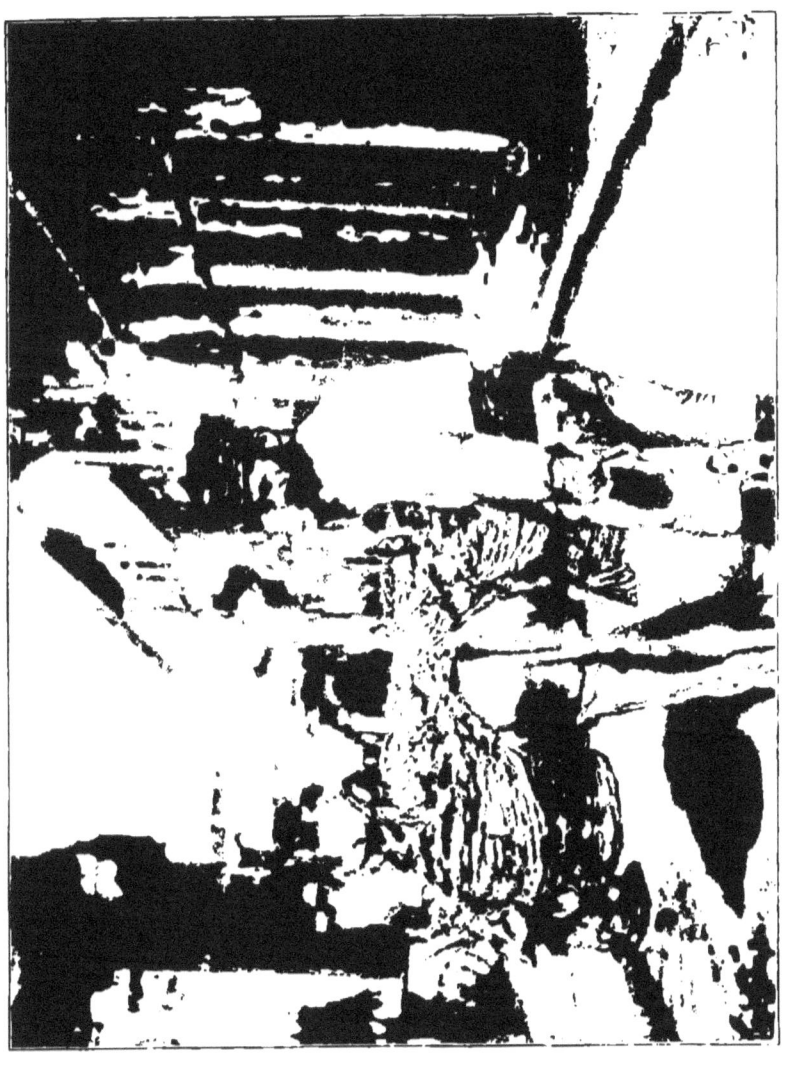

GRAPE VENDOR IN ATHENS

look out on the space in the centre. Each cell is ten feet deep, then a wall two feet thick, beyond which are the cells of the outer tier; that is, of the tier which does not face the interior of the amphitheatre. It is not really an outer tier; for, circumscribing this outer circle of cells is an aisle and then a massive wall, so that the so-called outer cells have not even the light or air of those facing the inner part of the circle. The interior of the cells is bare, a stool and a straw mattress, no pillow; but we saw no prisoners chained to the walls, nor were there staples, chains, or other evidences that such was the practice. The ex-prisoner from Naples evidently romanced in this respect: indeed, it would be useless cruelty to chain men in a dungeon when escape is practically impossible. The small window in each cell is eight feet from the floor and ingeniously arranged so that the light comes from above, not horizontally. The prisoner may manage to climb up to his window, but even there he can only look up at the distant sky: an outer shutter slopes upwards, keeping out all view of the scene around him. The cells have double doors, the outer one of solid wood, the inner one an iron grating. This inner door is to prevent a prisoner surprising a guard; also for religious services on Sunday, when the solid outer door is fastened six inches ajar. As in the Queen of Heaven prison, it is supposed that through these six-inch cracks and through the gratings of the inner doors, the prisoners can absorb religious ideas and reverential feelings from the mass celebrated in the chapel in the central tower of the circle. Those in the inner tier of cells can see little and hear less, while the prisoners in the still more distant outer tier, cut off by two solid walls and by a circle of ten-foot cells, must have vivid imaginations indeed to keep up with the priest and his ceremonies.

Once a day, rice or bean soup and a piece of bread is thrust through the trap of the cell door; and once a day there is an hour's walk in one of the forty triangular spaces; but even there the prisoner sees no living being save the guard watching him from a platform on the central tower. The walls separating one triangular space from the other are twelve feet high. The prisoner paces to and fro for sixty minutes like a caged beast, then two guards escort him back to his cell, and another convict takes his place in the exercise triangle. It was a pitiful sight, — those miserable men pacing to and fro, looking up at the blue sky, then at the massive walls that shut them out from freedom, from association with fellow-beings, from all that makes life worth living. The director said that two guards are necessary in escorting a prisoner from his cell to the exercise triangle in order to keep him from suddenly leaping over the railing and dashing his brains out on the stone pavements below. The circle of cells are in three stories; the upper floor some forty feet from the ground, whence a leap would, of course, be fatal. It sometimes happens that the unhappy wretch is quick enough to evade the two guards. Two such suicides occurred in one day, the week previous to our visit. Suicides sometimes occur in the cells; but these are rare, owing to the strict and frequent searches. The prisoner is searched each time he returns from the exercise triangle, although he has been under the eye of a guard the whole hour and seemingly has no possible chance to secure or secrete a weapon. He is also visited five times in the night, and thus never knows when a guard may not enter his cell or peep through the shutters in the door.

A few of the prisoners were patching clothes or making shoes, but the majority were sitting in their cells, staring vacantly at the walls or restlessly pacing to and fro. The director said arrangements were being made whereby work would be provided for all. This should be speedily done. If it be cruel to take the life of a man, no matter how criminal, how much more cruel is it to drive him to despair and self-murder! This, it seems, is what the Ergostola system often does. From motives of humanity Italy has abolished capital punishment by headsman and hangman; but, in point of fact, are not criminals put to death by isolation, idleness, and insufficient food? The system is only two years old, and therefore too young to afford accurate statistics; but the physician of San Stefano said he had no doubt that only a few will survive seven years of the Ergostola. Italy is not alone in this system. The reader will remember that in Portugal convicts are kept in perpetual isolation, and the same system, with more or less rigorous accessories, prevails in Belgium and several other countries. Mr. Nicholas Spilliopoulos, director of a prison which I visited in Greece, said that before the present Greek government began the reconstruction of prisons, he was instructed to study the different systems in Europe. He visited the penitentiaries of France, Switzerland, Italy, England, Ireland, Denmark, Sweden, Germany, and Austria; made a special study of the isolation system, and unhesitatingly condemned it as unadvisable, if not barbarous and unjust. In one prison visited by him were thirty-two lunatics, victims of the solitary system and the vices so frequently resulting therefrom. It seems to me, the fundamental principle which should govern the treatment of criminals is restriction and reform. The principle of revenge should not be entertained by a Christian nation: in proportion as revenge, even for evil deeds, prevails, in that proportion does the nation depart from true Christianity. If statistics of crime show that there are fewer murders with than without capital punishment, then, under the principle of protection to society, capital punishment is not only wise, but just. There are no facts to show that there is less crime under the Ergostola system than under a system where prisoners work in common; there are no facts to show that making men consumptives or lunatics in prison keeps other men out of prison. On the contrary, statistics show that there is an appalling amount of crime in Italy, despite the severe sentence of judges and harsh discipline of prisons. In 1888 English courts sentenced 150 persons for homicide; French courts, 175; while the Italian courts sentenced 1800! Each new year, when the law courts are opened, the magistrates give a *resumé* of the work performed by the courts during the preceding year. The Roman magistrates, in their opening addresses for 1891, stated that the courts of appeal and assizes of Rome had 407 more cases to deal with in 1890 than in 1889. The records for 1890 showed 82 murders and more than 4000 robberies in the single city of Rome.

The question, how to be just to the convict, how to teach him to be industrious, self-supporting, how literally to reform him, — make him over again, — without injuring honest free labor, is of vital importance: it is, however, hardly a question to be dealt with in these sketches of travel, especially as none of the prison systems in the Mediterranean countries afford even a suggestion as to its solution. But if a study of Mediterranean prisons will not afford a solution of the problem, how to utilize convict labor without injury to honest labor, it will, at any rate, make plain some errors to be avoided. A few years ago, the legislature of New York, aware of the evil, but utterly ignorant of the remedy, enacted a law prohibiting prisoners from working in any shape or form; and a politician in Missouri told an audience of workingmen, he hoped to see the day when the eighteen hundred felons at Jefferson City would not be allowed to turn a hand in productive labor. Could the advocates of this remedy visit an Italian Ergostola, could they see the unhappy men, hopeless in their narrow cells, nothing to do but think, think, always think, until disease racks their bodies and their eyes have a despairing look, until the brain sinks into a state of hopeless idiocy, — could they see this, they would not advocate isolation and idleness. Nothing so impressed on my mind the horror of a living death in a solitary cell, as an incident that occurred at San Stefano. As we were leaving a cell which the director unlocked at my request, the haggard prisoner followed us to the door, hands and legs twitching nervously, and humbly murmured thanks, because *his* cell had been selected to visit. Misery like this stirs a pity too painful for words. He thanked his jailer for merely showing his cell to a visitor.

The barren rock of San Stefano has no wells, and water must be brought from Naples; hence the supply given prisoners is meagre — only about twenty quarts per month for bathing. The one meal a day at 11.30 consists of rice soup, potatoes, and bread. On Sundays there is meat. Three men in the kitchen supply the wants of 228 prisoners: in an American penitentiary it would take at least twice as many cooks and waiters to supply food to that number of convicts. The Ergostola prisoner is allowed to spend three cents a day — if he has it. When he happens to have a little patching or mending or other job work, he can spend four cents. Here is the list and prices of articles from which he can select: —

Baccala, 100 grammes [1] (.22 pound)	12	centesimi.[2]
Cacio of cavallo, 60 grammes	18	"
Cacio of coltrone, 60 grammes	16	"
Black coffee, per cup	10	"
Cipolle (an herb of the onion species) 1000 grammes	10	"
Half litre milk	20	"
Lemons, 500 grammes (about two)	15	"
Macaroni, 250 grammes	16	"
Boiled potatoes, 1000 grammes	36	"
Salami, 100 grammes	35	"
Tonne fish with oil, 100 grammes	30	"
Two eggs	18	"
Half a litre of red wine	20	"
White bread, 1000 grammes (2¼ lbs.)	36	"
Black bread, 1000 grammes	30	"

When a prisoner is refractory and violates the rules, he is not allowed to purchase extra food; if the disobedience

---

[1] 1000 grammes = 2¼ pounds.
[2] One centesimo = fraction less than one-fifth of a cent.

amounts to more than a failure to arise and salute a guard on entering his cell, he is removed to a dark dungeon, where he must sleep on a stone floor and exist on a meagre ration of bread and water. I am glad to know that our visit gave at least a moment's respite to one poor creature who was condemned to the Cimmerian gloom of the dark dungeon. When the door was opened for our inspection, the prisoner started up from the stone floor where he had been lying and covered his eyes, blinded by the sudden and unaccustomed light. It is related of a prisoner released during the French Revolution that although confined thirty years in a dark dungeon, he preserved his reason by throwing on the floor a few pins, then groping for them in the dark. The unhappy man we saw in the dark cell at San Stefano seemed not to have even pins with which to amuse himself; he appeared to pass the time in a sort of dull stupefaction. The commutation system exists, but with such limitations that its effect upon the prisoner is greatly reduced. It is not applied to second-termers or to those condemned to less than three or more than thirty years, hence prisoners of those grades have no incentive to demean themselves well other than through fear of the dark dungeon.

The Ergostola of San Stefano is scrupulously clean, the cells large and well ventilated, the officials seemed to perform their unpleasant duties firmly but humanely. The reader will understand that the foregoing strictures are applied to the *system*, not to the individual prison of San Stefano. The director was most courteous and obliging; the room he placed at our disposal commanded a fine view of the rolling ocean; nevertheless we were glad when the ship stopped on its return from the Ponza Islands and enabled us to bid farewell to the sea-girt rock which holds so much human misery.

As the other Italian prisons differ only in detail from those above described, this unpleasant topic may be dismissed, after briefly referring to one or two of the more striking facts brought out by the investigation. Of 32,678 prisoners, 64 lost their reason in a single year; in addition to these 64 cases of downright madness, a number of prisoners were afflicted with mental maladies (82 cases of mania, 14 of melancholy, 21 of stupidity, etc.). A remarkable fact is, that, of the 64 cases of madness which occurred in *all* the penitentiaries of the kingdom, 16, or twenty-five per cent, occurred in the single prison of Parma, containing only 523 convicts. In other words, considering the Parma prison alone, more than three per cent of the convicts became lunatics in the course of a year. Commenting on this in his official report, the director of prisons states that the "grave fact cannot be attributed to heredity, but to enforced rules and rigid discipline." The length of time required for the severe discipline to deprive a convict of his reason varies : of 26 cases noted, 4 became lunatics after six months' imprisonment, 2 after a year, 11 after five years, 6 after ten years, 1 after fifteen years, and 1 after twenty years.

Thirty-three per cent of the average male, and 40.4 per cent of the female population of the penitentiaries are sick once a year. Death as well as sickness is more frequent among the women than among the men. Of every 100 sick women $10\frac{1}{2}$ die, while of 100 sick men only $8\frac{7}{10}$ die. The highest death rate is in the Piedmont women's prison ($71\frac{4}{10}$ per 1000, or 1 out of 14). The next highest is in the Sardinian prisons, $47\frac{9}{10}$ per 1000; the lowest in Veneto, $8\frac{3}{10}$ per 1000. The general death rate in all the prisons is 34 per 1000 men, and 51 per 1000 women. The significance of these figures appears when we remember that mortality in large cities rarely exceeds 22 per 1000, that figure including infants and octogenarians. Convicts are usually not only young, but from a class physically sound and strong. Of 17,715 galley slaves, only 125 were from learned professions, 23 were ecclesiastics, 246 public officers; the rest were from pursuits requiring physical strength. The farm furnished 10,040, or more than half. The fact that 34 out of every 1000 of these men, strong and in the prime of life, die in a year, is a strong arraignment of the disciplinary system adopted. Of the deaths during the year, 14 were suicides; 29 more attempted suicide, but failed, owing to watchfulness of the guards. The reader who remembers the prison bill of fare will not be surprised to learn that a large per cent of the sickness is due to stomach troubles. Of 10,210 cases of illness, 2087 complained of the " apparato digirente " (digestive apparatus).

Has the system of isolation prevented or lessened crime? The facts scarcely warrant the supposition. Experts reckon the proportion of " detained " to free inhabitants in Italy as 9 per 1000; in certain provinces the proportion is larger. In Abruzzi e Molise it is $16\frac{7}{10}$ per 1000. The cost of supporting this army of felons is enormous. In 1881, the last year for which I was able to obtain figures, the expense to the Italian people for prisons was 10,694,643.64 lire ($2,031,982.29).[1] Only a small part of this expense is paid for by labor of the convicts, their time, when not idle, being largely devoted to government work, such as building fortifications, printing official reports, etc. Italian judges lean toward long sentences. Of 17,729 men condemned to the galleys, only 5 had sentences less than five years; 2110 were sentenced for ten years, 4352 for fifteen years, 4745 for twenty years, 1839 for more than twenty years, and 4678 for life. A fact of especial interest to Americans is that relating to the movement of freed convicts. The charge has been made that convicts receive government assistance to emigrate to the United States, and there is reason to believe the charge true of some European states; the director of a German prison told me that the English language is no longer taught in the convict schools. I asked why.

" Because," replied the director, " it is difficult now to send our convicts to the United States; your laws are too strict. We

---

[1] Reckoning the lira at 19 cents (£1 sterling = 25.60 lire = $4.86).

are having the prisoners taught Spanish so they can be sent to South America."

If reliance can be placed upon the official report of the Italian prison director, America has nothing to fear from Italian convicts, as, after liberation, ninety-seven per cent return to their original homes, two per cent seek new homes in Italy, while only one per cent leave the kingdom. The great majority of these unfortunates are illiterate, 11,030 out of 17,715 being unable to read or write.

CHAPTER XV

Changes in Naples — How the Poor are housed — Italian Taxes — We hire a Boat — The *Principe Farnese* — Yachting on the Mediterranean — Capri and Sorrento — A Tramp over the Mountain — Mack wants a Nursery — A Ducking at Scaracatajo — What it costs to run Dr. Kelly's Yacht, and what it costs to run the *Principe Farnese*

THE proper housing of the poor is a difficult problem anywhere; it is especially difficult in a crowded city like Naples, and does not seem to have been solved by the enormous money grant made by the Italian government. One hundred million lire were appropriated by the general government to enable the Naples municipality to tear down the disease-breeding rookeries and widen the alleys and streets. The heart of Naples has been transformed as by an enchanter's wand. Where six years ago stood five, six, and even ten story tenements on alleys not ten feet wide, are now handsome buildings on boulevards fifty feet wide. Who has received the benefit of this Herculanean work? It is to be feared that the poor have actually been injured rather than benefited. Professor Villari, a senator who has given this question much thought, says that the government grant has caused the working classes of Naples to move further away, but that it has not bettered their condition. The senator adds : —

"Waiving the discussion as to the opportuneness from a social point of view of segregating the working classes from other classes of citizens, the system can only have a chance of success in cities which possess great factories and a real working-class population earning decent salaries. . . . But when you have to deal with the marruzzara, the carnacatotaro, the pizzaiuolo (shellfish, cooked meats, and cake sellers) . . . with an infinite series of microscopic trades which do not deserve the name of industries, with a multitude which lives from hand to mouth, selling edibles, string, pitch, fishermen's nets, earning a half-penny for some trifling service — the transferring all these poor creatures from the scene of their labors is to deprive them of the simplest possibility of existence. To say to the people of the districts of Mercato, Porto, Pendino, who, precisely in these poorest quarters, leave their children in some hole or other and ply their trades in the street, in the open air, 'Go and live in another quarter' is an irony, an insult, to their misery. Yet it is for this population that a roof must be found ; it is the problem of housing these people that has to be solved, and the solution of which is not commenced."

Senator Villari does not believe that the problem can be solved without the aid of government. He says : —

"Never has the problem of proper housing of the poor been solved by private speculation. At Naples especially, where space is so scanty, ground so dear, population so dense, the populace so poor, it is ridiculous to hope that private speculation can on the very smallest scale solve the problem. It is materially impossible to construct tolerable houses for the poor at prices which they can pay and at the same time repay the builders: and where are there commercial societies that will build at a loss? What happens is well known. The poor do not enter the new buildings ; they remain in their hovels, and when, as now happens, these hovels are demolished by the pickaxe, the poor herd go to other dens in ever-increasing numbers, thus making their condition worse; or many families crowd into one room in the new buildings, which become *fondaci*, often worse than those demolished, because, being dear, more people must be crowded into less space."

It seemed to me that crowding could not be greater than it was five years ago when I investigated the condition of the poor of Naples, often finding families of ten or twelve in one small room. I endeavored to learn what had become of these poor people, but failed: only one thing is certain, that they are not able to pay the increased rent demanded for the new buildings and have moved away. Notwithstanding the government grant of a hundred millions, rents were raised: rooms in the new buildings cost $4 to $6 a month. Five years ago rooms in the same location, but in the old buildings, on the narrow alleys, cost only $1.50 to $3 a month. The trend of population in America is steadily toward the cities, and unless checked, America will soon be confronted with this same problem which has proved so difficult of solution in Italy.

To one familiar with Italy's financial condition it is matter for surprise that any progress at all has been made toward remedying the evil of overcrowding in cities. With a population of barely 29,000,000 the public debt amounts to 9,053,000.000 lire. The interest alone amounts to 489,295,422.24 lire per year. Were the people of the United States similarly burdened merely in proportion to their population without regard to greater relative resources, the one item of interest on their public debt would cost $200,000,000 a year, or more than half the present actual expenses of government, pensions included. Italy makes no attempt to pay the principal of her debt; in fact, it is only by the greatest effort that the interest is paid. Italians are fairly up to the neck in taxes. The income tax is $13\frac{1}{5}$ per cent; that is, for every hundred dollars an Italian earns, $13.20

goes to the government. While unfinished, there is no tax on houses, but as soon as completed, the tax is heavy. The Marquis Pancaiticci has been living for years in a Moorish villa outside of Florence, paying no tax through the simple device of always having an addition in course of construction. The villa has in this way acquired fifteen new rooms, but being still "incomplete," does not yet appear on the assessor's books. Every one cannot adopt the noble marquis's method, consequently the house-tax on the average house ranges from seven to ten lire per capita. In Rome, three taxes alone, the land, income, and house taxes, amount to 34.30 lire per capita, and this amount is swelled to 92.42 lire by other taxes *not* including import duties. As if all this were not enough, taxes are levied to give bounties to certain favored classes. The bounty paid sailing-vessels amounted in 1888 to $436,934.55 (2,263,909.57 lire).

How does Italy raise this enormous sum of $18.48 per capita? In 1890 the post-office and telegraph receipts were 45,515,346.18 and 12,232,783 lire respectively — sums not enough to defray the expense of running those departments of the public service. Visitors to museums, art galleries, and antiquities paid in 1890, 348,995.40 lire entrance fees — not enough to pay the cost of excavations and guards. The taxes which bear the brunt of the government's expenses are the tariffs on foreign imports and the octroi duties on imports into cities and towns. Towns are divided into two classes, closed (with walls and gates) and open; there are 349 closed and 7891 open towns, all of which pay to the general government a portion of their octroi receipts. Some towns agree with the government upon a fixed sum, and these, called "Abbonati," manage their own octroi. When an agreement cannot be reached, the government places its own officers at the town's gates, collects the octroi, pockets its share and turns the rest over to the municipality. In 1890 the general government received from towns of the Abbonati class, 49,542,750 lire ; through the collection of its own officers 31,792,182, a grand total of 81,334,932 ($16,-453,637.08). The larger the town, the larger the amount paid. Genoa's octroi contribution in 1890 was 2,992,000, or 9.89 lire per capita. Rome's was 5,818,000, 17.92 lire per capita; Naples' was 18,726,720, or 23.60 lire per capita. This onerous tax, by increasing the cost of living in cities, is having the effect of pushing manufactures into the country, which in turn increases the cost of manufacture — coal, goods, and machinery having to be transported greater distances, houses having to be specially erected for workmen, etc., and lessens Italy's ability to compete with countries not burdened with so artificial a system.

An article imported from a foreign country into Italy is subject to three tariffs, — one at the frontier, another at the city gate for the city, and still another at the gate for the general government. The octroi tax in favor of the city may equal but not exceed one-half the amount paid the state. To this rule there are four exceptions, — flour, bread, macaroni, and rice. On those articles a sur-tax may be levied equal to one-fifth of their value, based upon the average value for the preceding five years. The amount of octroi paid the state varies according to the city's "class"; cities of 50,000 and over belong to the first class. The second class comprises cities of from 20,001 to 50,000 ; the third class, from 8001 to 20,000 ; the fourth class embraces all towns of 8000 and under. One who lives in a city of more than 50,000 inhabitants pays to the state 19 cents for every 100 pounds of flour he brings into the city, whereas one living in a town of less than 8000 pays only 14.3 cents. A similar difference exists on other articles, as will be seen from the following specimens of —

Octroi Duties levied by the State in the Different Classes of Towns.

ARTICLES.	QUANTITY.	1ST CLASS. Lire.	2D CLASS. Lire.	3D CLASS. Lire.	4TH CLASS. Lire.
Wine and vinegar	hectolitre [1]	7.00	5.00	4.00	3.50
" " "	per bottle	.15	.10	.05	.05
Grapes	quintal [2]	3.50	2.50	2.00	1.50
Beef	head	40.00	30.00	25.00	20.00
Calves one year old	"	22.00	16.00	14.00	12.00
Calves under one year	"	12.00	10.00	8.00	6.00
Sucking pigs	"	5.00	4.00	3.00	2.00
Sheep, goats	"	.50	.40	.30	.25
Pork	"	16.00	12.00	10.00	8.00
Flour	quintal	2.00	1.80	1.60	1.40
Butter	"	8.00	7.00	6.00	5.00
Sugar	"	10.00	8.00	6.00	4.00

The framer of these taxes must have strongly disapproved of pork; the tax of $3 per hog and $1 per sucking pig prohibits the consumption of those articles except by the rich. An Italian economical writer, the Marchese Vilfredo Pareto, after a careful investigation, published a table showing the income and condition of a typical mechanic's family of four persons in Florence, the expenses of the family, and the amount that the family paid in taxes. The four persons composing this family were all healthy, sober, and in regular employment. Nothing was expended for medical treatment and none of them smoked, which caused a sensible diminution of expense. The sum of their earnings was 2380 lire ($452.20). Their total expenses were 2366.50 lire ($449.63), of which 565.63 lire, or 23.9 per cent, were for taxes distributed as follows: 346.74 lire (14.7 per cent) to the state; 119.22 lire (5 per cent) to the city; 10.37 lire (0.4 per cent) to the province; and 89.30 lire (3.8 per cent) to the national producer. By this latter tax

[1] 1 hectolitre = 105½ quarts. [2] 1 quintal = 112 pounds.

Signor Pareto means the excess price which the national producer is enabled to charge owing to the heavy protective tariff at the frontier. The signor makes this estimate by comparing prices in London, where there is no duty, with prices in Florence. Italian farmers are protected by a duty of 50 lire per ton on foreign wheat; starting from this basis, Signor Pareto finds that of 387 lire spent for bread, 93.84 was to cover taxation which was divided as follows: 36.11 to the state, 13.49 to the town, and 44.24 to the national producer. On some items more was spent in tax than for the article consumed. The year's bill for salt was 13.20 lire; 11.11 of this was tax. Of 39.20 spent for petroleum 23.33 was tax; that is, but for the octroi, petroleum which cost 39.20 would have cost only 15.85 ($2.90 instead of $7.44). Signor Pareto, quoting from an English economical writer, presents a similar table for an English artisan's family. The comparison shows that the Englishman's taxes amount to 84.05 lire, or 4.4 per cent of his whole earnings, while of the Italian's income 565, or 23.9 per cent go to pay taxes.

Curious and unjust as is this system of taxation, it seems deeply rooted not only in Italy, but in several other states in Europe. When Queen Isabella was driven out of Spain, one of the first acts of the revolutionists was to abolish the octroi. When the monarchy was restored, so too was the octroi, and it flourishes in Spain to-day. The French republicans abolished the octroi in 1791; the Bourbons revived it in 1816, and it still exists in France. In Bavaria, as if the octroi were not sufficiently unjust, pressing hardest upon those least able to bear it, the aristocracy in some instances are actually relieved of any burden whatever, being accorded the privilege of introducing articles into towns free of duty, while mortals of common clay are stopped by the octroi officers, and made to pay a heavy tax. Octroi duties are levied in the Grand Duchy of Hesse, also in Wurtemberg, Saxe-Weimar, and the Grand Duchy of Baden. They do not exist in Denmark or Russia, and the revolution of 1848 inaugurated an agitation which led to their abolition in Belgium in 1860, and Holland in 1866. To an American or Englishman the vexation, not to speak of the expense, involved in a system that places at a town's every outlet, officers authorized to pry into your bundles and parcels, even into your pockets, is so great as to seem unbearable; yet, as shown, this odious system is fastened in all the principal countries of Europe.

"Vedi Napoli e poi mori" (see Naples and then die). The traveller who goes to Naples to hire a boat is likely to observe this well-known injunction; for of all aggravating, soul-wearing inventions, commend me to the Italian fisherman trying to get the better of you in a bargain. Mack, Perigarde, and I dressed in our most dilapidated and *negligé* style, in the hope that the Italian boatmen would be impressed with a sense of our impecuniosity, and not mistake us for English Milords. Our rough garb undoubtedly had its effect, still the impulse to demand three or four times as much as they were really willing to take was irresistible. For two days we walked the quays, looking first at this boat, then at that, and finding none to our liking. One was too broad and clumsy, one was worm-eaten and unsafe, another just suited us, but the owner would not go on a cruise. Finally, however, we found a boat at Castellamare that looked as if it would do, and the owner said he would be willing to go on the cruise whether it lasted a month or a year. It was an ordinary boat such as the Italians use on the Mediterranean, thirty-eight feet six inches long from stem to stern, ten feet beam, and sixteen tons' displacement. The keel was weighted to prevent capsizing, and the little cabin ran back to within three feet of the wheel, so that in rough weather, when the hatch was closed, there was little or no chance to ship a sea: the water ran off the slanting roof of the cabin as from a duck's back. When we had examined the *Principe Farnese* from top to bottom, and decided that it was a snug little craft,

and just the thing we wanted, I asked Luigi Conti, the owner, what rent he would charge.

"Mille lire," said Conti, darting at us a half furtive, half expectant glance.

"Mille lire?" I said musingly, "a thousand lire? That is about two hundred dollars. Of course, Luigi, that sum includes your services?"

"Oh no, signore," deprecatingly; "with me, tutto compresso, mille due centi lire."

"A thousand lire includes a boy as well as yourself?" I continued, pretending not to notice the interruption.

"Oh no, signore; non e possibile."

"And you will provide your own food?"

"No, no, signore; non e possibile."

"Well, then, I will tell you what we will do," I said, looking him in the face; "you ask a thousand lire for the boat alone; we will give you five hundred and fifty lire a month for the boat, including the services of yourself and a boy not less than sixteen years old."

We had been informed by an Italian gentleman that 550 lire ($105) was about the right sum for such a boat. Luigi shrugged his shoulders and burst into a pyrotechnical display of Italian — we must be mad to speak of 550 lire; it was ridiculous, absolutely ridiculous. The *Principe Farnese* was a beautiful boat, worth fully 5000 lire; it would not pay to rent it for a centesimo less than 1000 per month, but since it was for Inglese, he would let it go for 950; 950, but not a centesimo less, etc., etc. We smiled at this, and returned to Naples; where, while waiting for our proposition to work its way into Luigi's mind, we posted ourselves as to yachts, and the season suitable for boating on the Mediterranean. The last mail had brought an interesting article on yachts, by Dr. Kelly of the United States Navy: —

"A number one yacht has on deck three steel houses, teak

sheathed and mahogany lined; in the forward one is a smoking-room, furnished with divans and tables, and so framed with plate-glass windows as to give an uninterrupted view ahead and on each beam. Abaft this are a chart-room, cabin, and kitchen, between which a vestibule and carved oak stairway lead below to the owner's quarters. The saloon is thirty-one feet wide and eighteen feet long. Its floor is a mosaic of hard wood, and the sides and ceilings are wainscoted and panelled with polished native woods and finished in enamel of white and gold. A carved mantel and fireplace face the entrance. Overhead is a domed skylight; and, in every available spot, rugs, tapestries, pictures, cabinet lamps, and the one hundred and one accessories of the most opulent house accentuate the warmth and color. Forward of this are eight state-rooms built of cherry and walnut, trimmed in white and gold, and furnished with rugs and tapestries. Each has a hand-carved bed, dressing-table, chiffonnier, and wardrobe. In the floor is a porcelain bath, let in so deftly that the crack can scarcely be seen, even when the rug is removed. In a corner, a Scotch marble basin is supplied with hot, cold, and salt water. Electric bells and incandescent lamps are at command; and through a wide-rimmed, polished air-port, a charming measure of sea and sky is secured. A nursery nineteen feet long, eleven feet in width, completes the owner's special quarters. This vessel cruises at home and abroad and carries a crew of fifty."

"We might possibly get along without the porcelain bath," said Mack, with sorrowful gravity; "but we must have the tapestries and the nineteen-foot nursery, — we can never make this boat trip without a nursery. Does Dr. Kelly give the cost of his number one yacht?"

"Yes, $300,000 to build. The annual expense is not so much."

"Oh, I suppose not; the annual expense must be a mere trifle."

"Yes, a mere trifle; $100,000 a year."

After reading the description of Dr. Kelly's yacht, the *Principe Farnese* seemed "crowded and bilgy"; and when we saw Luigi again, we lowered our offer to 500 lire per month.

"Five hundred!" exclaimed Luigi, throwing up his hands and rolling his eyes; "you offered yesterday five hundred and fifty."

"True, Luigi, but yesterday is not to-day. We offer only five hundred to-day," and off we went to spend the day at Pompeii.

The next day a similar scene was enacted.

"Come, take it at eight hundred lire, only eight hundred," said Luigi.

"No, we shall give you only four hundred and fifty, not a centesimo more."

"Four hundred and fifty?" repeated Luigi, dazed. "Dio mio, signore, you offered five hundred and fifty the first day—"

"But this is not the first day."

"And five hundred the second day—"

"This is not the second day."

"*Sicuro, c' e vero — c' e vero* — true, too true," said Luigi, with a sigh. "Come, then, take it at five hundred and fifty lire, the sum you first offered."

But we refused: we did not tell Luigi of the sibylline books, but we played that sibylline game on him with great success.

"To-day," we said, "we offer you four hundred and fifty lire. If you do not accept, to-morrow we shall offer you but four hundred. Think before you refuse — four hundred and fifty lire are nine thousand soldi: nine thousand soldi are forty-five thousand centesimi — think of forty-five thousand centesimi every month, and meat and bread to your fill. That is what we offer to-day; to-morrow it will be too late."

Luigi could not withstand this: forty-five thousand centesimi seemed a big sum, and he closed the bargain on the spot. We adjourned to a café where an iron-clad contract was drawn up, renting us the *Principe Farnese* for four hundred and fifty lire ($85.50) per month, that sum to include the services of Luigi Conti and one able-bodied boy not less than sixteen. There were many formalities in connection with the writing and signing of this contract; various official stamps and seals had to be placed on the document. When everything was in shape, we proceeded to lay in a stock of supplies. Not much was needed, as our cruise was to be for the most part along shore. A keg of sea-biscuits, a box of macaroni, a cask of red wine, some sugar, dried beef, salami, and a barrel of water about completed our store of food. We expected to obtain vegetables, eggs, and other fresh supplies from day to day, at each stopping-place. The rest of the cargo consisted of our personal effects, two rubber vests that could be inflated to serve as life-preservers, two Bowie-knives, four forty-two calibre Smith & Wesson revolvers, several dozen boxes of cartridges, and the kodak with a supply of gelatine plates. These things were stowed snugly away in the forward part of the boat, and on the second morning after closing the contract with Luigi Conti, the *Principe Farnese* hoisted her lateen sail to the breeze, and glided out of the beautiful bay of Naples.

Our first trip was to Capri, only a few miles away. The *Principe Farnese* behaved beautifully. All of us were highly elated: Mack became so enthusiastic that he proposed to spend the night in the boat, but Perigarde and I overruled that idea, as we would have as many nights on the boat as we would want before the trip was over: so we went to the Blue Grotto Hotel, charmingly situated on one of Capri's bluffs. From the door of the hotel we could see grim old Vesuvius smoking in the distance, at his feet the dead city of Pompeii, and two or three living villages, beyond the beautiful city of Naples, and the bay with its thousand white-sailed boats skimming like birds over the water. On the beach at the foot of the cliff, pretty Capri girls, their throats circled with coral beads, sat stringing beads to sell to travellers. They were so pretty (the girls, not the beads) that we had great difficulty keeping Perigarde from bankrupting himself, buying coral beads and other ornaments. In the rear of the Blue Grotto Hotel is a grove of orange and lemon trees, back of these rises a lofty precipice two thousand feet above the sea, whence the tyrant Tiberius used to hurl his unhappy victims to the rocks below.

Tourists of the "personally conducted" sort allow three hours in which to see Capri. The steamer leaves Naples at nine in the morning, arrives at Capri at noon, and starts on the return trip at three, reaching Naples at six. My first visit to Capri was on the Naples steamer, but so delightful were the very first impressions that I gave up my return ticket, remained a whole week on the island, and regretted that I was unable to stay still longer. In addition to the picturesqueness of the place, Capri possesses the further advantage of affording cheap and good living. For a dollar a day one lives sumptuously at the Blue Grotto Hotel. The table is loaded with fruits and delicacies, and if at any time we wanted oranges or lemons, we had only to step into the grove at the rear of the hotel and pluck them at our pleasure.

There was a crowd on the beach when we departed. All stared at us, laughing and chattering like a lot of magpies. With a grin, Luigi said they had gathered to see the "three mad Inglese."

"Why do they think we are mad?"

"Maria Corlina, mia moglie [my wife] told them you were going to Africa in the *Principe Farnese;* she say I mad to go with you."

"Where is your wife?"

"Ecco," said Luigi, with a wave of his hand. We saw a passably good-looking Italian woman standing near our "langia" (small boat, or tender), a baby in her arms, and two youngsters tugging at her dress. "That is Maria Corlina," said Luigi. "She came over from Castellamare last night with the market boat. *Ella vorrà dirvi addio* — she wants to say good-bye."

Maria did not seem to view us with favor: probably she feared the three madmen from unknown lands would dump her husband in the sea and sail off with his boat. To the Italian peasant who lives a lifetime without going a day's walk from his birthplace, America and England seem as distant as the moon itself. Luigi appeared to enjoy the situation. Several times as we rowed out to the *Principe Farnese* he dropped his oars, to wave his hat and blow kisses to his wife and addios to the crowd. We left Capri at nine: when we cast anchor under the precipitous cliffs on whose summits rests the town of Sorrento, it was noon. So far we had not dined on board our "yacht." I proposed making a start in the bay of Sorrento. Sorrento is not only a fashionable resort with tourists, and therefore expensive, but the landlords have borrowed our American idea of trusts. The principal hotels are run by the brothers of a Sorrento family. We had not come all the way to Italy to find trusts, so we decided to have nothing to do with Sorrento hotels, and forthwith began to prepare our own dinner on the boat. Conti made a fire in the tiny stove, Mack got out the dishes, or rather the tin cups and pans, Perigarde opened a bottle of tomatoes, and I got out the box of macaroni. Francati, our cabin boy, did the cooking. The salt sea-air, the lovely surroundings, the utter freedom from the turbulent world, — youth, hope in the future, care we had left behind, — all these sharpened hunger, and that frugal food seemed a feast.

The rocks on which Sorrento stands rise perpendicularly from the sea. Here and there rifts in the rock afford approaches from the Marina to the streets and piazza. These frowning cliffs would give the city a rather formidable aspect but for the luxuriant orange, lemon, and nut groves which charm and captivate the eye with their exquisite colors of green and gold. The atmosphere is so soft and balmy, the whole scene so redolent with beauty and romance, one is almost tempted to settle down to inertia and dream life away. We resisted the temptation, and that same afternoon left Sorrento, Mack in the boat, Perigarde and I on foot across the mountains to Scaricatajo, where we expected to find Mack and the *Principe Farnese*. Although the coast from Sorrento around the Pointa de Campanella is not particularly fine, we regretted we had not gone with Mack in the boat, — this for the simple reason that if the coast was not unusually grand, the road over the mountain was not at all so. The first half-hour out from Sorrento leads the pedestrian upon a height whence a magnificent view is obtained of Ischia and Procida ; a few moments more, however, brings him between two high walls, and unless he is interested in studying Italian stones and masonry he will find the trip neither instructive nor entertaining. Only a few houses are passed. We were glad when we reached the stairs in the rock leading down to Scaricatajo. Mack and the boat were already off the beach ; they had had a spanking breeze, and made the trip in excellent time. The water at Scaricatajo was rough and caused trouble in boarding the *Principe Farnese*. Luigi and Francati rowed the langia as near the rocky cliff as they dared. Twice they endeavored to get the langia broadside to the sea and just beyond the break of the waves. This, however, was a difficult thing to do. Perceiving that even if they were successful, the langia would still be too far for us to reach her, we ended the matter by going to the boat, since it would not come to us. A plunge, a few vigorous strokes, and Luigi had me by the arm pulling me into the boat. Perigarde followed, and in five minutes we were safe aboard the *Principe Farnese*. This was one of the advantages of "roughing" it; we did not mind wetting our old clothes.

While we donned dry clothing, Francati lashed the langia

astern, Luigi let out his sail, and we started across the bay direct for Capo Sottile. The breeze from the west continued, and we rounded the cape before dark. After a glimpse of the village of Prajano with its olive and orange orchards, we passed along under the very shadow of the steep cliffs that line this part of the coast all the way to Amalfi. It was eight o'clock when we cast anchor in Amalfi's harbor. We ate supper and slept in the boat.

CHAPTER XVI

Amalfi — Macaroni-Makers — Burden-Bearers on the Via Molini — A Night Cruise to Pæstum — How Mack nearly lost his Ear — Puffed Preservers at Policastro — We take a Passenger — Paranzo's Strange Story — Pursued by his Wife — Reception at Fuscaldo — Mistaken for Princes — The Banquet, the Speech, and the Escape

AMALFI, which once had fifty thousand inhabitants, has now not more than ten thousand; nevertheless, it is a lively place, and possesses a number of manufactories of paper, soap, and macaroni. We understood quite well what the natives did with macaroni, we could also conceive that they might have a use for paper; but neither Mack, Perigarde, nor I could imagine what they did with the soap they manufacture. In fact, when we rowed ashore that morning, and passed up the street cut in the deep ravine which winds its way up to the highest part of the town and the summit of the lofty mountains beyond, we came to the conclusion that, however much soap they manufacture, they retain but little for home use. A more ragged and dirty, although picturesque, set of people cannot be found in Italy. With the exception of a few fishermen, almost the entire population is engaged in the manufacture of paper, macaroni, and soap. To an American the factories look antiquated and primitive, especially those of macaroni. The rooms where this staple Italian food is made are paved with brick or stone flagging; long poles run from one wall to another, seven or eight feet from the floor; over these poles the macaroni is strung to dry. As soon as you enter, you see the dark-skinned Italians with their short trousers, naked feet and legs, and bodies naked from the waist up, throwing the long strings of freshly made macaroni over the poles, and taking down those poles where the macaroni has dried. Cleanliness is not the most noticeable feature of these establishments. After watching the way in which the half-naked Italians handled the macaroni, slinging it over the long poles, often dropping it on the stone flagging, Perigarde's nose turned up, as he informed us of his determination to eat no more macaroni in the future. This resolution lasted just three hours; in other words, until dinner time. It could not well have lasted longer, for the tramp tourist in Italy must eat macaroni or nothing. It forms the principal article of food of the men who make it, as well as of those who have never seen the dirt that is mixed with it in the process of manufacture. The macaroni-maker earns two lire (thirty-eight cents) per day. He often has to support a family on this sum, so it is not surprising that macaroni forms his main if not sole diet. In the balmy climate of Southern Italy, a little clothing goes a long way: on a diet of macaroni and onions, the Italian workman manages to exist on thirty-eight cents a day as well, if not better, than does his American or English brother, in his more inhospitable climate, on twice or three times that sum.

After visiting the factories, we climbed the broad flight of stairs which lead to the Cathedral of St. Andrea. This ancient building dates back to the eleventh century. It was about that period and near this very spot that the celebrated Pandects of Justinian were accidentally discovered after having been lost to the world more than six hundred years. The manuscript of that wonderful compilation of ancient Roman laws which was buried for so many centuries until its accidental discovery, during the war between Amalfi and Pisa, now rests in the Laurentian Library, where it has, for hundreds of years, proved an inexhaustible source of information to the law-writers of all nations and climes. Every person who understands the spirit of law, understands the importance of the discovery of this mine of information, containing the legal wisdom of Rome accumulated during a thousand years. Every one knows how much we, to-day, are indebted to that manuscript, found in Amalfi eight hundred years ago, for the spirit and theory of our own laws; but, great as was the result to the world of that discovery, during the Pisan war, few modern Amalfians realize it; few even know what is meant by Justinian's Pandects.

On the narrow Valle dei Molini, just back of Amalfi, are a dozen paper-mills driven by a small stream. We followed this ravine some three-quarters of a mile to a point where it narrowed to a few feet, and whence we obtained a view of the quaint old town and the mills surrounded by orange and lemon groves. The path leading up the steep ravine crosses and recrosses the rushing stream and is usually filled with women carrying huge bundles of paper on their backs. Mack took several photographs of these poor women staggering under their burdens; he also "kodaked" two priests who were leisurely strolling down the path, cool and comfortable, in strong contrast to the bowed and wrinkled burden-carriers. Another photograph which Mack took told a tale. It was that of a dozen or so children who met us as we ascended the ravine, and who stopped to stare at the "Inglesi." The children were, some of them, not more than five years old, yet each carried in the arms a baby. The mothers were hard at work carrying those heavy bundles of paper down to the sea, so that the children and babies have to nurse each other.

When we returned down the ravine-like street to the beach, we saw the *Principe Farnese* at anchor where we had left her in the morning, but all our efforts failed to bring forth either Luigi or Francati — we shouted and yelled to no purpose. At length we hired a fisherman to row us out to the boat. To our astonishment, the langia was gone, and with it Luigi and Francati. It was not long, however, before they returned. They had tired of waiting for us, and made a trip to a cheap osteria (cheap eating-house) on shore to drink wine and chat. We reprimanded Luigi for leaving the boat, and asked if he wished us to break the contract and throw the boat back on his hands. This seemed to have a salutary effect, and I thought no more of the matter, but Mack was not satisfied. After housing the anchor and setting sail, he beckoned me to come into the cabin. When we were alone, the door closed, Luigi, Francati, and Perigarde on deck, Mack asked me what I thought.

"About what?"

"About this desertion business."

"They got lonesome and went off on a lark. I don't believe they will do it again, after the talk we gave them."

"Not if they merely went off on a lark; but is that what they went for? I fear there is something under this. We had better keep a sharp lookout."

"What do you suspect? Have you heard anything?"

Mack took an envelope from his pocket, produced therefrom a newspaper clipping, and handed it to me to read. He had received the clipping, that day at Amalfi, in a letter from America. It described how an English tourist who had chartered a boat to go to the Lipari Islands was murdered at sea by his crew for the sake of the gold he carried or was supposed to carry.

"To these Italians," said Mack, "we doubtless appear men of wealth. Suppose they chose to rob us and throw us overboard, who is to tell on them?"

This was rather startling: we agreed that caution would do no harm, so looked to our pistols and knives. In a hand-to-hand encounter, the razor-bladed Bowies would be more effectual than either gun or pistol. After assuring ourselves that the weapons were in good condition we went on deck, took Perigarde into our confidence, and arranged to take turn about in the watches. Luigi and Francati were holding a whispered conversation. Upon our approach they separated, and we fancied that Luigi looked rather guilty.

From Amalfi to Salerno there is one stretch of grand cliffs and mountains. Winding around these dizzy heights, often at a distance of five hundred feet above the sea, is a road cut out of the solid rock. It is a magnificent trip either by road or water. Originally we intended to follow the coast for the sake of this grand view, but to do so would add several hours to our journey, so we decided to make direct for Pæstum. At the best we could not arrive there before midnight, and in view of the suspicions which were now aroused neither of us liked the idea of an all-night sail with what might be two murderous pirates. By sundown we were out of sight of land, and for all we could tell or see might be in the open ocean. Luigi assured us that another hour or two would again bring the coast in view and that we would reach Pæstum not later than twelve or one o'clock. As the night shadows came on and the coast receded, we realized that we were five thousand miles from home, on a small boat with two strange Italians. We again read that newspaper clipping and shuddered at the account of the murder of the English tourist.

Mack stood first watch, while Perigarde and I went to our bunks in the cabin, where, thanks to our long day's wanderings, we were soon fast asleep. I do not know how long this sleep lasted, possibly not more than an hour, when I was suddenly startled by loud yells and screams for help. Jumping up, pistols in hand, I rushed to the cabin door, expecting to face desperate pirates. I was confronted by Luigi and Francati with Mack's long Bowie gleaming in the bright moonlight.

"Resta — aspetto —"

"Stop," I yelled, covering the two Italians with my pistol. Luckily they dodged before the pistol discharged; there was a terrible shout, and the next moment both pistol and knife were wrenched from my hands.

"*Dio mio*," exclaimed Luigi. "He is mad; hold him down, signore! The very devil is in him." Mack had seized me from behind, while Francati clutched hold of my wrists. I struggled wildly.

"For God's sake, what are you doing?" cried Mack.

Then my senses came to me. I realized the situation. I had been assailed, not by bold pirates, but by a stupid nightmare.

"I only regret," I said, snappishly, to Mack, "that I didn't clip off one of your ears. You deserve it, going around with your newspaper yarns, frightening the life out of a fellow. I have had enough of this pirate business. If Luigi and Francati want to cut our throats for the few old duds we have, let 'em do it. No more night watches or nightmares for me."

Mack agreed to this; but as we were now in sight of Pæstum, we sat up until we found ourselves safely anchored; then all hands turned in. Luigi and Francati, about whom we had been so suspicious, were the first to fall asleep. We soon followed their example. The light on the mast being trimmed, and everything in ship shape, both passengers and crew of the *Principe Farnese* were soon rocked asleep by the gentle swell of the waves in the harbor of ancient Pæstum. By the rise of another sun, our unworthy suspicions had fled forever: from that hour we put trust in our Italian boatmen, and that trust was not betrayed.

Going south from Policastro to Sicily, the coast is studded with numerous small towns, but the sixty miles intervening between Pæstum and Policastro contain scarce a single village. It was on this account that we wished to make no stop, after leaving Pæstum, until we rounded Cape della Licosa and anchored off Policastro. While Mack got out the kodak to take views of the ruins, the rest of us prepared our breakfast of macaroni, salami, and wine. The little stove did not take long to heat; the macaroni, seasoned with cheese, olive oil, and tomatoes, was ready even before Mack had finished with the kodak. We observed no ceremony on the *Principe Farnese;* there were no waiters in dress suits, no courses or changes of plates. As soon as Francati announced the macaroni ready, each of us took his tin plate, received from Francati's big ladle a bountiful supply, helped ourselves to a chunk of bread and salami, and, filling a tin cup with wine from the cask, retired to the deck, or some other convenient place, and there proceeded to lose our appetites as best we could.

After breakfast, leaving Francati to clean up and watch the things, we took Luigi in the langia and rowed ashore. Pæstum lies a mile and a half north of the Salso, a little stream, at whose mouth our boat landed. Twenty minutes brought us to the wall of the town; in an hour more we had circled around to the gate on the north, whence entrance to the city is made through the street of the tombs. These ruins date back more than five hundred years before Christ. The temple of Neptune is an interesting and imposing ruin. The thirty-six Doric columns of travertine stone still stand as they stood twenty-five centuries ago. The inner series of columns, which supported the roof, also remain to attest the artistic and architectural skill of the founders of ancient Pæstum. Mack took views of these classic ruins, built long before Rome was known or feared, centuries before Alexander was born, when Europe, so to speak, was in its infancy. Here, where once lived a busy populace, every trace of city life is gone, except the grand old ruins and temples. A solitary herdsman lives in a haystack-like hut, in the midst of the desolate plain, which was once the centre of the busy city. His thatched, conical hut, supported on poles ten feet above the ground, was so odd that Mack levelled the kodak for a photograph, whereupon the herdsman scampered down the ladder, and took to his heels, fancying the kodak some sort of a gun. His family were not so nimble, and their pictures were taken before they could descend the ladder.

It was noon when we returned aboard: Luigi spread the lateen sail, and got the *Principe Farnese* under way, while Mack and Perigarde, with equal promptness, began to prepare dinner. Francati had filled the cask with fresh water; he had also laid in a supply of finnochio and eggs, so that the dinner we had, after leaving Pæstum, was quite a swell affair. The stretch between Pæstum and Policastro was longer than any we had yet taken, longer than we would be likely to take, unless we decided to extend the trip to Greece or Africa. On this stretch, it was necessary to divide the day into watches; this we proceeded to do. Mack and I took the first watch, Luigi and Francati were to come on at six and go off at midnight. Perigarde undertook the management of the kitchen, the preparation of the food, etc., in lieu of standing watch.

When Mack and I took our first watch, the breeze was brisk, so we had little to do but give the wheel an occasional turn, and look at the lonely coast and still lonelier mountains, which, a few miles back from the sea, reared their lofty summits to the very clouds. In those first hours, when we were fresh, and when the *Principe Farnese* was behaving so well, Mack and I were enthusiastic. We voted yachting an immense success, and liked it so much that, when six o'clock came, we still tarried on deck, loth to crawl into the cabin and lose all that beauty of sea and land. What a difference there was between the first and second watch! The hours of the second watch, between midnight and six, seemed three times as long as those of the first. We thought day would never come. When it finally came, we were swift enough to turn in. Perhaps custom would make this breaking up of one's night easy, but we did not keep up the custom long enough to find it pleasant. We reached Policastro at noon, and before leaving, decided thereafter to run into some port every night; and, by so doing, not only avoid missing any of the scenery, but also avoid the necessity of being aroused out of bed at midnight to sit on deck and turn a wheel. We passed the Pointa di Spartivento at nine in the morning, then turned our course due east, and, a little after twelve, were lying at anchor in the bay of Policastro, a hundred yards from the town of that name.

The traveller in Italy who visits only such places as are convenient by rail or water, will never be able to fully realize the strangeness and quaintness to be found in less accessible parts of the kingdom. Policastro lies wholly out of the common route of travel. It is distant from the railroad, and few steamers ever touch there. Hence it is seldom visited by tourists. When we landed there, we were looked upon much as Barnum's white elephant is looked upon by the American small boy. The moment we stepped ashore, we were surrounded by a crowd of staring men, women, and children. We had not eaten dinner on the boat, and the first place we went to was a small trattoria (restaurant). During the progress of our dinner, in a spirit of boyish folly, we blew into the tube of our rubber life-preserver vests until our breasts and sides bulged out in the most surprising manner. The waiter stared until we thought his eyes would pop out. We gravely continued eating, now and then, unperceived, blowing a little more wind in our vests, until we looked like Falstaffs, instead of the slim fellows, who had first sat down at the table. So great was the waiter's surprise, he dropped the eggs on the stone-paved floor. The proprietor, a swarthy, dark-eyed man, came hopping forward, and cried : —

"Signore, pardono, it was an accident, it was — but Dio mio, signore — you — "

The Corinthian Canal

And the proprietor's eyes also seemed about to pop out.

"What's the matter, padrone?" we asked innocently.

"Signore, you grow, you get big, you — "

"Oh," we replied, "you think we grow rapidly? In our country, that is nothing. When Americans eat they grow fat. It does not last long, though. In a few minutes we grow lean again."

Mack and I slipped open the valve in the tube, and by gently pressing our arms against our sides, slowly drove the air out. Pietro and his master saw us shrink before their very eyes, and to say that they were astonished is to put the case mildly; they were dazed. The news rapidly spread, and in less than a quarter of an hour several hundred people packed the street in front of the trattoria, some pressed through the door, others flattened their noses against the glass window, to get a glimpse of the marvellous men who could become both fat and lean in the course of a few minutes. About seven o'clock we went down to the *Principe Farnese* to embark for Maratea, where we intended spending the night: the large crowd followed at our heels. I doubt if travellers were ever honored with more attention than we received at the hands of the inhabitants of Policastro.

Maratea is but a few miles from Policastro. We expected to make the trip before bedtime. When we saw Luigi, however, he said it would be impossible, as the wind was almost dead against us: accordingly we slept on the boat, and made an early start next morning. The event proved this the better plan. By four in the morning, the wind had shifted round to the north, and we had a spanking breeze that brought us to Maratea a little after nine. We had a leisurely breakfast, then went ashore. We told Francati to return with the langia in an hour, — that time we deemed ample for seeing the sights of the village, — and started up the ravine that leads to the piazza or square. The Apennines skirt all this part of the coast of

Italy and many if not most of the towns are perched on high hills or spurs of the mountains. The deep ravines that lead to the mountain peaks are utilized as approaches to the towns : in the case of Maratea there are several ravines. We asked an intelligent-looking man standing near the landing, which of the ravines was most direct. To our astonishment he replied in very good English : —

"You take the Strada Vittorio Emanuele to the left. It is only a short walk, but be careful to turn to the right at the first cross-street. The road to the left leads to Policastro."

"And when we turn to the right, are there still other cross-roads?"

"No, signore ; but permit me. I shall accompany you."

We made some show of not wishing him to put himself to this trouble, but as we really wanted him to go, we did not make our remonstrances very emphatic. It was not every day that we had a chance to speak English, and this Italian spoke almost as if to the manor born.

"I have been in England," he said in reply to the compliment we paid his English.

We expected him to add something further about himself, but in this were disappointed. He talked of Italy in general, of Maratea in particular, but of himself he said not a word except by way of explaining his English. In twenty minutes we had reached the piazza, in ten minutes more had seen everything in the town worth seeing.

"It is not much to see," said our new-found acquaintance, who had introduced himself as Filippo Paranzo. "Hardly worth walking up the hill, is it?"

"Oh, it is not so bad as that," we said. "The town is picturesquely located."

Paranzo smiled and shrugged his shoulders.

"You compliment because you think it pleases me ; that is not necessary. I do not live here."

"Ah?" we said inquiringly.

"No," he continued. "My home is in Florence. I have been here only three weeks."

We wondered if he were merely killing time, why he did not go to Rome or Naples. Paranzo smiled and again shrugged his shoulders.

"I dare not go there."

"Dare not?"

"Yes, dare not." Paranzo hastened to add: "I confess, though, that I am heartily sick of this place and desire very much to go to Syracuse, but the steamers do not stop here."

Was that a hint that he would like to go on our boat?

"Ah, do not think that I ask you to take me," he said, as if in answer to our thought. "I only say I would like to go with you. I speak the language; perhaps in Sicily you may have trouble."

Paranzo was so very agreeable, he spoke English so well, we felt embarrassed at having to refuse his request. He accepted the refusal very politely and changed the subject. When finally we started back down the ravine to rejoin Luigi, our new acquaintance parted from us with such words and manners as would have become a Chesterfield.

When we regained the *Principe Farnese*, it was to find that the wind had died out and we were unable to stir an inch. There was no knowing, however, when a breeze would spring up, so we did not go back ashore, but sat out on deck and looked at the mountains and talked of our plans and adventures. Dinner time, and still no breeze. After dinner Mack and Perigarde went into the cabin to take a nap. I got out my writing-materials and began jotting down notes; so absorbing was this occupation, I did not notice the appearance of a stranger until his boat was almost alongside us. To my surprise, on looking up I saw our acquaintance of the morning, Filippo Paranzo.

"I saw from the piazza that you had not departed, and so came down to see you," he explained.

"And I am glad you have come," said I. "You can imagine how monotonous it is lying here all day."

By this time, Paranzo had climbed over the rail on deck. I offered him a stool, and invited him to make himself at home.

"Ah!" he sighed, "if I only could. How I should like to go on with you."

I had not expected this turn; it was annoying. Paranzo instantly divined what I was thinking.

"You will excuse me," he said, "when you hear me, when you learn why it is I am so anxious to leave this place."

He then proceeded to tell one of the queerest stories imaginable. It was unusual enough to meet an English-speaking Italian, in such a place as Maratea, but the climax was not capped until Paranzo gave his reason for wishing to join our party. When I heard it I pinched myself to see if the adventure were real, or if I were not dreaming; but it was no dream this time. Paranzo sat there before me, a solid reality, and his earnestness of manner and troubled look indicated that what he said was true.

"My story," he said, "may appear like a scene from a comic opera. It is nevertheless only too true. You see me, in this out-of-the-way town; you wonder that I do not go to Naples or Rome. I will tell you; it is because I am safe here; safe at least for the present. In Rome or Naples I should not be safe a minute."

"You are, then, a fugitive from justice?"

"No, not from justice. I am a fugitive from — from my wife."

"You are fleeing from your wife?"

"Yes. For seven years I was a singer and sleight-of-hand performer in the theatres of London. One night I was unfortunate enough to attract the favorable attention of an old maid, who had brought her two little nieces to see the Christmas pantomime. The old maid was ugly, ugly as the Old Scratch, but she had money. She — she courted me, and — well, we married. I thought her money would make up for her lack of beauty. She kept telling me how happy I would be, but I did not get a penny; she kept it all tight, tight as sealing-wax. I was not happy, I was a slave, a poor slave, and ran away from London. She followed me to Florence, and hauled me back. I ran away again, what you call 'skip out,' to Rome; that woman followed: I came to Naples; she came, too: then I took the train to Reggio, got off at Coscile, and took the post-wagon to Maratea. But that terrible woman will track me down. She will trace me to Coscile, and from there to Maratea. My only chance is to leave in some private boat. If you knew that woman, you would pity me and take me away."

Paranzo looked so sorrowfully in earnest, I could but pity him. A tear or two stole down his olive cheeks. He was not ashamed to admit he had married an ugly old maid for her money; why should he, when in Europe public sentiment does not condemn a man for marrying money?

"If I once get out of Maratea," he said, "by some other means than the regular modes of travel, she will, after tracing me here, lose all clue, and I shall finally escape."

I instinctively sympathize with slaves, and delight in helping them to freedom, whether owned by masters or mistresses, so I went into the cabin, awoke Mack and Perigarde, and related the Arabian-Night adventure that had befallen us. The upshot was, we took the poor hunted husband under our protection, a passenger on the *Principe Farnese*.

"After all, you may regret coming with us," said Mack, laughingly, to Filippo Paranzo that evening at supper.

"Why so?" asked Paranzo.

"We may have to draw lots to see which of us shall be eaten by the others. This is the last piece of salami we have, and the rest of the larder is almost equally low."

Salami (a sort of sausage) was a favorite with us. We decided to stop at Fuscaldo to replenish the larder. The night was divided again into watches. It was eight o'clock the following morning, before that lazy breeze got us even started; and it was late in the afternoon before we arrived at Fuscaldo. As we rowed ashore in the langia, we observed a rather unusual commotion and a crowd assembled, as if awaiting some important event. Said Mack: —

"We have had a good many crowds out to see us, but none like that. Those people seem to be the big bugs of the town. They have a brass band."

As we neared the shore, the strains of the Italian national hymn reached our ears, and there was a great waving of handkerchiefs and flags. In another minute we had landed. Bidding Francati await our return, we started up the beach. A well-dressed man, with a red sash around his shoulders, stood somewhat in advance of the crowd. As we approached, he made a profound obeisance.

"Scusatemi," said Mack, "ma potete voi dirmi dove io posso trovare uno poco di salami?" (Excuse me, but can you tell me where I can get some salami?)

"Viva il principe!" shouted the man with the red sash.

"What does the fellow mean?" asked Mack of Paranzo. "He doesn't seem to understand his own language. I'm sure I spoke pretty plain Italian. Suppose you try him."

In a courteous manner, Paranzo explained to the gentleman in the red sash that our stock of provisions was exhausted, and we desired to lay in a supply of salami. The man with a sash made another profound bow.

"Capisco, capisco, — I understand," he said; "salami, that is good: all the salami in Fuscaldo is at your Excellencies' service. Long live your Excellencies, and thrice welcome to Fuscaldo."

With this he made a signal to the crowd, which thereupon

gave vent to three hurrahs, very much like our American "three cheers and a tiger."

"That is all very well," said Mack, "but let us hurry on and get the salami."

"Salami?" repeated the red-sashed man, solemnly. "You wish to eat salami: honor us with your Excellencies' attendance, and we shall provide you with the best salami in Italy."

With this, the band struck up a march, two dignified-looking men came forward and joined the man with the red sash; one of the two took Mack by the arm, the other took Filippo Paranzo, while Perigarde and I fell to the lot of the red-sashed man himself. Thus escorted, and followed by the brass band and the crowd of people, we started up the steep ravine of a street that leads to the piazza.

There we found a still larger crowd. Flags were floating in the breeze, women and children were dressed in holiday attire. By the fountain in the centre of the piazza, a small stand was erected, and hither our conductors escorted us. While Mack, Perigarde, and I received no small share of the attention, we could not help observing that it was to our new acquaintance, Filippo Paranzo, that the most marked and profound honors were paid. Paranzo bore his honors with grave dignity.

"Is it possible we have stumbled across some celebrity in disguise?" I whispered to Mack. Before he could reply we had reached the stand, and a short, pudgy, pompous man with hair brushed straight back from his forehead, the breast of his coat covered with badges, ribbons, and medals, stepped forward, took a roll of manuscript from his pocket and began reading what we would have guessed was an address of welcome, could we have imagined why we should be welcomed. He read so glibly, that with our imperfect knowledge of Italian, we did not understand a word he said. When he stopped, our astonishment, already great, was increased upon seeing our new-found acquaintance, Paranzo, step forward and begin rattling off something in Italian by way of reply to the address of the pudgy man with the medals. The only thing in Paranzo's whole talk that either Mack or I could understand was his closing sentence, in which he said that we were English gentlemen and could not speak the language fluently; he, therefore begged the indulgence of the Honorable Governor and Council of Fuscaldo. We were in a pretty state of mystification. There were one or two other speeches from men equally as solemn and self-important as the pudgy man with the medals. To all these speeches Paranzo responded with gracious smiles, bows, and nods of the head. From the speech-making in the piazza, we were escorted to the old castle that stands on the height just west of Fuscaldo. An interesting hour was spent rambling through this ancient relic of the Middle Ages, then we returned to the main part of the town to apartments in one of the oldest and most substantial-looking residences in the place. After our night watches on the *Principe Farnese* and after our journey through Fuscaldo and the castle on the height, we really needed rest and were about to tumble into bed when two of our most courteous entertainers appeared, and forthwith carried us off to a hall where was a large table spread for a banquet. Several hours passed at the table in eating and drinking and in toasts from the various town officers, which were all responded to in brief but graceful terms by our travelling acquaintance of Maratea — an acquaintance who we now felt certain was of no less rank than a prince; though how he happened to be in Maratea and why he took the voyage with us in our dingy boat was a mystery we could not fathom.

When the speech-making and banqueting were over, we were glad to get back to our room and be left to ourselves. Paranzo was given a room with Perigarde. I was put with Mack. The floor of our room was of smooth, square brick, laid with rugs and mats. A wide window opened on a balcony overlooking the street: there were two beds in the room. Hardly had we gone to bed, where we lay discussing the day's singular adventure, before the door softly opened and a voice whispered, "Get up and dress as quietly and quickly as possible." The voice was Paranzo's.

"What is the matter?" we asked.

"We have not a moment to lose. We must go at once. We may get caught. It would be dreadful."

We began to think the man crazy, but Perigarde, who accompanied him, explained in a hurried whisper: —

"Paranzo says we are mistaken for Prince Fallani, who is travelling with three English noblemen. The banquet and brass band were for them. They may arrive at any moment; we must hurry away. Paranzo did not say who we were; they think the prince wants to travel incognito."

While Perigarde was making this whispered explanation, Mack and I were hurriedly dressing. We made our exit as rapidly and quietly as possible, and in a quarter of an hour were on the beach looking for a boat to take us to the *Principe Farnese*. There was no boat to be had at that hour, so, after a hurried consultation, we plunged in the water, and ten minutes later were on board our boat gliding away from that enchanted city.

"Prince Fallani and his English friends," said Paranzo, "have been to the Lipari Islands and have been expected here for the last day or two. It seems the prince hired a boat at Reggio in which they sailed to Stromboli, whence they were to go to Fuscaldo, there to take the post-road to Cosenza. All those preparations were for Prince Fallini. Had the mistake been discovered while we were there, it would have gone hard with us."

"But you knew it was a mistake from the first."

Paranzo shrugged his shoulders.

"What was the harm in having a little fun with those fellows? The only sorrow is that we cannot be there to see them when they find it out in the morning."

That was a "sorrow" as Paranzo put it; but a few weeks after, we were enabled to learn the sequel of that adventure through a paper published in Reggio. Following is a translation of the article: —

"SENSATIONAL INCIDENT IN FUSCALDO.

"On Thursday of last week the Sub-Intendente, Council, and High Dignitaries of the Circondario of Fuscaldo in the province of Calabria-Citeriore were assembled to receive and honor Prince Fallani, who, with three English friends, was expected from Stromboli in the boat which his Highness chartered at this port ten days ago. In the early afternoon of Thursday, a boat answering the description of that chartered by the Prince for his short incognito trip, anchored off the beach of Fuscaldo; in a few moments four gentlemen went ashore. The party of four, three of whom, from their appearance and accent, were at once known to be Englishmen, were received and escorted to the Piazza Vittorio Emanuele, where an address of welcome was delivered by Signor Balthario, Sub-Intendente of the Circondario of Fuscaldo. Subsequently the visitors were conducted to the castle; in the evening there was a banquet at the hall. Upon the conclusion of the festivities the honored guests retired to their chambers, since which time they have not been seen or heard of.

"Early on Friday morning another boat anchored off the beach of Fuscaldo and another party of four rowed ashore. This party acted at first with some circumspection, as if wishing to avoid notice. The fact was not long concealed, however, that this was the genuine Prince Fallani. The question is, who were the impostors who landed at Fuscaldo on the afternoon of Thursday? Prince Fallani fears this impersonation of his party may lead to more harmful results than those at Fuscaldo, and has expressed a desire to see the offenders brought to justice.

"The imposture placed the Sub-Intendente and Council of Fuscaldo in an embarrassing position. The best wines and viands of the town were consumed in the banquet Thursday; so that his Excellency and party were provided with the merest relics of the feast originally intended for them."

CHAPTER XVII

Curious Asylum at Cosenza — Grave of Alaric the Goth — How Two Rivers guard the Barbarian's Bones and Booty — Life on our Boat — Swimming with the Fish — Midnight View of Stromboli — Volcanoes compared — Ascent of Stromboli — Lipari — Strange Conduct of the People — The Girl and the Deserted Quarry — Arrested on Angelo's Peak — Mistaken for Manutengoli — Two Nights in Jail — The Cave-dwellers of Volcano — An Island rises in the Sea

SCARCE had the heights of Fuscaldo disappeared from view than the white houses of Paola became visible in the distance. Paranzo said he had been to Paola, a dull town of eight or ten thousand inhabitants; when quite a young man he had stopped there on his way to Cosenza.

"Cosenza? Where is that?"

"About four hours' walk to the east," replied Paranzo. "Cosenza is an interesting town with historical ruins and a cathedral; apart from that, however, I shall always remember it because of a nearly fatal accident that befell me there. It was at the celebrated asylum of Dr. Martelli Forenzo. One of the patients seized me by the throat and nearly killed me."

Paranzo then went on to describe the weird scenery at the point where the Crati and Busentio rivers come together. Sila's rocky crags lift themselves sixty-two hundred feet into the clouds, — eternal sentinels over the place where two rivers were once swept from their course to afford a burial-place for Alaric the Gothic king.

"Half a mile from this spot," continued Paranzo, in that high oratorical way he sometimes indulged in, "is Dr. Forenzo's remarkable asylum. Aside from the interest afforded by a study of the patients, the grounds and ancient buildings are well worth visiting. A series of circles of trees planted many years ago has grown up, forming a striking arboreal outline of the Coliseum at Rome. I viewed this living model of the celebrated Flavian Amphitheatre from the outside, then entered through the main door, an arch of roses and fragrant vines, and rambled through the labyrinth composed of grass, hedges, flowers, bushes, and tall poplar trees. The traveller who gazes on the beetling walls of the real Coliseum can easily conjure in the imagination the sea of faces, the eighty thousand voices clamoring for blood, the hoarse roaring of lions and other wild beasts, the sullen, dogged faces of the gladiators, the high, resigned look of the martyr Christians. Nearly two thousand years have rolled by since Rome peopled the stone benches of the Coliseum, nearly twenty centuries since those scenes of horror transpired, but the stone walls, the benches, the very dungeons whence the unhappy victims were brought into the arena to be rent asunder, still exist, mute but damning evidences of the cruelty, the inhumanity, the barbarity, of the one-time mistress of the world."

Paranzo paused. Mack, Perigarde, and I gazed at him in astonishment. We had no idea we had picked up such an orator, and wondered if he were not reciting something from his stage repertoire.

"No such thoughts are awakened by Dr. Martelli Forenzo's arboreal coliseum," continued our orator. "The form and, as far as practical, the size are duplicated, but with soft and pleasing colors of green and gold, instead of stern, forbidding walls of granite. The outer wall of Dr. Forenzo's model is composed of a circle of high poplar trees. The inner circles are composed of trees each slightly shorter than the rest, so that the effect from the pit is that of a gradual incline. The first row is of short orange trees, the second row of lemon trees a few feet taller than the orange trees, the next row is still taller than the lemon, and so on, forming a green slope to the outer circle of poplar trees, which are nearly if not quite one hundred and twenty-five feet high."

Paola was now close at hand. We could see the houses in the ravine, the arched way winding up to the town, and the church high up on the mountain slope. Paranzo's description of Cosenza, of the resting-place of Alaric, and especially of Dr. Forenzo's asylum, was so graphic and interesting, we determined to anchor off Paola and make the tramp to Cosenza. To our surprise, Paranzo refused to accompany us; he even begged us not to attempt the trip.

"We are too near Maratea," he said. "After what happened there yesterday we ought to hurry away from this part of the country."

Mack, Perigarde, and I had no fears; it was not *our* fault that people mistook us for princes, so we ordered Luigi to tack for the shore. A little later we cast anchor within a few yards of the beach of Paola. Luigi had barely done this and gotten the langia alongside, when Paranzo beckoned me to one side and in a mysterious whisper said he thought it would be a good deal better if we kept on and did not stop at Paola.

"Especially," he added, "since you cannot see Dr. Martelli's asylum without a permit or letter of introduction. It will be a long, tiresome walk, and all for nothing."

"A long walk? Fifteen miles is nothing, and our American passports will take us through the asylum. If not, we shall at any rate see the arboreal coliseum. That of itself will be worth a fifteen-mile walk."

Paranzo's soft, dark eyes almost filled with tears at this; we began to think his adventure at the lunatic asylum had made him dread even the town again. Paola is situated partly in a ravine, partly on the slope of the mountain. From some of the streets a charming view of the sea is obtained. The sun was now well above Sila's peak; we paused on the height just beyond the village before plunging into the forest through which a road leads to Cosenza. The curious houses at our feet, the fisher-boats in the harbor, the smooth, sun-lighted waters of the Mediterranean, the mountains covered with grand old oaks, chestnuts, and pines, — all made a charming picture. The memory of that walk remains with us as one of the most delightful we ever took. The road is good, the scenery magnificent. To the west we still obtained occasional glimpses of the sea; to the east was Sila studded with grand forest trees on its topmost heights, villages and grazing flocks of sheep and goats on its slopes. Ancient Athens and Rome used to recruit their fleets with ships made of wood obtained from the forests on this lonely range of mountains, and though ancient Athens and Rome are cities of the past, the Sila forest which contributed to their greatness still remains to delight the eye of the traveller and to shelter the flocks of the peasants from the fierce heat of the Italian summer sun. When we reached Cosenza, we went to a hotel to wash away the dust and get something to eat before starting to the asylum. After dinner we asked the padrone of the hotel to direct us to Dr. Martelli's asylum.

"Asylum? What asylum?" said the padrone.

"The asylum for the insane."

"Never heard of such a place."

"Never heard of Dr. Martelli Forenzo's insane asylum?"

"Mai — never."

"Nor of Dr. Forenzo?"

"There is no doctor of that name in Cosenza."

"Has he moved away?"

"He has never been here; at least, not in my time. I was born here forty years ago."

Then we told the proprietor of the arboreal coliseum; he had never heard of such a place, and stared so hard as we described its beauties to him that I verily believe he concluded we were three escaped lunatics. At first we felt like going back and giving Paranzo a thrashing for playing his practical jokes on us, but remembering his sad face and dove-like eyes, we felt it would be almost as mean to thrash a woman. We were curious to see how he would act when confronted with his fictions. Although there was no arboreal coliseum and no Dr. Martelli, there were many other things by no means unworthy the walk from Paola. The Busentio River is as Paranzo described it; we saw the point where it is said Alaric and his treasures were buried. The river was turned from its course; afterwards, when the Gothic king had been safely interred under the bed of the stream, the waters were turned back again in their old channel, where they have swept for the past fifteen centuries, guarding the barbarian's bones and booty. We visited the old castle which with its thick walls has stood the shock of many a hard-fought battle, but which was unable to withstand the shock of the great earthquake of 1783. In that year the mountain itself was shaken to the centre and thirty thousand people were killed. There have been earthquakes in this vicinity as late as 1870. Although great damage was done in 1870, it was as nothing compared with the terrific loss of life and property during the convulsions and upheavals of a hundred years ago.

In the afternoon we started back for Paola, arriving there by nine o'clock, fatigued and with ferocious appetites after our twenty-eight-mile walk and our rambles through Cosenza. Luigi was waiting for us, and we lost no time in rowing out to the *Principe Farnese*.

Paranzo's method of justifying himself was worthy of his genius.

"Signori," he said, "I never intended you to believe that story. I was only telling a little romance. You astonish me when you say you really thought there was an arboreal coliseum and a lunatic asylum at Cosenza. It is impossible that you did not know I was merely romancing to pass the time; you only jest, you laugh at a poor fellow sad because always hunted by his wife."

It was impossible to feel anger toward such a man; we took care, however, not to be taken in by any more of his stories.

Our next stop was Pizzo, fifty miles south of Paola. In order to accomplish this without night-sailing we made an early start, weighing anchor and leaving Paola at four o'clock in the morning. For four or five hours we kept close to the coast, passing a number of picturesque villages, some perched high on spurs of the mountain, others cosily sheltered in the ravines or on the beach. We passed almost beneath the shadows cast by the cliff on which stands the town of Amantea. In 1806 the town on that lofty rock was converted into a fortress, to withstand the attacks of the French. The position on that high rock overlooking the sea was impregnable, and the French succeeded in capturing the Royalists only by a long siege and famine. South of Amantea the coast loses its mountainous character, and is not so picturesque as the country to the north. At nine o'clock we entered the Gulf of St. Eufemia. The Italian peninsula is only nineteen miles wide in this latitude, owing to the indentation of the eastern coast. The sail across the Gulf of St. Eufemia afforded a fine view both of the mainland and of the Lipari Islands. The unfavorable winds compelled us to do a good deal of tacking, so that we did not reach Pizzo until after dark. Apart from the fact that it was in this lonely hamlet that Joachim Murat was shot seventy-five years ago, the place possesses no particular historic interest. Its position on top of high sandstone bluffs, approached from the sea by winding steps, is picturesque, though not more so than a dozen other places we had already visited; accordingly we decided not to remain longer than was necessary to replenish our larder and get a few hours' sleep. The volcano of Stromboli was our next point, and this lay directly out to sea fifty miles west of the mainland. We started next morning by sun-up, hoping to make the entire run by daylight. This would have been done with a half-way

Deck of the "Minerva"; Smyrna in the Distance.

decent wind, but, when about three hours out from Pizzo, the wind died out, and we found ourselves, for the first time, absolutely becalmed.

"It is fortunate," said Mack at dinner, after the *Principe Farnese* had been five hours almost motionless on the smooth, still sea, "that we replenished our provisions at Pizzo. There is no telling how long this calm will last. Without a good supply, we might perish or turn cannibals."

Perigarde took this seriously, and went back into the cabin to take a look at the stores, and make a calculation as to how long they would last. The reader may remember that Dr. Kelley's yacht had a porcelain bath-tub let into the floor. Our boat had no porcelain tub; nevertheless, we did not lack baths. The prow of the *Principe Farnese* stood at least six feet above the water, and from this point we took a dive every morning. The water swarmed with fish; they came up to us, swam around us, displayed no more fear than if we had been of their own kind. In fact, the fear was rather on our side, for some of the fish were monsters. Luigi or Francati were always on the lookout, ready to haul us aboard in case of attack. A shark must turn over before it can bite, and an expert swimmer who does not go too far from his boat need have no difficulty getting out of danger before the enemy is on his back ready to attack. The jelly-fish were the most strange and interesting. Some, shaped like tiny umbrellas, propelled themselves backward, forward, or upward, by undulating, or, as it were, by raising and lowering the top or umbrella portion of their being. Other jelly-fish seemed mere shapeless masses of sticky, transparent substance. We spent a good part of that day while becalmed between Pizzo and Stromboli swimming about and watching the curious organisms in the water.

About nine o'clock a breeze blew up, which soon became a bit sharp and brisk. We sat on the prow of the boat, our feet hanging over, watching the white foam which the increasing speed of the *Principe Farnese* caused the keel to dash up in fountains of spray. The shadows closed around us. There was no moon, the night was inky dark; in all that world of blackness the only bright thing was the lantern swung from the masthead. The sombreness of the scene had its effect upon all in the vessel; conversation died out; Luigi and Francati stopped their songs; the only sound breaking the dead stillness of the night was the swish of the waves as the keel ploughed its way through the water. Suddenly the silence was broken.

"Yonder rises the sun," said Perigarde.

"The sun? at midnight?"

"And in the west?"

Yes, sure enough, there, over to the west, was a great light, like the sun's. Only a few hours ago we had seen the red glow of twilight fade into night, and now in the western horizon is again a roseate light. The roseate glow grew brighter and brighter, until finally it burst upon us that this second sunset or sunrise was the fire of old Stromboli. Never shall we forget the grandeur of that scene — all around, a world of blackness except to the west, where towered that gigantic pillar of fire and flame. The most powerful electric light is but as a rush candle beside Stromboli, the beacon light that we beheld that night, raising its majestic head three thousand feet above the sea, and casting showers of fiery stones and lava half as high again, until all the heavens were lurid. We anchored off the north end of the island, at the very base of the volcano; then, though loth to lose the sight of that magnificent mountain of fire, we felt the necessity of rest and sleep, and crawled into our bunks.

Hills and vales are picturesque, the ocean is grand, mountains are majestic, the beetling crags of the Alps and the tremendous cañons of the Colorado are immense and awe-inspiring; but it is not until you have gazed down into the

fiery depths of a volcano, not until you hear the awful
rumbling and roaring and witness the mighty upheavals of
molten lava and see the pillars of flame shooting up from the
fiery hells, the hail of red-hot stones falling thick and fast in
burning showers, — it is not until you have witnessed these
phenomena, that you can say you have seen nature in its most
awful grandeur. The largest volcano of which there is any
record is Haleakala (House of the Sun) on the island of Maui
in the Pacific Ocean. The cone of that volcano rises ten
thousand feet above the sea, and so immense is the crater the
city of New York could be put within it and have ample room
to spare. In comparison with Haleakala, Stromboli, Vesuvius,
and all other known volcanoes, grand as they are, are mere toys.
Within Haleakala's crater, a vast pit two thousand feet deep
and thirty miles in circumference, rise half a dozen cones, any
one of which if considered alone would appear a volcano of
no mean size. But the fires of Haleakala are extinct, and
Kilauea, on the island of Hawaii, enjoys the distinction of being
the largest active volcano in the world. Though much smaller
than Haleakala, Kilauea is prodigious in comparison with
Vesuvius or Stromboli. The crater of Kilauea is eighteen
miles in circumference, and within this vast pit a veritable sea
of fire rages and roars, its waves of flame rising high, beating
against the rocky shores, and here and there shooting columns
of molten lava high in the air. Sometimes so great, so
tremendous, are the forces at work that the whole restless
flaming mass boils up and over the crater's walls six hundred
feet high, and rushes madly down the mountain's side, a
Niagara of flame. Perhaps the sublimest spectacle ever
witnessed was that which occurred a few years ago when
Kilauea overflowed its crater and produced a stream of molten
lava fourteen miles long, from its source to the lofty cliffs
whence it leaped into the sea. For days this cataract of fire
rushed down the side of the mountain, four thousand feet high,

and poured itself into the ocean, heating the water for miles around and boiling thousands of luckless fish.[1]

While Stromboli cannot compare with Kilauea, it is nevertheless well worth visiting. The cone rises three thousand feet, and like Vesuvius frequently ejects showers of stones and red-hot masses of lava. These ejections are accompanied by loud detonations, so that the traveller may well imagine he hears the cannon's roar or the peal of thunder. Despite these constant showers of stones and lava Stromboli's cone may be visited with perfect safety, as the sirocco blows the smoke and stones to one side of the crater, permitting fine views from the other. Spallanzani in 1788 spent days at a time on the brink of Stromboli, gazing into the fearful cauldron and noting its workings and peculiarities. The data thus obtained served as the foundation of the writings which subsequently won for Spallanzani the title "Father of Vulcanology."

Stromboli is noted, not alone for its volcano, but from the fact that it was the seat of Æolus, the ancient god of the Winds. The description of Homer, barring poetic license, is not inapplicable even now : —

> "A floating isle high raised by toil divine,
> Strong walls of brass, the rocky coast confine."

It was here that Ulysses obtained the bags of wind which proved so disastrous on his homeward voyage and kept him for years a wanderer on the face of the waters. During the Middle Ages the cone of Stromboli was regarded as an entrance to purgatory : the crusaders who passed near the island on their return from the Holy Land declared that they could hear the groans and lamentations of the miserable souls suffering for their sins on earth. If purgatory is half as hot as the molten lava, or if the groans of the wicked are half so awful as

---

[1] For account of the author's journey to these Pacific Island volcanoes, see " The Tramp at Home," Chapter XX.

the rumbling and roaring of old Stromboli, I would earnestly urge the reader to mend his ways and secure some quieter and cooler destination.

It was almost three o'clock in the morning when we anchored under the shadows of Stromboli and turned in to sleep. The constant boom, boom of the volcano's discharges broke up our sleep; so, notwithstanding the long night vigil, we arose by six and prepared for the ascent of the cone. The ascent begins almost at the water's edge: in some places it is excessively steep and difficult, at others it is more gradual, but everywhere there is fine powdered ashes, everywhere you sink into these ashes until your shoe-tops are covered, your shoes filled.

"This volcano business," said Perigarde, panting, "is a humbug, Meriwether, and we ought to tumble you in for bringing us on such a fool's errand."

Yet we all reached the top and looked around, above, and below. The grandeur of the scene made both men stop their grumbling, and wonder and gaze in silence. We did not marvel that it was once regarded as the entrance to purgatory. In fact, Stromboli's crater might readily be taken for the portal way to Sheol itself. The view from the summit of the cone is grand and beautiful beyond words to describe — at least, beyond my words. It is to be regretted that Byron never climbed a volcano — his genius alone were worthy to describe them. From the top of the cone, the Mediterranean seems to stretch out into limitless space except toward the east and south, where, within easy reach of the eye, are Panaria, Salina, and other of the Lipari islands. After eating the bread and salami we had brought and taking one last look at the crater, we began the descent, making great leaps and bounds down the precipitous sides of the cone, sometimes jumping or sliding ten feet at a time. We reached the sea-level in less than thirty minutes. Paranzo, who had respectfully but firmly declined to do anything so foolish as climbing three thousand feet merely to see a lot of fire and lava, still lay stretched in the langia fast asleep. We lost no time arousing him and rowing to the yacht. A few minutes later we weighed anchor, spread the lateen sail, and started for Lipari, which we expected to make by early bedtime.

We passed Panaria, a barren, uncultivated island which Pliny says was upheaved from the sea 126 B.C. The jagged crags of this desolate rock rise to a height of one thousand feet above the Mediterranean. By eight o'clock the *Principe Farnese* lay at anchor off the Pointa Castagna, the extreme northern cape of the island of Lipari. The fatiguing ascent of Stromboli, together with the long vigil of the preceding night, left us rather stiff and sore. We ate supper, hung our light on the masthead, and turned in to get a good night's rest before beginning the tramp to Monte Sant' Angelo.

Lipari is not large; its extreme length is only eight or ten miles, its width only five or six; nevertheless it is an interesting place and one which we shall never forget. A little episode and adventure is all well enough, but as Shakespeare says, there may be too much even of a good thing. Before leaving Lipari, we agreed we had had too much adventure.

"Henceforth," said Mack, "I shall be content to follow in the beaten ruts. A little more humdrum life and a little less episode would, with me, fill a long-felt want."

But this is anticipating. Mack did not make this remark until we had spent a night off the coast of Capo Castagna and six hours on the island itself. Capo Castagna, the northern point of the island, is not a town; it is a desolate point jutting out into the sea. A rugged path leads from the cape across high mountains to the town of Lipari. It was our intention to take this trip across the mountains and have the boat meet us at the town. Luigi was instructed to set sail as soon as we were ashore: to his failure to start promptly was due in part the trouble that overtook us. With anything like a rough sea, it is difficult to effect a landing at Capo Castagna. Fortunately, when we landed, not a ripple disturbed the water: we rowed alongside the rocks and stepped ashore as easily as if we had been alongside a dock. The path begins to ascend a short distance from the sea, and in a few minutes we were on a height affording a view of Panaria and Liscabianca, the islands we had passed the evening before. While trudging up this rugged path a sudden turn brought us face to face with a young woman and two boys, the oldest not more than fourteen: all three were pulling at a rope fastened around a large block of pumice-stone.

"Questa non e troppo grande per ella?" (Is not that too large a load for you?) I asked.

The girl stopped and stared.

"She does not understand my Italian; you try her, Paranzo."

Paranzo put the question, but with no better result. By this time the girl and the two boys, who, at first glimpse of us, stopped as if rooted to the ground, seemed to recover one of their powers, that of locomotion. They turned and fled up the path like three startled deer, leaving their rope and block of pumice-stone behind them.

"What's the matter with them?" said Perigarde. "What was that jargon you scared them with?"

"That jargon," I replied with dignity, "was a polite remark to the effect that this pumice-stone was entirely too heavy for a young girl to haul over a rough path like this. If the girl was frightened, it must have been at your stare. You looked at her as if you had never seen a girl before."

"No harder than she looked at us," said Perigarde. Presently he added: "But what if I did stare at her? She made a pretty picture, with her bare round arms, her olive cheeks and dazzling teeth. By Jove! it beats the world how beautiful these Italian peasants are — when they are young. Pity it doesn't last longer."

" A pity, but quite natural. It would be strange if beauty could long withstand such strains," and I pointed to the big block of pumice-stone which the girl had been pulling.

" There must be quarries of this pumice-stone in the neighborhood," said Paranzo. " If we follow quickly, we may track that girl to her home."

There was a quarry; but, to our surprise, when we reached it, not a soul was in sight. The workmen had not been long absent; tools were lying about, ropes, tackles, freshly made chips of stone. We called down several caves, black holes that went down we knew not how deep; but there was no response, so we continued our way. The incident seemed peculiar. When, finally, we were on the summit of Monte Sant' Angelo, two thousand feet above the sea, Mack said : —

" The more I think of that girl, the stranger seems her conduct. Are we so uncouth that people should run from us?"

" I don't know about you," said Perigarde ; " speaking, though, for the rest of us, there is certainly no good reason why a girl should run from us."

" And yet she *did* run, run like a startled deer."

We were not in full dress, still we did not think our appearance justified, not only the girl and two boys, but a whole camp of quarrymen, in abandoning their work and burying themselves in their shafts. We gave up trying to solve the riddle, and occupied ourselves with the easier task of gazing at the panorama of sea and land stretched beneath us. The lofty peak of Monte Sant' Angelo is in the centre of the central island of the entire group. From its summit the eye can reach from the smoking volcano on the island of Vulcano, eight miles to the south, to the fiery cone of Stromboli, twenty-five miles to the north. The Capo Castagna was distinctly visible, and, to our surprise, the *Principe Farnese* scarcely less so. It seemed a mere speck, but we recognized it as our boat. On the western side of the islands we saw the mist arising from the hot springs of San Calogero. Towards the southeast was the town of Lipari, and the intervening terraces forming a a grand natural amphitheatre, extending from the harbor to the summit of Monte Sant' Angelo. Half-way between the summit and the town on one of the terraces is the site of extensive baths built by the Romans. These baths were once partially excavated, and the *débris* of twenty centuries removed. The ruins began to attract tourists; and Bishop Todaro, dreading the demoralizing effect that foreigners might exercise upon the simple natives, ordered the work to cease and refilled those portions that had been unearthed, so that strangers might have no inducement to visit the island. Looking beyond these ancient baths, our gaze rested on the town. It was a charming sight; the terraces covered with reed trellises and currant vines, with fig and olive trees; and the town, with its churches and cathedrals, — so charming that, as we sat there on the grass, it absorbed our thoughts to the exclusion of all else. We did not hear the sound of approaching footsteps on the soft grass; hence were startled when half a dozen carabinieri emerged from the thicket close by, levelled their guns, and cried : —

"Mani sopra" (hands up).

After an instant's pause, up went our hands; it was no time to question — obedience was the thing for that moment. The next moment, we realized that all four of us were prisoners, tied together. We demanded the reason of our arrest; the commander of the squad said gruffly that we would find out in Lipari. One of the soldiers went a little in advance: the other five placed themselves at our sides and in the rear; then we began to descend towards Lipari.

The entire slope of the mountain, from the sea to Sant' Angelo's peak, is laid off in terraces, where flourish luxuriant fig trees, currants, cotton, and grape vines, whence is obtained the celebrated Malmsey wine. It must be admitted, however, we gave these beauties of nature little attention. The sensation of being prisoners was so novel that we found it difficult to adjust ourselves to the situation. On more than one occasion, we were unpleasantly reminded of the fact, by one of the soldiers jabbing his sword at us. This was when I turned about for the third time to ask Paranzo to speak in Italian and demand the reason of our arrest. Paranzo, who knew the ways of his country better than I, discreetly refused to make any such demand: when I saw that the brute of a soldier meant to jab me with his sword, if I did not keep quiet, I bridled my tongue, and continued the rest of the journey in silence. The carabinieri were anything but silent. They kept up a constant chatter. The descent of the slope being accomplished, we crossed a small plain, lying between the beginning of the ascent and the fort; passed the bishop's palace, which stands on the site of the ancient Roman baths, and near the old Greek necropolis; and, half an hour later, found ourselves in a cell of the castle built by Charles V. after Barbarosa sacked the place in 1544. After the door was locked Mack came to me, and said in a whisper: —

"I don't trust Paranzo. Is he running away from his wife or from the police? People are judged by the company they keep. Haven't we made a mistake in taking up with a man who, for all we know, may be a brigand?"

At this moment Paranzo approached.

"Do you know," said he, "I have an idea as to what this means? I overheard what the carabinieri said, and am almost sure they think we are manutengoli."

"Manutengoli? What the mischief are manutengoli?"

"Manutengoli are the friends of brigands, — peasants and others who harbor brigands. A peasant may not be a friend of a brigand, yet may be forced to shelter him. The government does not discriminate, deeming a peasant who shelters a brigand, willingly or unwillingly, a manutengolo, and confines him on an island."

We subsequently visited other islands used by the Italian government as residences for enforced colonists or "Domiciliati Coatti," as they are called. There are upwards of two thousand such colonists. Napoleon's little kingdom of Elba holds 181, Ventotene has 144, Pentellaria 195. The rest are scattered about in other small islands belonging to Italy. Though as a rule the Domiciliati Coatti have the liberty of the island, they are sometimes restricted to narrower limits; at night a guard locks them up; if the " enforced colonist" has a wife, she is also locked up. Paranzo's theory proved true, as we found when brought before a stern official who questioned us as to when we had come to Lipari and for what purpose. Lipari is one of the islands for enforced colonists. When the peasants reported our landing at a lonely end of the island, the officers imagined we had come to help some prisoner escape. We explained that we were plain American citizens travelling for pleasure, adding that our boat was probably in the harbor, where an officer could easily satisfy himself as to the truth of our statement. To our surprise, the reply to this was that carabinieri had been sent to capture the yacht as soon as the peasants brought word of her arrival, but the *Principe Farnese* had at once put out to sea, and had not since been heard of. This fact added to the judge's suspicions. When asked to explain, we could only reply that we had given our captain orders to sail at once to Lipari, and did not understand why he had not done so. Further questioning elicited nothing more of consequence; we were remanded to the castle, there to await the arrival of the boat or any other development that might satisfy the authorities as to our identity.

Where was Luigi? This question was not answered until the following day: he had had bad winds, then no wind at all, which accounted for his delay in reaching Lipari. When he arrived, the passports were brought ashore and our predicament pleasantly ended.

"I propose to use my freedom," said Mack, "by leaving this confounded island at once. The Bishop of Todaro gave himself unnecessary trouble filling up those Roman baths to keep visitors away. Were it known what receptions are given strangers here, there would not be one tourist a century."

According to Homer, when Ulysses landed in these parts some years ago, he met with a reception very different from that accorded us.

"This happy port affords our wandering fleet
A month's reception and a safe retreat."

Our reception was scarce twenty-four hours in length, and the retreat anything but safe. "Times have sadly changed since Ulysses was here," said Perigarde. "Then visitors were given a palace; now they are given a jail."

While waiting on the quay for Francati to come with the langia, debating whether or not we should go to the island of Vulcano, a shabbily dressed, sad-faced man approached us.

"Scusatemi, signori" (excuse me, signori), he said. "I do not understand the language you speak, but I understand Vulcano. Is it true that you go to Vulcano?"

"Perhaps. Why do you ask?"

"Ah, signori, will you be so good as to take me?"

Was this another Paranzo who wanted to settle himself in the *Principe Farnese?* This man, however, asked only an hour or two's passage, so we agreed to take him. On the way to Vulcano he told his story. For five years he and his wife had been working for the Scotch firm that owns the volcano and manufactures sulphur, alum, and boracic acid from the numerous products that line the sides of the crater. Teresa, his wife, had borne him one child, a little girl, who was the one bright spot in their lives. For three years the bambino cheered the hard-working father on his return at night to the gloomy cavern he called home. Then came a strange sickness

STREET SCENE IN SMYRNA

that shrivelled the little one's limbs and wrung the parents' hearts with sorrow.

"The bambino got worse and worse," continued Vellino, "and Teresa did nothing but cry when she saw its pale, thin little face. We had a little money, our friends helped us, and three weeks ago I took her to the hospital at Messina." Here the poor man choked; two tears trickled down his cheeks.

"You took her to Messina? What then?" we asked gently.

"And then," returned Vellino, "and then — she died. She was buried in Messina yesterday."

The island of Vulcano, as its name indicates, is of volcanic origin. The volcano composes the island. On all but the north side the mountain rises abruptly from the sea. The north coast is less abrupt, and a path leading from the beach to the summit of the cone six hundred feet high is not unusually steep or rugged. As at Stromboli, Paranzo declined to join in the fatiguing tramp, and we left him to take his nap. We accompanied Vellino to the cave in the side of the mountain that he called his home. There are many of these caves, mere nooks and crevices in the lava, which serve as human habitations. When we entered the den where our companion lived, our hearts were heavy at the thought that fellow-creatures, creatures like ourselves, should know no other home than this.

The roof was formed by a mass of lava that stopped short in its fiery course down the mountain and congealed in the air. Banks of lava were built up to this natural roof, thus walling the place in. A hole in the roof served as a chimney; in one corner of the dark cave lay a heap of rags called a bed, in another corner was a rude table and two three-legged stools. From pegs in the wall hung three or four greasy bags containing goat's cheese.

We shall never forget poor Teresa's look as she saw Vellino and did not see the child.

"Il bambino — dove il bambino?" (the child, where is the child?) she cried.

The unhappy Vellino hung his head, big tears trickled down his cheeks, but not a word did he speak.

A bereaved mother is always a pitiful sight to see, but somhow that poor father's sorrow seemed doubled; he not only mourned for his dead child; he mourned for the anguish of the child's mother; it was anguish to him to hear her ask about the little one whom he had left in the quicklime-pit of the pauper cemetery of Messina. Vellino took her hand in his, and led her back into their cave; we walked away saddened at the sight of sorrow no mortal had power to soothe.

We climbed to the mountain's summit. As we stood on the brink of the crater with its blue and green flames and molten lava, we recalled the fact that the whole island is the result of one sudden and fierce earthquake. What if the same force that hurled the island up out of the water were to uproot it from its moorings and again submerge it under the sea? The thought was not a pleasant one nor was it impossible. Only a short time after our visit an island was suddenly thrown up from the sea in this enchanted region, and after a few weeks was as suddenly submerged. The London "Graphic" of October 24th, 1891, speaking of this remarkable occurrence, says: —

"A volcano has appeared in the Mediterranean between the Sicilian and Tunisian coasts. Last week several earthquake shocks affected the island of Pentellaria, and shortly afterwards a small volcano emerged from the sea about two miles from the island, throwing up smoke and stones and causing general disturbance around. The inhabitants of Pentellaria have asked for government steamers to carry them away in case of danger."

CHAPTER XVIII

A Sirocco Storm — Running before the Wind — The *Principe Farnese* weathers the Gale — A Tramp in Calabria — Scilla and Charybdis — Messina's Strait — Sicily — Cruising along the Coast — A Town of Nut-Crackers — How St. Agatha saved Catania — Perigarde meets a Fräulein — Syracuse — Perigarde astounds us

WHEN we boarded the *Principe Farnese*, Luigi set sail for Messina. By direct line the distance is scarcely seventy miles, and ordinarily might be made in eight or ten hours. We did not make it, however, for two or three days. We had not proceeded above an hour before the wind from the west increased almost to a gale. The sky assumed a hazy appearance, the air became hot and scorching, as if it had passed over a furnace, as it really had,— the furnace of the Sahara Desert. We were at last face to face with the oft-heard-of and much-dreaded sirocco. The *Principe Farnese* made a brave attempt to keep on her course, but the force of the gale increased from moment to moment, and it was not long before we were glad to take in our sail, turn the prow to the east, and run straight before the wind. We did not adopt this course a moment too soon: lashed by the gale, the waves rose to a fearful height; had we continued the attempt to tack to the southeast, we should have run broadside with the swell, and been deluged if not disabled, or perhaps swamped. The rain fell in torrents, waves dashed over our sides and stern, the cabin was stifling, outside we could scarce keep on our legs. Having never before seen the *Principe Farnese* in a storm, we were a little alarmed; Mack and I expanded our rubber vests with air. Doubtless we appeared ridiculous enough, looking, as we did, bloated and drenched; but no one laughed at us. Paranzo and Perigarde had no life-preserver, and fearing they might be washed overboard, crawled into the cabin, where they lay limp and pale with sea-sickness and fright, although Luigi declared there was no danger.

"How long do these siroccos last?" Mack asked.

"Sailors say from one to three days; seldom longer."

"If it keeps up like this for three days," said Perigarde, "where shall we wind up? At this rate, we ought to sight Gibraltar by morning." But Luigi was too good a sailor: the way he manipulated that lateen sail and tacked to the south almost at right angles to the wind was wonderful. About three o'clock in the morning we saw the lighthouse of Cape Vaticano: the gale had taken us in two hours at least thirty-five miles out of our course.

"The bay of Nicotera is just beyond Cape Vaticano," said I. "Can't we find anchorage there?"

"Not with a sea like this," replied Luigi. "Our best chance is at Palmi, at the south end of the bay."

So to Palmi we set our faces, and a long and tedious time we had getting there. We tacked against the wind to avoid the rocks of Cape Vaticano, and our course off the cape lay directly south, while the wind was from the west-southwest. The reader can imagine what speed and progress we made under the circumstances. After two nights on the Mediterranean our gallant little craft dropped anchor off Palmi at five o'clock in the afternoon. Palmi is a picturesque town, but not one of us felt then the least desire to see the people or scenery. We patched up what damage had been done by the storm, ran up the lights, and early as it was, turned into our bunks, and slept like logs until nine the next morning.

The tremendous shaking up gave us a temporary distaste for the sea: we determined to send Luigi with the *Principe Farnese* to Scilla while we went there on foot. This proved a happy idea, as the distance was not great, — only fifteen miles, — and the entire way lay through most charming scenery. Some miles to the northeast of Palmi, in a lonely valley surrounded by mountains, are the imposing ruins of an ancient monastery : nearer at hand are the ruins of another monastery destroyed by the great earthquake of 1783. Palmi itself is one of the most picturesque places in Italy : its position high on the slope of Monte Elia commands a view as far as old Stromboli on the north, and on the south as far as its giant brother, Ætna. A glance at the map will show what a stretch of land and sea this view comprises, — Scilla, Charybdis, Lipari, Messina, and a host of other places celebrated in song and story. Willingly would we have lingered in this delightful region, but time was flying, and our plan required us to push on to Sicily and the East. A four hours' tramp through chestnut and olive groves brought us to Scilla, which Homer describes as a terrible monster, part virgin, part wolf, part dolphin. Scilla has evidently changed since the time of Homer ; for it is now neither virgin, wolf, nor dolphin. It is simply a massive rock standing boldly out of the sea opposite the whirlpool of Charybdis. The reader doubtless remembers the description of this rock in the twelfth book of the " Odyssey " : —

> " High in the air the rock its summit shrouds.
> In brooding tempests and in rolling clouds
> Loud storms around, and mists eternal rise,
> Beats its black brow and intercept the skies.
> The summer and the autumn glow in vain;
> The sky forever hovers, forever clouds remain."

Æolus and his wind-bags must have upset Ulysses and caused him to take a gloomy view of things. So far from being eternally wrapt in mists and clouds, Scilla is a bright enough sort of place overhung usually by the brightest of blue Italian skies. The castle of Scilla, on a high promontory overlooking the town, was thrown in ruins by the 1783 earthquake, which was so terrific that the rock was rent asunder ; the sea rolled up like a tidal wave and drowned more than a thousand people.

"Between Scylla and Charybdis" is an expression used to denote an uncomfortable, if not dangerous, position. We did not find it either; there were some swift eddies and currents, but the *Principe Farnese* glided along quite as safely as on the open sea. Luigi said it was not always so; sometimes fierce gales sweep through the strait, and the waters are lashed into boiling whirlpools that sometimes overwhelm the strongest bark. Luigi said that a few months before such a storm had dashed three vessels against the rocks and drowned the crews. With a good breeze behind us we brought up in the Messina harbor a little before sundown. Unlike most quays, that of Messina is not given up to ship-chandlers, boarding-houses, and grog-shops. On the contrary, it is the most beautiful boulevard in the city, lined with handsome buildings and thronged on summer evenings with carriages and pedestrians. The Corso Cavour, Via Garibaldi, and Corso Vittorio Emanuele are modern-looking streets; for, notwithstanding Messina is as old as Rome — founded 723 B.C. — it was almost totally destroyed by the great 1783 earthquake; when rebuilt, the architecture was in the modern style. Those streets which withstood the earthquake are narrow and crooked. While rambling through this older and more interesting portion of the city, we stopped in a workman's "trattoria" for supper. On the wall over our table was pasted a copy of the New Orleans "Picayune" containing pictures of a Mardi Gras procession. Perigarde wanted me to ask the padrone if he had friends in New Orleans. I declined to put the question.

"And you are quite right," said Paranzo. "As a rule the Italians know little and care less about that New Orleans lynching; but this fellow evidently has friends in New Orleans — it may be some of them were lynched; in which case he will not have much love for Americans."

We did not boast of our nationality to that fierce-eyed Sicilian padrone. Since five o'clock that morning we had walked from

Palmi to Scilla, sailed through the strait, seen Messina, and were now ready to cruise along the coast of Sicily. That is, all were ready but Perigarde, who declared he wanted a brief respite from boating. As the *Principe Farnese* was to sail early next morning, Perigarde bade us adieu and slept at the hotel: of course we suspected he had another love affair on hand. He said he would go down to Syracuse by rail and meet us there. Whenever Perigarde flew off at a tangent, we knew some woman was the cause. We sailed south in the early morning, the coast of Italy gradually receding from view, while Mt. Ætna loomed up nearer and grander. Immediately south of Messina the mountains recede from the sea, and for ten miles the shore is low and sandy, except in those places where the indefatigable peasants have covered the sand with earth almost to the edge of the salt sea and planted vineyards and gardens. A curious feature of this portion of Sicilian scenery is the " Fiumare " — a rocky ravine ordinarily dry, but which, after a heavy rain, is suddenly filled with a foaming and turbulent torrent. We saw a dozen of these " Fiumare " as we sailed along the coast. One we climbed to the summit. At the sea the " Fiumare " was fully five hundred yards wide, but as we ascended it grew rapidly narrower, until at an elevation of a thousand feet it was a mere ravine, the sides of which were terraced and planted with almond, orange, and lemon trees. We made our way over the huge boulders in the bed of the ravine, deposited by the last torrent, and continued the ascent until we literally walked into the clouds.

Our halting-place the first night out from Messina was at Giardini, the village whence Garibaldi began his expedition to Calabria in 1860. Early the following morning we began the ascent to Taormina. " We " must not usually be understood as including Paranzo; for that indolent Italian was too fond of ease to care for climbing; but in the case of Taormina even Paranzo was stimulated to exertion, and accompanied us up the steep and rugged path that leads to the ancient town on its rocky perch, five hundred feet above Giardini. No sooner had we reached the summit of the bluff, and passed into the town through an ancient gate, than we heard proceeding from almost every house an odd tapping or pecking noise — tap — tap — peck — peck — with curious regularity. Paranzo laughed at the guesses we made as to the cause of this peculiar noise.

"It is merely the noise of cracking nuts," he explained.

We in turn laughed at Paranzo. The noise in one house might be explained by the cracking of nuts, but were we to believe the entire population of Taormina engaged in cracking nuts? Paranzo said we could believe what we liked, but that the tap-tap, peck-peck noise we heard on every side came from the cracking of nuts. To prove his assertion, he pushed open the door of a house, and there to our astonishment, we saw twenty or thirty men, women, and children sitting on the floor, each with a flat stone in the lap, a round stone in the hand, and by their sides, bags of almonds, which they were busily engaged in cracking. We learned that during the season Taormina busies itself almost entirely with the almonds that grow in such abundance on the neighboring mountain slopes. Everywhere during our stroll there was the noise of tapping, and everywhere were the people busy nut-cracking. Expert crackers earn as much as two lire a day: all are paid by the amount of nuts cracked.

The Greek theatre at Taormina makes Roman ruins seem modern, and impresses upon the traveller the fact that the further south one goes in Europe, the older are the evidences of civilization. Buckle says the beginning of civilization was the date tree, which by the abundance of its fruit enabled man to spare a moment from the search for food, and begin the process of lifting himself out of a state of savage ignorance. Civilization began in warm countries where nature met man more than half way to supply his wants: why is it that the causes that gave rise to civilization did not prevent its decay? Why is it that to-day the highest civilization is found, not in Egypt or Italy, where the soil need only be scratched to produce a harvest, but in England and America? England, fog-covered, small, and seabound, outranks every country of Europe in energy and intellectual power, while America, so recently covered with the primeval forest, outranks the world in every practical art conducive to man's political and physical comfort. Some of the columns of Taormina's Greek theatre stand as they stood two thousand years ago. The stage, situated on the very edge of the precipice, whence one can hear the beating of the waves four hundred feet below, is well preserved; so too is the amphitheatre of seats hewn in the solid rock. Beyond the theatre rises a cliff two thousand feet high; beyond that is the mighty peak of Ætna ten thousand feet above the sea.

The distance from Taormina to Catania is only thirty miles; yet the journey consumed fourteen hours, because part of the time there was no wind, and when at last a breeze sprang up it was almost dead against us, requiring tremendous tacks to make a headway. We could see from the *Principe Farnese* the various lava streams that at one time or another have flowed down Ætna's side to the sea: one of these, over twenty centuries old, was the river of fire that drove back the Carthagenians when on their march to Syracuse. Later on, just before reaching Catania, a tack to the east brought us almost under the shadows of the Cyclopean bluffs, the huge rocks jutting to a height of two hundred feet out of the sea, which the one-eyed Polyphemus hurled after Ulysses when the latter had driven the spike in the giant's eye, and then made his escape from his cavern by hiding under the belly of a sheep.

Catania, like Messina, is ancient yet modern; that is, though founded by the Chalcidians 720 B.C., it has been destroyed by convulsions of nature: the present city dates from the earthquake of 1693, which shook all Sicily and literally destroyed

Catania. On this occasion St. Agatha did not extend her beneficent protection to the city of Catania. Twenty-four years before, on March 8th, 1669, Ætna upheaved a small mountain, and sent forth a river of molten lava. The fiery stream had proceeded fourteen miles, and was rapidly approaching the seemingly doomed city, when the aid of her patron saint was invoked. St. Agatha's veil was thrice waved towards the torrent, and immediately the lava congealed, and Catania was saved. In 1693, the veil of St. Agatha was not used, and the unfortunate city was laid low in ruins. The relics of St. Agatha are preserved in the cathedral, and in the church of St. Carcere we saw the model of her feet in marble. She is greatly revered in Catania. Once a year the pious citizens array themselves in white, and march through the streets with her relics and silver sarcophagus.

South of Catania the shore is flat, often marshy. In several places we saw pyramids of salt glistening in the sun. The sea-water is let into shallow basins, where it evaporates, leaving the basins encrusted with salt. When we arrived at Syracuse, and while standing looking up and down at the long garden that girts the harbor, we saw among the throng of promenaders Perigarde with a hearty-looking young lady walking by his side. Perigarde was radiant as he introduced to us Fraulein Freck, the rosy blonde by his side. The Fraulein was staying at the same *Pension* at which Perigarde was stopping. He had made her acquaintance in Messina, and of course left us on her account.

"Fraulein Freck," added Perigarde, smiling joyously, "is as deeply interested in archæology as I am; in fact, we study it together." This was the first we knew of Perigarde's interest in archæology, but we let that pass. "She thinks the Greek theatre immense, simply immense. So do I," he added, with a radiant face. The Fraulein smiled and blushed.

While Mack was saying something polite to the Fraulein,

Perigarde seized the opportunity to inform me in a whisper, that the Fraulein was a wonderful girl. "She knows everything, positively everything; she is governess to Herr Boehne's little girl; they esteem her highly; she's down here on her vacation." I thought of the American baroness he met at Lisbon, and his "soul's mate" at Granada, but had not the heart to throw those lovely ladies in the poor fellow's face right before the honest, wholesome face of Fraulein Freck.

"Herr Percegott," said the Fraulein, beamingly, "ees so very instructive. I profit my mind very much by Herr Percegott's knowledge of many things."

This was charming: here was this young hearty German girl discovering after a few days' acquaintance Perigarde's great knowledge, which Mack and I had failed to discover during the months we had been together.

"That is the way women always get ahead of men," said Mack. "They are intuitive — everybody admits that — they see things men cannot see at all."

The healthy Fraulein was right when she said the Latomie of Syracuse are immense: they are so immense one can easily lose one's way in their caverns and grottos. In the Latomia dei Cappucini were once confined seven thousand Athenians after their defeat, 413 B.C., by the Syracusans. We obtained the key, opened the little iron door, and descended a zigzag path hewn in the rock, leading down one hundred and fifty feet below the level of ancient Syracuse, to one of its vast, curious quarries. The strange and gloomy place called to mind the Garden of the Gods in Colorado. In these old Syracusan caverns, however, the massive shafts, the fantastic figures, are not freaks of nature, but the work of man wrought more than twenty centuries ago. It is known that the rock quarried from the Latomie was used in building ancient Syracuse, but it is difficult to understand why the excavators left these wonderful shafts and figures. The walls are from ten to twenty feet out of the perpendicular, sloping inwardly to the top: here and there stand solitary shafts and obelisks one hundred and fifty feet high. Some of these caverns are hewn in the shape of tents and pavilions; in places the rock is quarried to within a few feet of the surface of the earth, leaving a bridge of the natural stone spanning an artificial gulf.

The bottoms of these vast quarries are now planted with orange, lemon, and pomegranate trees; the walls, bridges, and shafts are festooned with vines which seem to draw their subsistence from the bare rocks.

The Latomia del Paradiso contains the celebrated "Ear of Dyonisius," — a grotto hewn in the rock in the shape of a human ear. This vast expanse of ear is two hundred and ten feet long, seventy-four feet high, and thirty-five wide. It is said to have been constructed by Dyonisius, whose tyrannous nature led him to devise means whereby a prisoner's faintest whispers could be heard by the guards, and reported to him. The acoustic properties of the ear grotto are certainly remarkable: the softest sound can be heard from one end to the other, two hundred and ten feet distant. The custodian clapped his hands, and the sound, magnified a hundred-fold, reverberated through the tortuous grotto like a peal of thunder. A hundred yards from this place are the Roman and Greek theatres, — both better preserved than most ruins, from the fact that their amphitheatres are not built by putting one layer of stone on another, but are hewn out of the solid rock. In the cliff, at the top of the Greek theatre, the rooms cut into the rock in the shape of pavilions, and perhaps once used as "Green rooms" by the Greek actors, are now converted into pigstys. Cicero, on his return from Athens, indulged in melancholy reflections over the ruins of the Acropolis. Rome was then mistress of the world, but Cicero felt that the day might come when Rome's power would be a thing of the past, as Grecian greatness then was. The once

SCENE IN CYPRUS

mighty city of Syracuse has shrunken to an insignificant town; her ancient tombs and Latomie, the chief objects of interest she possesses. It was here Marcellus stationed his army; here Archimedes erected the engines which lifted the Roman ships and hurled them on the rocks; on this spot stood reflecting-glasses that concentrated the sun's rays on the Roman fleet, and set the vessels on fire. We made a little calculation: geologists say that the coast of Sicily has risen forty feet within the historic age; ten feet of that rise must have been since the time of Archimedes. The coast of Syracuse even now is low, not more than fifteen or twenty feet above the sea; hence two thousand years ago it could not have been more than five or ten feet high. How could so small a height afford a position for engines with arms long and high enough to reach out over the sea and lift up the Roman galleys?

The laws governing marriage are different in the different countries of Christendom, but all governments claim the right to more or less restriction of the marital relation. In some countries a man must obtain his parents' consent, the woman must be of a certain age, etc. Whether such restrictions conduce to happiness or not is an unsettled question; but when one sees two young people rush into a life-long contact, after a few days' acquaintance, one is rather doubtful as to the wisdom of too much freedom being allowed on that vital subject. True, our friend Perigarde was twenty-one; true, he had enough worldly substance to maintain a wife; equally true that Fraulein Freck was over twenty-one, but — we were positively dumbfounded one morning, when Fraulein Freck and Perigarde appeared with beaming faces, and the latter announced that they were man and wife. They had been tied together by a clergyman in the house, and in the presence of Herr Boehne and his wife and daughter, the Fraulein's ex-pupil, who had come down the day before from Messina.

"You see, I've won her," said Perigarde to me privately as

he fairly bubbled over with joy, pride, and triumph. "Yes, I've won her. You fellows are too prosaic; you don't know how to manage with women. She's the most wonderful woman,— knows everything, positively everything."

"Herr Percegott so instructive," said the ex-Fraulein. "I need so mooch instruction. I like mooch to instruct my mind. Herr Pereegott instruct my mind all dee time."

We heartily congratulated these two children of Nature who were so fond of instruction, and gave them the best supper we could get up on the *Principe Farnese*. In view of the fact that American baronesses and "souls' mates" still roam over this world, liable to upset the equanimity of our friend Perigarde if left entirely to himself, we concluded the substantial and wholesome Fraulein might prove the best protection he could have : we took a hopeful view of his future, and rejoiced that he was safely anchored in matrimony.

CHAPTER XIX

Voyage to Greece — Birthplace of Venus — Milo — A Soldier Passenger — Mysterious Disappearance — Our Greek Sailor put in Jail — The Home of Perseus — Cruising 'mid Classic Scenes — Syra — The Shrines of Delos — Storm on the Ægean — Aristotle's Skull and Tomb — We bid Farewell to the *Principe Farnese* — Cost of Yachting

PERIGARDE'S marriage was followed next day by another surprise : Paranzo disappeared without a word of explanation or farewell. This double desertion necessitated the employment of an additional sailor; Luigi was fortunate enough to find a man who spoke Greek. In fact, Xera was a native of Hermupolis, but from long association with Italian sailors spoke Italian as fluently as Greek. He proved a happy acquisition because of his ability to act as interpreter, and his intimate knowledge of the channels and coasts of the Cyclades.

Before starting from Syracuse for Greece, we laid in an extra supply of water, wine, and provisions, because, although a safe enough tub, the *Principe Farnese* was anything but fast; we reckoned on six days as the least possible duration of the voyage. The event proved this a wise precaution; a week saw us barely half way, and it was ten days before we sighted the island of Cerigo. We had not expected to take this course: our plan was to sail for Crete; but after knocking about two days waiting for northerly winds, we decided to take whatever wind arose and go whither it wafted us. This policy was adopted throughout the trip among the Grecian Isles. If we turned into our bunks at night, intending in the morning to visit an island to the north, and if, next morning, there was a good breeze to the south, we went to some island in that direction; generally the island thus visited by chance was as interesting as the one we had planned to explore; at any rate, we avoided wearisome delays, waiting favorable breezes, or tacking against headwinds.

Cerigo's coasts are rugged and steep. Venus, after her birth from the ocean, was wafted ashore there and had no trouble climbing the rocky heights and having a temple erected to mark the spot: to mortal sailors the task is not so simple. By Xera's advice we avoided the island's dangerous coasts and steered direct for Athens, winding up, however, at Milo. Having no particular preference, and thoroughly enjoying the lazy life at sea, this plan of accepting the first strong wind, no matter whither it blew, added an element of uncertainty and brought us to many places we had not planned to see. We spent two days in Milo stretching our limbs, cramped after the long voyage from Syracuse, exploring caverns and examining ruins which indicate the ancient grandeur of this now neglected island. The marble theatre, the ruins of which still exist, once seated more people than inhabit the Milo of to-day, and the statues and tombs discovered display an artistic taste in striking contrast to their rude modern surroundings. Lucky indeed was the Venus de Milo in being carried to Paris; so exquisite a work of art, even though of cold stone, must have blushed to find itself relegated to the garbage pile by a lot of unappreciative barbarians. It was only when M. Brest, the French consul, displayed anxiety to secure the statue, that the Meliotes suspected its value. They decided to send it to the Turks as a propitiatory gift: it was being conveyed in a small boat to a Turkish vessel lying in the harbor, when M. Brest received a message from the French ambassador to Turkey authorizing the purchase of the Venus at any price. Had that message arrived at Milo half an hour later, one of the most beautiful statues of the ancients would now be in Constantinople instead of in the Louvre at Paris. Not far from the spot where the Venus was found in 1820 a Roman horseman was excavated; but both horse and rider still remain where found, Roman statues being considered by the Greeks too recent to be worthy of a place in museums of antiquities.

The catacombs of Milo are extensive; the portions already excavated contain upwards of a thousand graves. In the galleries are inscriptions, niches for lamps, monograms, etc., just as in the catacombs of Rome. The superstitious Meliotes look with awe upon these gloomy caves, especially at noon and midnight. They fancy that ghosts issue forth at those hours. Even Xera, despite his acquaintance with the world, feared the midday and midnight ghosts, and begged us to let the catacombs alone. More awe-inspiring to us than these ancient tombs was Zephyria, Milo's capital, until, in the early part of the present century, a terrible pestilence literally depopulated the city. The stone houses are still there, the church of St. Charalambos still exists, but its doors are closed, there are no worshippers, no people, no living things except lizards, droning flies, poisonous insects; a desolation exists in this old Christian city as great as that of the pagan Pompeii. The Meliotes attribute Zephyria's pestilence to the curse of a priest; the traveller is more apt to attribute it to the unwholesome surroundings — a low plain, a stagnant stream in winter, an alkali salt marsh in summer. From a neighboring mound hot steam issues. Rheumatic peasants visit this mound, descend into its miniature crater, and enjoy a natural Turkish bath. It is said to cure many ills; people, however, do not care to live all the time in a Turkish bath; hence this noxious region is no longer populated. The wonder is that a town was ever built in such a place.

As we were starting in the langia for the *Principe Farnese* the afternoon of our return from Zephyria, a soldier came down to the water's edge, and said something which Xera translated as a request to be taken aboard.

"Where does he wish to go?" I asked.

"To Seripho," replied Xera. "I told him you were going there."

I bade Xera say we were as likely to go to any other island — that all depended on the wind, but the soldier said he would take the chance; so we gave him a place on deck. As usual, we did not go where we planned; at least, not direct. Easterly winds decided us to anchor for the night at Siphenos. Next morning we found our soldier passenger missing. What made the matter something of a mystery was the fact that in taking French leave, he also took Xera's clothing, leaving, however, his uniform in exchange, so that next day our worthy Greek sailor strutted around in all the glory and brass buttons of a soldier. But though in soldier's uniform, he was as much a sailor as ever, and brought the *Principe Farnese* to anchor off Livadion, a fisher village on Scripho, within two hours after leaving Siphenos. We ate dinner on the boat; then Mack and I went ashore to explore this island so famous in Greek mythology. It was in Seripho that Danaë was driven by the tempest after giving birth to Perseus, and here that the inhabitants were turned to stone by the head of Medusa.

A mile or two north of the town of Scriphos is a squalid village with one street, a precipitous and rugged path, and houses with roofs made of a yellowish mud that melts and trickles down the walls every time it rains. Scriphos, the capital, is no better. The main street is only six feet wide at its widest point; at its narrowest, it is scarcely three feet, and in front of each house a lot of pigs block the way. It was a difficult and unpleasant feat, scrambling down this malodorous street, jumping over the pigs and occasionally almost upsetting and tumbling into their filthy mire. On returning to Livadion, the fisher village at the beach, we rowed out to the yacht, and to our surprise found it deserted by all except Francati. In reply to our inquiries as to the whereabouts of Luigi and Xera, Francati said they had been taken away by a band of soldiers; for what reason or whither they had gone he did not know.

"We saw them coming in a small boat," said he, "but had no idea they were coming to us, until they stopped and clambered on deck. As soon as aboard, they pounced first on Xera; then, after some words, which, being Greek, I did not understand, on Luigi. Luigi shouted from the boat as they rowed ashore that the soldiers were taking them to prison."

We started back for the shore to seek the explanation of this curious arrest. Being absolutely ignorant of Greek, we could make no inquiries, and it was difficult to find the prison; when at length we stumbled across it, the guards, who seemed to expect us, conducted us at once to an inner room, where on a wooden bench sat Luigi and Xera, the pictures of despair. When they saw us, their faces lighted.

"We knew you would come," Luigi cried, starting up, and grasping our hands, and laughing and crying together. "Xera said they would shoot him; I said No, the Signori Americani will never permit it; they will save us, and — ecco, here you are. Did I not tell you, Xera?"

"But what is the matter?" we demanded. "Why are you here?"

"They say I am a deserter," answered Xera, dolefully. "That thief, that murderer, your Excellencies took aboard at Milo, is the cause of it all. It is he whom the soldiers seek."

Xera's epithets were a trifle strong, though pardonable under the circumstances. We assured him the matter would be set right in no time, and we really thought it would. But when it came to the point, the thing was easier said than done. Xera was our sole means of communication with the officers, and when we bade him tell the story about the soldier at Milo, and his running off at Siphenos with his clothes, Xera replied quite as dolefully as before that he had already told that story, and that the officers had laughed in his face. However, he told them again, and during the narration Mack and I made sundry signs and gestures meant to corroborate Xera's story, but which unfortunately served rather to convince the officers that we were lunatics or pirates. The officers said they had received orders to look out for a runaway soldier. One had been caught on our boat who could give no reasonable account of himself, hence would be held as a deserter until his innocence was established. The situation was more awkward than we had at first thought. True, there were four of us to vouch for Xera, but we could do so only through Xera himself. We thought the matter might be settled could we find another interpreter, so set out to find one. For two hours we walked through the neglected streets, over the grunting pigs, stopping every passer-by with the question, "Parlate Italiano? — do you speak Italian?" and pushing on as soon as the answer came in a flood of Greek. It was useless trying any other foreign language and almost useless trying Italian. Finally, however, we found a boy who had made voyages with Italian sailors, and with this mite of an interpreter we hurried back to jail, and again explained the situation. To our dismay, the officers remained obdurate, and poor Xera went back into his pen, moaning and sniffling, and declaring he knew they were going to shoot him. We felt sure the affair would come to no such tragic conclusion; nevertheless, it was extremely unpleasant not only to Xera, but to us. Seripho is not now the interesting place it was when Perseus lived there; we were tired of it, and anxious to get away. Next morning Xera was liberated through the arrival of a boat from Siphenos with news of the deserter's arrest. The officers said that several years' imprisonment would be the soldier's punishment for deserting. To avoid future complications, we bought Xera a suit of clothes, and left in Seripho the uniform that had caused such trouble.

To the lovers of the picturesque there can be no more fascinating experience than a boating trip in the Ægean. On every hand some island mountain rises from the sea; every island is rich in scenery, oft weird and rugged, and every grove, every glen, is colored with the romance of Greek mythology. What matters it if you have not the swift-ploughing keel of a racing-yacht? On summer seas amid such surroundings there is as much pleasure on a slow-going fish boat; at least, so Mack and I thought, as the *Principe Farnese* lazily drifted on toward Syra. We sat on deck, occasionally reading or writing, but more often giving ourselves up to the delicious languor of the warm summer air, gazing at the wonderful scenery. The hundreds of islands are so close together, the intervening channels so narrow, we might well fancy we were sailing on the canals of a Grecian Venice, were the Grecian Islands built up with houses as are the islands on which stands the city of Venice. It was night when we entered Syra's harbor; the gay little city's terraced streets were lighted with lamps that looked from the sea like stars. The mountain slope upon which the city is built is steep and rugged; many of the lights which, while entering the harbor, we actually mistook for stars, were at the top of the terraced streets eight hundred feet above the sea.

Syra, with its twenty-five thousand inhabitants, second city in Greece in point of population, is perhaps the first as regards commercial importance. Being the central island of the Cyclades, it is the distributing point of the group, and enjoys a toll on all trade that circles round its shores. The Marina, or quay, is a bustling place, alive with boatmen, sailors, and marketmen from neighboring islands. Syra is so sterile the other islands supply it with provisions. Almost every house on the Marina is a restaurant; even in those that are not restaurants cooking is constantly going on. The merchants sit out in front of their shops, holes scarcely ten feet square, and when not waiting on customers, kill time by cooking on curious little three-legged stoves, making dreggy coffee and boiling a mixture of herbs and fish resulting in a compound much liked in the Greek Islands.

Only the merchants can afford this rich diet; the mechanics and wharf laborers live much simpler. A shoe cobbler, whose "establishment" consists of a seat on the street, was surrounded by a few tools and old shoes, a loaf of bread, and a hatful of grapes. He seemed quite contented as he basked in the sun, pegging away at the old shoes and munching his bread and grapes. Every time we saw him he was eating bread and grapes and working as he ate. We paid two cents a pound for the big, luscious grapes; the shoemaker, not being American, pays only one cent.

The islanders wear a singular costume; yet instead of laughing at themselves, they laughed at us. This was because we did not wear shoes of untanned rawhide with the toes turned up two inches, sharp-pointed, and ornamented with black tassels; our legs were not wrapped in coarse canvas, we wore no white kilt, and our sleeves were not flowing and big enough to hold a peck of potatoes. Had we dressed thus, we would have slightly resembled the natives and perhaps attracted less attention. By some of the peasants the baggy breeches of the Turk are preferred to the kilt. In Syra's plaza stands a statue of Pentellic marble representing Miaoulis, the naval hero furnished by the Isle of Hydra in the war of independence, 1821. The hero wore baggy breeches, and may have looked heroic in the flesh and in the heat of battle; but represented in cold stone, he looks bloated and ridiculous.

As all roads lead to Rome, so in Syra all steps lead to the Cathedral of St. George; at any rate, enough steps lead there to fatigue even practised pedestrians. The cathedral is in the top part of the town, approached by a street of narrow and steep steps. We toiled up those steps, found the cathedral locked, then continued our walk to the topmost point of the island, a point nearly fifteen hundred feet above the sea, whence we saw not only all of Syra, but a dozen other islands of the Archipelago. The mountain on which we stood seemed almost like one solid rock. There is not enough earth on it to grow weeds, yet its sides are seamed here and there with stone walls laboriously built with the abundant boulders. Even on the steepest slopes, slopes where we had to crawl on hands and knees, we saw these walls, and marvelled not only at the patience and labor that had put them there, but at the folly of building them. Mack suggested that pasturing was so poor the cattle were weak, and the walls were built to keep them from falling down the mountain. The trouble with this theory is that there are *no* pastures and *no* cattle. Afterwards, in other islands, equally mountainous and sterile, we saw stone walls three feet high. Questioning failed to find the cause of their existence. One man said they were built to mark the divisions of property; when we asked why sane people wanted to divide "property" consisting of a slab of rock a thousand feet high and almost perpendicular, the man said he did not know.

From Syra we made a side trip to Delos, the birthplace of Apollo; the whole excursion there and back and several hours on the island took a long day. Delos is now as free of live as of dead men. Traces of the ruins of a castle indicate that it was inhabited in the Middle Ages, but at the present time it shows no sign of human life except during the occasional visits of fishermen.[1]

The temple of Apollo, once reckoned one of the seven wonders of the world, and the other early Greek ruins have disappeared, but those of a somewhat later date remain; the traveller, as he gazes upon the mosaic pavements and marble columns still existing in Delos, is reminded of Pompeii. For many generations the women of Delos, when enceinte, also aged and feeble persons, were banished to the isle of Rheneia, in order that deaths and births might be avoided as far as possible on the sacred island of Delos. Those who had been buried in Delos before its sanctification were dug up and carried to Rheneia; but as Byron says, even gods must yield. Delos fell from its high estate. In later days not only did the philosopher Pherecydes die on the sacred island; he died of a loathsome disease. His disciple Pythagoras buried him near the temple of Apollo; then, disgusted that so wise a man could not keep himself free from vermin, left Greece forever.

It was our intention on leaving Syra to sail north to Giura and see that gloomy rock, ancient Rome's most dreaded place of banishment, then veer to the west, pass between Zea and Thermia, and so enter the Gulf of Ægina, on the way to Athens. A storm and contrary winds changed this plan. We reached Giura safely enough, clambered up its rocky heights, and gained a vivid idea of how the old Romans felt when banished there, by imagining how *we* should feel were Luigi to sail off with the *Principe Farnese* and leave us to broil and starve to death on that huge boulder in the sea. This much of our plan was carried out within a few hours after leaving Syra. But in the afternoon, instead of going west to Zea, we sailed north as far

---

[1] We were afterwards told that Delos is not entirely deserted, that the island is rented to a shepherd, and that it is also occupied by an old man hired to watch the ruins. These two lonely inhabitants must have been absent at the time of our visit; at least, we saw nothing of them.

as Eubœa. The experience on this voyage reminded us that summer was gone and with it the pleasant, if not the safe, season for boating. Good weather is often found in October and November, but it is never certain; storms often blow up suddenly. I think boatmen will find it well to leave the Ægean not later than the middle of October.

Although there was little danger to be apprehended on so staunch and large a boat as ours, there was a great deal of discomfort. The wind swelled almost to a gale, the sea was high and choppy, the great waves that now and then broke over the deck drenched us. The day following this storm was so cloudless and brilliant we determined, now that we had been blown so far north, to lengthen the voyage a few days by a cruise to Chalkis. Grecian waters afford no more charming excursion. The channel between Eubœa and the mainland is narrow, and from early morn until late night of that brilliant October day the *Principe Farnese* sailed between two coasts, now rugged and bare, now gentle slopes and cosy harbors, again rising into mountain peaks five thousand feet high.

In Chalkis we were greatly interested not only in the modern population, descendants of the people who once threw a bridge across the Euripus, fortified it with castles, and defied the power of Athens, but in the discoveries of Dr. Charles Waldstein, particularly in his discovery shortly before our visit of the tomb of Aristotle. Many archæologists have believed that Aristotle drowned himself in the Euripus, because of his disappointment at not being able to discover the cause of the ebb and flow of the tides. Dr. Waldstein rescues the philosopher's memory from the charge of suicide. His tomb was found some miles out of Chalkis, where Aristotle is known to have had his country seat. In addition to inscriptions, other evidence that the grave is really that of the philosopher is afforded by its contents. A portion of the skull was found, and near it a band of pure gold an inch and a half wide, also a diadem

ABDULLAH AND THE AUTHOR SETTING OUT FOR THE PYRAMIDS

with leaves of ivy. A metal pen, styluses, and implements of writing lay near, while in a niche of the sarcophagus stood a statuette of the philosopher. When Dr. Waldstein described his discovery, and submitted the evidence to the Royal Institute of London, it made a profound impression and convinced the savants that the world not only has the tomb of Aristotle, but the very skull whence were evolved those ideas that for twenty-two hundred years have been a force in the world.

On the return from Chalkis our route lay along the coast of Attica, and part of the time we sailed close to the long, sandy beach of Marathon. We saw the mound from our boat, and that being all there is to see, did not land. Classical students make the tedious and expensive trip from Athens to Marathon simply out of sentiment; the field differs little to-day from any other field, and the traveller's satisfaction consists merely in the knowledge that he is standing on the spot where Greece rolled back the Persian invasion. By land Marathon is only twenty-five miles from Athens; by water it is probably one hundred, as the entire southern end of Attica must be circumnavigated. Winds were favorable; we reached Zea, where we intended stopping, in the night of the second day out from Chalkis. Zea has a snug little harbor almost land-locked; it is not easy to find by day; at night it is difficult; and though there was a bright moon, we beat about several hours before Xera had the *Principe Farnese* safely anchored.

Zea's mountains are so steep and rise so precipitously from the sea that boats cannot land except at the harbor. From a distance the island seems rugged and sterile, but a climb to its capital three or four miles from the harbor, on a mountain fifteen hundred feet high, shows more vegetation than is found on many of the Cyclades. A peculiarity of the island is its gnarled oaks that grow very large acorns, furnishing abundant food for the pigs that wallow in the streets of Zea. Like most of the island towns, Zea is built perpendicularly, so to speak:

the streets are like ladders, and the houses cling to the sides of the mountain instead of standing on level spaces. A Zean can step out of his back door on to the roof of his neighbor's house, and a man with long legs can descend from the upper to the lower part of town without stepping on the streets at all, the houses forming an excellent if large stairway. In ancient times the people of Zea had the extraordinary custom of committing suicide on reaching the seventieth year. Old age was held in disrepute, and persons of both sexes voluntarily put a period to their days as soon as it became evident that nature meant to let them pass seventy. This is one of the customs not observed to-day; there are a great many old people in Zea; they live long because of their mild climate and quiet, regular lives. Among the few relics of past greatness is the colossal statue of a lion; the granite monster, thirty feet long, stands on a lofty height commanding a superb view of the island, the sea, and the coast of Attica.

We made but one stop on the voyage from Zea to Piræus. The *Principe Farnese* was sailing along in the Ægean Gulf, I was looking through the glasses at the bold cliffs and bald-pated mountains of the island of Ægina, when Mack, who was gazing in the opposite direction, declared he saw a temple on the Attic coast. We tacked to the east, and in three-quarters of an hour hove to under a bluff on the summit of which, three hundred feet above the water, stood a series of majestic columns. At first we were at a loss how to scale that precipice and how to designate those columns and the marble portico that so unexpectedly met our gaze on this lonely height. A little work solved both problems. A rugged path and hard climbing brought us to the top of the bluff, and an examination of our maps brought us to the conclusion that the ruins were those of the Temple of Minerva. We were standing on the promontory of Sunium, where Neptune was worshipped, and in front of which the Athenians were wont to hold their regattas and trials of strength on the sea.

A few hours later our boating trip came to a close at Piræus. Xera brought the *Principe Farnese* close to the dock, where our papers were examined and where we began the task of getting our goods and chattels ashore. This done, captain, crew, and passengers of the gallant little craft adjourned to one of the curious Greek restaurants — kitchen in front, dining-room in the rear, pigs, dogs, and goats everywhere — and indulged in a farewell jollification. Luigi, Francati, and Xera had served us faithfully, and we felt a genuine regret when they accompanied us to the Athens train and the moment for parting came. The worthy boatmen doubtless felt sorry too, but their sorrow was tempered by the fact that after our departure they fell heir to sundry goods, clothing, blankets, and odds and ends of no small value to them, but of no further use to us.

When England turned the Ionian Isles over to Greece, a number of the departing English officers left their yachts at Corfu. We were told these yachts can be rented very cheap, and the reader who purposes taking a boating trip in Greek waters will do better to get his boat at Corfu or Athens than at Naples. A twelve-ton boat can be hired at Athens for $50 to $60 a month, and for cruising among the islands that tonnage is sufficient. The *Principe Farnese* was large enough to sail in any waters, and cost 450 lire (about $86) a month. This sum was divided between three, so that the cost to each was only $29. Living on the boat cost us on an average $50 a month, so that the total cost of our yachting trip was only $45 per month per person. If the reader is not satisfied with a rough fishing-boat, he can rent an eight or ten ton yacht for from $125 to $150 per month. For the former sum we were offered a handsome boat that made easily eight knots an hour and was furnished with bedding, table service, etc. The address of the owner of this boat may be obtained from Thomas Cook & Son, Naples.

CHAPTER XX

Athens — Curious Costume of the Greeks — Their Prison System — The Bay of Salamis and the Hill where Xerxes sat — Rue Byron in Athens — The Corinthian Canal — A Stupendous Work — We climb Pentelicon's Peak — Primitive Ways and Means — How Money is changed

THE Greeks are more appreciative of their antiquities than were their Turkish rulers. In the beginning of this century the Sultan gave Lord Elgin a firman " to take away pieces of stone." This was a broad expression, and Lord Elgin made the most of it. His vandalism, while adding priceless treasures to the British Museum, damaged the Parthenon more than the Venetians and Turks combined. Such vandalism cannot be repeated now. Departing travellers are searched, and if found attempting to carry antiquities out of the kingdom, are heavily fined. We heard of a Frenchman who was caught just as his steamer was about to sail. The old vases and bric-a-brac found in his trunk were confiscated, and the unlucky antiquarian fined 6000 drachmæ (about $960).

The popular idea that something serious happens when "Greek meets Greek" is a mistake. We saw hundreds of Greeks meet, and nothing serious happened, although very amusing subjects were afforded the kodak. A Greek gentleman's costume resembles that of a ballet dancer. He wears a short white linen or muslin skirt, stiff with starch and standing out almost at right angles from the body. These skirts, though less than two feet long, often contain as much as forty yards of cloth, the plaits are so broad and numerous. His legs are encased in white stockings, on his head is a jaunty bonnet, and dangling at his side is a short sword. Were a troupe of ballet girls to clap false beards on their faces, belt swords on their waists, and rush out on the street, they would afford an idea of what one sees every day on the streets of Athens. It is difficult for Westerners to realize that they are gazing on real men. We never wearied looking at them, especially in the cafés, where they stretched out their long stocking-covered legs, smoothed down their plaited skirts, and solemnly puffed their narghilla pipes. Mack tried to kodak a fat old fellow, but desisted when the Greek drew his sword, scowled, and intimated that further glances at his legs and petticoat would result in gore. This was in a café where the well-to-do classes drink black coffee early in the morning. They do not eat breakfast until noon and dinner until six. Workingmen seem to prefer milk to coffee. There are little shops where they take their bread and buy a pint of milk for two and a half cents. At noon laborers on buildings and in workshops stop half an hour to eat grapes, bread, cheese, figs, and to light their pipes from a pan of coals at some tobacconist's. Matches are taxed and are very dear; hence smokers usually go to tobacconists for lights.

The Athenian mechanic earns about three drachmæ per day; that is, about half a dollar. Nominally the Greek drachma is equivalent to the French franc, but so depreciated is the currency. a Napoleon, twenty francs, commands a premium of six or seven francs; that is, it buys from twenty-six to twenty-seven drachmæ. On the principal street corners are the stands of money-changers, who have an odd way of making change. They simply tear in two the notes of large denomination. The first time a banker cashed my draft with parts of notes, I refused the money, but soon learned that this halving of bank notes is sanctioned by law and that the two halves of a ten-drachmæ bill pass as freely as if each half were stamped "five drachmæ." The money-changers have not been scourged from the temples of Athens. When we entered the cathedral we saw near the door several priests driving a brisk trade in candles. The priests had their long hair tied up with strings, their black caps sat back on their heads, the sleeves of their flowing gowns were turned up, their eyes had a business look as they leaned on the counter counting their money and candles. The purchasers lighted their candles and stuck them about the church. The recent death of one of the royal family brought an unusual number of worshippers to the cathedral, so that it blazed with the light of more than a thousand candles.

When I applied to the Greek Minister of the Interior for permission to inspect prisons, I should have fared badly but for Mr. P. Gennadius, Secretary of Agriculture, who, having spent four years in the Illinois College of Agriculture, speaks English; Mr. Gennadius not only procured the necessary permits, but accompanied me on my visit to the chief penitentiary just outside of Athens. The director, Mr. Nicolas Spiliopoulos, was most courteous and obliging, conducting us through the entire institution, but he spoke no English: Mr. Gennadius kindly translated the director's explanations. The Greek prison system, unlike that of the other Mediterranean countries, avoids the extremes of isolation and too free communion. Greek prisoners cannot mingle freely as do Spanish convicts; on the other hand, they are not kept in perpetual isolation as in many Italian prisons. The Greek prisoner's cell consists of a wooden cage seven feet long and five feet wide. One large room holds six of these cages, three on a side, a narrow aisle between the two rows, and the doors perforated with holes to allow circulation of air. The holes also make it easy for the prisoners to see and talk with their *vis-a-vis* across the aisle whenever the guard is absent, which is most of the time; for after the soldier in white stockings and ballet dancer's skirt has assured himself that all is right in a room, he locks the door and leaves the six convicts to themselves. It would not be difficult to break out of the wooden cages; but as that would not release them from the large room and would bring severe punishment in the morning, the attempt is seldom made: a casual inspection during the night has been found sufficient to preserve order.

Although the government has a regulation convict uniform, the prisoners are by no means dressed alike, for the reason that the gray-checked suit is not furnished until the convict wears out the clothing worn on first entering. The Greek government is in such financial straits it is forced to economize even in such petty ways as this. The penitentiary was built by private subscription, the government undertaking only to support the institution when completed. Mr. Spiliopoulos stated that the prison's annual cost to the tax-payer is 100,000 drachmæ ($15,500). One-fourth of this sum is for guards and administration, the rest for food and clothing of convicts. The average number of prisoners is three hundred, so that 250 drachmæ is the yearly expense per capita for food and clothing. The daily cost of food is 61 lepta (9 cents), which amount, though small, seems large, considering the prisoner's meagre rations. He has only two meals a day. When noon, the hour for the first meal, arrives, each prisoner is marched from the workshop to his cell, locked up, then given a kilogramme (2⅓ pounds) of bread and a bowl of "revithia"—a soup composed of oil, tomatoes, and a sort of bean called "revithia," whence the soup derives its name. An hour and a half is allowed for the consumption of this meal, then back to the workshops until dinner at six, of olives, cheese, or sardines, and what is left of the kilogramme of bread served in the morning. Only once a week is a small piece of meat served by the government; the prisoner, however, may buy meat any day. Convicts receive each week one-fourth of the net proceeds of their labor; on leaving prison, they receive another fourth: the other two-fourths are retained by the government. It is provided, though, that the prisoner's receipts shall not exceed 70 lepta per day, and any sum in excess of that amount is appropriated by the government. When the king's son attained his majority a year or two ago, there was a brisk demand for Chinese lanterns to illuminate the capital. Mr.

Spiliopoulos set sixty convicts to work making lanterns, and in a short time twenty-nine thousand were ready. The sixty prisoners received 3000 drachmæ, while the government's share amounted to 6000 drachmæ.

The principal work at present is the manufacture of shoes and brushes. The latter display very neat workmanship, but as they are made in thirty different styles, I was obliged to decline the director's kind offer to give me one of each to show the sort of work performed by Greek convicts. A trunkful of brushes would be a rather expensive article of luggage to carry about Europe. In 1890 the Greek government's income from convict labor was only 10,000 drachmæ. The smallness of the amount is due to the fact that the prisoners are idle a large part of the time. The government is seeking a way to provide work, but thus far has not succeeded. When shoe-making was first attempted, a loud outcry was made by the free shoemakers, and now convicts are allowed to make shoes only for the army. To avoid as far as possible the ill effects of idleness, a school and an exercise court are provided. In the former a competent teacher instructs the illiterate; in the latter a guard stands with a long switch like the ringmaster of a circus, and makes the convicts circle around him one hour a day. The prisoners are in single file, three feet apart, and so well trained that the guard controls them by a mere motion of his switch as though it were a magic wand. At a signal from that switch the three hundred convicts march slowly and sedately or run furiously as if to escape a dangerous foe.

The penitentiary is in the middle of the sun-baked plain between Athens and the sea. Before returning to Athens we rode over to the Bay of Salamis. While the horses rested in the shade of a gnarled olive tree, we climbed over rugged boulders to the summit of the hill whence Xerxes overlooked the battle of Salamis. On top of the hill Mack hauled out his Thucydides, and after reading a while, looked up and said : —

"There seems to be a doubt as to whether Xerxes sat on this hill or on that one there. To be sure, we had better climb the other hill too."

It is well to make certain of important points; hence we climbed the second hill; then, to make assurance doubly sure, we rambled about *all* the hills that line the Bay of Salamis. We did not recognize the hill, but as we were on all of them, I think we may say we climbed the one whereon Xerxes sat. Afterwards we took other trips, one to Pentelicus and one to Corinth. A steam tram runs from Athens through a plain dotted with adobe huts and gnarled olive trees, to Kephisia, a small town where wealthy Athenians have summer homes and some pretence of verdure and vegetation. The pedestrian part of the trip began at Kephisia, and though Pentelicus is less than four thousand feet high, the ascent is so steep and rugged that we were thoroughly fatigued by the time we reached the summit. The view more than compensated for the fatigue of the climb. There is probably no spot on earth that overlooks more historic ground than the peak of Mt. Pentelicus. The circle swept by the eye embraces on the one hand the most important part of the mainland of Greece, while in the sea islands as far away as Crete loom up clear and distinct on unclouded days. On the way down we made a detour to visit the ancient quarries where Pericles got his marble for the Parthenon; in this detour we lost our way, but one of the quarrymen (Pentelicus still affords Athens marble) guided us back to Kephisia. This was the only guide we had in Greece, and it is humiliating to record that his name was plain Tarnos. Most travellers in Greece have guides named Thucydides or Aristotle or Demosthenes, and in their books they tell how Miltiades blacked their boots, how Alcibiades waited on them at the hotel, and how Euripides, or some other "des," served as cabman in drives about Athens. The only places we came across such distinguished names were on the street lamp-posts, and it was gratifying to note that her respect for ancient celebrities has not caused Greece to forget modern friends. Conspicuous among the streets of Athens is that named after Byron, who is remembered by the Greeks with an affection and respect that, despite his great genius, has never been accorded him in his native land.

On the trip to Corinth we might have imagined ourselves in Arizona, but for the blue domes on the churches and the strange costumes of the people. Eleusis, Megara, and the other towns passed are dilapidated places set down in sterile plains. The desert-like appearance of the country was partly due to the season, the close of the long annual drouth. But even under its most favorable aspect those boulder-covered hills and plains must look rugged and stern rather than picturesque and beautiful. The peasants in the fields were working with implements of the same pattern in use two thousand years ago. Grain is cut with a hand-sickle and threshed with sticks or flails.

There are no Corinthian columns in the Corinth of to-day; in fact, there are no columns of any sort. The only remaining original Corinthian columns are those on the site of ancient Corinth, three miles from the modern village of that name. Twelve of the columns were standing in the last century. An earthquake shook five down, so that now only seven stand just as they were placed twenty odd centuries ago. Mack and I saw neither the standing nor the fallen columns. There was but one day to spare, so instead of going to ancient Corinth we walked through the canal that is being dug between the Corinthian and the Saronic gulfs. Although only four or five miles long, this canal deserves to be reckoned as one of man's greatest works. Its construction, originally projected by Alexander the Great, was seriously considered by Julius Cæsar, but not actually begun until after the ship-railway (Diolkos), on which goods and small boats were transported across the Isthmus, proved clumsy and unprofitable; then Nero began the task of cutting through the rocks and hills. The difficulties, however, were too great for that age; Nero abandoned the task after digging out a few hundred yards, and it was not until recent years that work was resumed. When completed, the cutting will be nearly three hundred feet deep and sixty-five feet wide. The water will have a depth of twenty-five feet. The greater part of this stupendous work has already been accomplished; the engineers say two more years will see it completed.

When we entered the cutting from the Corinthian end and looked down toward Kalamaki, the air was filled with smoke and clouds of dust, and there was a rumbling sound caused by the explosions and falling masses of stone and earth. An army of Montenegrins, Greeks, and Italians are digging away at the Isthmus, and the noise of their work is as the noise of battle. Tracks have been thrown into the canal, and as the blasting which goes steadily on like the roar of artillery, dislodges mountains of earth and stones, the debris is lifted by steam-dredges on to trains of cars and hauled rapidly away. The curiously costumed workmen whom we saw digging and cutting and pouring powder into the blast holes receive four drachmæ (about fifty-nine cents) per day. The entire work will cost sixty million francs in gold.

A few days after returning to Athens I bade farewell not only to Greece, but to Mack, my friend and fellow-voyager, whom a cablegram called to America.

CHAPTER XXI

Smyrna — Imprisoned by the Turks — Barbarity of the Moslem — How Taxes are farmed and Peasants robbed — Mr. McNaughton the Missionary — A Good Samaritan — From a Foul Dungeon to the Deck of the *Minerva* — I step on an Austrian — Chios and Rhodes — Through the Ægean Sea — Prison Circles of Rhodes

ENGLAND'S occupation of distant and semi-civilized lands is often regarded unfavorably by Europeans and by some Americans. I think, though, that those of my countrymen who travel in the Orient will wish the "occupation" policy extended further than it does now. Wherever English sway or influence is felt, whether in Cyprus, Egypt, India, or still remoter lands, the traveller may go with some assurance that he will not be robbed or maltreated. That this assurance is lacking where Western influence is lacking the following narrative will show.

The Egyptian steamer on which I took passage from Greece arrived at Smyrna Saturday, October 10, 1891, at nine o'clock in the morning. It was my intention to transship immediately to the Austrian-Lloyd steamer *Minerva*, bound for Jaffa; but as my supply of ready money had dwindled to a few francs, I found myself obliged to go ashore for a visit to the banker's. At the custom house I complied with the demand for papers, by exhibiting the regular American passport issued by the Department of State at Washington, but the customs officials declared this insufficient, because lacking a Turkish consul's visa. He said the "fine" for attempting to enter Turkish territory without such visa was £1. I protested I did not mean to remain in Smyrna, that I merely transshipped there, and was going ashore only in order to get money. When this explanation proved unsatisfactory, I requested my passport, which had been taken from me, stating I would not go ashore at all, but would

CLIMBING THE GIZEH PYRAMID

have myself conveyed at once aboard the Austrian steamer. Instead of permitting this, the officer conducted me to a room in another part of the building, where the chief of police renewed the demand for money, and where, finding myself in the hands of brigands, I agreed to accede to their demand as soon as I had procured funds at the bank. To my surprise this was not satisfactory. They ordered me to pay the money on the spot — a physical impossibility, not having that sum about me. I showed my letter of credit and circular notes of Thomas Cook & Son, and asked to be escorted to their Smyrna correspondents, Messrs. Patterson & Company. This request was roughly refused, an armed guard was called, and an order written by the chief of police committing me to prison. Thither, a distance of more than a mile, was I conducted through the streets like a condemned criminal and compelled to carry two heavy valises and the kodak that constituted my baggage and which I wished transferred from the Egyptian to the Austrian steamer. We passed a number of Turks and Arabs, who eyed me curiously, and some of whom turned and followed to see what was to be done with the European thus heavily loaded and guarded. Once at a cross-street, when stopped by a train of camels all tandem, tied together by a rope, I took out the kodak and was about to photograph the scene, when one of the soldiers gave a yell, shook his fist at me and roughly ordered me to put the camera back in its place.

Arrived at the prison, I was first placed in a room of one of the officers, but after several ineffectual demands for money the turnkey became savage and led me out of the official's room into a den that might well pass for the Black Hole of Calcutta. Although only thirteen feet square and about ten high, this den contained thirty-one prisoners. There was not room enough to sit; indeed, there was scarce room to stand, and the space under the one small, iron-barred window was literally jammed with men trying to escape the foul air within and get a whiff of the comparatively pure air without: comparatively, for the window opened, not on a street or court, but on a narrow prison corridor only less foul than our dungeon. There was no closet in the den, and the filth and odor that prevailed is absolutely indescribable. In this foul hole, amid vermin-infested cut-throats and criminals, I was an object of wonder to the turbaned prisoners and of persecution by my jailers, who came at frequent intervals to renew their demands for money. The fact that they refused to let me send for the American consul or to Patterson & Company satisfied me that the so-called "fine" was entirely illegal, not justified even by Turkish law. They evidently feared that at either the consul's or the bank, protection would be extended and their attempted robbery balked and exposed.

The reader will remember that prisoners in the island dungeon of San Stefano are allowed twenty quarts of water a month; the prisoners in the Smyrna den are apparently not allowed twenty quarts a year — a more filthy and malodorous set of men could scarce be found in either Europe or Asia. Their scanty clothing was ragged and tattered, their hair long and unkempt. One Turk had an enormous nose which, at some period of his career had been cut off and then sewed on again. The deep red seam gave his naturally brutal face a still more repulsive aspect. Another of my fellow-prisoners was a boy not above thirteen years old; another was a blind Turk, with legs naked to the thighs, then short, baggy breeches to the waist: from the waist up there was merely a coating of dirt. At twelve o'clock bolts and bars rattled, the door opened, a turnkey ordered all to march out, and I thought freedom at last in sight. But it was not. The turnkey only wanted to count us. After standing the prisoners in a row in the narrow, dirty corridor, he began shoving them one by one back into the den, accompanying his enumeration by sundry cuffs, kicks, and curses, which I deemed myself lucky to escape. The unfortunate Turk with the sewed-on nose seemed to attract the turnkey's special attention. Seizing him by the neck with his left hand, with his right he gave him several resounding blows on the head and face, then kicked him into the dungeon. The other prisoners were servile enough to laugh at this brutal and uncalled-for treatment, imagining thereby to win some degree of favor for themselves: in this they were disappointed; few escaped, nearly all were kicked and cuffed as though they had been creating a disturbance instead of, as was actually the case, bearing their imprisonment with the most servile humility.

During the time I was in that den I heard not a word of complaint; all seemed to accept the filth and foul air as a matter of course: even the brutal cuffs of the jailer evoked sickly smiles instead of murmurs. A young man of about eighteen, with a face that did not seem that of a criminal, was brought in at two o'clock. The first thing that struck his attention was the Turk with the remarkable nose. This nose with its end hanging on by threads, was so extraordinary, the young man was unlucky enough to exhibit his surprise before the turnkey closed the door. The turnkey seemed as furious as if it had been *his* nose that was stared at; re-entering the den, he gave the young man so sudden and severe a blow as to send him staggering against the wall. As usual, the other prisoners gave a subservient smile. I had had no breakfast and was both hungry and thirsty, but the turnkey, in return for what loose change I happened to have,—a franc or so,—gave only a crust of dry bread. Water was too great a luxury for a man guilty of my offence. I suffered greatly from thirst during that long and sweltering day. Once the jailer took me out to the street, pointed to the penitentiary, a large building on a hill several hundred yards away, and said that I would be transferred there if money were not speedily forthcoming. As a "bluff" this threat failed; for the den in which I was already consigned seemed to me the extreme limit of filth and horror. The penitentiary could not be worse.

It may be necessary to keep the Turk alive in Europe to preserve the balance of power; yet, after two trips into Turkey in Europe and Asia, I cannot help wishing the strong hand of Western civilization extended to the East. As an instance of the oppression which the occupation of Turkey by a Western power might abolish, I may mention that flowing from the farming out of taxes. The Turkish government exacts one-eleventh of all products, and no one can touch his ten-elevenths until the government's one-eleventh has been taken. After the harvest a peasant goes to the tax-gatherer and tells him his wheat is in the field ready to be taxed. But the tax-gatherer refuses to make any estimate; he is too busy — has other fields to visit. In short, the wheat will lie on the ground until it rots unless the peasant bribes the tax-gatherer to come and take the government's share. So severe is the punishment meted to one who removes a crop before the government tax has been levied that families often suffer hunger with abundance of fruit and wheat before their eyes. One inspector went to a field and marked off about a third instead of an eleventh of the crop. The peasant remonstrated. "Very well," said the tax-gatherer, "keep it all; I have not time to measure it again," and off he went. The peasant did not dare touch the wheat until the tax had been collected. At the end of a week he went to the tax-gatherer and begged him to come and make the division on his own terms. The result of this system is that fertile fields are left untilled, and the people produce no more than enough to support bare existence.

Here is another grievance which would be abolished by Western occupation of Turkey: The government recruiting officer sends word to a town or village that so many soldiers must be provided — say two hundred. The number he is authorized to demand is only one hundred; but the village authorities know it is useless to resist the government officer, who usually arrives in the village several days before the drawing, to afford the wealthy an opportunity to buy their freedom. One man I heard of gave the recruiting officer a flock of eighty sheep — his entire wealth — to buy off his son. The ballot-box has a partition; the names of those who have given bribes are on one side, the names of the poor on the other. The Mahometan priest who supervises the drawing puts his hand in the box, draws out a ballot numbered and named, and announces the result, — "Suli Abdul, no number," which means freedom. Priest and officer congratulate Suli Abdul; then the priest puts his hand in the box again, and this time draws a ballot from the other side of the partition, — "Mahmud Dost, No. 75" (seven years in the army); and, while Mahmud Dost weeps and bids farewell to his family and friends, the pious priest prays for his welfare and safety. By the above process the recruiting officer sometimes takes away eight or nine hundred dollars from a single village. One officer I met paid his servants 200 piastres a month (his own official salary was only 125 piastres). This is as great a feat as that performed by those American congressmen who become millionnaires on $5000 a year.

About four o'clock, through the bars of the window to which I had climbed for a whiff of air, I perceived a well-dressed gentleman in the corridor, apparently a visitor to the prison on business. I succeeded in attracting his attention, and, when he came under the window, begged him to bring the American consul. The gentleman seemed astonished to see a Caucasian in the prison, and expressed his willingness to go for the consul. I gave him my card with a few lines scribbled on it. The turnkey, entering the corridor at this moment, demanded to know what was going on.

The gentleman stated that I had given him my card to take to the American consul.

"Ah! I was just going with him to the consul's. You can give me the card." (The turnkey spoke fairly good English.)

The unsuspecting gentleman gave him the card and went away, whereupon the jailer turned toward me viciously, tore up my card, and threatened me with dire punishment if I made another "attempt to escape."

The first sign on the Smyrna quay that one sees from the harbor bears the name " B. Diogenes." Judging from my experience, Diogenes selected a poor place in which to seek his honest man.

After eight hours' imprisonment my jailer seemed to reach the conclusion that I really had no money in my pocket; the door was opened and I was roughly ordered to get out, which I was glad enough to do.[1] I hurried at once to the American consulate, only to learn that the consul had sailed for Greece at five o'clock that afternoon. It was now too late to visit the bank ; I had not enough money to pay for a night's lodging, and was strolling on the quay, looking for a good place to sleep, when my eye chanced to light on a sign in English, —

"SMYRNA REST."

A large, jovial-looking man was standing in the door of the "Smyrna Rest." I asked in English if I could rest there.

" No, young fellow ; you cannot get lodging here. This is a rest for the soul, not the body. See here," pointing to gospel

---

[1] I transmitted an account of this affair to Secretary of State James G. Blaine, who at once placed the matter in the hands of our Minister to Turkey. After much diplomatic red tape the Turkish Prime Minister, on behalf of his master, the Sultan, wrote the Secretary of State a letter which I am confident was prepared by Mark Twain. The Prime Minister, after flourishes and expressions of good will towards the American people, says : —

"Mr. Meriwether was merely invited to establish his identity. Upon establishing it, he was allowed to depart without paying a fine."

"Invited!" Possibly the highwayman who presents a cocked pistol and demands your money or your life imagines he is " merely inviting " you to make a choice.

As the Prime Minister was good enough to add that his master, the Sublime Porte, profoundly regretted the occurrence; also as the Smyrna jailers were shrewd enough to hold me until the departure for Greece of the American quotations and inscriptions on the walls. "But do not worry. The Lord will provide. I shall take you to one of His servants."

I briefly told the man my story. Just at this moment a gentleman and lady approached, and the jovial man took off his cap with an air of affection and respect.

"How are you, James?" said the gentleman, in a kindly voice. "Is all well at the Rest?"

"All is well, Mr. McNaughton. Here is a young American in trouble. I was just about to take him to you," with which he related the story of my imprisonment. Mr. McNaughton was a missionary from Canada; the lady was his wife. They were as kind to me as if I had been an old friend instead of a stranger, made me go home with them, where I got a warm bath (I felt as if I needed to be boiled a week after that prison experience) and a good supper. The company of these Christian people was indeed a contrast to the Moslem brutality of Turks. It is too much the custom of thoughtless persons to deride and sneer at missionaries. It seems to me the man or woman who voluntarily submits to banishment from home and all association with civilized people to preach the gospel of Christianity to savages or semi-savages merits our reverence as a true follower of Christ. I shall never again hear missionaries derided without thinking of the "Smyrna Rest" and of Mr. and Mrs. J. P. McNaughton. Mr. McNaughton has been four years with the American Mission in Smyrna, and in that time has acquired a wide influence among the Turks, Greeks, and Armenians. The next morning the religious services held at the Rest were in five languages. I felt a genuine regret on leaving that genial and hospitable home.

Consul, preventing me from obtaining witnesses and testimony, I could but do as the Department of State suggested in acquainting me with the result of the negotiations — accept the Turkish government's apologies, and forgive if not forget the indignities to which I was subjected in Smyrna.

Thomas Cook & Son bring much business to the Austrian-Lloyd Steamship Company. On occasions Cook's tourists are so numerous that their agents book all the first-class cabins and even charter an entire ship; yet, when I went to the Lloyd office in Smyrna, stated I could not call on Messrs. Patterson & Company (Cook's Smyrna correspondents), as it was Sunday, and requested the acceptance of Thomas Cook & Son's circular notes or a draft against their letter of credit for passage to Jaffa, the request was refused, and I found myself in a position where I had either to wait in Smyrna fifteen days for another steamer or raise money for passage on the steamer then about to leave. By means possibly not unknown to some of my readers I succeeded in lightening my baggage two napoleons' worth, paid twenty-five francs for a deck passage, and boarded the *Minerva* just as she weighed anchor, as I thought, for Jaffa — as I thought, for the *Minerva* did not go to Jaffa at all.

Almost every inch of her deck was covered with variegated specimens of humanity, — Turks, Arabs, Armenians, Greeks, and Russian Jews. Fortunately, I had preserved one of the rugs from our boating trip. This I spread on the deck at the extreme end of the prow of the vessel, the only place not pre-empted. It was not pre-empted, as I speedily found, on account of the wind, from which in that exposed point there was no protection, and which grew strong and cold as the steamer's speed increased and as the day darkened into night. After some hours I succeeded in falling asleep even in that cold and cramped position, but the sleep was neither long nor deep. At ten o'clock Chios was reached, and I was made aware of the fact by two sailors walking over me to reach the ropes and chains confining the anchor. I made a desperate grab to save the kodak, upon which one of the sailors came within an ace of treading, then concluded to spend the remainder of the night pacing the aisle in front of the engines. There I should at least keep warm and not be trod upon by the hobnailed shoes of sailors. A curious sight was that as I picked my way among the sleeping throng. Here, bathed in the moonlight, lay a venerable Turk, with three wives and eight children, barricaded by half a dozen mattresses, baskets, blankets, and other household goods. Immediately beyond this camp lay a lot of Russian Jews in long greasy coats, queer top-heavy caps on their dirty heads, scanty, ragged quilts covering their bodies. Then came more Turks and Arabs, some Albanians and Greeks, and finally an Austrian "Handwerksbursch" (strolling mechanic). I learned this last sleeper's nationality through the fact that I stepped on him. The deck was so thick with sleeping bodies it was hardly possible to avoid this. But the Austrian Handwerksbursch was none the less angry and indignant.

"Was der Teufel ist denn los?" he exclaimed.

"Ah, I beg pardon," I said, also speaking in German. "I stepped over three men; it was impossible for my legs to reach further, hence I landed on you. I see you are a German."

"No; Austrian. And you?"

"American."

At this the Handwerksbursch sat up, rubbed his eyes, and stared as though the man from the horned moon had appeared.

"Wenn Sie Amerikaner sind, was machen Sie denn hier?" (If you are an American, what are you doing here?)

"Seeing the world," said I.

"Just what I am doing. I didn't know that Americans did such things. I never saw one before."

I was a curiosity to him, — the only American he had ever seen without a Baedeker and a pair of opera-glasses. He was a friendly, good-hearted fellow, told me his name, — Marko Popovitch, — asked me mine, and, when he learned that I had no bed or "post," invited me to share his, — an invitation which, under the circumstances, I was glad to accept. For an hour or two we lay awake, looking at the starlit heavens and at the mountains of the island of Chios, in the shadows of which we were then gliding. We listened to the weird songs of the Turks, now in lusty tones near by, now in faint refrain from a distant part of the ship. Marko related tales of his wanderings, and at last we fell asleep, not to awake until the cold gray of morning. Thus passed my first night in the steerage of a vessel crowded with people of the Orient.

Discomforts of the steerage were almost forgotten the following day, so beautiful, so enchanting, was the scenery. On every side were islands with majestic mountains. Sometimes the passage-way between these islands narrows to a few hundred yards, so that the Ægean seems more like a river or series of lakes than a sea. Early in the morning we saw Nikaria, where the first flying-machine was invented. This machine differed from all its successors in the fact that it was not a failure; that, on the contrary, it was too much of a success. Iscarios, after resting awhile on the summit of the lofty peak near which we passed, resumed his flying trip, onward and upward, until he got so near the sun that the heat melted the wax on his wings and plunged him headlong into the sea, perhaps in the very spot now ploughed by the *Minerva's* keel.

In one narrow strait we saw on the one hand the coast of Asia and the town of Budrum, birthplace of Herodotus; on the other hand was the island of Kos, with lofty mountains, and Ko, its capital, the birthplace of Hippocrates. Ko not only gave birth to the greatest physician of antiquity; it was also the seat of medical knowledge and was held sacred to the first physician of all, Æsculapius. The approach to Rhodes surpasses even the eastern Ægean in grandeur of scenery. The sea between the island and the coast of Asia Minor narrows into a mere strait, on both sides of which rocky mountains lift their heads until lost in the clouds. Two towers stand on either side of the harbor, where 280 B.C. the two feet of the Colosus erected by Chares are said to have stood. Besides the great Colosus,

Rhodes, in the height of its prosperity, contained three thousand statues: no trace of these now remains. The Colosus was overthrown by an earthquake less than a century after its erection, but its pieces are said to have remained where they fell until a comparatively recent period, when they were sold to a Jew and transported to Syria on the backs of nine hundred camels. Rhodes is now used as a place of banishment by Turkey, and the interior of the town consists of a maze of narrow alleys and walls, each having its signification, each constituting the boundary line beyond which certain classes of criminals dare not go. The outer circle comprises the greater part of the city; the prisoner possessing the liberty of that circle is comparatively free, but the inner circles are small and restricted. Soldiers guard the boundaries of each district, and fire at prisoners crossing the boundary to which they are limited. Marko and I strolled through the winding alleys, stared at the grave Turks sitting in front of their doors smoking narghilla pipes, then bought several loaves of bread and a basket of grapes, and started back for the steamer.

CHAPTER XXII

Howajani Sulah and the Russian Prince — Fifty Hours' Fast — Marko falls in Love — The Marriage in Cyprus — I receive a Proposal — Russian Jews and Moslem Turks — Horrors of a Deck Passage — Turks capture the Ship — A Day in Syria — First Glimpses of the Nile — Cholera Quarantine at Alexandria — Mr. Abbott proves a Friend

MARKO was a German Mark Tapley. No discomfort dampened his joyous nature, no rebuff abashed him. He made friends with the passengers and sailors, pried into the kitchen, and, though driven out at first, turned up again smiling and pleasant, and within two days was an established fixture there, peeling potatoes and washing dishes in return for food.

One day he came to me, leading by the hand a Turkish woman closely veiled. From behind the depths of the veil came muffled sounds of weeping.

"Herr Amerikaner, a poor Turkish woman — lost her money — nothing to eat — you must help her."

I was surprised at this request, for Marko knew of my impecunious condition, but he speedily explained the nature of the help desired. He did not expect money from me, but a letter in English to a Russian prince, who, he said, was among the first-class passengers. Following is the letter written at Marko's dictation: —

"To the Prince of Blank: —

"A Turkish woman, travelling alone with no friends on the *Minerva* ventures to address Your Highness in the misfortune which has overtaken her. Yesterday morning, while making her toilet, her entire supply of money — £1½ — fell out of her pocket and rolled into the sea. She has absolutely nothing left with which to buy food, and begs Your Highness' aid, for which she will ever bless and thank you.

"Howajani Sulah,

"*Per L. M., American Secretary pro tem.*"

It proved much easier to write this letter than to deliver it. When Marko went back to the first-class cabin and asked one of the waiters to call the prince, the waiter brusquely replied that steerage passengers had no business bothering their betters. Then Marko returned to me accompanied by the Turkish woman, who, by this time, was weeping harder than ever. The good-hearted Austrian said he knew that I could succeed, — I spoke English and could talk first to one of the American passengers; so at length I, too, started back to interview the Russian prince. Marko pointed him out to me. He was not at all like one's ideal prince, not a bit noble or grand looking; on the contrary, he was small, thin, sallow, had lantern jaws, a white moustache waxed and twisted, thin, gray hair brushed

Scene on the Way to Mimbres

forward apparently to hide a section of two unusually large ears. A jaunty steamer cap was on his head; a yellow canvas bag was thrown over his shoulders.

"Is that your Russian prince?" I asked.

"Ja, Herr."

"And you want *it* to help Howajani?"

"Ja, Herr."

"Well, I will ask him, but he won't do it; he is too leathery and dried up to have any sympathy."

Such actually proved the case. He took the letter, read it; then said dryly, —

"Why do you give this to me?"

"This poor woman seeks aid. She has lost — "

"Yes; but why come to *me?* This is addressed to the Prince of Blank."

"And are you not the prince?"

"The d——, no," with which he turned on his heel and walked off.

We afterwards learned that this supposed prince was, or had been, an interpreter in Constantinople. The deck passengers were told of Howajani Dost's misfortune, and in a few minutes she was the recipient of enough bread, grapes, and cheese to last the rest of the voyage. The poor are usually ready to help their fellows in distress — sometimes more ready than the rich who can better afford it.[1] This is because those who have themselves suffered want have more than a speculative appre-

---

[1] After my transfer to the cabin I learned that Howajani Dost went herself to the first-class passengers, presented the letter I had written to a gentleman in a tweed suit and knee breeches, who was taken to be the Russian prince by the deck passengers after they learned the true position of the Turkish dragoman. The second guess was as incorrect as the first; for the gentleman in the tweed suit was not a Russian prince, but a plain American citizen, Rev. Dr. Edward Abbott of Cambridge, Mass. He was also a sympathetic gentleman, as were the other American passengers. Among them Howajani collected twenty francs.

ciation of what want means. I had opportunity to appreciate this fact before the voyage of the *Minerva* was ended; for between Rhodes and Cyprus, some fifty hours, I had no food whatever. This happened through the theft of my bread and grapes. Fifty hours may not be long for a professional faster, but it is longer than the non-professional cares to starve. I tried to allay the pangs of hunger by remembering that Mr. Tanner voluntarily starved forty days, and another gentleman went Tanner five days better and starved forty-five days. I am sorry to say the noble endurance of those gentlemen had no effect in subduing my rebellious appetite. At the end of the fast I procured at Cyprus some bread and grapes, which to a hungry man is a luxurious feast.

Marko took the loss of our bread and grapes composedly. He had made friends with the cook, and there were too many odd pieces of bread and meat to talk of suffering hunger. He could not understand why I would not join him in hanging around the kitchen and eating scraps flung him by the cook.

Often have I observed children of the poor flattening their noses against confectioners' windows, and women in rags with babies looking wistfully into restaurant doors, but I do not think I appreciated their feelings as much then as I do since my own experience in the hunger line. When the cabin waiters passed about with hot dishes, the aroma of the food made keener my already sharp appetite. The problem of the times is not the production, but the distribution of wealth. The first-class passengers had soup, three or four kinds of meat, vegetables, fruits, nuts, coffee,— more than they could eat, more than was good for them,— whereas the deck passengers were half starving. This is the way all over the world,— too much on the one hand, too little on the other. Enough is produced; the problem is how to distribute it. The two hundred and odd deck passengers, when it came to the pinch, took the solution of this problem in their own hands, as will be shown later.

At Rhodes the deck passenger-list received an accession in the person of a very pretty Greek girl on her way to Cyprus. Marko lost no time making the acquaintance of this dark-eyed damsel. In fact, it was not long before he established over her a sort of protectorate. He cuffed two or three Greeks and Turks who were impudent, arranged with the cook to give her supper, and, finally, when he found she had no bed, surrendered to her his own mattress. The result of these attentions was romantic. Just after the *Minerva* cast anchor at Limmasol the young coppersmith came to me, looking jollier than ever.

"I am going to get married, Herr Amerikaner, and I want you to attend the wedding."

"Married? To whom? When and where?"

"To Artemis Xanthapoulu, to-morrow, perhaps to-day, in Limmasol."

Artemis Xanthapoulu was the name of the young Greek girl who had boarded the steamer at Rhodes. She had been visiting relations there : her home was in Cyprus. She and the Austrian Handwerksbursch had in that fifty-hour journey quietly made up their minds to get married. Limmasol, though now under English rule, is an ugly Turkish town, containing nothing worth seeing ; so I readily agreed to go on to Xanthapoulu's house as soon as my long fast was broken. It was a hot and fatiguing walk to the peasant's home, a mile or more from town, in the centre of an arid, sun-baked plain ; but Artemis and Marko noticed neither the sun nor the heat. They walked along hand in hand, laughing and chatting, happy as two children. I brought up the rear in company with the Turkish porter who carried the young girl's bundle of clothing. Lord Bacon recommended people never to marry ; Aristotle advised careful consideration and delay until forty years old. Aristotle and Bacon would be astonished at the recklessness with which their advice is disregarded in Cyprus. Artemis's arrival was expected, and long before we reached the adobe hut we saw several women and half a dozen children advancing to meet us. After greeting Artemis they gave Marko and me inquiring glances.

"This is Marko," said Artemis simply. "And this," pointing to me, "is Marko's friend."

She spoke in Greek, which Marko translated for me into German. There was some rapid conversation between Artemis and her mother and sisters, and by the time we reached the hut we were not only friends, we were members of the family. Marko kissed Mrs. Xanthapoulu, called her "mother," dandled the babies, and made himself as much at home as though he were a son-in-law of ten years' standing. The news of the intended marriage created quite a flutter. One of the children was sent for the father, then at work in the fields, and for the neighbors and relations. In the meantime we were plied with preserves and questions. Preserves are always offered visitors in Cyprus houses, and I presume questions are also in order when a stranger suddenly drops in with the announcement of his intention to marry the householder's daughter. I disposed of the preserves (they were sweet and good), but I could not answer the questions. They were literally all Greek to me. My observations of the house — a low, two-roomed adobe affair, filled with rude furniture and odds and ends, no attempt at neatness or ornamentation — was interrupted by a sudden and startling proposition. Marko, who had been rattling away in Greek with one of the prettiest of the several girls around us, turned and said in German : —

"Eleni says she will marry you. She is the sister of Artemis's mother. Why not take her and stay here?"

There were many imperative reasons why this generous offer could not be accepted; but the suddenness of the proposition so took me aback I was unable to give one of them. Apparently, getting married on ten minutes' notice was to Marko neither unusual nor unreasonable. He began to make arguments — I could open a photograph studio in Limmasol (the kodak had created the impression that I was a photographer), he would help me in the work and in interpreting the languages; moreover, Eleni Skufa was pretty and attractive. There was no doubt about this — she had regular features, soft, dark eyes, and a wealth of black hair, which fell below her waist. Notwithstanding all these inducements I felt obliged to decline the honor.

Mr. Xanthapoulu arrived, and was introduced to his prospective son-in-law. Then the matter was talked over. Artemis's dowry, a few cheap dresses and other articles of clothing, was taken from a bag hanging from a nail in the wall, and spread out on the table for inspection. It was a pitifully small trousseau, but the warm-hearted mechanic was highly pleased. Rings were exchanged, a priest sent for, and the matter finally settled. Then we all sat down to the wedding banquet of preserves, radishes, bread, and sausages. The whole family accompanied me back to the steamer, where Marko gathered together his few belongings, and bade his fellow-travellers good-bye before returning ashore with his bride.

The scenery of Cyprus is less interesting than that of the more eastern islands. There are mountains in the interior, but the coast is flat and arid. After four hours along this coast, the *Minerva* cast anchor at Larnacca, where I went ashore for another glimpse of Cyprus life. Larnacca is under any circumstances a dull and uninteresting village; after the gay festival of a few hours before at Limmasol, it was positively depressing. The desire for communion with one's fellows is so inherent and strong, one overlooks mental grades and social ranks, aye, even overlooks race and language. After the jovial Handwerkbursch's desertion, I took up my old quarters at the extreme end of the prow of the ship, and it was not long before the Turks and I were carrying on an animated conversation. To be sure, they talked in their language, and I in mine, but even that was better than sitting dumb like an oyster: besides, it established between us a friendly feeling. A venerable Turk with three wives and eight children offered me lunch. This I declined, but he would take no refusal when it came to his beloved "masticom," a white, colorless, and pungent liquid much liked in the Orient. It was so strong that, instead of taking it down at a mouthful, I was compelled to sip drop by drop, greatly to the amusement of the children. They laughed, rubbed their stomachs, smacked their lips, and tried to make me understand by signs that "masticom" was a liquid fit for the gods, that it was not to be sipped with reluctance, but swallowed with delight.

The Russian Jews spoke German; hence I fared better with them than with the Turks. They told how they had been kicked about from pillar to post; how difficult it had been for them to get out of Russia, yet how impossible to remain. One gray-bearded patriarch told how the Russian "Christians" had first beat him, then set fire to his house. Said he:—

"'They came to my restaurant near Luskov in Poland, and ordered drink and dinner. After they had eaten they refused to pay. I insisted, but that only brought me trouble. They jumped on me, beat me, and that night returned and set fire to my house. Everything excepting some clothing was lost."

"What was done to the rascals?"

"You mean the Christians?" said the gray-bearded Jew. "Nothing was done to them, but I and my family received notice from the police that we must leave at once. When we reached the frontier, the German soldiers would not let us cross, then the next day the police demanded my papers. I had none. You cannot stay anywhere in Russia without papers. They made me move on. I went from place to place and at last back to Luskov. 'What are you doing back here?' demanded the police. 'You have no pass for Luskov.' I told them how the Germans had marched us back across the frontier, and how the Russian police had driven me out of every town and village I had entered. It was no use. They knew nothing, they said, except that my pass for Luskov had been revoked — and once more I set out, never allowed to remain longer than twenty-four hours in any one place. My business at Luskov before that unhappy night was worth 6000 roubles ($3000). When at last I succeeded in leaving Russia at Odessa, I had barely enough money to pay passage to Jerusalem."

What would be thought of a jailer who should put his prisoner in an iron cage, then order him to get out, and whip and maltreat him for failing? This is the treatment accorded by Russia to the Jews. Other nations refuse to accept them ; Russia refuses to keep them ; what are the poor Jews to do? When the *Minerva* landed at Caifa, the officers there said that there were enough Jews in Palestine, and refused to let them land. When I left the ship at Alexandria they were still on board. It is to be hoped these unhappy mortals will find some land that will grant them the right of living. The men who persecute the Jews pretend to follow the Christ who said, " Do unto others as you would have others do unto you."

Shortly after leaving Cyprus, one of the cabin passengers came forward to the steerage deck to photograph its motley array. I thought it would be a good thing to have a kodaker kodaked, so just as the cabin passenger took a snap shot at the Turks, I took a snap shot at him. He saw it and opened his eyes with astonishment.

" By Jove," he remarked to the gentleman accompanying him, " by Jove, if that fellow hasn't stolen a kodak ! "

He was scarcely to be blamed for his suspicions. A week on deck without bath or water is enough to make any one look like a robber. The next day a most exciting event caused me to return the cabin passenger's visit. When the *Minerva* entered the harbor of Beirut, a cordon of police boats was observed, and before anchor was cast men shouted to us that the cholera was raging in Damascus, and that if our boat stopped a moment at Beirut all foreign ports would be closed to us. This news decided the captain not to land. In this decision, however, he was reckoning without his host, or, more literally, without his two hundred and odd steerage passengers, Turks who were bound for Beirut and who meant to go there or know the reason why. The Turks surrounded the captain, yelling, gesticulating, and demanding to be set ashore. Finally the captain compromised. A telegram was sent to Constantinople inquiring if the mere landing of passengers would incur quarantine in Egypt. In the mean time the *Minerva* was to lie at anchor surrounded by police boats to see that no one went ashore or came aboard. For five long hours we floated there, so near yet so far from the interesting city, its white houses and minarets glistening in the southern sun. Then a boat was seen approaching; a message came across the water that if a single passenger landed the ship would have to go into quarantine. Again the captain declared he would not land, and again was he reckoning without his two hundred Turks. In a moment the wildest confusion prevailed. The angry Turks made a charge on the kitchen; butcher-knives were seized, shovels, crowbars, marlinspikes, belaying-pins, and the captain and cabin passengers found themselves in a state of siege. Though not a cabin passenger, I was a Caucasian, and sided with the Europeans against the Asiatics. I seized my club and revolver, made my way up on the captain's bridge, and awaited the onslaught. I hope the reader will be perfectly confident that I would have performed deeds of heroic valor had there been a chance, which there was not. The captain and crew were too few in numbers to hazard a fight, so capitulated, agreed to let the Turks land, and quiet was restored. An hour later every Turk was on *terra firma*. I went for a walk on the Damascus road, constructed by the French after the massacre of ten thousand Christians in Syria on the 9th of July, 1860. Previous to that time Damascus was comparatively inaccessible to Western armies. Moslem fanaticism held full sway. The wholesale slaughter of July, 1860, aroused the civilized world. France sent an army which wreaked immediate vengeance and built this road, so that in the future troops might be massed in the Syrian capital before instead of after massacres. There has been no occasion for troops since 1860. The French road and the powerful fleets that patrol the Mediterranean have inspired Oriental fanatics with a wholesome respect for the might and wrath of the West.

Beirut, with its curious Eastern life, its labyrinthian streets, often arched and covered, its background of hill and mountain, is well worth seeing; still the price we paid was dear, — a long and tedious quarantine at Alexandria. No one knew just how long the quarantine would last. Some said ten days; others, twenty-one; others, the number giving rise to the word *quaranta* (forty). A sailor informed us we would be put into tents, no trees, broiling sun, no food but bread and water, for which we should have to pay fabulous prices; that the day before quarantine was raised we would all be put into a large room and smoked and fumigated. The reality was bad enough, still it was not quite as bad as represented by the sailor. His story, however, caused us to suffer by anticipation.

The *Minerva* did not touch at Jaffa. When we landed at Caifa, the agent of the Lloyd Company came aboard, announced that our boat would not stop at Jaffa, and directed the passengers for that port to disembark at Caifa. The Turks at Caifa refused to let the Jews land there, which settled the question for them. With me it was another matter. I asked how the Lloyd Company proposed to forward me from Caifa to Jaffa, whether by land or sea. The agent drily replied it did not propose to forward me at all. I said I had not bought a ticket for Caifa, did not wish to go there, and if the steamer did not touch at Jaffa, the port to which it had contracted to take me, I would go on to Alexandria. The agent said this could be done only on payment of the extra fare. I declined to pay, for the good reason that I had no money, also because I deemed his demand illegal. The agent then went so far as to threaten to have me set to work firing the ship's engines. The poor Jews were also threatened, but we defied him to carry out the threat, and stood on our right to be transported to Jaffa according to contract. The agent of the Lloyds gave cholera and quarantine regulations as reasons for not stopping at Jaffa. The validity of these reasons seemed to us doubtful in view of the fact that the captain had touched at Beirut, the nearest port to Damascus and the port against which all other ports were enforcing the strictest and longest quarantine. Our firmness saved us from paying the unjust demand for extra fare, but we were not numerous enough to do as the Turks at Beirut, — force the captain to stop at our destination. Consequently from Caifa, the settlement of so many odd religious sects and fanatics, the *Minerva* steamed direct for Alexandria.

At five o'clock Sunday morning, October 18th, I was awakened by sailors walking over me to get at the signal light, and, happening to look out at the sea, noticed that the usually blue water of the Mediterranean was almost yellow. It was mud from the Nile, and the low sandbanks and hills that were visible from the other side of the ship formed our first glimpse of hoary, historic Egypt. For six hours the *Minerva* glided along in full view of those sandy banks; then the mole of Alexandria became visible, reaching its long arm out in the sea; soon thereafter we were riding at anchor in the city's outer harbor. As at Beirut, a cordon of police boats surrounded us to see that no one went ashore. One of the boats sent aboard a sallow soldier with a fez on his head and a bed under his arm. This fellow informed us that we were prisoners of the Egyptian quarantine. He remained with us to the bitter end. When I started down the ship's steps to throw a letter into a police boat he grabbed me by the arm and led me away as if fearing my approach, even only to the foot of the ladder, would contaminate the entire city of Alexandria. I was obliged to throw my letter overboard from the ship's railing above. Fortunately the crew of the small boat were expert catchers, my letter was mailed to Cook's Cairo agent, and the very next day I was provided with money. Then I went to the captain of the *Minerva*, proffered the difference in fare, and requested to be transferred to the cabin. To my astonishment this was refused. The captain said: —

"If you are transferred, the other deck passengers will wish to be transferred also."

"If they pay for it, why not? Your regulations say that any passenger may transfer from an inferior to a superior class upon paying the difference in fare."

The captain said this was not meant for deck passengers. The transfer was peremptorily refused, and I was confronted with another and indefinite period of extreme discomfort, — sleeping on the deck, nothing but hardtack to eat, never a chance to wash my face and hands, owing to the scarcity of water and the fact that the pump was broken. The situation was far worse than while at sea. At sea we had a breeze; in the harbor off the sandbanks of Alexandria we had no breeze, no protection from the fierce African sun, and none from the clouds of coal-dust that rose from the barges being unloaded into the *Minerva*. It was pitiful to see the hungry, wistful looks of the poor men and women as they loitered near the kitchen, hoping to receive a bone or a crust from the cook. I heard one girl, a comely lass of fourteen or fifteen, her face white and pinched with hunger, offer the cook a kiss if he would give her a piece of bread. One man, eighty-two years old, a veritable patriarch, with long, snow-white hair and beard, quite collapsed with hunger. A crisis seemed at hand, when chance put a better face on the situation.

Among the cabin passengers happened to be a Mr. Edward Abbott who, as editor of the Boston *Literary World*, had reviewed "A Tramp Trip" containing my likeness on the frontispiece. Mr. Abbott remembered the book and remembered me. The third day of quarantine we chanced to meet. On hearing my story, he consulted with other Americans aboard, then went to the captain, protested against my continued detention in the steerage, and demanded that I be transferred to the cabin at once. The captain yielded to this pressure, I paid the difference in fare, and obtained, for the first time in ten days, a bath and sufficient food. That evening, at the request of the cabin passengers, I gave a brief description of my experience in the steerage, also of the condition of the unfortunate deck passengers. These well-fed people could scarcely believe that within two hundred feet of their table, loaded not only with abundance but with superfluities, fellow-beings were on the verge of starvation. When the fact was fully brought home to them, immediate and active measures were taken to better the situation. Moral pressure was brought to bear on the captain. Hardtack and potatoes were served to the needy, and a subscription was raised among the cabin passengers to buy bread, tea, and fruit for those of the sufferers who were sick or aged. If Mr. Edward Abbott of Cambridgeport, Mass., Dr. R. C. Pearson of Ashville, N. C., Mr. Merrill of the Hotel Vendome, Boston, and the other American passengers on the *Minerva* chance to see these lines, they will know that their kindness and prompt action were appreciated.

If the head officers of the Austrian Lloyd steamship line chance to see this book, I hope it may cause them to make an inquiry into the condition of deck passengers, and issue orders for their better treatment when unexpectedly detained, as in the case of the *Minerva*, far beyond the schedule time, without food or the means of procuring it.

The sanitary council in Alexandria sat upon our case, and on

EGYPTIAN WATER CARRIER

the fourth day we were informed that, in consideration of the fact that the *Minerva* had disembarked passengers at Beirut, but had not taken on new passengers, our quarantine would be commuted to eight days. This term passed slowly enough; still it was so much better than the forty days first expected, we bore it with patience.

CHAPTER XXIII

Naked Alexandrians — "A.D." Sights in Egypt — The Ride to Cairo — Why Abdullah's Ass is losing his Ears — Fantastic Scenes — Fragments of a King — Rameses at the Bulak Museum — Mahmud jerks me up the Pyramids — Memphis — Under the Libyan Desert — Tombs of Sacred Bulls — Crocodile Pits of Maabdeh — Devoured by Vampires — Suez Canal — Paranzo again — Captured by his Wife — Conclusion

THE standard of modesty — some will say decency — is very different in Southern Europe from the standard in North Europe and America. In Italy one sees openly, at every street corner, things which in the north are closely veiled from view; but notwithstanding this preparation, the first glimpses of Egypt's children of nature astonished me. It is said that Alexandria has been Europeanized, and so it has been. Some of the streets are broad, lined with modern buildings, and a large per cent of the population are Greeks and Italians; but despite this there are sights in Alexandria that would make a sensation even in free and easy Italy.

Within an hour after landing from the wearisome quarantine, I ran across a squad of swarthy men, some with hideous wigs, some with ghastly daubs of white paint under their eyes, some with rude drums — all absolutely naked. They marched slowly down the street, stopping at each corner, where the men with the drums made a deafening noise, while the painted wig-wearers hopped and jumped about like naked demons. The crowd that surrounded the performers showed no surprise at the entire absence of clothing, and after witnessing similar scenes in Cairo I came to the conclusion that, if one would be conspicuous in Egypt, it must be done other than by appearing on the streets naked.

Alexandria's chief, if not only, monument, Pompey's Pillar, an ugly, red granite shaft, one hundred and four feet high, stands on a low hill surrounded by squalid hovels. Alexandrian chroniclers have endeavored to invest this column with interest, by asserting that it was erected to the great Pompey whose statue ran blood when Cæsar was assassinated. Unfortunately for this theory, antiquarians, while rummaging around in the mouldy past, discovered documents showing that the monument was not erected until three hundred and fifty years after Pompey's defeat by Cæsar and his assassination on the coast of Egypt. Then the chroniclers told another pretty story: after Diocletian conquered the rebellious city, he ordered his legions to massacre the Alexandrians until their blood filled the streets to his horse's knees. The massacre had barely begun when the emperor's horse stumbled and wet his knee in the blood of one of the first victims. Diocletian graciously consented to regard this as a fulfilment of his command, and forthwith had the massacre stopped. The Alexandrians, out of gratitude, erected the pillar, and placed on its summit a bronze statue of the horse that had saved them. So said the chroniclers until antiquarians brought them to grief again, by showing that the Pompey who erected the column was a Roman consul of the fourth century; moreover, that it was originally surmounted by the statue of a man, not a horse.

A fourth century column seems modern even in Italy; in Egypt it is pitifully new, and the traveller, after learning the facts about Pompey's Pillar, feels that he has been inveigled there under false pretences. The American, one of the *Minerva* passengers, who accompanied me on this stroll, gave our guide a good scolding, told him he had not come to Egypt to see anything modern and new.

"If you have anything B.C. in your town," he said severely, "take us to it; if not, be honest about it, tell us, and let us move on. We don't want to waste time on A.D. sights in Egypt."

The guide would not admit it, but we soon found for ourselves that the Alexandria of to-day is essentially a modern city erected on centuries' accumulations of *débris* upon the site of the Alexandria of the ancients. An express train covers in four hours the 128 miles between Alexandria and Cairo; and, could the brakemen speak English, one would hear the cry, "All out for Cleopatra's tomb!" Many travellers stop over at one of the stations to see the recently discovered sarcophagus of Egypt's celebrated queen. The Egyptian cars are on the American plan, — long and open, with seats on both sides of an aisle. There are other reminders of America, — cotton-fields, sugar-cane, and negro plantation hands in scant cotton shirts and breeches; but for all that one is in no danger of imagining one's self in Louisiana or Florida. Apart from the familiar features just mentioned, the American traveller is reminded more of a circus than of home. Camels and buffaloes amble along, driven by just such fantastic-looking Arabs with turbans and flowing gowns as head the circus procession when it enters the ring; and the towns look just as strange and unreal as the artificial villages erected in the Oriental sections of expositions.

On leaving Alexandria the train passes between Lake Mareotis and Lake Abukir. After that there is not much water; and even through closed doors and windows the dust penetrates in such volumes one can scarcely see or breathe. When I crossed the Yuma desert in Southern California, I thought that the only place where, with windows closed, blinds down, doors locked, sand and dust could accumulate half an inch deep on the car floors and seats. The trip to Cairo demonstrated that Yuma is not the only place where this feat is accomplished. Occasionally a little relief is afforded where the train runs parallel with the Mahmudiyeh Canal, which seems to absorb some of the sand and give the suffocated traveller a breathing-spell. The banks of the canal are high enough to prevent one seeing the water from the car window, so that the boats with their lateen sails seem to be drifting along on the land. Now and then a gang of naked men are seen on the artificial embankment, tugging at a rope tied to a loaded boat; but you do not see the water. Were "seeing believing," you would believe the fellahs were dragging their burden over dry land. After an hour the train stops at Abu Homs, a group of mud hovels ten or twelve feet high, each roof reached by a ladder; and you rush out on the platform and buy several bottles of soda-water at champagne prices and try to dislodge some of the sand and dust that is choking your throat and clogging your mouth. But an ocean of soda-water would scarce cope with Egyptian sand and dust, and by the time Cairo is reached nothing but a boiling Turkish bath can restore the traveller to anything like his normal condition.

Most impartial observers admit that England's occupation of Egypt is a blessing to the Egyptians. There is grumbling by Egyptian Beys, who under the present *régime* are debarred from wholesale swindling and oppression of the miserable fellahs; but the masses are benefited. The Khedive owned one-fourth of the arable land of Egypt until 1879, when the International Finance Commission forced him to disgorge. The Nilometer on the island of Roda, opposite Cairo, was formerly shut off from public view, and the Nile rise represented higher than the truth warranted, because taxation is regulated by the height of the inundation; to-day the Nilometer is open to view, and taxation is adjusted with fairness and honor. There are many other indications that English rule is evolving order out of chaos. In fact, if comparison is made with neighboring countries still under Turkish rule, it may be said order is already evolved, and life and property are as secure in Cairo as in Rome or Paris. English soldiers walk the streets, sit in cafés, drill in open squares, and even in front of sacred mosques. While resting one day under the great dome of Gami Mohammed Ali, the famous alabaster mosque, sounds of bugles and drums floated in on the soft November air and drowned the droning noise of the Mahometan professors and their classes squatting on the cool alabaster floor. The English occupy the citadel near the mosque, and the sound of the bugles was a call to arms. After my shoes were restored to me I left the mosque and, so to speak, stepped in two minutes out of the Orient into England; for amid the red coats, within hearing of the rich Irish brogue of a sergeant drilling the awkward squad, it was easy to believe for a moment that the alabaster walls of Mohammed Ali, the turbaned priests, the half-naked donkey boys, were all a dream. I was recalled to Egypt by a reminder from Abdullah Ali, my donkey boy, that time was flying, and that the tombs of the Khalifs, whither we were going, were some distance away.

The donkey "boy" is one of the most charming institutions of Egypt, and Abdullah Ali is one of the most charming of donkey boys. He is forty years old and has a family of grown children, so is a "boy" only in a technical sense; but he can run like a youth of twenty. His donkey is a fine traveller, and might be considered good-looking but for the fact that one of his ears has been gradually clipped away. The custom in Egypt is to cut a piece from a donkey's ear every time it commits a trespass. The unfortunate beast owned by Abdullah Ali has, owing to this system, lost all of his right ear, and is slowly but surely being deprived of the left one. However, as Ali justly remarked, donkeys do not travel on their ears, and we reached the tombs of the Khalifs in time to see the sun set on that weird, desolate scene. No sheiks are now employed to guard the domes and minarets erected over the dead Khalifs, and the strange and fantastic city of the dead is falling in ruins.

Abdullah attached himself and his donkey to me during my stay in Cairo, and made my name well known on the streets and public squares. If, perchance, I escaped from the hotel without encountering him in front of the door where he usually lay in wait, it was not long before I heard a shrill voice crying, "Master Lee, Master Lee!" or "Wait, my master, wait, Abdullah is coming!" It was of no avail to declare I did not wish to ride, that I preferred walking; Abdullah smiled and made respectful salaams, but he did not let me walk; it gave him a pain to see his "master" walk — walking was for him, Abdullah Ali, the poor donkey boy. White masters should travel in state. I usually succumbed after being followed half a mile with such arguments, and assumed the state (a seat on an ass's back), to which my position as a "white master" entitled me. Donkeys cost only three piastres (about sixteen cents) an hour, so even an economical traveller can ride in state in Egypt.

Abdullah's amiability knew no bounds. For $10 a month he offered to go to America and be my slave; the thought of his wife did not deter him. She could get along without him, and for $10 a month, he, on his part, could get along without a dozen wives. One of the places I agreed to visit on Abdullah's ass was the petrified forest; but inquiry developed the fact that there is no petrified forest, — merely a few stumps of interest to geologists, — so I substituted for the day's programme a trip to old Cairo. To my surprise, Abdullah demanded extra pay because of the change of plan. I said that, inasmuch as he had prepared for the long journey by giving his donkey extra rations, I would pay the same amount asked for the trip to the petrified forest.

"Oh no," replied my amiable servitor, "that is not enough.

It is a hard trip to the petrified forest. My donkey has eaten a big breakfast for that journey and will be sick if he makes a little one. It is a little trip to old Cairo!" Court records show queer damage demands, but none like this, to pay for a donkey's indigestion.

On the return from the isle of Roda and old Cairo, we turned through a gateway that leads ten or fifteen feet below the level of the surrounding country, to a Coptic village. It was in this squalid hamlet that the Virgin Mary sought refuge on her flight to Egypt. A Coptic priest conducts visitors into the dark crypt of the ancient church and points out the niche in the wall where the Virgin and the infant Jesus rested. The floor of the crypt is below the level of the Nile, hence, except in the dry season, it is several inches under water — a damp, unwholesome place, as the Virgin doubtless found during the month she remained between its damp walls.

The European quarter of Cairo is laid out in such wide streets, lined with such modern buildings, that the traveller remaining in that quarter may easily forget that he is in Africa; he cannot do so, however, in the Arab quarter, in the passage-ways — they cannot be called streets — that wind about, making a labyrinth in which one quickly becomes bewildered and lost. Although these passageways are only three or four feet wide, Abdullah discouraged a proposal to walk; he would feel hurt, humiliated, if people saw his "white master" shopping on foot, so, as usual, I stayed on top of the donkey while Abdullah walked a little ahead, giving forth shrill cries to warn common mortals out of the way. It was a tight squeeze; in the narrowest places the donkey almost wedged between the two rows of shops, so that before we could proceed, pedestrians had to jump upon the little platforms where the merchants squat cross-legged waiting for customers. When we stopped to look at the curious little booths we completely blocked the way; this, however did not seem to trouble any one. The merchants liked it, thinking we might buy something, and persons wishing to pass did so by jumping up on the little platforms and walking through the shops. In some of the shops, mere dens ten feet square, silversmiths were working away at toy bellows and forge, making those queer little tubes resembling bits of gas-pipe, that Egyptian women wear between their eyes on their nose. A string passing through the tube and tied behind the head holds it in place, and also supports the black veil that reaches from the face almost to the ground. All one can see of an Egyptian woman are her two eyes gleaming through the holes in her veil on each side of the section of gas-pipe. A brass tube on the nose seems not sufficiently uncomfortable, so the tube is provided with little teeth, sharp-pointed cogs, that stick into the flesh, making it red and sore. No phantom party could look more strange or weird than these Egyptian women closely veiled, the only bright thing about them, their eyes and gas-pipes. One shop we visited contained two men squatting on the floor, facing each other, a stick of wood between them, which the two men were lazily sawing in two. A third man weighed the wood with a spring scale suspended from a rude tripod, and sold it by the pound.

The hotel porter said it was impossible to go to the pyramids on a donkey, but as to go in a carriage costs five dollars, and as Abdullah guaranteed to get me there for one dollar, I determined to try the donkey. The faithful Abdullah Ali gave me no cause to regret my determination; he gave his ass a good night's rest and an extra large breakfast : thus fortified we set out at six o'clock in the morning and galloped almost all the way. The endurance displayed by Egyptian donkey boys is astonishing. Their meagre diet consists mainly, if not solely, of a rank sort of oil, and bread made of maize mixed with a bean flour that gives it a greenish color. Despite this scanty regimen, they can run all day without showing as much fatigue as a beef-eating European would show in an hour. Abdullah went tearing along, his white gown streaming behind him, shouting at the top of his voice, "Master Lee is coming! my white master is coming to see the pyramids!" Had those venerable monuments been built and kept for the special purpose of being visited by his "white master," Abdullah could scarce have cried out with more gusto. The reason of his cries was, that he looked on the selection of his ass as a great victory; he wanted all Cairo to know we were on no mere ride about town, but were going to the pyramids.

In all the eighteen hundred miles between Khartum and the Mediterranean the Nile has but one tributary, hence it is not an imposing stream; near Cairo, however, it attains its greatest width, one thousand yards, and is a noble looking river. A long bridge, guarded at its approaches by two enormous bronze lions, spans the river and leads to the road of the pyramids. As we crossed in the early morning the bridge was thronged with the incoming tide of market-men bringing supplies to the capital. Some of the long trains of camels were loaded with provisions, others with dried buffalo manure to be used as fuel, others bore burdens of sugar-cane, the ends of the long cane sweeping the ground. There were hundreds of peasant girls carrying baskets of dates on their heads. Near the west end of the great bridge is the Bulak Museum, where a few days later I saw King Ounas and Rameses II., the Pharaoh of the Bible. Rameses being comparatively modern,— that is, of the 19th Dynasty, only 1500 B.C.,— is well preserved. His nose is as aquiline and straight as it was thirty-five hundred years ago. But poor King Ounas is much older than Rameses (5th Dynasty, 4000 B.C.), hence is sadly out of repair. The humiliating but justly descriptive label given him by the museum director reads "*Fragments* of King Ounas!"

The pyramids are Egypt's chief attraction to tourists, and the government endeavors to make access to that attraction as pleasant as possible. The road thither is lined with trees, the branches of which meet overhead and afford protection from the burning sun. Men with hog-skins holding five or six gallons of water go about laying the dust, and although the means are primitive, the end is accomplished because there are so many men, and they keep filling their hog-skins from the backwater of the Nile and emptying them on the road from early morn till late at night. At the time of my visit the Nile's inundation had made of the pyramid road a long embankment through a muddy lake. For miles around the country on both sides was several feet under water, one odd result of which was that the road fairly swarmed with rats that had abandoned the fields and villages to escape being drowned. At our approach they scampered about in droves so thick that we came near trampling them.

While still half a mile from our destination we were met by Arabs who spied us from the pyramids and came to offer their services. At Abdullah's suggestion I employed one of the fellows, not because I needed him, but because that would divert the attention of the crowd from me to others. The idea was a happy one. No sooner had I made a selection than the struggling, importuning mob turned from me to seek a new victim, while my new servitor said, "This way, my master, this way," as if the pyramids were in a cave and could not be found without a guide.

At first glance the pyramids do not seem so large, so overpowering, as you have been taught to expect; but when you approach nearer, when you stand at their base and let your glance run up the jagged, sloping sides to the top, you realize that they are the largest as well as the oldest monuments of man. This is more emphatically realized by the time two Arabs have pulled and hauled you to the top. The Arabs who jerked me up said they had pulled Mark Twain up. They said Mark Twain had been able to write interesting things after seeing them run up and down the Great Pyramid in ten minutes, and for five dollars offered to repeat the performance, which would enable me to write interesting things. When the kind offer was declined, one of the men, Mahmud, volunteered to cut my name on the top; he said Napoleon's and the Prince of Wales' names were there, and I could have the same honor for a dollar. Mahmud declared he could hardly believe his ears when I declined so high an honor at so low a price, but, as the dollar was not forthcoming, he was obliged to believe them; then he tried to sell me antiquities five thousand years old for fifty cents. Finally he said he would be satisfied if I gave him Egyptian money for a shilling that he had received from an English traveller. This was a modest request and would have been complied with had not investigation shown the shilling was counterfeit. It was not the first time swindlers have attempted to transfer money from my pockets to their own, but it was the first time the attempts were so barefaced and persistent and the swindlers so openly furious at their lack of success.

After gazing at the view,—on the one hand indescribably desolate, a sea of rolling, shifting, burning sand, on the other hand fields and villages supported by the life-giving Nile,—I began the descent, and Mahmud and his companion got even with me for not buying their spurious antiquities and changing their counterfeit coins. They pulled and jerked me about under pretence of keeping me from falling and breaking my neck, until my bones felt dislocated and my muscles sore. I was glad enough, after a brief visit to the Sphynx, to mount Abdullah's donkey and return to Cairo.

My next excursion was to Memphis, and this time Abdullah and I parted, since a donkey is not a good means of locomotion on a river. A party of twenty was made up at Shepheard's Hotel, a boat was chartered for $100, or five dollars apiece, and we sailed slowly up the strong current of the Nile. Little remains of Memphis save its tombs, which have been preserved by their fifty feet covering of sand. On the site of that part of the city that lay near the river is a forest of date palms, containing a miserable mud village and the gigantic statue of Rameses lying prone on the earth, where it fell in front of its temple thousands of years ago. There is nothing else of interest in the forest; it is not until one leaves the forest and enters the Libyan desert that one feels repaid for the trouble of the trip. Here is the pyramid of Sakara, the oldest monument of man; a few miles further in the shifting sands is a shaft, with difficulty kept open, admitting to the vast and gloomy tombs of the sacred bulls. In long galleries, forty feet underneath the sands of the Libyan desert, are the huge sarcophagi, some weighing fifteen tons, which hold the mummies of the sacred bulls. Our courier warned us to stick together, to hold our candles up, and carefully watch for pitfalls and caverns, unless we wished to get lost and remain behind in that fearful place full of bats and mummies. Said he:—

"Such things have happened. You linger to examine a curious hieroglyphic and are startled on looking up to find yourself alone. Your party has moved on, and you may or may not find it again. These chambers are of vast extent. One could wander in them for days without finding the exit."

This warning reminded me of the crocodile pits of Maabdeh, in which an English member of Parliament, a Mr. Leigh, and others, lost their way. Mr. Leigh finally escaped, but two of his party were never found, and were supposed to have been attacked and devoured by the myriads of bats which infest the tombs. The mummied crocodiles and priests in those horrible pits are piled up in great heaps; the outer layers are mangled and torn to pieces, whether by the bats or other beasts is unknown. The inner layers seem intact, and extend no one knows what distance in the heart of the mountain. M. Mariette, who discovered the tombs of the bulls, must have had strong nerves. He lived ten years in a hut in the desert and still kept his reason. Ten weeks would be enough to upset most men. Even one day of that wilderness of sand, of those mines of mummies, had a depressing effect upon our party, which was not dispelled until we were safe aboard the boat bound for Cairo.

Shortly after the trip to Memphis I bade Abdullah Ali and donkey an affectionate farewell and started for Port Said, going as far as Ismaila by rail, thence on the Suez Canal. The canal trip affords the pleasantest way of seeing and appreciating the Arabian desert. There is no sand, no dust, no jolting on a camel's back; yet you can see the great desolation of desert as well as if you were with a caravan ten days west of Cairo. From the steamer deck we looked over the low banks of the canal, as far as the eye could reach, a burning waste of sand. The monotony of this dreary scene was varied by passing steamers and by the huge dredge-boats that patrol the canal and clear it of the ever-shifting sand. Each dredge-boat has a big pipe, like an arm, 150 feet long, projecting some distance over and beyond the banks. As the sand is scooped up from the bottom of the canal by iron buckets revolving on an endless chain, it is dumped into the long arm and so carried to the shore. By night the scene was even more interesting. The desert was no longer visible, but the canal seemed alive with steamers. Every ten or fifteen minutes one would loom up out of the darkness, its electric light gleaming in the centre like the eye of Polyphemus.

Port Said is an ocean station. Like a railway station, it is full of life and activity one moment; the next it is dull and lifeless. A steamer from China or India arrives, and the streets swarm with several hundred passengers, anxious to stretch themselves after four weeks aboard ship. For an hour or two the shooting-galleries, saloons, concert halls, are thronged; then the steamer whistle blows, the passengers hurry aboard, and Port Said is dead — to come to life again, however, perhaps in half an hour; for the commerce of two worlds passes here, and vessels arrive and depart at all hours, day and night. While awaiting the Orient steamer *Cuzco*, on which I had engaged passage to Naples, I saw my former passenger, Paranzo. He was singing, and giving acrobatic performances in one of the numerous music halls. As soon as the show was over he came down into the audience where I was sitting and bubbled over with protestations of joy.

"Ah, amico mio," he cried, pressing my hand, "who could have imagined such happiness? At last I really behold you! At last I clasp your hand and embrace you!"

"Never mind the embracing, Paranzo," I said, holding him at arm's length; "what I want you to do is to explain your mysterious disappearance at Syracuse."

A tearful film came over Paranzo's soft dark eyes.

"Ah, signore," he sighed, "that is what I most wish; the signore must not think me ungrateful — ah, no! That dreadful woman!"

"What woman, Paranzo?"

"My wife, signore; she pursue me all the time. I no escape, she find me — what you call pounce on me suddenly."

It was a peculiarity of Paranzo now and then to drop into pigeon English, though at times he talked very correctly.

I was curious to hear the sequel to his marital story, and when he said he would relate his adventures after dinner, I took him to a restaurant, where, after disposing of macaroni, salad, wine, and other things dear to the Italian palate, he settled himself comfortably in his chair, sighed, and over his sad eyes came that film which never failed him when talking of his wife, and which, despite the secret suspicion that Mrs. Paranzo was as imaginary as Sarah Gamp's Mrs. Harris, somehow aroused my pity — he was such a gentle, feminine fellow.

"The day you went to the Greek theatre," said Paranzo, "I strolled about Syracuse happy — ah, so happy! I say my wife find me never again. I stop before one shop-window. While

I look some one grab my arm. I turn and see my wife. Signore, I most faint dead, but my wife, she hold me up. 'Villain,' she say, ' come with me, else I give you to caribinieri and put you in prison all your life.' I not like that, so I go with her to the *pension* where she stay. She put me in her room — ah, signore, I suffer, I suffer! My wife she talk, talk all day, all night; I sleep no one wink."

And this was the way he used the Queen's English, after that eloquent and fluent speech on Cosensa!

"And no food, Paranzo? Did she give you no food to stand all that talk?"

"Yes, signore, she rang the bell and ordered supper,— a good supper, — but I not eat; my stomach sick, she talk so. Next day she go out and lock me in. I look down the window. It very high, but I jump and run away. Then I find a great sorrow. They tell me the signori Americani sail to Greece. I sail too. I think to see you in Greece. But on that ship I see the brother of my wife. He say my wife know when I run away — I run to Greece; so she go by steamer and her brother go by ship to catch me. Ah, amico mio! this make me so miserable. I think of that woman, of England, all time fog, all time talk, talk; and so one night I jump — dive down deep, and see ship go off, and my wife's brother think me dead: but I have on jacket like the signore. See; I bought it in Syracuse."

Paranzo opened his coat and displayed a life-preserver vest suspiciously like the one Mack had lost on the *Principe Farnese;* but I had not the heart to hint a suspicion that would add to the sorrows of the soft-eyed Italian.

"Yes," resumed Paranzo, with a sigh, "I put trust in my vest. I rise to the surface and blow it up and float — float comfortable till a steamer pick me up, and, Dio mio! what you think? That steamer pick me up come from Catania and have my wife. I see her and faint dead away. She take me to

Greece; then she say she take me to England: but in the night I slip away on Egyptian steamer and come here, and my wife think I kill myself. I leave her note say I go kill myself."

At this moment a shrill whistle announced my steamer's arrival.

"Paranzo," I said solemnly, "are you my friend?"

"Si, signore, to death! Paranzo always your friend."

"We are about to part, Paranzo — part forever. In a few minutes I board the steamer. My eyes may never be blessed with a sight of you again. I have one last favor to ask of you — "

"Amico mio! Speak! Paranzo die for you."

"No, Paranzo; I do not ask death of you: I only ask for one grain of truth. Have you a wife? Did you ever have a wife? Is she not a fancy?"

"Signore," said Paranzo, tears in his voice as well as in his eyes, "my feelings hurt. You distrust me. Ah, signore! how happy I would be if my wife — that old English cat — was nothing, was one air-bubble, one breath — so." (puffing out a breath); "but she too real, too hard, solid flesh. I feel her grip on my arm; it black and blue yet. Signore, you look here; you see her picture!"

This was said triumphantly. I gazed on the kodak portrait of a lady, which Paranzo drew from a side pocket.

"How was this taken, Paranzo? When and where?"

"You like? Keep it, signore. I no want it more. A signore Americano on the steamer kodak it while my wife talk, talk, telling me she give me to the carabinieri if I try run away again."

If Mrs. Paranzo is like her portrait, Paranzo can scarcely be blamed for running away. The soft-eyed fellow accompanied me down to the dock and threw me salutes and farewells as the *Cuzco* began the voyage that ended my trip on the Mediterranean.

INDEX

Ægean, cruise on, 298.
Alcalde, the, 109.
Alexandria, 345.
Almeria, 151.
Amalfi, 248.
Anarchists, Spanish, 166.
Andora, republic of, 187.
Aristophanes, theory of love, 149.
Aristotle, tomb of, 308.

Barcelona, 157.
Baroness, the, 60, 87.
Beirut, 340.
Bicycles, American tariff on, 183.
  French tariff on, 184.
  Italian tariff on, 189.
  cost of transporting in Europe, 211.
Bolsena, 209.
Bull-fighter, pay of, 144.
Bull-fights in Spain and Portugal, 53.
Byron, street of, in Athens, 318.

Cafés in Spain, 135.
Cairo, 348.
Capri, 245.
Carthage, 152.
Catania, 293.
Ceuta, prisons of, 122.
Chalkis, 308.
Charybdis, 289.
Cleopatra, tomb of, 347.
Chiusure, 202.
Civil guards in Spain, 73.
Cordova, 88.
Corinth, 318.
Costume in Greek Islands, 305.
  in Athens, 313.
  in Egypt, 345.
Cost of living in Lisbon, 22.

Cost of living in Spain, 69.
  in Italian village, 208.
  in Italian prisons, 216, 219, 229.
  in Greek prisons, 315.
  in American prisons, 219.
Cost of clothing in Portugal, 29.
  of travelling in Spain, 181.
  of trip New York to Portugal, 16.
  of boating on Mediterranean, 243, 311.
Cotton mills in Spain, 129.
Courtship in Spain, 136.
Crime in Italy, 232.
Crocodile pits, 356.
Cyprus, 335.

Dance, the Spanish, 106.
Death rate in Italian prisons, 231.
Delos, island of, 306.

Egypt, English occupation of, 320.
Eubœa, 308.
Euripus, 308.

Fair in Ronda, 96.
  in Tangiers, 117.
Food of convicts in Italy, 216, 219, 229.
  in America, 219.
  in Morocco, 120.
  in Spain, 124, 144.
  in Greece, 315.
  in Portugal, 40.
Foundling asylums, 50.
Fruit, value of in Europe and America, 81.

Garibaldi, tablet of, 194.
Genoa, 196.
Gibraltar, 110.

Granada, 140.
Gaucin, adventure in, 106.

Hours of labor in Spain, 67.

Illiterates in prisons, number of, 233.
Insurrection on steamer, 340.

Kodak, 9, 14, 89, etc.

Labor in Lisbon, 17.
 in Spain, 67, 83, 129.
Lake Garda, 197.
Liberty in Italy, 196.
Lipari, adventure on island of, 278.
Lisbon, 13.
Lotteries, 49.
Lunatics in prisons, 231.

Marathon, 309.
Marriage in Cyprus, 335.
 in Morocco, 114.
May 1st, troubles on, in Europe, 172, 221.
Memphis, 356.
Mentone, 187.
Messina, 290.
Milo, island of, 299.
Monte Carlo, 185.
Morocco, 113.
Montefiascone, accident at, 211.
Montserrat, monastery of, 177.
Mount Oliveto, monastery of, 201.
Mosque of Cordova, 88.

Naples, changes in, 233.
Nice, 184.

Octroi tax in Spain, 70.
 in other countries, 236.

Pantheon, 212.
Passports, 1.
Pentellicus, ascent of, 317.
Perseus, in the home of, 302.
Pestum, ruins of, 254.
Pompey's Pillar, 346.
Post-office, bad management of, in Spain, 93.

Post-office, receipts of, in Italy, 236.
Prisons in Italy, 214.
 in Greece, 314.
 in Morocco, 120.
 in Spain, 122, 142, 153, 160.
 in Portugal, 36.
 in Smyrna, 321.
Pyramids, 353.
Pyrenees, across the, 103.
Port Said, 357.

Radicafani, 207.
Renting boats, 240.
Rents in Barcelona, 170.
 in Lisbon, 20.
 in Malaga, 133.
 in Naples, 235.
 in Seville, 73.
Rhodes, 330.
Rome, 212.
Ronda, 94.
Russian Jews, 338.

San Quirico, 205.
Scilla, 289.
Seriphos, 301.
Seville, 66.
Sherry, how made, 82.
Sicily, 291.
Society in Spain, 134.
Sorento, 240.
Stage-coaching in Spain, 90.
Strikes in Spain, 83, 131, 169.
Stromboli, ascent of, 277.
San Stefano, dungeon of, 224.
Smyrna, 320.
Suicide in prisons, 232.
Syra, island of, 304.
Syracuse, 294.
Syria, 341.
Suez Canal, 357.

Tangiers, 113.
Taormina, 291.
Taxation in Italy, 236.
Tobacco factories in Spain, 67.
Toulon, 183.
Tyrol, a day in, 197.

INDEX

Unions, labor, in Lisbon, 19.
  in Xeres, 83.
  in Malaga, 131.
  in Barcelona, 167.

Valencia, 156.
Virgin's Cave, 178; Virgin's crypt in Egypt, 351.
Volcanoes of the world, 275.

Wages in Lisbon, 18; Spanish tobacco factories, 68; of Spanish bricklayers, 92; Spanish coopers, 83; Spanish vineyards, 84; Spanish convicts, 142; Spanish cotton mills, 130; Spanish bull-fighters, 144; Italian field-hands, 203, 208; Italian convicts, 220; Italian bar-mill rollers, 195; Italian macaroni-makers, 249; Greek mechanics, 313; Greek convicts, 315; American convicts, 219.

Xeres, 82.
Xerxes, 317.

Zea, 309.

Typography by J. S. Cushing & Co., Boston, U.S.A.
Presswork by Berwick & Smith, Boston, U.S.A.

www.ingramcontent.com/pod-product-compliance
Lightning Source LLC
Chambersburg PA
CBHW020544300426
44111CB00008B/794